Amsterdam

F. Lemmens/ERNOULT FEATURES

MICHELIN TYRE PLC
38 Clarendon Road - WATFORD Herts WD1 1SX - U.K.
Tel. (01923) 415 000
www.ViaMichelin.com

Manufacture française des pneumatiques Michelin

Société en commandite par actions au capital de 2 000 000 000 de francs
Place des Carmes-Déchaux – 63 Clermont-Ferrand (France)
R.C.S. Clermont-Fd B 855 200 507

Dépôt légal juillet 2001 – ISBN 2-06-000233-8 – ISSN 0763-1383

Printed in the France 07-2001/3.3

Compograveur - Imprimeur : LE SANGLIER, Charleville-Mézières

Cover design: Carré Noir, Paris 17e arr.

THE GREEN GUIDE: The Spirit of Discovery

The exhilaration of new horizons, the fun of seeing the world, the excitement of discovery: this is what we seek to share with you. To help you make the most of your travel experience, we offer first-hand knowledge and turn a discerning eye on places to visit.
This wealth of information gives you the expertise to plan your own enriching adventure. With THE GREEN GUIDE showing you the way, you can explore new destinations with confidence or rediscover old ones.
Leisure time spent with THE GREEN GUIDE is also a time for refreshing your spirit, enjoying yourself, and taking advantage of our selection of fine restaurants, hotels and other places for relaxing.
So turn the page and open a window on the world. Join THE GREEN GUIDE in the spirit of discovery.

Contents

Ph. Gajic/MICHELIN

Bell-tower of Westerkerk, Prinsengracht

A night out at the Odeon

The City of Amsterdam 98

The Suburbs 198

R. Lemmens/IMAGE BANK/AEF

Trying the local speciality, *hareng à la hollandaise*

Ph. Gajic/MICHELIN

Façade stone on the Lindengracht

Maps and plans

COMPANION PUBLICATIONS

Plan of Amsterdam no 36

– a complete street map of the city (1cm = 150m) with all major thoroughfares, one-way streets, large car parks, major public buildings, post offices etc.

– a street index

– practical information

Map of the Netherlands no 908

– a 1:400 000 scale map with a list of place names and an enlarged map of Amsterdam.

Maps of the northern and southern Netherlands nos 210 and 211

– a detailed 1:200 000 scale map with a list of place names. Map no 210 includes an enlarged map of Amsterdam.

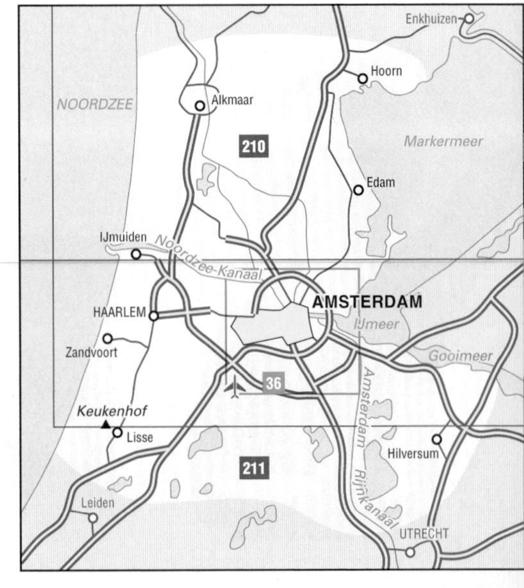

LIST OF MAPS AND PLANS

District maps

Local maps

Plans of museums and sights

Using this guide

● The **summary** maps at the front of this guide have been designed to assist you in planning your trip.

● The **Practical Information** section includes information on getting to Amsterdam, transport around the city, guided tours, boat trips and shopping. There is also a calendar of events, a bibliography, and selected hotel and restaurant recommendations.

● The **Introduction** gives information on the geographical, historical and cultural background of Amsterdam.

● The principal natural and cultural attractions in the Netherlands are presented in alphabetical order in the **Sights** section. The clock symbol ⓥ placed after the name of a sight indicates that opening times and prices for visiting that sight are included in the **Admission times and charges** section at the back of the guide.

● The **Index** at the back of this guide contains a comprehensive list of specific place names, historical figures and and other important information.

We greatly appreciate comments and suggestions from our readers. Contact us at:

Michelin Travel Publications, 38 Clarendon Road, Watford, Herts WD1 1SX, England.
☎ 01923 415 000
Fax 01923 415 250
TheGreenGuide-uk@uk.michelin.com
www.ViaMichelin.com

X. Richer/HOA QUI

Key

	Sight	Seaside Resort	Winter Sports Resort	Spa
Highly recommended	★★★			
Recommended	★★			
Interesting	★			

Tourism

Admission Times and Charges listed at the end of the guide

Sightseeing route with departure point indicated

Ecclesiastical building

Synagogue – Mosque

Building (with main entrance)

Statue, small building

Wayside cross

Fountain

Fortified walls – Tower – Gate

Visit if time permits

AZ B Map co-ordinates locating sights

Tourist information

Historic house, castle – Ruins

Dam – Factory or power station

Fort – Cave

Prehistoric site

Viewing table – View

Miscellaneous sight

Recreation

Racecourse

Skating rink

Outdoor, indoor swimming pool

Marina, moorings

Mountain refuge hut

Overhead cable-car

Tourist or steam railway

Waymarked footpath

Outdoor leisure park/centre

Theme/Amusement park

Wildlife/Safari park, zoo

Gardens, park, arboretum

Aviary, bird sanctuary

Additional symbols

Motorway (unclassified)

Junction: complete, limited

Pedestrian street

Unsuitable for traffic, street subject to restrictions

Steps – Footpath

Railway – Coach station

Funicular – Rack-railway

Tram – Metro, Underground

Bert (R.)... Main shopping street

Post office – Telephone centre

Covered market

Barracks

Swing bridge

Quarry – Mine

B F Ferry (river and lake crossings)

Ferry services: Passengers and cars

Foot passengers only

3 Access route number common to MICHELIN maps and town plans

Abbreviations and special symbols

G	Police station (Marechaussee)
H	Town hall (Stadhuis)
J	Law courts (Gerechtshof)
M	Museum (Museum)
P	Provincial capital (Hoofdplaats provincie)
P	Provincial council (Provinciehuis)
POL.	Police station (Politie)
T	Theatre (Schouwburg)
U	University (Universiteit)
	Landing stage
	Outstanding frontage
	Park and Ride

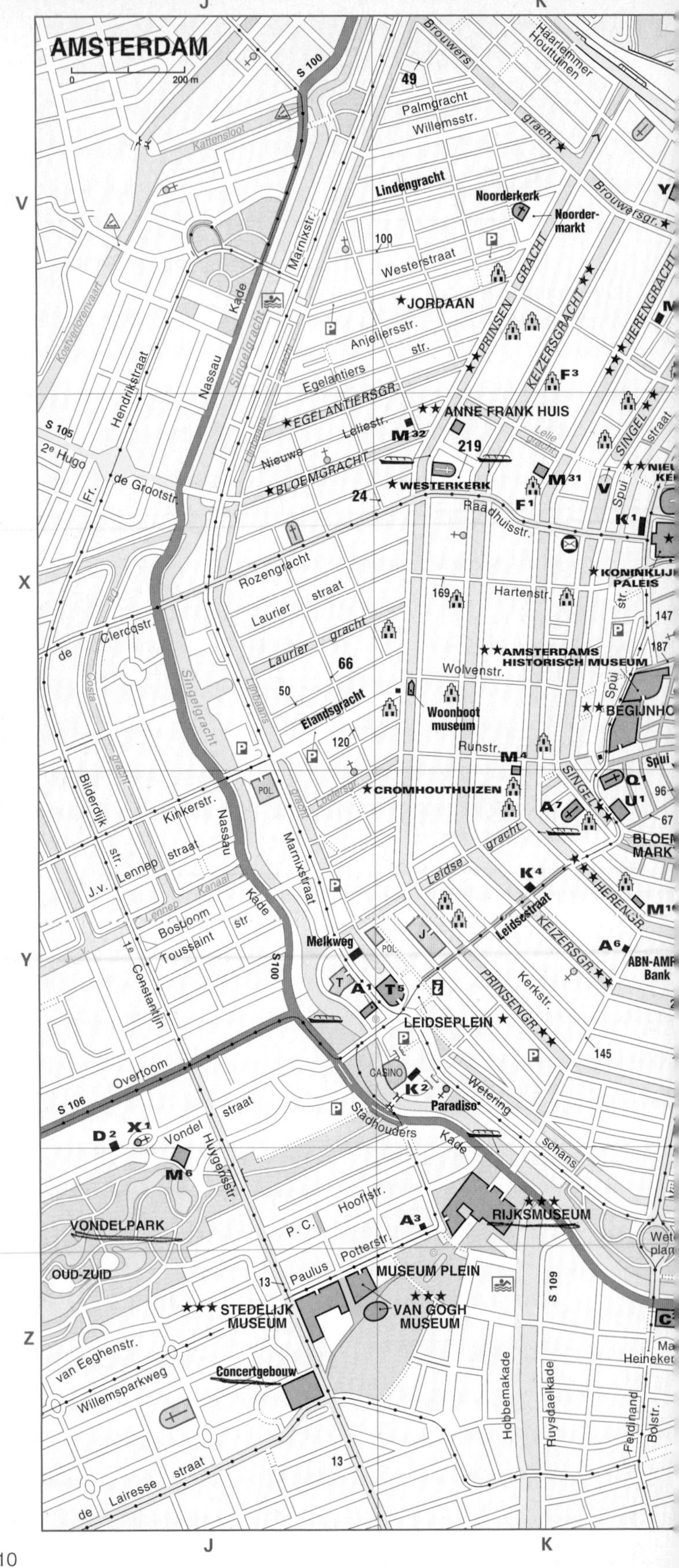
AMSTERDAM
0
200 m
J
K
V
X
Y
Z
Noorderkerk
Noordermarkt
Lindengracht
Palmgracht
Willemsstr.
Brouwersgracht
Westerstraat
JORDAAN
PRINSENGRACHT
KEIZERSGRACHT
HERENGRACHT
SINGEL
Anjeliersstr.
Egelantiersstr.
EGELANTIERSGR.
ANNE FRANK HUIS
Nieuwe Leliestr.
BLOEMGRACHT
WESTERKERK
Raadhuisstr.
KONINKLIJK PALEIS
Rozengracht
Lauriergracht
Elandsgracht
Hartenstr.
AMSTERDAMS HISTORISCH MUSEUM
Wolvenstr.
Woonboot museum
BEGIJNHOF
Runstr.
CROMHOUTHUIZEN
Leidsegracht
Leidsestraat
Marnixstraat
Nassaukade
Singelgracht
Kattensloot
Kostverlorenvaart
Hendrikstraat
2e Hugo de Grootstr.
de Clercqstr.
Bilderdijk
Kinkerstr.
J.v. Lennepstraat
J.v. Lennepkanaal
Bosboom Toussaintstr.
1e Constantijn Huygensstraat
Overtoom
Melkweg
LEIDSEPLEIN
CASINO
Paradiso
Weteringschans
Stadhouderskade
RIJKSMUSEUM
Vondelstraat
VONDELPARK
OUD-ZUID
P.C. Hooftstr.
Paulus Potterstr.
MUSEUM PLEIN
STEDELIJK MUSEUM
VAN GOGH MUSEUM
Concertgebouw
van Eeghenstr.
Willemsparkweg
de Lairessestraat
Hobbemakade
Ruysdaelkade
Ferdinand Bolstr.
Kerkstr.
ABN-AMRO Bank
Spui
BLOEMMARKT
S 100
S 105
S 106
S 109

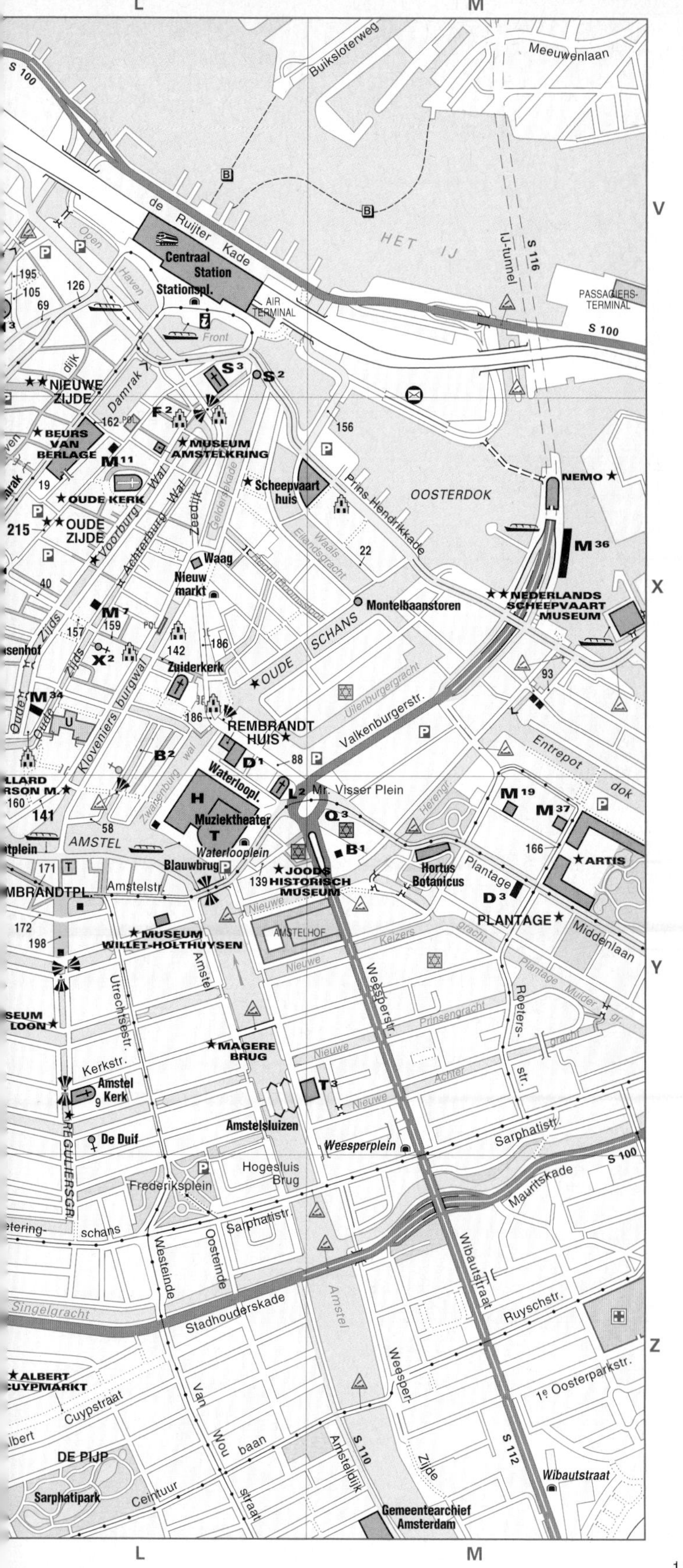
L
M
V
X
Y
Z
Buiksloterweg
Meeuwenlaan
de Ruijter Kade
HET IJ
IJ-tunnel
S 116
S 100
PASSAGIERS-TERMINAL
Centraal Station
Stationspl.
AIR TERMINAL
Open Haven
Front
Damrak
NIEUWE ZIJDE
BEURS VAN BERLAGE
MUSEUM AMSTELKRING
OUDE KERK
OUDE ZIJDE
Voorburgwal
Achterburgwal
Zeedijk
Geldersekade
Scheepvaart huis
Prins Hendrikkade
OOSTERDOK
NEMO
Waag
Nieuwmarkt
Montelbaanstoren
NEDERLANDS SCHEEPVAART MUSEUM
OUDE SCHANS
Zuiderkerk
Kloveniersburgwal
REMBRANDT HUIS
Uilenburgergracht
Valkenburgerstr.
Entrepot dok
Waterloopl.
Muziektheater
Mr. Visser Plein
Herengr.
AMSTEL
Waterlooplein
Blauwbrug
JOODS HISTORISCH MUSEUM
Hortus Botanicus
Plantage
ARTIS
PLANTAGE
Middenlaan
Amstelstr.
REMBRANDTPL.
MUSEUM WILLET-HOLTHUYSEN
AMSTELHOF
Nieuwe Keizersgracht
Weesperstr.
Plantage Muidergr.
Roeterssstr.
Utrechtsestr.
MAGERE BRUG
Prinsengracht
Kerkstr.
Amstel Kerk
Amstelsluizen
Weesperplein
Sarphatistr.
REGULIERSGR.
De Duif
Frederiksplein
Hogesluis Brug
Mauritskade
Westeinde
Oosteinde
Singelgracht
Stadhouderskade
Wibautstraat
Ruyschstr.
1e Oosterparkstr.
ALBERT CUYPMARKT
Cuypstraat
Van Woustraat
Weesperzijde
Amsteldijk
S 110
S 112
DE PIJP
Sarphatipark
Ceintuur baan
Wibautstraat
Gemeentearchief Amsterdam

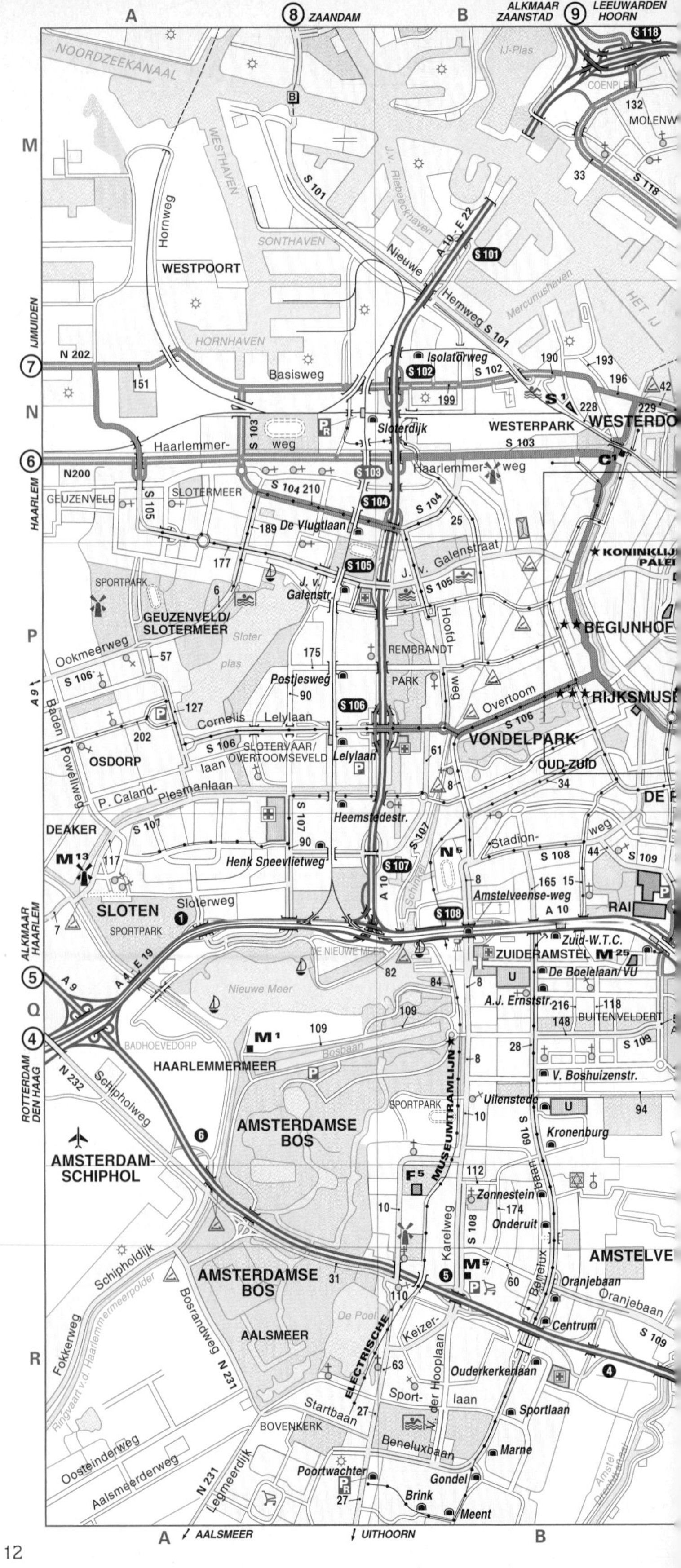
A
ZAANDAM
B
ALKMAAR
ZAANSTAD
LEEUWARDEN
HOORN
NOORDZEEKANAAL
IJ-Plas
COENPLEIN
MOLENW
WESTHAVEN
SONTHAVEN
HORNHAVEN
Hornweg
WESTPOORT
J.v. Riebeeckhaven
Nieuwe Hemweg
Mercuriushaven
HET IJ
IJMUIDEN
N 202
Basisweg
Isolatorweg
WESTERPARK
WESTERDO
Haarlemmer-weg
Sloterdijk
N200
HAARLEM
GEUZENVELD
SLOTERMEER
De Vlugtlaan
J. v. Galenstraat
J. v. Galenstr.
KONINKLIJ PALEI
SPORTPARK
GEUZENVELD/ SLOTERMEER
Sloter plas
BEGIJNHOF
Ookmeerweg
Postjesweg
REMBRANDT PARK
Hoofdweg
RIJKSMUS
Overtoom
Baden Powellweg
Cornelis Lelylaan
OSDORP
SLOTERVAAR/ OVERTOOMSEVELD
Lelylaan
VONDELPARK
OUD-ZUID
P. Calandlaan
Plesmanlaan
Heemstedestr.
DEAKER
Stadionweg
Henk Sneevlietweg
Schinkel
Amstelveense-weg
RAI
SLOTEN
Sloterweg
SPORTPARK
ALKMAAR
HAARLEM
DE NIEUWE MEER
Zuid-W.T.C.
ZUIDERAMSTEL
De Boelelaan/VU
Nieuwe Meer
A.J. Ernststr.
BUITENVELDERT
BADHOEVEDORP
Bosbaan
HAARLEMMERMEER
V. Boshuizenstr.
ROTTERDAM
DEN HAAG
Schipholweg
SPORTPARK
Uilenstede
Kronenburg
AMSTERDAMSE BOS
MUSEUMTRAMLIJN
AMSTERDAM-SCHIPHOL
Zonnestein
Onderuit
Karelweg
Beneluxbaan
AMSTELVE
Schipholdijk
AMSTERDAMSE BOS
Oranjebaan
Ringvaart v.d. Haarlemmermeerpolder
Bosrandweg
Centrum
De Poel
AALSMEER
Keizer-
Fokkerweg
Ouderkerkerlaan
ELECTRISCHE
V. der Hooplaan
Sport-laan
Sportlaan
Startbaan
BOVENKERK
Beneluxbaan
Oosteinderweg
Aalsmeerderweg
Legmeerdijk
Poortwachter
Marne
Gondel
Brink
Meent
Amstel
AALSMEER
UITHOORN

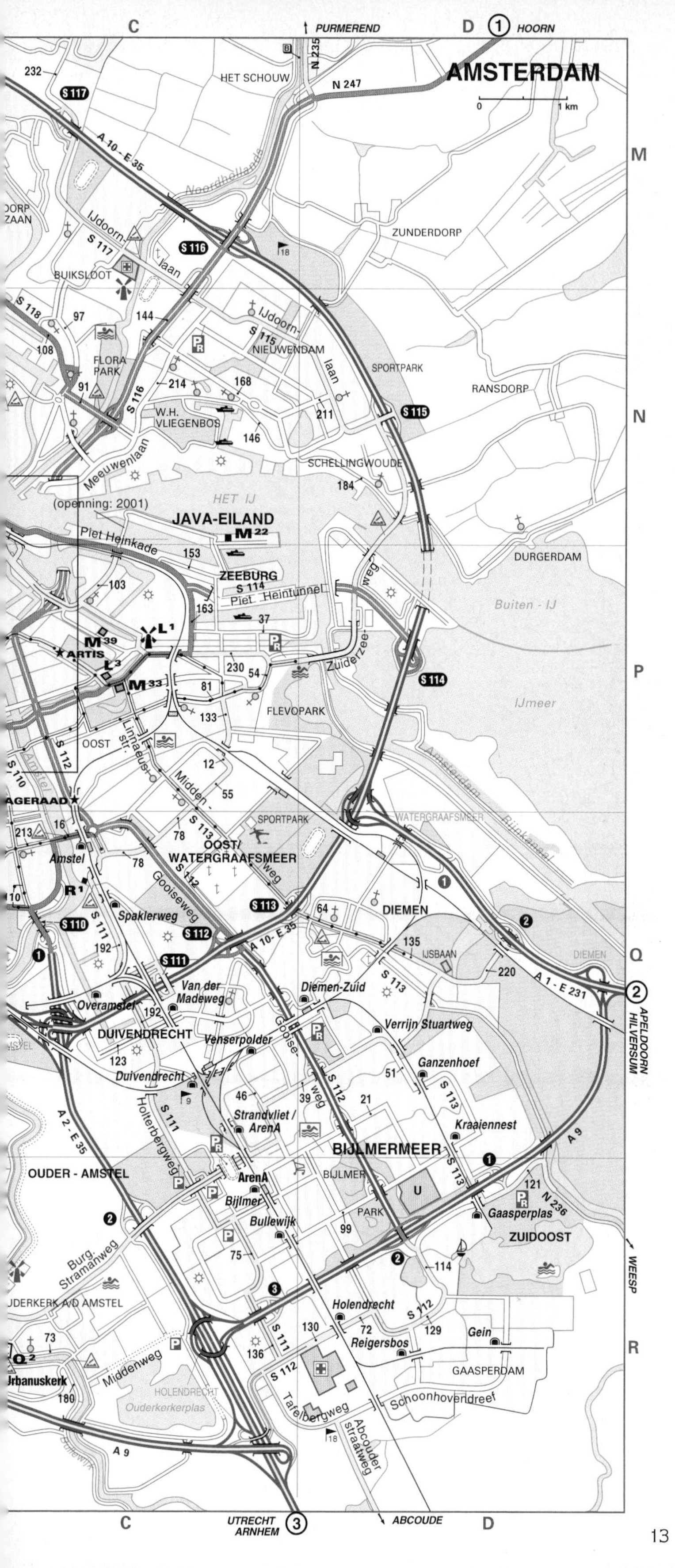

AMSTERDAM
PURMEREND
HOORN
HET SCHOUW
ZUNDERDORP
BUIKSLOOT
NIEUWENDAM
RANSDORP
FLORA PARK
W.H. VLIEGENBOS
SCHELLINGWOUDE
HET IJ
JAVA-EILAND
ZEEBURG
DURGERDAM
Buiten - IJ
ARTIS
FLEVOPARK
IJmeer
OOST
OOST/ WATERGRAAFSMEER
DIEMEN
DUIVENDRECHT
BIJLMERMEER
ZUIDOOST
OUDER - AMSTEL
GAASPERDAM
HOLENDRECHT
Ouderkerkerplas
(opening: 2001)
APELDOORN HILVERSUM
WEESP
UTRECHT ARNHEM
ABCOUDE

INDEX OF STREETS INCLUDED IN THE MAPS OF AMSTERDAM

SIGHTSEEING WITH AMSTERDAM STREET MAPS

(M) = See Museums (T) = See Theatres

The great town houses lining the canal banks

The Europe of the 17C had only two cities that were truly independent, **Venice** and **Amsterdam**. In a monarchical Europe these two powerful, rival cities, each the capital of a Republic, were controlled, as Vilfredo Pareto put it, by foxes in a world of lions. One had a Roman Catholic aristocratic elite; the other was headed by a Protestant upper middle class. This major contrast in the middle of so many similarities is reflected in the many canals flowing through the two cities.

Like the Serene City, Amsterdam attracts visitors from all over the world because of the almost magical atmosphere inherent in towns and cities built on the water. One of the main attractions of the city is of course a tour of the four majestic canals known as the **Singel**, **Herengracht**, **Keizersgracht** and **Prinsengracht**. The quaysides lining these four waterways are backed with magnificently designed buildings imbued with a Nordic sense of moderation, erected for people who would find quite unacceptable the splendour of the Venetian *palazzi* on the Grand Canal, a veritable "triumphal waterway" that is unthinkable to the Calvinist mind.

Ph. Gajic/MICHELIN

The Blue Room in the Willet-Holthuysen Museum

All the charm and interest of the great town houses in Amsterdam lie behind their brick and sandstone frontages, in their interiors elegantly decorated by artists such as Jacob de Witt or the Frenchman Daniel Marot, and in their gardens richly decorated with fountains and statues. However, the number of town houses open to the public is fairly small. Only a few museums housed in the former homes of wealthy merchants give an insight into the living conditions of the ruling class which gave Amsterdam its Golden Age. These museums include the Museum Van Loon, the Museum Willet-Holthuysen, the Bijbels Museum, the Theatermuseum and the Kattenkabinet. However, there is one opportunity to see what is usually out of bounds during the *Gardens Open Day* in the middle of May *(for information, contact the VVV. See Practical information for address)*.

Sightseeing programmes

TWO-DAY PROGRAMME

Two days, which will be a weekend for most people, enable visitors to acquire a fairly good idea of the main sights in the city and appreciate its often fascinating aspects.

Day One **The historic city centre**

We suggest that you begin your stay in Amsterdam with a boat trip along the canals, followed by a tour of the historic city centre

Morning Start at the central railway station for a **boat trip★**

Return to the central railway station: **Museum Amstelkring★** and **Oude Kerk★★**

Stock Exchange★ (Beurs van Berlage)

Dam★, **royal palace★** (Koninklijk Paleis) and **Nieuwe Kerk★★**

Afternoon **Local history museum★★** (Amsterdams Historisch Museum)

Beguine convent★★ (Begijnhof)

Flower market★ (Bloemenmarkt) on banks of the **Singel★★**

Evening A stroll along the Amstel to the romantic **Magere Brug★** and return via the **Herengracht★★★**, a majestic sight at night

Day Two **Canals and major museums**

Morning Start at central railway station and take the Museumboot (boat) to the Prinsengracht stop (stop no 2): **Anne Frank Huis★★**

Take the Museumboot again to the Museumplein (stop no 4), by the **Rijksmuseum★★★**

Afternoon **Rijksmuseum★★★** and **Van Gogh Museum★★★**

Take the Museumboot to the Muziektheater (stop no 6) and stroll along Kloveniersburgwal and **Oudezijds Voorburgwal★** to see the amazing variety of sights in the city centre

Evening A classical music concert (Concertgebouw), or a rock concert or variety show (Paradiso or Melkweg)

FOUR-DAY PROGRAMME

A long weekend is ideal. It gives you time to soak up the city's atmosphere, spend more time on one or other of the sights, and discover the contrast between the city and its suburbs.

Day One **The historic city centre**

Same programme as for the first day above

Day Two **Rijksmuseum and the surrounding district**

Morning The huge, superb **Rijksmuseum★★★**

Afternoon A stroll via Leidseplein, Leidsegracht, **Prinsengracht★★**, **Reguliersgracht★** before returning to the **Rijksmuseum★★★** (the ticket is valid all day) for another look at the major works of art or a chance to complete the tour of this gigantic museum

Evening A classical music concert (Concertgebouw), or a rock concert or variety show (Paradiso or Melkweg)

Day Three **From the Van Gogh Museum to the Batavia**

Morning **Van Gogh Museum★★★**

Afternoon Weather permitting, have a cycle ride *(see Cycling in Amsterdam)* or, if you prefer museums, continue with the programme below

Stedelijk Museum★★★

Reguliersgracht★ and **Oude Schans★**

Nederlands Scheepvaart Museum★★

Evening A stroll through the historic town centre: Nieuwemarkt and **Oudezijds Voorburgwal★**

Day Four Haarlem and the Quaysides

Morning It is easy to get to Haarlem by train *(departures every 30min; 15min journey)*: have a stroll around the quiet suburb of **Haarlem★★** and visit the **Frans Hals Museum★★★**

Afternoon **Haarlem★★** and return to Amsterdam:
Keizersgracht★★, **Museum Van Loon★**
Prinsengracht★★, **Anne Frank Huis★★**

Evening Take a stroll in the Jordaan district: **Bloemgracht★**, the area around the old warehouses: **Brouwersgracht★**. End your visit with a walk along **Herengracht★★★** and **Singel★★**

When walking around the city, watch out for cyclists and tramways. Cyclists tend to ignore pedestrians and show total disregard for the highway code, while trams are seldom restricted to the same traffic lanes as other traffic which makes them a danger for anybody not accustomed to them.

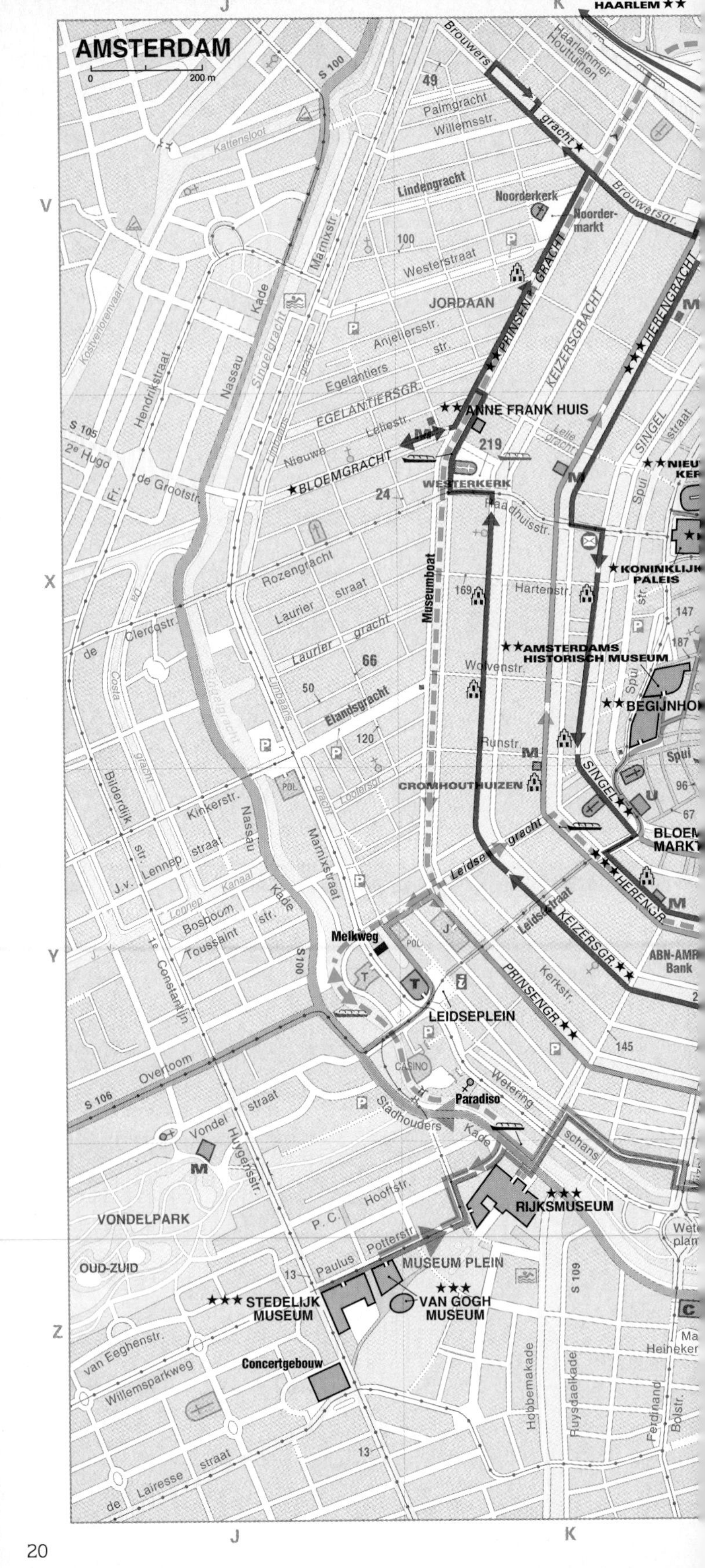

AMSTERDAM
0
200 m
HAARLEM ★★
★★ ANNE FRANK HUIS
WESTERKERK
JORDAAN
★BLOEMGRACHT
★★PRINSENGRACHT
KEIZERSGRACHT
★★HERENGRACHT
Noorderkerk
Noordermarkt
★KONINKLIJK PALEIS
★★AMSTERDAMS HISTORISCH MUSEUM
★★BEGIJNHOF
CROMHOUTHUIZEN
Museumboat
LEIDSEPLEIN
Melkweg
Paradiso
CASINO
★★★ RIJKSMUSEUM
MUSEUM PLEIN
★★★ VAN GOGH MUSEUM
★★★ STEDELIJK MUSEUM
Concertgebouw
VONDELPARK
OUD-ZUID
ABN-AMRO Bank
Heineken

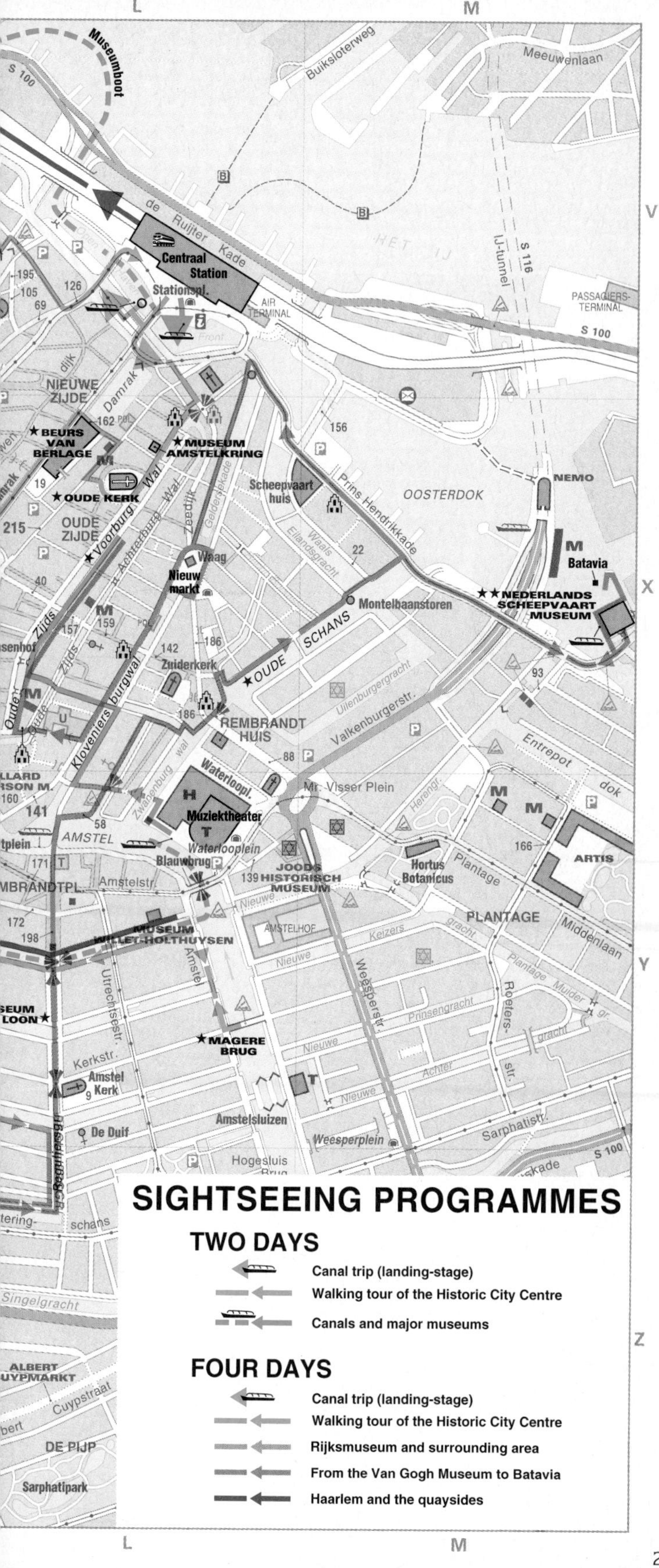
L
M
V
X
Y
Z
Museumboot
S 100
Buiksloterweg
Meeuwenlaan
de Ruijter Kade
Centraal Station
Stationspl.
HET IJ
IJ-tunnel
S 116
AIR TERMINAL
PASSAGIERS-TERMINAL
S 100
Front.
NIEUWE ZIJDE
Damrak
★ BEURS VAN BERLAGE
★ MUSEUM AMSTELKRING
★ OUDE KERK
OUDE ZIJDE
Voorburgwal
Achterburgwal
Zeedijk
Geldersekade
Scheepvaarthuis
Prins Hendrikkade
OOSTERDOK
NEMO
Batavia
★★ NEDERLANDS SCHEEPVAART MUSEUM
Waag
Nieuwmarkt
Montelbaanstoren
Waals Eilandsgracht
OUDE SCHANS
Zuiderkerk
Kloveniersburgwal
Uilenburgergracht
Valkenburgerstr.
REMBRANDT HUIS
Entrepot dok
Waterloopl.
Muziektheater
Mr. Visser Plein
Zwanenburgwal
AMSTEL
Waterlooplein
Blauwbrug
JOODS HISTORISCH MUSEUM
Hortus Botanicus
Plantage
ARTIS
PLANTAGE
Middenlaan
Amstelstr.
MUSEUM WILLET-HOLTHUYSEN
AMSTELHOF
Nieuwe Keizersgracht
Plantage Muidergr.
Utrechtsestr.
Amstel
Weesperstr.
Roeterstr.
Prinsengracht
★ MAGERE BRUG
Kerkstr.
Amstel Kerk
De Duif
Amstelsluizen
Weesperplein
Sarphatistr.
Hogesluis Brug
S 100
Singelgracht
ALBERT CUYPMARKT
Cuypstraat
DE PIJP
Sarphatipark
SIGHTSEEING PROGRAMMES
TWO DAYS
Canal trip (landing-stage)
Walking tour of the Historic City Centre
Canals and major museums
FOUR DAYS
Canal trip (landing-stage)
Walking tour of the Historic City Centre
Rijksmuseum and surrounding area
From the Van Gogh Museum to Batavia
Haarlem and the quaysides

Leidseplein in summer: the "tourists' rest"

Guillot/DIAF

Practical Information

Planning your trip

TOURIST BOARDS

Although Amsterdam is only a short journey away, it is worthwhile preparing a holiday in advance. To obtain the necessary documents and check out certain information, begin by contacting the **tourist offices** which have numerous brochures providing up-to-date information on tourist and cultural events.

London – Netherlands Board of Tourism, 18 Buckingham Gate, London SW1 (postal address: PO Box 523, London SW1E 6NT), ☎ (020) 7931 0661 & (0891) 717777, fax (020) 7828 7941, www.holland.com/uk

Toronto – Netherlands Board of Tourism, 25 Adelaide Street East, Suite 710, Toronto, Ont. M5C 1Y2. ☎ (416) 363 1577.

Amsterdam – Netherlands Board of Tourism, Vlietweg 15, 2266 KA Leidschendam, ☎ (070) 370 57 05, www.holland.com/nl

ANWB – This is the Netherlands Royal Touring Club. ANWB, Wassenaarseweg 220, 2596 EC Den Haag; ☎ (070) 314 71 47. www.anwb.nl

VVV – In the Netherlands, the **tourist offices** or "VVV" provided the latest information on tourist and cultural events or available accommodation in Amsterdam and the various other towns mentioned in this guide.
In Amsterdam, VVV offices are located on **Stationsplein** (opposite Centraal Station and in the station itself), **Leidseplein/Leidsestraat**, **Stadionplein** and at **Schiphol** Airport. They are open every day and can be reached on ☎ 0900 400 40 40. The main VVV website is at www.vvv.nl and the VVV Amsterdam site is at www.visitamsterdam.nl
Addresses, telephone numbers and web sites of the tourist offices of the suburbs of Amsterdam appear at the end of the guide in the Admission Times and Charges section.

WEB SITES

You can of course look for addresses on your own, but for those in search of specific information on transport, hotels or tourist attractions, listed below are some useful addresses. Some sites are written exclusively in English. You can find museum addresses here as well as in the Admission Times and charges section at the end of the guide.

– **www.amsterdam.nl**: Amsterdam's official web site offering a wide range of information including cultural news and practical information.
– **www.bmz.amsterdam.nl**: the site of the organisation in charge of historic monuments. Offers detailed information on the city's historic heritage.
– **www.fiets.amsterdam.nl**: All you need to know about cycling in Amsterdam.
– **www.gvb.nl**: the official site of Amsterdam's public transport authority. Information on trams, buses, metro and ferries.
– **www.ivv.amsterdam.nl**: the site of Amsterdam's road infrastructures. Information on driving, public transport and cycling.
– **www.ov9292.nl**: information on public transport as well as transport in the rest of the country.
– **www.visitamsterdam.nl**: VVV's Amsterdam site (in English) with information on hotels, tourist attractions and cultural events.
– **www.wereldstad.nl**: a daily calendar of recommended things to do and see in Amsterdam.

FORMALITIES

There is no longer any border control in the Netherlands although drivers are expected to slow down at customs. It is however obligatory to carry some official documents.

Documents – Nationals of EU member states should carry a European identity Card or a passport that is currently valid or which has expired within the previous five years. Unaccompanied minors must have parental authorisation issued by their local police station.
For Canadian nationals a National Identity Card or a valid passport are sufficient.
Holders of British, Irish and US passports require no visa to enter the Netherlands, although visas may be necessary for visitors from some Commonwealth countries, and for those planning to stay for longer than three months. Visitors are advised to check visa requirements with their travel agent or with their local Dutch embassy or consulate. US citizens should obtain the booklet **Your Trip Abroad**, which provides useful information on visa requirements, customs regulations, medical care etc for international travellers. Apply to the Superintendent of Documents, PO Box 371954, Pittsburgh, PA 15250-7954, ☎ (202) 512 1800; Fax (202) 512 2250; www.access.gpo.gov

DISABLED VISITORS

Most public buildings, museums, galleries and theatres provide good facilities for the disabled, and the sights accessible to wheelchair users are indicated by the symbol ♿ in the **Admission Times and Charges** section at the back of the guide. **The Red Guide Benelux** also indicates rooms and facilities suitable for the disabled. The ANWB publishes a brochure entitled **Reiswijzer voor gehandicapten** (Travel Guide for the Disabled) which provides useful information on tourism, leisure activities and sports facilities suitable for the disabled. Further information is available from the **Nederlands Instituut voor Zorg en Welzijn** (The Netherlands Healthcare Institute), ☎ (030) 230 66 03, and the information department for the disabled of the ANWB, the **Afdeling Gehandicaptenvoorlichtin**, ☎ (070) 314 14 20.

Drivers – Drivers must have a three-part driving licence (EU licence) or an international driving licence. They must also have the international car insurance document known as the "Green Card" which is issued by insurance companies. The vehicle must have a regulation nationality identity plate at the rear.
To obtain information during your stay in the Netherlands, contact the ANWB whose address is indicated above.

Pets – A certificate proving that your pet has been vaccinated against rabies is a mandatory requirement. The certificate should be dated more than 30 days but less than one year before your arrival in the Netherlands.

Health care expenditure – Before leaving home, contact your local Social Security Office or Post Office and ask for an E111, a form which proves your health care entitlements.

GETTING TO AMSTERDAM

By plane – Most major airlines have direct flights to Schiphol Airport, 18km/10mi southwest of the city.
We would draw your attention to the plane/hotel packages offered by certain travel agencies. These packages may appear to be more expensive at first sight, but can turn out to be very attractive because hotel accommodation is usually expensive in Amsterdam.
KLM – KLM UK, Amsterdam Way, Norwich NR6 6JA. Central booking office: ☎ 0990 074 074.
BRITISH AIRWAYS – British Airways plc, Waterside, PO Box 365, West Drayton UB7 0GB. Central booking office: ☎ 08457 222 111.
AIR CANADA – 979 de Maisonneuve Ouest, Montréal, Quebec H3A 1M4. Central booking office: ☎ (514) 393 3333.
Schiphol: City Centre links – Schiphol Airport is famous for its huge duty free area. It is also a very practical airport since it has only one terminal, laid out around Schiphol Plaza on the ground floor. It is here (Arrival 1) that you will find the Holland Tourist Information desk *(open daily 7am-10pm)*, where travellers can book hotels and excursions or purchase public transport tickets, phone cards and the Amsterdam Pass *(see below)*.
The railway station is underneath Schiphol Plaza (buy tickets at the automatic ticket machines on the Plaza). A regular quarter-hourly suburban train service runs from the airport to the central station in Amsterdam. The journey lasts 20min.
There is a taxi rank opposite Schiphol Plaza. Taxis take at least 20min to reach the city centre; it can take three times as long during rush hours.
A coach service is provided by KLM from the airport to the main hotels in the city centre.

By train – All trains from Belgium arrive at the Centraal Station (usually referred to as the "CS").
There are daily trains from London to Amsterdam via Brussels. The journey lasts approximately 7hr. For information and booking, contact Eurostar ☎ 08705 186 186.

By coach – Eurolines provides a regular service from London and Dublin. Depart from the Eurolines terminal in Victoria Bus Station (London) daily at 8.30am, 10.30am, 8pm and 10.30pm; for information, ☎ 01582 404 511. Depart from the Bus Éireann terminal (Dublin) daily at 8.45am and 8.45pm; for information, contact the local Bus Éireann Travel Centres. The Eurolines agency in Amsterdam is at Rokin 10 (near the Dam); for information, ☎ (020) 627 51 51.

By car – From London, the drive to Amsterdam takes approximately 5hr 45min plus the crossing to the continent via the Channel Tunnel. From Dublin, the journey lasts 14hr 45min excluding the sea and Channel crossings. A toll is charged for the use of motorways in France.
The route recommended by Michelin is as follows:

London-Amsterdam (477km/296mi) – Use Michelin maps 404, 51 and 907. Leave London via the A 102 then A 2 to Rochester. Take the M 2 to Chatham, leave at exit 3 and follow the A 229. From Maidstone, take the M 20 to Folkestone and cross the channel on Le Shuttle. After leaving the terminal in France, continue along the A 16 to Calais and Dunkirk. Beyond the Belgian border, this becomes the A 18 to Ostend. Follow the A 10 through Brugge to Ghent then the A 14 to Antwerp. Follow the signposts for Antwerp North and take exit 7 (Antwerpen Noord) to join the N 49. Follow the Breda signs and pick up the A 1 which takes you across the Dutch border. Follow the A 16 to Tilburg and Eindhoven then the A 58 to Breda and the A 27. Exit on slip road 26 (Lexmond) and follow the signs to Utrecht West and Amsterdam. The A 2 skirts Utrecht and continues to Amsterdam.

Dublin-Amsterdam (951km/591mi) – Use Michelin maps 986, 987, 923 and 210. Leave Dublin via the N 11 to Blackrock then take the N 31 to Dun Laoghaire (ferry crossing). Leave the ferry terminal in England via the A 5 then the A 55 to Chester. Take the A 41 signposted Birmingham then the M 54 and M 6 via Birmingham and Coventry to Rugby. Pick up the M 1 via Northampton to Hemel Hempstead where you join the M 10 to St Albans, Harlow and Brentwood. From the M 25 join the A 282 to the Dartford Tunnel (toll charge). Pick up the A 2 to Rochester and follow the same route as indicated above.

For other routes, consult the Michelin web site on www.ViaMichelin.com

DRIVING IN THE NETHERLANDS

Speed limits: 120kph/75mph on motorways (100kph/62mph in the vicinity of large towns) – 80kph/50mph on the open road – 50kph/31mph in built-up areas.

Tolls: Motorways (autosnelweg) are toll-free; however there are tolls for certain bridges and tunnels in the Netherlands.

Overtaking and right of way: Only pass trams on the right unless there is insufficient room. Trams generally have priority.
Be careful of cyclists who pass on the right and have priority over motorists when the latter want to turn off the road.

Petrol: The following kinds of petrol are on sale in the Netherlands:

UK	Netherlands
Super	**Super gelood**
Unleaded 98 octane	**Super + (loodvrij)**
Unleaded 95 octane	**Euro 95 (loodvrij)**

Some useful words and phrases on the road:

Autosnelveg	Motorway
Betaald parkeren	Parking at a charge
Doorgaand verkeer	Through traffic
Eenrichtingsverkeer	One-way street
Inhaalverbod	No overtaking
Knooppunt	Junction
Let op! Gevaar!	Caution! Danger!
Omleiding	Diversion
Overstekende wielrijders	Cyclists path
Richting	Direction
Uitrit	Exit
Verboden	Prohibited
Voorrang geven	Give way
Werk in uitvoering	Roadworks
Zachte berm	Soft verge

Breakdown service: The main organisation is the ANWB (Koninklijke Nederlandsche Toeristenbend), the Royal Dutch Touring Club, which operates road patrols *(Wegenwacht)* on main roads. The address of the ANWB principal office is listed above.
In case of accident or breakdown, phone for assistance from one of the roadside telephones. Drivers can also contact the ANWB office, *Alarmcentrale*, ☎ (070) 314 14 14 (365 days, 24hr) where they will find operator assistance in their own language.
Road patrols (Wegenwacht) can also be contacted on a toll-free number, ☎ (0800) 08 88 (24hr).
Foreign visitors who are not members of ANWB will have to pay a subscription charge and will receive a membership card valid for two months. Members of affiliated clubs, such as the Automobile Association (AA), with a valid International Circular Letter of Credit (IRK), obtain free assistance.

Road maps – distances: Michelin map 907 covers all the Benelux countries at a scale of 1:400 000. Map 908 covers the Netherlands at a scale of 1:400 000.
The Netherlands is also covered at a scale of 1:200 000 by maps 210 (covering the area between Amsterdam and the northern border of the country) and 211 (covering the area between Antwerp and Amsterdam).

Getting around Amsterdam

BY CAR

It is strongly recommended that you do not drive in Amsterdam. The traffic jams are no worse here than in most large European cities, but the public transport system is really excellent, and it is very difficult to drive along the many narrow streets in the city centre. Moreover, in an effort to discourage people from bringing their cars into the city, the City Council has voluntarily limited the number of car parking spaces near and along the canal banks, and all car parking is subject to the rather steep charge of 2.25fl/hour. Moreover, cars are usually clamped within a few minutes of overrunning the parking time; they are taken to the police pound within 24 hours. The yellow clamp, known as the "*wielklem*", is a familiar sight and it will cost you 122fl to have it removed. If you do find yourself in this predicament, we advise you to phone Klem-hulp (Clamping Services) ☎ (020) 667 10 01), a company which will enable you to avoid wasting time and effort in the formalities demanded by the department responsible for the management of the car parking space ("*parkeerbeheer*": the address is indicated on the ticket placed on your windscreen) which you had the misfortune to choose. The Klem-Hulp company will free your car within 45min for the modest sum of 30fl (this is in addition to the fine). In order to avoid this inconvenience, it is recommended that you purchase a **one-day parking permit** (dagparkeerkaart) from your hotel.
It is also worth knowing that the number of vehicles broken into by thieves searching for cameras, bags and car radios is unbelievable. If you do choose to travel into the city by car, fill your pockets with change to feed the ever-hungry parking meters which operate every day of the week from 9am to 11pm (and from noon to 11pm on Sundays).
If you arrive in Amsterdam by car, use the Park and Ride facilities (Parkeer + Reis) indicated on our city map *(at the beginning of the guide)*. For further information consult the Infrastructure, Transport and Traffic web site at www.ivv.amsterdam.nl

Car hire – This is a very useful solution for those who come to Amsterdam by plane or train but would like to visit the outskirts.
The main car hire agencies in the city centre are as follows:
- **Avis**: Nassaukade 380: ☎ (020) 683 60 61.
- **Budget**: Overtoom 121: ☎ (020) 612 60 66.
- **Europcar**: Overtoom 51-53: ☎ (020) 683 21 23 (near Leidseplein).
- **Hertz**: Overtoom 333: ☎ (020) 612 24 41.
- **Kuperus**: Middenweg 175: ☎ (020) 693 87 90.
- **Safety**: Papaverweg 3b: ☎ (020) 636 63 63.

PUBLIC TRANSPORT

The Municipal Transport Company *(Gemeentevervoerbedrijf Amsterdam)* has a very practical network of public transport. Most of the tram and bus routes run from the central station. Opposite the station is the main information office where tickets, "strippenkaart", and one-day travel cards can be purchased *(see below)*. For timetables, routes and tariffs, consult the GVB web site (www.gvb.nl), the VVV or the public transport information service at ☎ 0900-9292 or www.ov9292.nl

Tickets – For the purposes of public transport, Amsterdam is divided into zones. *Zone Centrum* (5700), for example, covers the city centre. The price of the ticket varies according to the number of zones crossed.

A youthful touch in the old Spuiskaat

The **Strippenkaart**, which costs 12.50fl, is valid throughout the country, on buses, trams, and underground services. It is a pass with 15 vouchers (there is a larger one with 45 vouchers) that can be purchased from the transport office at the address indicated above, in railway stations, in post offices and in many tobacconists' shops. If you are travelling within a single zone, you fold back the first voucher and stamp the second one on a punching machine on board the vehicle. The stamp indicates the date, time and zone (you can travel for one hour with this voucher). If you are travelling through two zones, you will have to stamp the third voucher; for three zones, you stamp the fourth voucher etc. It sounds complicated but you will very quickly get used to the system.
The **Dagkaart** is a one-day pass for one person. Other passes are available for 2, 3 etc up to 9 days. It is only stamped once, during the first trip. If you are staying in Amsterdam for more than two days, this soon becomes a very worthwhile solution because it is valid for all zones. A 1-day pass **(Circle-Amsterdam ticket)** costs 12fl.

Trams – The tram network in Amsterdam is the easiest way of getting around the city and its suburbs, with the exception of the area around the city centre canals where walking is the best solution. The trams only run along the main streets.
You can get on or off a tram by any of its doors (except on a few routes running older tramcars which require passengers to get on at the rear). The intermediate step keeps the door open and prevents the tram from starting off. Use the yellow machines inside the tram to stamp your ticket. The driver usually announces the name of the stop and the main museums nearby, but these announcements are not easy for visitors to understand.

Circle-Tram 20 – Since 1997, with visitors in mind, the transport company has been operating a service along a circular route that takes in most of the main sights, museums and large hotels in the city. Tram no 20 provides a 10min service every day from 9am to 7pm. The route has 31 numbered stops. The number of the stop is called and it is easy to see where one is by consulting the map displayed on board the tram.

Bus service – Trams do not run through Amsterdam-Noord, a district which admittedly contains very few buildings of interest to tourists. The bus is the best means of transport if you want to see the suburbs. You should show your ticket to the bus driver when you get on.

Underground – The underground network is not very extensive. The trains run to Amstelstation and the Bijmelmeer district (in particular to the Amsterdam Arena, home ground of the great football club, Ajax). Stamp your ticket in the machines near the steps to the platforms.

Not forgetting the railways – Departing from the central station, the train offers easy access to the surrounding areas of the capital. These include towns and villages described in this guide, such as Alkmaar, Haarlem, Hilversum, Hoorn, Zandvoort, etc. The other stations in Amsterdam are Lelylaan, De Vlugtlaan, Sloterdijk, Zuid-WTC, RAI, Duivendrecht and Diemen-Zuid.
For further information regarding timetables, tariffs, bicycle transport, special offers etc., telephone the public transport information service on ☏ 0900-9292 or consult the web site at www.ns.nl (Netherlands Railway) or www.ov9292.nl (Public transport information).

BY BIKE

The Netherlands seem to meet all the criteria for happy cycling and, like many cities in Scandinavian countries, Amsterdam is a paradise for cyclists.
We advise you to read the beginning of the chapter entitled "Cycling in Amsterdam" where you will find a few recommendations that may be useful. You could also consult the web site **www.fiets.amsterdam.nl**

Cycle hire – The only problem is the vast choice! Here is a small selection of addresses within Amsterdam:

Take a bike: *Stationsplein 12, ☎ (020) 624 83 91*. This is the cycle hire office in the central station *(to the right of the entrance when you are facing the building)*. A full-day hire costs 10.50fl. The main advantage is that you can keep the bike until 10pm and, moreover, it is fitted with a basket big enough for a small rucksack. Do not hesitate to inspect the bike that is offered to you because there are very few in good condition. If you are not accustomed to back-pedalling in order to brake, ask for a bike with brakes on the handlebars. Deposit: 150fl in cash or by credit card.
Yellow Bike: *Nieuwezijds Kolk 29, ☎ (020) 620 69 40, www.yellowbike.nl* Only a short distance from the central station (in a narrow street between Nieuwendijk and Nieuwezijds Voorburgwal). The advantage of Yellow Bike is that it can provide a cycling tour of Amsterdam with a tourist guide (32.50fl for a 3hr tour). The disadvantage is that you will be riding a bright yellow bike and will not, under any circumstances, be able to pass for a local.
MacBike: *Mr. Visserplein 2: ☎ (020) 620 09 85 (near Rembrandthuis) and Marnixstraat 220 (south of Jordaan, opposite Lauriergracht), www.macbike.nl* A full day's hire of a bike with no gears and back-pedal brakes costs 12.50fl. Pay a few florins more to obtain a bike that meets your requirements. Deposit: 50fl in cash or by credit card.
Holland Rent-a-Bike: *Damrak 247, ☎ (020) 622 32 07 (in Berlage's Stock Exchange building)*. The same remarks apply. The only difference is the cost: 13fl for a full-day's hire. Deposit: 50fl if you show your identity card; 200fl if you do not have your identity card on you.

BOATS

With the boats of Canal Bus and Museumboot you can cruise the canals of the city. In the summertime with their sliding roofs these vessels offer a particularly pleasant mode of transport.

Canal Bus – *Weteringschans 24, ☎ (020) 626 55 74, www.canal.nl* This company operates three routes (green, red, blue) with eleven stops (Rijksmuseum, Leidseplein, Westerkerk, Anne Frank Huis, Centraal Station, Rembrandthuis, Nemo, Nederlands Scheepvaartmuseum, Stadhuis (Town hall), Artis. The blue line runs between the central station and the Nemo while the other two follow slightly different routes along the city's canals. The one-day ticket (which remains valid until noon on the following day) costs 25fl; the blue line ticket costs 15fl. It can be worthwhile buying a combined one-day ticket + admission to several museums and tourist attractions which gives a 15% saving.

Museumboot – *Rederij Lovers, ☎ (020) 530 10 90, www.lovers.nl* The "museum boat" runs from 10am to 5pm along a single route with seven stops (Centraal Station, Anne Frank Huis, Museumplein, Herengracht, Waterlooplein and Nederlands Scheepvaartmuseum). The price depends on the length of the journey. You can travel in either direction on the route.

Artis Express – *Rederij Lovers, ☎ (020) 530 10 90, www.lovers.nl* This regular boat route runs from the central station to Nederlands Scheepvaartmuseum and Artis.

Water Taxi – *Rederij Lovers, ☎ (020) 530 10 90, www.lovers.nl.* Water taxis run from 8am to midnight and can take up to 25 passengers. This is a very expensive way of travelling. The landing-stage is located opposite the central station.

Boat and pedal boat trips

Boat trips – Several companies operating from various landing-stages offer short cruises along the canals of Amsterdam. Most of them are to be found in the basins opposite the central station. Not all of them offer the same routes and services so ask for information at the ticket offices (the next departure time is always displayed).
Lovers *(located opposite the central station)* is a company well-known for its low prices. Because of this, its boats are often full, which can be a disadavantage. **Reederij P Kooij** *(opposite Rokin 25)* provides a more refined service on board a higher class of boat (the cabin roof can be removed in the summer, for an "open-top" cruise), and at a higher price. Here are a few more companies with the addresses of the landing-stages: **Amsterdam Canal Cruises** *(Nicolaas Witsenkade 1a)*; **Holland International** *(opposite the central station)*; **Meyers Rondvaarten** *(Damrak, Jetty 5)*.

Pedal Boats – The **"Canal Bike"** provides an amusing way of touring the canals in fine weather. There are four landing-stages: Rijksmuseum, Keizersgracht/Leidsestraat, Leidseplein and Anne Frank Huis. It is possible to hire a pedalo at one landing-stage and return it to another one. You can also purchase a map of the canals (3.50fl) with a description of five itineraries when boarding your pedalo. A trip costs 12.50fl an hour per person and 10fl an hour for more than two. A 50fl deposit is required. For more information: *Weteringschans 24, ☎ (020) 626 55 74, www.canal.nl*

General information

CURRENCY

The national currency unit is the florin ("*gulden*" in Dutch) which is divided into 100 cents. There are 1 000, 250, 100, 50, 25 and 10 florin notes and coins to the value of 5, 2.50 and 1 florin. In June 2001, the exchange rate was 3.60fl to the British pound.
Following the launch of the euro at the beginning of 1999 and in preparation for its full introduction in the Netherlands in January 2002, many prices now appear in both florins and euro. In June 2001, 1€ was valued at 2.2fl.

Banks – Bank hours vary from one place to another and from one branch to another; however they are generally open Mon 1pm-4pm or 5pm, Tue-Fri 9am-4pm or 5pm. Many banks have cash machines. Visa and Eurocard / Mastercard are widely accepted as well as cards belonging to the Cirrus banking network (see logos on machines).

Some useful addresses:
American Express: Amsteldijk 166; ☎ (020) 504 86 66.
Diners Club Card: ☎ (020) 654 55 11.
Eurocard Nederland: Eendrachtlaan 315, Utrecht; ☎ (030) 283 55 55.
Visa Card Services: Wisselwerking 32, Diemen; ☎ (020) 660 06 11.

TELEPHONES

To phone the Netherlands from abroad – Dial 00 31 followed by the area code without the 0 and the subscriber's number.
Area codes of towns covered in this guide are as follows: Amsterdam (020), Alkmaar (072), Haarlem (023), Ijmuiden (0255), Lisse (0252, Hilversum (035), Zaandam (075).

To phone abroad from the Netherlands:
GB: 00 44
USA: 00 1
Canada: 00 1
Australia: 00 61
Republic of Ireland: 00 353
followed by the area code without the 0 and subscriber's number.

In the Netherlands – Most public telephones operate with phonecards (in units of 10, 25, or 50fl) available from post offices, railway stations, bookshops, newsagents and tourist offices. 0800 numbers are toll-free, numbers beginning in 0900 have special rates. To make reverse-charge call dial 0800 04 10 (freephone).

POST OFFICE AND TELECOMMUNICATIONS

Post Offices – These are open from 8.30am to 5pm weekdays, 8.30 am to 12pm on Saturdays. The main post office *(Hoofdpostkantoor PTT)* is located at Singel 250/256; it is open on weekdays from 8.30am to 6pm (8pm on Thursdays) and on Saturdays from 10am to 1.30pm. It includes the poste restante service which is open from 8am to 7pm on weekdays and 9am to noon on Saturdays. Another large post office can be found at Oosterdokskade 3 (east of the central station); it is open from 8.30am to 9pm on weekdays and 9am to noon on Saturdays.

Postal rates – Letters (up to 20g) and post cards for destinations within the European Union cost 1fl to send.

MUSEUMS

The "Museumjaarkaart" – Despite its price, which appears fairly steep at first sight, the "Annual Museum Pass" may be of interest to those who enjoy cultural visits. It is a personal pass that entitles the holder to free entry to some 440 museums through-

USEFUL NUMBERS

Emergency Services (Ambulance, police, fire brigade) – ☎ 112
Traffic reports – ☎ 0900 88 55
Public transport travel information – ☎ 0900 92 92
Breakdown service (24hr a day) – ☎ 0800 08 88
Dutch Directory Enquiries – ☎ 0900 80 08
Weather information (KNMI) – ☎ 0900 80 03
Ticket service (Bookings for shows) – ☎ 0900 300 12 50

out the Netherlands for a one-year period. More than 40 of the museums mentioned in this guide are included and the pass pays for itself if you visit at least 10 museums. It costs 30fl for under-24s, and 70 fl for adults. It can be purchased from the VVV *(remember to take an identity photo with you)* or from museums participating in the scheme.

Nederland Museumland – This guide, updated annually, includes brief descriptions of all the Netherlands' museums, castles and zoos as well as information on admission times and charges. It can be purchased in bookshops, large museums and tourist offices.

Museums on the Internet – The following sites give listings of all museums and exhibitions in the Netherlands:

– **www.hollandmuseums.nl**: The museum web site of the Netherlands Tourist Board.
– **www.museumland.nl**: The online version of the Nederland Museumland publication
– **www.museumserver.nl**: Links to all museums with their own web sites as well as an online publication, Museumkr@nt

CONSULATES IN AMSTERDAM

Although Amsterdam is the capital of the Netherlands, it does not have any embassies. They, together with the Crown, government, Parliament and ministry buildings, are all in The Hague. However, Amsterdam has 46 consulates including the following:

United Kingdom – Koningsplein 44, 1075 AE Amsterdam. ☎ (020) 676 43 43.

USA – Museumplein 19, 1071 DJ Amsterdam. ☎ (020) 575 53 09.

Denmark – Radarweg 503, 1043 NZ Amsterdam. ☎ (020) 682 99 91.

Norway – Keizersgracht 534, 1017 EK Amsterdam. ☎ (020) 624 23 31.

Canada has no consulate in Amsterdam. Its consulate is located at Sophialaan 7, Den Haag. ☎ (070) 361 41 11.
Ireland has no consulate in Amsterdam.

ADDITIONAL INFORMATION

Public holidays – 1 Jan, Good Friday, Easter Sunday and Monday, 30 Apr (Queen's birthday celebrations, national holiday), 5 May (Liberation), Ascension, Pentecost Sunday and Monday, 25 and 26 Dec.

Shops – Most shops are open Tue-Sat 9am-6pm and are closed Monday morning and Sunday. They remain open until 9pm on Thursday (late shopping or "koopavond"). In the centre of Amsterdam shops are also open Sunday 1pm-5pm.
Supermarkets are open from 8am-8pm (Sat until 6pm and until 9pm on late-night shopping days) and are closed on Sunday.

ENTERTAINMENT

Concerts, theatre productions, dance and films are listed in the free monthly paper called *Uitkrant* (also online at www.uitkrant.nl), available from theatres, bookshops and cafés and every three weeks in the English-language magazine *What's on in Amsterdam* which is available from the VVV, certain bookshops and most hotels.

Tickets – For most shows seats can be booked either at the VVV or at the **Amsterdam Uit Buro** (AUB). The **AUB ticketshop** is located at the Stadschouwburg theatre in the Leidseplein *(open daily 10am-6pm)*. You can also telephone the Uitlijn service on ☎ 0900-0191 (daily 9am-9pm). The very useful web site run by **Ticket Service** (**www.ticketservice.nl** or ☎ 0900-300 12 50) allows searches by date, location and title in three different categories: theatre, concerts and films. It also offers several links to cinemas, theatres and concert halls all over the country.

Further reading

History

Dutch Revolt – Geoffrey Parker (Penguin Books 1990)

Amsterdam – Geert Mak, Philipp Blom (Trans) (Harvill Press 1999)

The Netherlands: Revolt and Independence, 1550-1650 – Martyn Rady (Hodder & Stoughton Educational 1990)

A Bridge Too Far – Cornelius Ryan (Wordsworth Editions Ltd 1999)

Arnhem – Christopher Hibbert (The Windrush Press 1998)

The Diary of a Young Girl – Anne Frank, Otto Frank (Ed), Mirjam Pressler (Ed), Susan Massotty (Trans) (Penguin Books 1997)

The Battle of the Bulge – Charles B MacDonald (Phoenix Press 1998)

Patriots and Liberators – Simon Schama (Fontana 1992)

The Embarrassment of Riches: An Interpretation of Dutch Culture in the Golden Age – Simon Schama (Fontana 1988)

Travel

Through the Dutch and Belgian Canals – P Bristow (A & C Black)

Of Dutch Ways – H Colijn (Harper & Row)

Holland – A Hopkins (Faber & Faber)

Art and architecture

Mondrian – John Milner (Phaidon Press 1994)

Vincent: the Complete Self Portraits – Bernard Denvir (Courage Books 1997)

From Rembrandt to Vermeer – Jane Turner (Ed) (Macmillan Reference Books 2000)

Rembrandt – Michael Kitson (Phaidon Press 1992)

The Paintings of Willem Van De Velde – MS Robinson (Philip Wilson Publishers 1990)

From Van Eyck to Brueghel – (Phaidon Press 1998)

Dutch Painting – Christopher Brown (Phaidon Press 1993)

Dutch Painting – RH Fuchs (Thames and Hudson 1978)

Dawn of the Golden Age: Northern Netherlandish Art 1580-1620 – Ger Luijten, Ariane Van Suchtelen, Reinier Baarsen (Rijksmuseum 1994)

Dutch Art – Sheila D Muller (Ed) (Garland Publishing Inc 1994)

Rembrandt's Eyes – Simon Schama (The Penguin Press 1999)

De Stijl 1917-1931: The Dutch Contribution to Modern Art – HLC Jaffe (Harvard University Press 1986)

Fiction

Headlong – Michael Frayn (Faber Paperbacks 2000)

Tulip Fever – Deborah Moggach (Heinemann 1999)

Girl with a Pearl Earring – Tracy Chevalier (HarperCollins 1999)

An Empty House – Marga Minco (Peter Owen 1986)

The Black Tulip – Alexandre Dumas, David Coward (Ed), Franz Demmler (Trans) (Oxford Paperbacks 2000)

The Assault – Harry Mulisch, Claire White (Trans) (Random House 1986)

The Two Hearts of Kwasi Boachi – Arthur Japin, Ina Rilke (Trans) (Chatto & Windus 2000)

Dutch Treat – Tristan Jones (Sheridan House 2000)

The Following Story – Cees Noteboom, Ina Rilke (Trans) (The Harvill Press 1994)

Calendar of events

Our list includes only the major events. For more comprehensive information, contact the relevant tourist offices *(see tourist board information above)*.

February

Amsterdam .... **Carnival**.

March

Amsterdam .... **Stille Omgang**. A silent procession (on the nearest Sunday to 15 March) commemorating the Amsterdam Miracle.

Last Saturday in April

Noordwijk-Haarlem .... **Grand floral procession**.

3rd weekend in April

Netherlands .... **Nationaal Museumweekend**. Free admission to all museums.

30 April

Amsterdam .... **Koninginnedag** (Queen's Day). To celebrate the birthday of Queen Beatrix, all the country's young people converge on Amsterdam, filling the city with a crowd out to enjoy itself. Orange is the only colour to wear on this occasion.

Mid-April to mid-September, Fridays 10am - noon

Alkmaar............................ **Cheese market** (Kaasmarkt). Tradition and folklore, a combination that never fails to please.

2nd Saturday in May

Netherlands .... **National Windmill Day** (Nationale Molendag). The windmills are open to the public.

1st week in June

Amsterdam .... **Arts Fair in the RAI**. Contemporary art at the exhibition centre. ☎ (020) 549 12 12. The Dutch are very fond of modern art in all its forms.

June

Amsterdam .... **Holland Festival**: concerts, operas, ballets, drama productions. For bookings, contact: Holland Festival, Kleine Gartmanplantsoen 21, 1071 RP Amsterdam. ☎ (020) 530 71 10, or contact major travel agencies in foreign countries.

EUREKA SLIDE

Preparations for Koninginnedag (30 April)

June-August

Amsterdam .... **Vondelpark Openluchttheater** (open-air theatre): free concerts in Vondelpark. ☎ (020) 523 77 90.

July

Haarlem .... **Internationaal Orgelfestival** (International organ competition) (even-numbered years only). ☎ (023) 516 05 74.

July-August, Wednesdays

Edam .... **Cheese market** (Kaasmarkt).

2nd half of August

Amsterdam .... **Prinsengrachtconcert**. Free concert in front of the Pulitzer hotel.

Last weekend in August

Amsterdam .... **Uitmarkt**. Opening of the theatre season.

1st Saturday in September

Aalsmeer-Amsterdam......... **Bloemencorso** (Floral procession). The procession starts in the town that has the world's largest flower market (Aalsmeer).

2nd weekend in September

Netherlands .... **National Heritage days**.

Mid-October

Amsterdam .... **Amsterdam marathon**.

December

Amsterdam .... **Show jumping competition**. International events organised in the RAI. ☎ (020) 549 12 12.

3rd Saturday before 5 December

Amsterdam .... **Official entry of St Nicholas** on Prins Hendrikkade. In the Netherlands, children adore St Nicholas who is much more important than Father Christmas.

Where to stay

HOTELS

When staying for a few hours or a few days, the current edition of **The Red Guide Benelux** is an indispensable complement to this guide. It is updated every year and offers a range of hotels and restaurants with an indication of their standard of service and comfort, their location and their prices as well as telephone and fax numbers. The red symbol indicates that the hotel is particularly pleasant or peaceful.
Towns underlined in red on Michelin maps 908, 907 (Benelux), 210 and 211 are listed in the current edition of *The Red Guide Benelux* with a choice of hotels and restaurants.
Selected hotels below have been classified in three categories in order to provide a range of hotels for every budget.
The **Budget** category includes hotels in which the cheapest rooms are priced at a maximum of 95fl. They are usually plain little hotels with all modern amenities. **Moderate** refers to particularly pleasant hotels in which prices range from 195 to 325fl. Each of these hotels has its own charm and a little extra something that caught our eye.
Under the heading **Expensive** you will find a few luxury hotels which provide high-class amenities and ensure an unforgettable stay. It goes without saying that the prices charged in these hotels correspond to the excellence of their amenities and service.

Netherlands booking centre – Allows you to book hotel rooms, bungalows and apartments at no extra charge. NRC, Postbus 404, 2260 AK Leidschendam, Netherlands, ☎ (070) 419 55 00; fax (070) 419 55 19; www.hotelres.nl

ANWB/VVV – The tourist boards can also assist you in making hotel reservations. The ANWB hotel guide **(ANWB Hotelgids)**, also available online at www.anwb.nl, lists all hotels in the Netherlands.

Budget

Hotel Aalders – *Jan Luijkenstraat 13-15, 1071 CJ Amsterdam; ☎ (020) 673 40 26, fax (020) 673 46 98, www.hotelaalders.nl 53 rooms.* The Stedelijk Museum, Van Gogh Museum and Rijksmuseum are all situated near this simple and comfortable hotel.

Amstel Botel – *Oosterdokskade 2-4, 1011 AE Amsterdam; ☎ (020) 626 42 47, fax (020) 639 19 52, www.amstelbotel.com 176 rooms.* This floating hotel is a former cruise ship, with 176 rooms providing all mod cons.

Nicolaas Witsen – *Nicolaas Witsenstraat 4, 1017 ZH Amsterdam; ☎ (020) 623 61 43, fax (020) 620 51 13. 31 rooms.* This comfortable hotel is situated in a quiet street only a few minutes' walk from the museums and bustling streets of Rembrandtplein and Leidseplein.

Moderate

In Amsterdam

Ambassade – *Herengracht 341, 1016 AZ Amsterdam; ☎ (020) 555 02 22, fax (020) 555 02 77, www.ambassade-hotel.nl 59 rooms.* Located in a row of ten 17C canal houses, this charming hotel is remarkably well-situated on the Herengracht close to the centre. The attractive breakfast room makes for an elegant start to the day.

Arena – *'s-Gravesandestraat 51, 1092 AA Amsterdam; ☎ (020) 694 74 44, fax 020/663 26 49, www.hotelarena.nl 121 rooms.* This hotel, located near Oosterpark, is housed in an old orphanage dating from 1890. Rooms are spacious and have a restrained designer décor. The complex also includes a café-restaurant with a garden and terrace as well as a disco. Private parking.

Canal House Hotel – *Keizersgracht 148, 1015 CX Amsterdam; ☎ (020) 622 51 82, fax 020/624 13 17, www.canalhouse.nl 26 rooms.* This splendid 17C hotel is furnished with antiques. All the rooms are different. Breakfast is served in a room overlooking the garden.

La Casaló – *Amsteldijk 862, 1079 LN Amsterdam; ☎ (020) 642 36 80, fax (020) 644 74 09. 4 rooms.* This floating hotel has four rooms in the Dutch, Oriental, African and Caribbean styles. In fine weather, breakfast on the water is a pleasant way to start the day.

Piet Hein – *Vossiusstraat 53, 1071 AK Amsterdam; ☎ (020) 662 72 05, fax (020) 662 15 26, www.hotelpiethein.nl 37 rooms.* A comfortable hotel situated near the Vondelpark and the main museums.

Toro – *Koningslaan 64, 1075 AG Amsterdam; ☎ (020) 673 72 23; fax (020) 675 00 31. 22 rooms.* Set on the edge of the Vondelpark, this old bourgeois villa dating from the beginning of the century has an almost family atmosphere. From its patio there is a delightful view of a lake.

In the vicinity

De Fortuna – *Spuistraat 3, 1135 AV Edam; ☎ (0299) 37 16 71, fax (0299) 37 14 69. 23 rooms.* Located 22km/14mi from Amsterdam, this pleasant hotel is a complex of six 17C houses on the banks of the canal.

De Klughte – *Van Ogtropweg 2, 1949 BTO Wijk aan Zee; ☎ (0251) 37 43 04, fax (0251) 37 52 24. 17 rooms.* This small "turn-of-the-century" villa on the edge of the dunes is steeped in incomparable charm. Friendly atmosphere and a chance to step back in time!

Spaander – *Haven 15, 1131 EP Volendam; ☎ (0299) 36 35 95, fax (0299) 36 96 15. 80 rooms.* There is an interesting view of the village. The hotel also has a collection of paintings.

't Jagershuis – *Amstelzijde 2-4, 1184 VA Amstelveen; ☎ (020) 496 20 20, fax (020) 496 45 41.* 12 rooms. This small inn on the banks of the Amstel provides a magnificent image of traditional Holland.

Expensive

American – *Leidsekade 97, 1017 PN Amsterdam; ☎ (020) 556 30 00, fax (020) 556 30 01, wwwinterconti.com 186 rooms.* A prestigious hotel located on Leidseplein. Its magnificent Art Deco grill-room is the meeting place of leading cultural figures and politicians.

Amstel – *Prof Tulpplein 1, 1018 GX Amsterdam; ☎ (020) 622 60 60, fax (020) 622 58 08, www.amstelhotel.nl 64 rooms.* Situated on the banks of the Amstel, this "classic" hotel has one of the best-known restaurants in the country, La Rive. Amenities include a fitness centre with swimming pool, jacuzzi, sauna, gym and Turkish bath.

Europe – *Nieuwe Doelenstraat 2, 1012 CP Amsterdam; ☎ (020) 531 17 77, fax (020) 531 17 78, www.leurope.nl 94 rooms.* Located only a short distance from the historic city centre of Amsterdam, this luxury hotel has a restaurant beautifully situated on the Amstel. Called *L'Excelsior*, it is famous for its wine cellar. Indoor heated swimming pool, sauna, solarium and fitness centre.

Pulitzer – *Prinsengracht 315-331, 1016 GZ Amsterdam; ☎ (020) 523 52 35, fax (020) 627 67 53, www.pulitzer.nl 222 rooms.* This magnificent hotel occupies 25 houses dating from the 17C and 18C. In addition to a restaurant, *De Goudsbloem*, the hotel has a garden, a piano-bar and a café.

The Grand – *Oudezijds Voorburgwal 197, 1012 EX Amsterdam; ☎ (020) 555 31 11, fax (020) 555 32 22, www.thegrand.nl 169 rooms* . This luxurious hotel is housed in the former Prinsenhof. Rooms overlook the canal or internal garden.

OTHER TYPES OF ACCOMMODATION

Youth hostels – *See below.*

Bed and Breakfast – Most VVV offices have listings of families offering bed and breakfast style accommodation *(kamers)*. Reservations can also be made through Bed & Breakfast Holland, Theophile de Bockstraat 3, 1058 TV Amsterdam, ☎ (020) 615 75 27; fax (020) 669 15 73 (bookings only); www.bedandbreakfast.nl

Camping – Camp sites are indicated by the symbol ▲ on Michelin maps 908 and 210. A list of camp sites in the Netherlands is available from VVV tourist offices or from the Netherlands Board of Tourism.
Camping in places other than official camp sites is not allowed in the Netherlands. However landowners may obtain exemptions from this law from their local councils.
The ANWB publishes two guides, Campinggids Nederland and Kleine Campings, the latter covers small sites such as on a farm. You can also consult these two guides online at www.anwb.nl/city/kamperen. For addresses of camp sites in the environs of Amsterdam see below.

Youth hostels

The following are open to members of the Netherlands Youth Hostel Association (**NJHC**, *Postbus 9191, 1006 AD Amsterdam, ☎ (020) 551 31 55, www.njhc.org*). Non-members can also stay here, at extra charge. The youth hostels have no age limits. They are equipped with dormitories as well as rooms sleeping from 2 to 8 people.

NJHC Stadsdoelen – *Kloveniersburgwal 97, 1011 KB, ☎ (020) 624 68 32, 184 beds.* Near the "Red light district".

NJHC Vondelpark – *Zandpad 5, 1054 GA Amsterdam, ☎ (020) 589 89 96, 493 beds.* The busiest and most attractive hostel for its location.

Camp sites

Camping-Jachthaven Uitdam – *Zeedijk 2, 1154 PP Uitdam;* ☎ *(020) 403 14 33, fax (020) 403 36 92.* 23ha site 6km/4mi from IJsselmeer. Caravans for rent.

Gaasper Camping Amsterdam – *Loosdrechtdreef 7, 1108 AZ Amsterdam;* ☎ *(020) 696 73 26, fax (020) 696 93 69.* Situated on the shores of a lake. Public transport 300m.

Het Amsterdamse Bos – *Kleine Noorddijk 1, 1432 CC Aalsmeer;* ☎ *(020) 641 68 68, fax (020) 640 23 78.* This is a municipal site near the airport and Amsterdamse Bos leisure park.

Vliegenbos – *Meeuwenlaan 138, 1022 AM Amsterdam;* ☎ *(020) 636 88 55, fax (020) 632 27 23.* Very popular with young people (few caravans).

A SHORT GLOSSARY OF TERMS

At the hotel – In een hotel

Do you have a single room? – **Heeft u voor mij een eenpersoonskamer?**
Do you have a double room? – **Heeft u voor mij een tweepersoonskamer?**
Do you have a room for X people? – **Heeft u voor mij een kamer voor X personen?**
With bathroom – **Met badkamer.**
With shower – **Met douche.**
How much? – **Hoeveel kost dat?**
May I see the room? – **Mag ik de kamer zien?**
Is breakfast included? – **Is het ontbijt inbegrepen?**
At what time do you serve breakfast ? – **Hoe laat wordt het ontbijt geserveerd?**
I'm looking for a hotel for one night at less than X florins. – **Ik zoek een hotel waar ik voor minder dan X gulden per nacht kan logeren.**

Eating out

Amsterdam is traditionally a cosmopolitan city where you can enjoy a traditional Dutch meal as well delicious food from all over the world. Asian food in particular is well represented with specialities from Indonesia, China, Japan, India and Thailand. Restaurants listed below have been chosen for their setting, atmosphere, authentic food or unique character.

The Red Guide Benelux – Contains a wide selection of restaurants that will enable you to discover the authentic flavours of the Netherlands.
The red Bib Gourmand 🙂 found in the guide indicates a good meal at a reasonable price.

Neerlands Dis – The 140 restaurants of this nationwide chain are easily recognisable by their red, white and blue soup tureen emblem. They offer a selection of traditional Dutch dishes.

RESTAURANTS

Budget

City centre

Cobra – *Museumplein,* ☎ *(020) 470 01 14*. This café-restaurant has chosen as its theme the CoBrA movement, which is in evidence not only in the works of art but also in the floor decoration, the chairs and the wine labels. The tableware was designed by Corneille. There is also a sushi bar, a boutique and a large covered terrace in the summer.

De Roode Leeuw (Hotel Amsterdam) – *Damrak 93,* ☎ *(020) 555 06 66*. A grill-room on the bustling Damstraat, serving Dutch specialities such as capucijners: broad beans served with bacon and onions.

Haesje Claes – *Spuistraat 275,* ☎ *(020) 624 99 98*. Simple Dutch cuisine offering good value for money.

Hosokawa – *Max Euweplein 22,* ☎ *(020) 638 80 86*. Japanese cuisine. Teppan Yaki.

Indrapura – *Rembrandtplein 40-42,* ☎ *(020) 623 73 29*. Indonesian cuisine.

Kantjil & De Tijger – *Spuistraat 291-293,* ☎ *(020) 620 30 74*. Indonesian cuisine.

Raan Phad Thai – *Kloveniersburgwal 18,* ☎ *(020) 420 06 65*. Thai "fast food". Very good value for money.

Moderate

City centre

Bordewijk – *Noordermarkt 7,* ☎ *(020) 624 38 99*. Restaurant with designer interior and an atmosphere typical of the current population in the Jordaan district. Modern cuisine. Dinner only.

Café Roux – *Oudezijds Voorburgwal 197,* ☎ *(020) 555 35 60*. This restaurant, situated on the ground floor of The Grand hotel *(see above)*, serves tasty food in a beautiful Art Deco setting. Note the wall painting by Karen Appel near the entrance.

De Gouden Reael – *Zandhoek 14,* ☎ *(020) 623 38 83*. Well situated in the old harbour. This restaurant offers French regional cuisine with a different menu every month.

In de Waag – *Nieuwmarkt 4,* ☎ *(020) 422 77 72*. Located in the public weights and measures office, this attractive café-restaurant has a menu consisting of fish from the IJsselmeer. Wine bar, reading table and a large terrace in the summer.

Kaiko – *Jekerstraat 114,* ☎ *(020) 662 56 41*. Japanese sushi bar.

Keyzer – *Van Baerlestraat 96,* ☎ *(020) 671 14 41*. Located near the Concertgebouw, this old tavern is popular with music lovers.

Lana-Thai – *Warmoesstraat 10,* ☎ *(020) 624 21 79*. Excellent Thai cuisine. Ask for a table in the back room overlooking the Damrak Basin.

Le Garage – *Ruysdaelstraat 54-56,* ☎ *(020) 679 71 76*. A modern grill-room with an artistic atmosphere and a cosmopolitan clientele. The owner presents a TV cookery programme.

Mangerie De Kersentuin (Hotel Garden) – *Dijsselhofplantsoen 7,* ☎ *(020) 664 21 21*. A favourite address with locals. Lively, convivial atmosphere, local cuisine.

Sea Palace – *Oosterdokskade 8,* ☎ *(020) 626 44 77*. Chinese restaurant on the waterfront with fine views of the city.

Tom Yam – *Staalstraat 22,* ☎ *(020) 622 95 33*. An elegant restaurant with a zen garden serving exotic cuisine in a mixture of styles.

De Vijff Vliegen – *Spuistraat 294-302,* ☎ *(020) 624 83 69*. Dutch cuisine in an atmosphere typical of Amsterdam. A labyrinth of magnificently decorated rooms in the 17C style. Dinner only.

Ph. Gajic/MICHELIN

De Vijff Vliegen or "The Five Flies"

In the vicinity

De Jonge Dikkert – *Amsterdamseweg 104a, ☎ (020) 641 13 78.* Unusual: located in a 17C windmill. Modern cuisine.

Ron Blaauw – *Kerkstraat 56, Ouderkerk a/d Amstel, ☎ (020) 496 19 43.* A good place for a meal during a visit to this delightful little village on the banks of the Amstel.

Imko's – *Halkade 9c, IJmuiden; ☎ (0255) 51 75 26.* Located in a modern building with a panoramic view of the fishing harbour. Fish and seafood.

Kraantje Lek – *Duinlustweg 22, Overveen, ☎ (023) 524 12 66.* Set at the foot of a dune, this 450-year-old inn is a pancake house and is very popular with local people who like to come on family outings.

Expensive

In the city centre

Dorrius (Hotel Holiday Inn Crown Plaza) – *NZ Voorburgwal 5, ☎ (020) 420 22 24.* Located near the main railway station, the restaurant is more than one hundred years old (the interior has been restored). It offers typical Dutch specialities.

't Swarte Schaep – *Korte Leidsedwarsstraat 24, ☎ (020) 622 30 21.* French cuisine in a 17C Dutch interior.

In the vicinity

De Hoop op d'Swarte Walvis – *Kalverringdijk 15 (Zaanse Schans), Zaandam, ☎ (075) 616 56 29.* A great culinary classic stands on the water's edge in a magnificent 18C house that is part of the picturesque village of Zaanse Schans.

De Nederlanden – *Duinkerken 3, Vreeland, ☎ (0294) 23 23 26.* Located on a river bank beside a swing bridge, the restaurant serves French cuisine. It is also a hotel with seven charming bedrooms. Not to be missed!

Klein Paardenburg – *Amstelzijde 59, Amstelveen, ☎ (020) 496 13 35.* Lacquered furniture and silverware make this restaurant on the banks of the Amstel a delightful old-fashioned bistro.

A SHORT GLOSSARY OF TERMS

In the restaurant – In een restaurant

May I see the menu? – **Zou u mij het menu willen geven?**
May I have the menu? – **Kunt u mij de kaart geven?**
A non-smoking table, please! – **Een tafel voor niet-rokers, alstublieft.**
The bill, please! – **De rekening, alstublieft.**

Water – **water**	Plate – **bord**
Wine – **wijn**	Salt – **zout**
Bread – **Brood**	Pepper – **peper**
Fork – **vork**	Butter – **boter**
Knife – **mes**	Milk – **melk**
Spoon – **lepel**	Chair – **stoel**
Glass – **glas**	Table – **tafel**

Time for a drink

Amsterdam has a large number of cafés; the city is said to have a total in excess of one thousand. All of them, from the grand designer café to the traditional "brown" establishment, provide a warm, friendly atmosphere in which everybody chats to those around. A very pleasant tradition cultivated by a large number of cafés is the reading table at which customers can take a look at the newspapers, including international papers. Most cafés offer snacks or have a short menu. Some of them indicate this in the window by the term "*eetcafé*".
In the evening, apart from the "Red Light District", night life is at its busiest on Leidseplein and Rembrandtplein. On Leidseplein is the Stadsschouwburg, around which there are numerous small theatres, cafés, cinemas and discos. In the summer months, outdoor cafés are busy until well after midnight. Nearby, those who enjoy a flutter can play in one of the largest casinos in Europe. Rembrandtplein is famous for its restaurants and bars with vast terraces. It is equally well known for its discos.

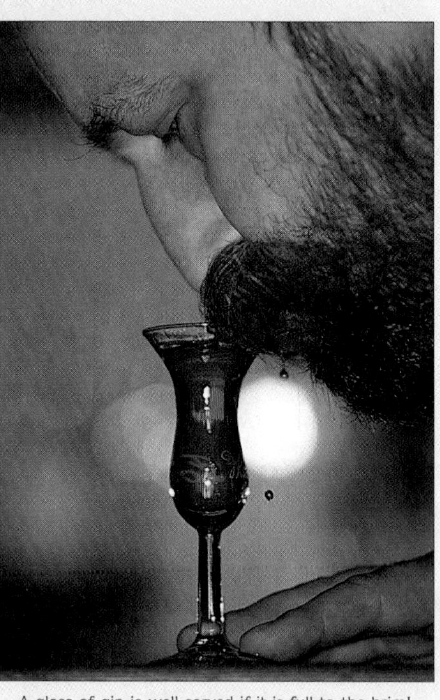
Ph. Gajic/MICHELIN

A glass of gin is well served if it is full to the brim!

BROWN CAFÉS

Brown cafés are typical of the Netherlands. In an authentic brown café the walls are bare, the wood panelling worn smooth by the passing years and the hands of customers, and the floor covered with sand. Although they serve coffee and hot chocolate, most customers order beer and schnapps. Many of these cafés are small and even with only a very few people in them appear crowded, creating the convivial atmosphere that is their main characteristic. The city centre and Jordaan district contain the most authentic brown cafés.

Café Hoppe – *Spui 18-20.* Very popular with the literary world (writers, journalists). In the summer, customers move outside onto the pavement, creating what the Dutch call "stand-up receptions".

Chris Anno 1624 – *Bloemstraat 42.* Unusual for its entertainment: on Sunday afternoons, customers can hear live performances of extracts from operas or operettas.

De Admiraal – *Herengracht 563.* This café resembles a distillery. It serves schnapps from one of the oldest distilleries in Amsterdam.

De Druif – *Rapenburgplein 83.* Its atmosphere and old-fashioned decoration seem to have stood the test of time.

De Karpershoek – *Martelaarsgracht 2.* With its ceramics on the walls and sand covering the floor, this café (1629) takes us back into the 17C. The atmosphere becomes lively when local office workers arrive.

Eik en Linde – *Plantage Middenlaan 22.* Located near Artis, it is very well known for the television programmes broadcast from it. In the middle of the café is a billiard table.

Het Molenpad – *Prinsengracht 653.* This café, in the heart of the area filled with antique shops and designer furniture stores, serves as an art gallery for young local artists. Terrace overlooking the canal.

De Dokter – *Rozenboomsteeg 4.* A tiny café with a plethora of decoration. It is the ideal place to stop and rest in a busy pedestrian area (Kalverstraat).

't Gasthuys – *Grimburgwal 7.* The café is long and narrow with a wooden counter worn smooth and, hanging from the ceiling beams, bank notes from all over the world. Very popular with students from the nearby university.

't Papeneiland – *Prinsengracht 2*. Its location on the canal bank, old-fashioned decoration (Delft ceramics, old paintings etc), its furnishings and its old stove make this a very romantic brown café.

't Smalle – *Egelantiersgracht 12*. Standing on the bank of a canal, this small café has a small terrace overlooking the water.

Ph. Gajic/MICHELIN

't Papeneiland, a "brown café" on the banks of the Prinsengracht

PROEFLOKALEN

These bars have existed since the 17C. Customers can drink (and buy) schnapps and flavoured spirits, many of them distilled on the spot.

De Drie Fleschjes – *Gravenstraat 18*. Few seats, lively atmosphere. Everything happens at the counter. The wall is lined with jugs bearing labels suggestive of their contents: cream of roses, cream of vanilla, perfect love, ratafia etc.

De Ooievaar – *St-Olofspoort 1*. A small long-established bar where many locals come for a beer with a schnapps as a chaser (wide selection).

Wynand Fockink – *Pijlsteeg 31*. This bar offers a wide selection of schnapps and spirits made locally for tasting and purchase. A very busy bar. Located only a short distance from the Dam, this small café is a haven of peace with a pleasant garden in summer. Tables are set out in the middle of trees, shrubs and rippling fountains.

LUXURY CAFÉS

Café Américain – *Leidsekade 97 and Leidseplein 26*. This magnificent grill-room with a combination of Art Nouveau and Art Deco ornamentation is one of the sights of Amsterdam. It is an elegant place which is well worth a visit despite the slightly steep prices.

Café Dantzig – *Zwanenburgwal 15*. A very large café with a reading area. Its terrace on the banks of the Amstel is an ideal place to rest after a stroll through the flea market in Waterlooplein.

Ph. Gajic/MICHELIN

The *American Café* in the chic but expensive American Hotel

Café Luxembourg – *Spui 22.* Midway between a brown café and a luxury café, this is a pleasant venue, particularly in the late morning. The breakfast is very good.

De Jaren – *Nieuwe Doelenstraat 20-22.* This is a spacious venue that is very popular with Amsterdam's young people. Its superb two-storey terrace on the banks of the Amstel is crowded in fine weather. Relaxed atmosphere with music.

De Kroon – *Rembrandtplein 17.* Located in a building that contains radio and television studios, De Kroon is an institution. The clientele could not be more varied, and the room on the first floor is a particularly strange sight. From the terrace, there is a fine view of the square.

BEER BARS

Gollem – *Raamsteeg 4.* A bar with very mixed decoration although everything has some connection with beer. Selection of 200 beers.

In de Wildeman – *Kolksteeg 3.* Good selection of beers and schnapps. Traditional music at weekends. This bar has a non-smoking room, which is a rarety in Amsterdam.

PUBS

Mulligans – *Amstel 100.* An Irish pub with very popular live music on Friday and Saturday evenings. Serves draught Guinness – of course.

O'Reilly's Irish Pub – *Paleisstraat 103-105.* An Irish pub in which stouts flow by the gallon, especially on concert nights. A popular venue with Amsterdam's large Irish community.

The Balmoral – *Nieuwe Doelenstraat 24.* A very elegant Scottish pub with live concerts every Wednesday at 9pm.

Three Sisters – *Rembrandtplein 17.* Superb pub with a grandiose frontage and vast terrace. Very busy, especially before the nearby discos open their doors.

BARS FOR ALL TASTES

Badcuyp – *Eerste Sweelinckstraat 10.* A bar that offers a different type of music every evening: blues sessions; salsa; jazz sessions; disco evenings.

Café du Nemo – *Oosterdok 2.* One of the very few cafés providing a view of the city.

De Sluiswacht – *Jodenbreestraat 1.* Located on a canal bank near Waterlooplein, this small café has a delightful terrace. No, you have not drunk too much – the house really does lean at an angle!

Café Ter Kuile – *Torensteeg 8.* This fairly banal café has a superb terrace on the bridge spanning the canal in the summer. Very popular with students from the nearby Arts Faculty.

De Engelbewaarder – *Kloveniersburgwal 59.* A quiet atmosphere. Jazz session on Sunday afternoons.

De IJsbreker – *Weesperzijde 23.* Very popular with those who enjoy contemporary music. Wonderful terrace on the banks of the Amstel in summer.

De Prins – *Prinsengracht 124.* A bar with a good atmosphere. Superb view of Anne Frank Huis and Westerkerk.

De Reiger – *Nieuwe Leliestraat 34.* An old-fashioned bistro in a quiet little street. Very pleasant place for a snack if you are strolling in the area.

De Twee Zwaantjes – *Prinsengracht 114.* A bar-café with a fairly muted decor of stained glass through which filters soft light. Musical evenings.

Flying Dutchman – *Martelaarsgracht 13.* One of the favourite haunts of Amsterdam's English-speaking community.

Hard Rock Café – *Max Euweplein 57-61.* Music and decoration are in honour of rock music. A popular place with rock 'n roll fans.

Hof van Holland – *Rembrandtplein.* A café decorated with gadgets given by the many supporters of the city's football clubs (especially Ajax).

Morlang – *Keizersgracht 451.* A café in an old house with modern decoration. Fairly young clientele. Superb terrace on the river bank. All this makes the bar a particularly popular venue.

Proust – *Noordermarkt 4.* This is a modern café with jazz and blues music.

Cyber – *Nieuwendijk 19.* The cyber café has a dozen computers available for internet fans.

VOC Café In de Schreierstoren – *Prins Hendrikkade 94-95.* A café consisting of two rooms in very differing styles. The bar is decorated with antiques; the other room resembles a private lounge. Two pleasant terraces, one of them on the canal bank, complete this magnificent venue.

Walem – *Keizersgracht 449.* A large designer bar. At the back of the room is a door into a pleasant summer garden. Terrace overlooking the canal.

Ph. Gajic/MICHELIN

The interior of *VOC Café*

COFFEE SHOPS

Although they serve coffee, the main purpose of these cafés is the sale of cannabis, a drug which has been taken off the streets and is sold in registered *koffieshops*. It would not be appropriate to give a selection of this type of café – anyway, it is open to debate as to what the criteria for selection should, or could, be.

CAKES AND PASTRIES

Beune – *Haarlemmerdijk 156*. If you can ignore the old-fashioned decoration, this is one of the best cake shops in the city.

Holtkamp – *Vijzelgracht 15*. Good Dutch cakes and home-made chocolates.

Lanskroon – *Singel 385*. Only the steel-willed would be able to resist taking a bite of the forest fruits tart. Gluttony is no longer a vice here. There are a few tables at which to do more than feast the eyes.

Multi Vlaai – *Kinkerstraat 173*. Sells several varieties of the traditional Vlaai, a tart from the province of Limbourg.

Oldenburg – *Beethovenstraat 17*. A leading biscuit specialist. At Christmas, the shop produces a marzipan to die for.

Entertainment

All cultural events in the city are listed weekly in the *Uitkrant* and in the English-language magazine *What's on in Amsterdam*.

DANCING

Those who enjoy dancing will find plenty to keep them busy in Amsterdam. The city's many discos each have their own style and music, with every kind of music represented (house, hip-hop, techno, disco etc).

Dansen bij Jansen – *Handboogstraat 11*. Disco with a student clientele. Particularly busy during the Happy Hour early in the evening.

Escape – *Rembrandtplein 11*. Amsterdam's largest disco. Commercial music and superb laser show.

iT – *Amstelstraat 24*. The city's most extravagant disco: colourful, mind-blowing evening with professional dancers, go-go girls, drag queens and everything connected with night-life. Gay evenings on Fridays and Saturdays.

Mazzo – *Rozengracht 114*. The young person's disco. Futuristic design with lasers and lights.

One of the auditoria in the Odeon: no lack of atmosphere here

Odeon – *Singel 460.* Bar and disco with three storeys, each with its own style of music. More conventional evenings also organised here.

West Pacific – *Haarlemmerweg 8-10.* Trendy café with an equally trendy clientele. It is turned into a disco from Thursdays to Sundays (from 11pm). 1970s music.

CASINO

Holland Casino Amsterdam – *Max Euweplein 64.* One of the largest casinos in Europe: slot machines, roulette, black Jack etc. Its "Lido" theatre-restaurant stages famous shows.

CABARETS

Boom Chicago – *Lijnbaansgracht 238, ☎ (020) 530 73 00.* One of the most famous comedy shows in Amsterdam, in the cabaret style.

Comedy Club – *Max Euweplein 43-45, ☎ (020) 638 39 71.* Comedy cabaret with a very relaxed style. The customers are close to the performers.

MUSIC

Jazz

Alto Jazz Café – *Korte Leidsedwarsstraat 115, ☎ (020) 626 32 49.* A small, elongated bar decorated with musical instruments and jazz posters. Live concert every evening. Pleasant, bohemian atmosphere.

Bimhuis – *Oude Schans 73, ☎ (020) 623 13 61.* The top jazz club in Amsterdam. The performers are often world-famous. Some evenings, it is the customers who provide the music. A "must" for those who enjoy jazz.

Bourbon Street – *Leidsekruisstraat 6-8, ☎ (020) 623 34 40.* A bar with music and a 1920s atmosphere in which to hear blues and jazz or rock'n roll.

Casablanca – *Zeedijk 26, ☎ (020) 625 56 85.* A famous old jazz bar which also has jazz sessions on Tuesday and Sunday afternoons. The karaoke evenings are very popular with the locals.

Rock, pop etc

Amsterdam ArenA – *Arena Boulevard 1, ☎ (020) 311 13 33.* World-famous stars perform in this stadium which can cater for 50 000 people.

Arena – *'s-Gravesandestraat 51, ☎ (020) 694 74 44.* Weekend concerts in this multi-purpose venue: hotel for young people, restaurant, café, dance club.

Akhnaton – *Nieuwezijds Kolk 25, ☎ (020) 624 33 96.* A centre dedicated to world cultures. Live concerts and dance evenings.

De Melkweg – *Lijnbaansgracht 234, ☎ (020) 531 81 81.* A famous arts centre offering all forms of entertainment: dance, theatre, cinema, modern music concerts etc.

Paradiso – *Weteringschans 6, ☎ (020) 626 45 21.* Housed in a former church the most famous rock groups enjoy performing here (the Rolling Stones used the venue to film one of their video clips). Dances are also held here.

Classical music and opera

Koninklijk Theater Carré – *Amstel 115-125, ☎ (020) 625 52 25.* The largest auditorium in the city seating 1 700. Musical comedies and variety shows. Most popular for its circus spectaculars.

Muziektheater (Stopera) – *Amstel 3, ☎ (020) 625 54 55.* Major operas and ballet performances. The Nederlandse Opera, Nationale Ballet and Nederlands Dans Theater, all of them highly renowned, perform here regularly.

Stadsschouwburg – *Leidseplein 26, ☎ (020) 624 23 11.* A very varied programme (plenty of opera).

Beurs van Berlage – *Damrak 213, ☎ (020) 627 04 66.* The former Stock Exchange is now used for numerous cultural events including classical music concerts. The Netherlands Philharmonic Orchestra is one of the guests.

Concertgebouw – *Concertgebouwplein 2-6, ☎ (020) 671 83 54.* The main venue for classical music thanks to its perfect acoustics and the outstanding quality of its famous orchestra, the Royal Concertgebouw.

Felix Meritis – *Keizersgracht 324, ☎ (020) 623 13 11.* Classical music concerts in a magnificent 18C auditorium.

THEATRES

These addresses are given as a guideline for those visitors who understand Dutch.

Bellevue – *Leidsekade 90, ☎ (020) 530 53 01.* Experimental theatre and variety shows.

De Brakke Grond – *Nes 45, ☎ (020) 622 90 14.* The café-restaurant of this Flemish cultural centre is very popular with performers of all nationalities.

De Engelenbak – *Nes 71, ☎ (020) 624 13 24.*

Frascati – *Nes 59, ☎ (020) 624 13 24.* Experimental theatre.

De Stadsschouwburg – *Leidseplein 26, ☎ (020) 624 23 11.* The oldest theatre in the city (vaudeville and musical comedies).

Vondelpark's Open-air Theatre – *Marnixstraat 427, ☎ (020) 523 77 90.* Each summer, this magnificent park hosts classical music concerts, drama productions and children's shows. All these entertainments are free of charge.

CINEMAS

There are not many cinemas in Amsterdam. Box-office successes are shown in their original language and sub-titled in Dutch. Numerous cinemas show art and experimental films for film lovers.

Bellevue Cinerama – *Marnixstraat 400.* A large cinema showing recent films.

City – *Kleine-Gartmanplantsoen 15-19.* Located near Leidseplein, this is the city's largest complex.

G. Dubbelman-Melkweg

De Melkweg, one of Amsterdam's night-time hot spots

Desmet Studio's – *Plantage Middenlaan 4a.* Located near the zoo, this is the cinema for knowledgeable film lovers.

Kriterion – *Roetersstraat 170.* Art and experimental films.

Nederlands Filmmuseum – *Vondelpark 3.* The city's film library. Films shown daily. On Sundays, jazz concert in the adjacent café.

The Movies – *Haarlemmerdijk 161.* Early 20C decoration.

Tuschinski – *Reguliersbreestraat 26 – 28.* Magnificent Art Deco building.

Shopping

Most stores are open on Mondays from 1pm to 6pm and from Tuesdays to Saturdays from 9am to 6pm. City centre shops are open on Sundays from 1pm to 5pm. Some shops have late night opening on Thursdays (9pm).

DEPARTMENT STORES AND SHOPPING ARCADES

De Bijenkorf – *Dam 1.* The equivalent of Debenham's.

Magna Plaza – *Nieuwezijds Voorburgwal 182. Open daily.* Shopping centre with 40 stores including a Virgin Megastore and two restaurants in a splendid building.

Maison de la Bonneterie – *Rokin 140.* One of Amsterdam's foremost department stores.

Metz & Co – *Leidsestraat 34-36.* Designer furniture, decorative objects, gifts etc.

Pauw – *Van Baerlestraat 66.*

Vroom & Dreesmann – *Kalverstraat 201.* There are branches all over the Netherlands. Slightly less exclusive than De Bijenkorf.

FASHION

The **Museumkwartier** and, to be more precise, **Hooftstraat** and Van Baerlestraat are the places to go if you are looking for haute couture houses (Versace, Gucci, Boss etc), leading footwear names, jewellers (Cartier) and fashionable boutiques. The pedestrian streets such as **Kalverstraat** and Nieuwendijk are dotted with numerous off-the-peg clothes shops.

Awareness Winkel – *Weteringschans 143.* All the clothing and accessories are made of organically-grown cotton.

Cora Kemperman – *Leidsestraat 72.* Women's off-the-peg clothes shop.

Panara – *PC Hooftstraat 124.* Leather goods shop with very chic, unusual items.

Pauw – *Van Baerlestraat 88-90.* An unusual off-the-peg clothes shop.

Reflections – *PC Hoofstraat 66-68.* For curiosity's sake only, given that no prices are displayed.

Shoebaloo – *Koningsplein 7 and PC Hooftstraat 80.* A designer boutique with an excellent selection of fashion footwear.

MUSIC

Concerto – *Utrechtsestraat 52-60.* Very wide selection of CD's and LP's (new and second-hand).

FAME Music – *Kalverstraat 2-4.* Every style of music has its own department: classical, jazz, techno, military bands, variety artists etc.

Jazz Inn Motion – *Middenweg 129.* Excellent selection of jazz records.

JEWELLERY

Most of the refined, and unusual, jewellery shops are to be found in Rokin.

Bonebakker – *Rokin 88.* Magnificent jewellery, sometimes with very modern designs.

Hans Appenzeller – *Grimburgwal 1.* This shop will make the jewellery you have always dreamed of, especially for you.

Jorge Cohen – *Singel 414.* A specialist in Art Deco jewellery and modern jewellery inspired by old designs.

Harry Tromp Juwelier – *Rokin 48.* Wide selection of jewellery of every style.

DIAMOND MERCHANTS

Amsterdam is one of the world's leading centres for diamonds. The Koh-i-Noor, which is now part of the British crown jewels, was cut here. You can buy a diamond from any of the following addresses.

Amstel Diamonds – *Amstel 208.*

Amsterdam Diamond Center – *Rokin 1-5;* ☎ *020/624 57 87.*

Coster Diamonds – *Paulus Potterstraat 2-4.*

Gassan Diamonds – *Nieuwe Uilenburgerstraat 173-175.*

Van Moppes Diamonds – *Albert Cuypstraat 2-6.*

ANTIQUES

Most antique shops are on the banks of the main canals (Singel, Herengracht, Keizersgracht and Prinsengracht), especially in **Spiegelstraat**, **Nieuwe Spiegelstraat** and **Kerkstraat**.

Aronson – *Nieuwe Spiegelstraat 39.* Furniture and porcelain.

Blitz – *Nieuwe Spiegelstraat 37a.* Porcelain and Chinese ceramics.

De Munt – *Muntplein 12.* Delft faïence, pottery and tiles.

Eduard Kramer – *Nieuwe Spiegelstraat 64.* A specialist in Dutch tiling from the 15C to the present day.

Inez Stodel – *Nieuwe Spiegelstraat 65.* Silverware and jewellery.

Israël – *Nieuwezijds Voorburgwal 264.* A specialist in old books.

Premsela & Hamburger – *Rokin 98.* Antique jewellery.

Toebosch – *Nieuwe Spiegelstraat 33.* Antique watches and barometers.

DESIGN

Djoeke Wessing – *Huidenstraat 20.* Furniture.

Kis – *Paleisstraat 107.* Utility objects with avant-garde and humorous designs.

The Frozen Fountain – *Prinsengracht 629.* Although prices are high, the items and furniture on show are well worth a look.

CHEESES

Abraham Kef – *Marnixstraat 192.* The best cheeses from Holland and elsewhere.

Mylunch – *Rozengracht 32.* A cheesemonger established 150 years ago. Excellent selection. If you are in Amsterdam between mid-June and mid-July, try some "May" gouda.

Wout Arxhoek – *Damstraat 19.* There is a dazzling array of cheeses in this apparently insignificant shop. Worth a taste: Frisian cheese with cloves.

CYCLES

Bankras Tweewielers – *Nieuwe Hoogstraat 21.* The best place to buy a bike. Also sells all the accessories required to ensure that your cycle is fully equipped.

Lohman – *De Clercqstraat 70-76.* New and second-hand bikes for sale.

SOUVENIRS

De Klompenboer – *Sint-Anthoniesbreestraat 51.* Artisan clogmaker. Demonstrations of the clogmaker's craft.

Galleria d'Arte – *Prinsengracht 170.* Delft porcelain.

Heinen – *Spiegelgracht 13.* Extensive selection of Delft porcelain.

Ph. Gajic/MICHELIN

Cigar-lovers should not miss the shop run by Hajenius the cigar manufacturer

Oude Amsterdam – *Nieuwendijk 75.* Local liqueurs: schnapps and fruit-based spirits.

PGC Hajenius – *Rokin 92-96.* A "must" on any trip to Amsterdam: everything for cigar and pipe smokers. There are several rooms in this magnificent store decorated with wood panelling, including one room with air conditioning for top-of-the-range products.

SOME UNUSUAL SHOPS

Art Unlimited – *Keizersgracht 510.* Thousands of artistic post cards (displayed by subject matter, photographer, country etc).

Christmas Palace – *Singel 508-510.* A Christmas shop, selling Christmas goods all year round!

De Hoed Van Tijn – *Nieuwe Hoogstraat 15.* Dozens of hats of every shape and every colour.

De Witte Tanden Winkel – *Runstraat 5.* Very wide selection of toothbrushes for children and adults. Many of the brushes are highly unusual.

Geels & Co – *Warmoesstraat 67.* A magnificent shop selling tea and coffee. Don't miss the small museum on the first floor.

Gulden Vlies – *Warmoesstraat 141.* A condom specialist providing advice and a wide selection of products.

Joe's Vliegerwinkel – *Nieuwe Hoogstraat 19.* Kites for the most enthusiastic kite flyers.

Bulterman Filatelie – *Nieuwezijds Voorburgwal 302.* Heaven for philatelists.

Rodolfo's Skateshops – *Magna Plaza.* A "fun" shop selling roller skates, roller blades and related products.

ART GALLERIES

Atelier Amsterdam – *Weteringschans 221.* Naive art. The artists and managers of the galleries are all disabled.

Boekie Woekie – *Berenstraat 16.* Books and posters created using a range of different techniques.

Delaive – *Spiegelgracht 23.* A gallery specialising in the 20C.

Paul Andriessen – *Prinsengracht 116.* Contemporary art.

Prestige Art Gallery – *Reguliersbreestraat 46.* Paintings and sculptures from the 17C to the 20C.

Rob Jurka – *Singel 28.* Contemporary paintings and drawings.

BOOKSHOPS

À la Carte – *Utrechtsestraat 110-112.* The largest and most comprehensive tourist bookshop in the Netherlands.

Athenaeum – *Spui 14-16.* Wide selection of international magazines and books.

De Slegte – *Kalverstraat 48-52.* Very large selection of second-hand books.

Lambiek – *Kerkstraat 78.* A "must" for strip cartoon collectors.

Premsela – *Van Baerlestraat 78.* Very wide selection of art books.

MARKETS

The best way to discover Amsterdam's colourful inhabitants.

Albert Cuypmarkt – *Albert Cuypstraat; Mondays to Saturdays from 9.30am to 5pm.* Food and clothing. The Albert Cuypmarkt attracts 20 000 people every week. *Also see De PIJP.*

Antiekmarkt Nieuwmarkt – *Nieuwmarkt; May to September, Sundays from 9am to 5pm.* Antiques, old objects, ornaments.

Bloemenmarkt – *Singel, between Muntplein and Koningsplein; Mondays to Saturdays from 9.30am to 5pm.* The flower market, a sight not to be missed.

Boekenmarkt – *Oudemanhuispoort; Mondays to Saturdays from 10am to 4pm; Spui, Fridays from 10am to 6pm.* Two markets specialising in old books. The first one is very popular with students from the nearby university.

Boerenmarkt – *Nieuwmarkt; Saturdays from 9am to 6pm.* Organic farm products.

De Looier Kunst- en Antiekcentrum – *Elandsgracht 109; daily (except Friday) 11am to 5pm.*

Postzegelmarkt – *Nieuwezijds Voorburgwal; Wednesdays and Saturdays from 1pm to 4pm.* For philatelists and numismologists.

Rommelmarkt – *Looiersgracht 38; Saturday and Sunday 11am to 5pm.* Bric-à-brac.

Fleamarket – *Waterlooplein; Mondays to Saturdays from 9am to 5pm.* Second-hand clothes, ornaments, old records etc. Something of everything for those who enjoy looking for that hidden treasure. *Also see WATERLOOPLEIN.*

Amsterdam and sport

FOOTBALL: Ajax

The club famous for Johan Cruyff and the De Boer brothers has since 1996 had the pleasure of playing in its ultra-modern stadium, the Amsterdam ArenA in Bijlmermeer. Its museum will delight football fans. League matches are usually played on Sundays at 2.30pm.

HOCKEY

The Dutch are excellent grass hockey players. To see a match, ask for details from: Amsterdamse Hockey- en Bandyclub, *Nieuwe Kalfjeslaan 1,* ☎ *(020) 645 66 15.*

KORFBALL

Invented by a Dutchman in 1901, korfball is a combination of netball, volleyball and basketball. It is worth seeing if you are a foreign visitor. Matches are played from September to June at 2pm at the Sportpark, J Banckersweg and there is no admission charge. For information on the sport, contact the Vereniging Amsterdam-Zuid Korfball, *Kinderdijkstraat 29;* ☎ *(020) 646 15 15.*

TENPIN BOWLING

Bowling Knijn – *Scheldeplein 3;* ☎ *(020) 664 22 11.* 18 bowling alleys.

SWIMMING POOLS

De Mirandab – *De Mirandalaan 9;* ☎ (020) 546 44 44. A pool complex with a magnificent wave pool.

Zuiderbad – *Hobbemastraat 26;* ☎ *(020) 679 22 17.* This city centre swimming pool is housed in an early 20C building.

ICE RINK

During particularly harsh winters, many of the locals enjoy skating through the city along the frozen canals. If you cannot take advantage of this very unusual situation, you will have to be content with an ordinary ice rink.

Jaap Eden – *Radioweg 64;* ☎ *(020) 694 96 52.* The largest manmade ice rink in the Netherlands.

TENNIS AND SQUASH

Borchland – *Borchlandweg 6;* ☎ *(020) 563 33 33.* Located near the ArenA Stadium, this sports complex offers tennis, squash, badminton and bowling.

Nieuw Tenniscentrum Amstelpark – *Karel Lotsylaan 12;* ☎ *(020) 644 57 08.* One of the largest tennis complexes in the Netherlands: 36 indoor and outdoor courts.

Amsterdam for children

EATING OUT

Kinderkookkafé – *Oudezijds Achterburgwal 193;* ☎ *(020) 625 32 57.* In this restaurant, the children do the cooking which parents can then taste. All the necessary equipment is made available to them (hob, oven, kitchen utensils etc) and is scaled down to suit their size. For children aged 5 to 12.

MUSEUMS AND ATTRACTIONS

Amsterdam Marionettentheater – *Nieuwe Jonkerstraat 8;* ☎ *(020) 620 80 27.* Puppet theatre speaks a universal language, unhindered by linguistic borders.

Artis – *See PLANTAGE.* In this superb 19C park, children can see one of the oldest zoos in Europe. The **Artis Express** *(see Practical information: Boats)* is an opportunity for a boat trip from the central railway station to the zoo.

Aviodome – *See SCHIPHOL.* Aviation for children. They can try out simulators set up next to actual aircraft cockpits.

Kindermuseum – *See PLANTAGE, Tropenmuseum.* For children aged 6 to 12 only.

Madame Tussaud Scenerama – *See DAM.* The history of the city and famous people from the modern world, who seem almost larger than life!

Nederlands Scheepvaartmuseum – In addition to the many models, the tour of the famous ship belonging to the India Company, the Amsterdam, enables children to dream of sea voyages, pirates and privateers thanks to the many attractions organised by people dressed in period costume.

Rialto – *Ceintuurbaan 338-340.* A cinema with a programme designed for children. Open Wednesdays, Sundays and during school holidays.

SHOPPING

Coppenhagen 1001 Kralen – *Rozengracht 54.* Beads, beads and more beads, of every sort and in a myriad of colours. A "must" for girls who want to make their own jewellery.

Kleine Nicolaas – *Cornelis Schuytstraat 19.* Magnificent shop filled with cuddly toys and wooden toys.

Party Balloon – *Rozengracht 65.* Balloons of every shape, size and colour.

World Heritage List

In 1972, the United Nations Educational, Scientific and Cultural Organization (UNESCO) adopted a Convention for the preservation of cultural and natural sites. To date, more than 150 States Parties have signed this international agreement, which has listed over 500 sites "of outstanding universal value" on the World Heritage List. Each year, a committee of representatives from 21 countries, assisted by technical organizations (ICOMOS – International Council on Monuments and Sites; IUCN – International Union for Conservation of Nature and Natural Resources; ICCROM – International Centre for the Study of the Preservation and Restoration of Cultural Property, the Rome Centre), evaluates the proposals for new sites to be included on the list, which grows longer as new nominations are accepted and more countries sign the Convention. To be considered, a site must be nominated by the country in which it is located.

The protected cultural heritage may be monuments (buildings, sculptures, archaeological structures etc) with unique historical, artistic or scientific features; groups of buildings (such as religious communities, ancient cities); or sites (human settlements, examples of exceptional landscapes, cultural landscapes) which are the combined works of man and nature of exceptional beauty. Natural sites may be a testimony to the stages of the earth's geological history or to the development of human cultures and creative genius or represent significant ongoing ecological processes, contain superlative natural phenomena or provide a habitat for threatened species.

Signatories of the Convention pledge to cooperate to preserve and protect these sites around the world as a common heritage to be shared by all humanity.

Some of the most well-known places which the World Heritage Committee has inscribed include: Australia's Great Barrier Reef (1981), the Canadian Rocky Mountain Parks (1984), The Great Wall of China (1987), the Statue of Liberty (1984), the Kremlin (1990), Mont-Saint-Michel and its Bay (France, 1979), Durham Castle and Cathedral (1986).

In Amsterdam, UNESCO World Heritage sites are:

The Defense Line of Amsterdam (1996)

In the Netherlands, UNESCO World Heritage sites are:

The former island of Schokland (1995)

Kinderdijk windmills (1997)

Ir. D.F. Wouda steam pumping station (1998)

The Beemsterpolder, Noord-Holland (1999)

Rietveld Schröderhuis, Utrecht (2000)

Keizersgracht

Introduction

Amsterdam's coat of arms

Visitors will often see the emblem from the coat of arms during a visit to the city. It includes three St Andrew's crosses set on a vertical black band in a red shield.

THE ORIGINS

Coats of arms bearing St Andrew's crosses appeared in the Amsterdam region in the 13C when this type of shield belonged to a local family. In the following century, the seals of certain aldermen bore the same motif. Its exact origin remains unknown. However, it is highly likely that the crosses did not refer to St Andrew, St Peter's brother who was martyred on an X-shaped cross; instead they were chosen because of their symbolic simplicity. In those days, most of the population was illiterate and it was important to choose a visual sign that was sufficient to indicate the origin of goods or people immediately and without ambiguity.
However, the oldest surviving seal of the town, dating from **1347**, has none of these crosses. It consists of a boat (a symbol of trade) and the lion of the Counts of Holland under whose authority the Amstel region had been placed in 1317. It was c 1419 that the town's seal first bore the three St Andrew's crosses, accompanied by the medieval boat which continued to decorate the Amsterdam seal until the end of the 18C.

THE BOAT, A LEGEND AND A REALITY

Having fled his country, a Norwegian prince is said to have drifted for days on end with a dog and a Frisian fisherman in a boat in a poor state of repair that finally came ashore on the banks of the IJ. He set foot on dry land c 1200 and founded Amsterdam. This legendary episode is indicated on the tympanum of a house at no 235 Prinsengracht.
In more real history, by the 14C, the town already had strong trade links with the Baltic. The cog, a single-masted boat that was unusually broad in the beam, had considerably reduced transport costs by decreasing the risks of shipwreck. Moreover, trading towns such as Lübeck in the Trave Estuary on the Baltic Sea or Damme near Bruges used seals depicting this type of boat to mark their goods. It was, therefore, in honour of these vessels that the municipal authorities of Amsterdam placed a boat on their seal.

A CROWNED COAT OF ARMS

In the mid 15C, after **Philip the Good**, Duke of Burgundy, had captured Holland and Zeeland, Amsterdam became the economic capital of Holland. Although it was not a member of the German Hanseatic League Amsterdam was one of the main Dutch centres for Hanseatic trade. The town quickly gained power and importance, making it a rich rival for Hamburg and Bremen.

In 1488, **Emperor Maximilian I** of Austria, who was yet again short of money, had to withstand rebellion in Flanders, especially in Ghent. Amsterdam took advantage of the situation by offering him a loan of the 10 000 Flemish *livres* he required. In order to thank the people for their gesture and loyalty, he granted them the right, one year later, to place the "crown of his empire" on the town's coat of arms. The wording was important because, in 1493, Maximilian succeeded Frederick III as Emperor of the Holy Roman Empire. The population soon began to question, rather late in the day, the crown to which they were entitled. Was it the Habsburg crown or the crown of the Holy Roman Empire? The hesitancy, one might even say anxiety, continued unabated until Charles V mounted the throne of the German Holy Roman Empire in 1519. It was then that the crown with the blue mitre appeared above the three St Andrew's crosses on the Amsterdam coat of arms: in 1555, for example, one of the stained-glass windows in the Old Church *(Oude Kerk)* or in 1631 at the top of the bell-tower of Westerkerk *(illustration, see p. 4)*. The origin of the red and black already being used for the coat of arms at that time has remained a mystery to the present day, but historians tell us that the single lion acquired a twin in the early 16C.

THE DEFINITIVE COAT OF ARMS

Over the years, new versions of the coat of arms appeared, especially when **Louis Bonaparte**, King of Holland, abdicated in 1810. Since the country was annexed to the French Empire, Napoleonic bees were immediately inserted between the St Andrew's crosses and the crown.

Changes continued until, eventually, nobody was very sure what the correct coat of arms of the capital city was like. At the end of the 19C, the director of the city's archives was commissioned to trace the original document relating to the coat of arms, drawn up in 1489 during the reign of Maximilian I. The research revealed that the Habsburg crown had changed in 1806 when Franz II had waived his right to the throne of the Holy Roman Empire. In 1898, the coat of arms was finally and definitively designed with the Austrian Imperial crown. The blue mitre and lions became gold.

On 29 March 1947, in order to pay homage to the attitude of the people of Amsterdam during the Nazi occupation, **Queen Wilhelmina** granted the city the right to add to its coat of arms the motto *Heldhaftig, Vastberaden and Barmhartig* (heroic, firm and charitable).

AN URBAN MOTIF

The three St Andrew's crosses constitute a wonderfully simple motif which the city has used to the full as its symbol. Visitors will see it all over the city, on tourist office brochures, on the thousands of *Amsterdammertjes* (literally "Amsterdam children"), the posts that prevent cars from parking on pavements, on council vehicles, on the pennants of the Ajax football club, on the many clogs sold to tourists, in the form of the lamp standards erected along the Rokin, on the electricity junction boxes, on house fronts where they constitute an architectural feature, and so on.

Ph. Gajic/MICHELIN

A decorative coat of arms

The city's three St Andrew's crosses have almost become a trade mark

Historical table and notes

2200 BC	A nomadic people settles to the north of the great rivers. They make pottery with rope decoration
300 BC	Arrival of the Germans and Celts south of the Rhine.
1C BC	The Romans occupy the areas between the Rhine and the North Sea.
12	The **Batavi** tribe is mentioned.
69	Led by one Julius Civilis, the Batavi rebel against Roman domination.
3C	Like the other tribes who fought Rome, the Batavi are taken over by the **Franks**, who controlled Europe during the Dark Ages. With the **Saxons** and **Frisians**, they are the main inhabitants of the area at this time.
382	St Servaas transfers his bishopric from Tongres to Maastricht. This is the beginning of Christianity in the country.
561	Division of the Merovingian kingdom into Neustria (west of the Scheldt) and Austrasia (east of the Scheldt), now the Netherlands.
843	**Treaty of Verdun**. The Carolingian Empire is divided into three parts: one Germanic, one French, and one central area stretching from the North Sea to the Mediterranean and including the present-day Netherlands. Later, the central area loses land to the south and becomes Lotharingia.
879-82	Great **Viking invasion**: The Vikings use Utrecht as their base and raid neighbouring regions, especially Dorestad (now Wijk bij Duurstede).
959	Lotharingia is divided into Upper Lotharingia (Lorraine) and Lower Lotharingia or Lothier, which corresponds approximately to the Netherlands as it is today.

Formation

1015-75	Founding of the **County of Holland** and extension at the expense of the County of Flanders (in Zeeland) and the bishopric of Utrecht.
1152-90	Reign of Frederick I Barbarossa. He is crowned Emperor.
c 1205	Gijsbrecht van Amstel builds a castle near the confluence of the Amstel and IJ. Its precise location has never been identified.
1222	In order to contain the Zuiderzee Marshes, the **first dike** (dam) is built on the Amstel. Amstelledamme later becomes Amsteldam then Amsterdam.
1225	Dating of the oldest archeological remains in Amsterdam.
1247	**Willem II**, Count of Holland, leader of the Holy Roman Empire.
1275	First appearance of the town's name in an official document dating from 27 October by which Floris V, Count of Holland, exonerates the inhabitants from paying customs and excise duties.

1299 Triple countship of Holland, Zeeland and Hainaut.

1300 Amsterdam obtains from the Bishop of Utrecht a **charter** granting it borough status.

1309-78 The Popes settle in Avignon. The beginning of the Great Schism of the Western World.

1323 The Count of Holland grants the town the right to impose tolls.

1334 Founding of the Oude Kerk, the oldest church in the city.

1337-1453 Hundred Years War.

1345 The miracle of the wafer: thrown into the fire because it had been regurgitated by a dying man, the eucharistic wafer is not consumed by the flames. This attracts crowds of pilgrims to the town.

1350 Amsterdam is a centre for the export of Dutch beers to the Baltic.

1380 Building of the Nieuwe Kerk.

1400 Beginning of the Italian Renaissance (Quattrocento) in the works of the Humanists (Dante, Petrarch and Boccaccio).

1400 The town has a population of some 5 000.

1421 First great fire in Amsterdam.

The domination of the House of Burgundy

1428 **Philip the Good**, Duke of Burgundy, captures Holland, Zeeland and Hainaut, to the detriment of Jacqueline of Bavaria.

1452 After a gigantic fire, a law is passed requiring the use of brick and tiles in place of wood for construction work.

1453 The Fall of Constantinople, the capital of the Christian Orient.

1467 **Charles the Bald** succeeds Philip

1477 Death of Charles the Bold. In the same year, his daughter Mary of Burgundy marries Maximilian of Austria, a member of the Habsburg dynasty, who inherits most of the Burgundian States, including the Low Countries, when his wife dies in 1482.

1480 Town walls are built around Amsterdam.

1492 Christopher Columbus discovers America.

Under Habsburg rule

1494 Philip the Fair, son of Mary and Maximilian, reigns over the Low Countries. Two years later, he marries the daughter of Isabella of Castile, Juana, later known as "Joan the Mad".

1502 The town has a population of 12 000.

1515 Charles I of Spain, Philip the Fair's son, inherits the Low Countries. In 1519 he becomes Holy Roman Emperor and takes the title **Charles V**.

1515 A struggle between François I of France and the future Charles V in an attempt to be elected Emperor and dominate Europe.

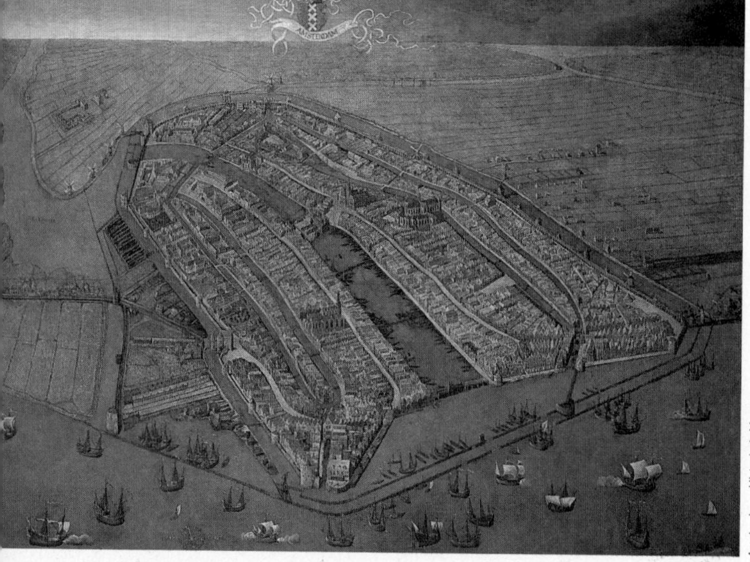

Amsterdams Historisch Museum

The oldest map of the town (c 1538) by Cornelis Anthonisz.

1520 First translation into Dutch of the writings of Luther.

1534 Anglican schism: King Henry VIII becomes the head of the Church of England.

1535 The **Anabaptists** (radical Protestants) who fomented a riot on the Dam are arrested and executed. More than 40 years of religious strife are to follow.

1546 Amsterdam has a population of 14 000.

1548 Charles V groups the 17 provinces in the Low Countries with Franche-Comté and creates an independent "Burgundy Circle".

1555 Charles V transfers the Low Countries (in particular) to his son, Philip II, soon to become King of Spain. Two years later, Margaret of Parma becomes Regent of the Spanish Low Countries.

1568 **William the Silent** takes military action: start of the Eighty Years War. Eight years later, he besieges Amsterdam which remains faithful to Philip II. The counts of Egmont and Hornes (supporters of William) are beheaded in Brussels.

1568-73 Repression under the orders of the Duke of Alba.

1572 St Bartholomew's Day massacre during which 3 000 Huguenots are assassinated in Paris.

Amsterdam during the Republic of the United Provinces

1578 Creation of the *Waterstaat*, the water board responsible for protecting the region against flooding and for continuing with drainage work.

1579 Union of Utrecht: alliance of the Protestant provinces in the north. One year earlier, the Calvinists seize power in Amsterdam during the Alteratie or peaceful revolution which leads to the **adoption of the Reformed Religion**.

1580 The town has a population of almost 30 000.

1581 Creation of the **Republic of the United Provinces**, a federation of the seven provinces independent of Spanish rule. Amsterdam experiences an influx of immigrants fleeing from persecution. Among them are rich merchants from Antwerp and Portuguese Jews.

1585 Antwerp is recaptured by the Spaniards and this, with the closure of the Scheldt, gives Amsterdam an almost complete monopoly in maritime trade between the North Sea and the Baltic.

1588 Destruction of the "invincible" Spanish Armada.

1596 Arrival of Cornelis de Houtman on Java.

1598 Edict of Nantes: Henri IV instigates freedom of conscience and pacifies the kingdom of France.

1602 Founding of the **Dutch East India Company** funded by public subscription. The first Jewish community is established in Amsterdam.

The IJ or the port of Amsterdam (1610). Hendrick Cornelisz. Vroom

1609	Founding of the **Bank of Amsterdam**. The town becomes Europe's leading financial market. The **Twelve Years' Truce** is signed with Spain.
1612	The town has a population of 50 000.
1613	Beginning of the first phase of construction of canals around Amsterdam.
1618	Beginning of the Thirty Years' War.
1619	Batavia is founded in the Dutch East Indies.
1621	Founding of the **Dutch West India Company**. Grotius goes into exile in France where he remains until 1634.
1624	Founding of New Amsterdam on the island now known as Manhattan. Occupation of the northeast of Brazil (until 1654).
1629	**Descartes** settles in Amsterdam, followed two years later by Rembrandt.
1632	Birth of **Spinoza** in Amsterdam.
1639	Holland can be considered as the world's leading maritime power.
1642-49	Civil war in England.
1642	**Rembrandt** paints *The Night Watch*.
1643-1715	The 72-year reign of Louis XIV, the Sun King, leaves its mark on France and Europe as a whole.
1648	End of the Eighty Years War. Under the terms of the **Treaty of Münster**, Philip IV recognises the independence of the United Provinces.
1650	The city has a population of 220 000. William II attempts a *coup d'état* against Amsterdam. The city puts up resistance by opening its sluice-gates and flooding the region.
1651	The English Parliament passes the Navigation Act which is disastrous for Dutch trade. All goods leaving or entering England must be carried on board English ships.
1652-54	Jan van Riebeeck founds the Cape Colony in 1652. First war with England. Until 1672, the Low Countries are governed without a *stathouder* (governor).
1658-1759	Occupation of Ceylon.
1662	Construction of the City Hall. One year later, beginning of the second phase of the construction of canals around Amsterdam.
1665-67	Second war with England. Under the terms of the Treaty of Breda, New Amsterdam (now New York) is exchanged for Dutch Guiana (now Suriname).
1672-78	Louis XIV wages war against the United Provinces. In 1672, Amsterdam withstands attack by Louis XIV's troops by reopening its sluice-gates. Third war with England (1672-74).
1685	**Revocation of the Edict of Nantes**: some 5 000 French Huguenots seek refuge in Amsterdam.

Amsterdams Historisch Museum

The 18C, or the decline of the Republic

1694-1725 | Reign of Peter I, better known as Peter the Great, the creator of Russian splendour.

1701-13 | War of Spanish Succession: alliance between several countries, including the United Provinces, against Louis XIV.

1702 | The *stathouder*, William III, dies without an heir. Emperor Charles VI of Austria sets up another East India Company in Ostend. This is a hard blow for the Dutch economy which has already suffered badly as a result of the wars.

1707 | Act of Union between England and Scotland.

1713 | The **Peace of Utrecht** recognises the independence of the northerm provinces.

1720 | This year marks the beginning of the commercial and industrial decline of the United Provinces and, therefore, of Amsterdam, the largest city in the Republic.

1740-48 | War of Austrian Succession.

1740-86 | Beginning of the reign of Frederick von Hohenzollern. In a few years, Frederick the Great makes Prussia the Empire's second largest power.

1751-87 | The United Provinces suffer a civil war opposing the supporters of the House of Orange and the "Patriots", liberal reformers demanding greater democracy.

1762-96 | Reign of Catherine of Russia, a patron of the arts and letters.

1783 | Peace of Versailles: the United States of America gain their independence.

1787 | Frederick William II, King of Prussia, occupies Amsterdam in order to support the Prince of Orange against a Patriot uprising.

1789 | French Revolution.

1791 | Beginning of the dissolution of the Dutch East India Company.

French domination (1795-1813) and the short-lived union with Belgium

1795 | The French enter Amsterdam and turn the United Provinces into the Batavian Republic. In 1801, the country is divided into eight *départements*, the equivalent of counties.

1804 | Napoleon I is crowned Emperor of the French.

1806 | **Louis Bonaparte**, Napoleon's brother, becomes monarch of the Kingdom of Holland which takes Amsterdam as its capital in 1808. The city pays a heavy price to France.

1810 | Louis Bonaparte abdicates. The country is annexed to the French Empire.

1811 | Napoleon receives the keys of the city. Amsterdam is no longer the "county town" of the Zuiderzee *département*. Two years later, the local population revolts and chases out the occupying forces.

1814 | The southern provinces are reunited with the provinces in the north to form a single kingdom. William of Orange becomes sovereign of the United Provinces. Amsterdam is made the country's capital.

1814-15 | Congress of Vienna.

1815 | Battle of Waterloo. At the Congress of Vienna, William of Orange is acknowledged as the King of the Netherlands (including Belgium) under the title of **William I**.

1825 | Opening of the Noord-Holland canal.

1828 | Occupation of the western part of New Guinea.

1830 | A wave of revolution sweeps through Europe.

1830 | Revolution in Belgium. The country gains its independence.

The Netherlands, an independent kingdom

1839 | First rail link in the Netherlands, running between Amsterdam and Haarlem.

1845 | Amsterdam suffers a wave of protests in favour of democratic reform. A constitutional committee is set up, chaired by **Johan Thorbecke**.

1850 | The city has a population of 245 000.

1851 | First World Fair in London.

1870-71 Last stages of the unification process in Italy and Germany. Rome is declared the capital of unified Italy. The German Empire is proclaimed in Versailles and extended to include Alsace and Lorraine.

1870-76 Amsterdam's harbour becomes prosperous again thanks to council policy and the opening of the northern canal in 1876.

1883 The international exhibition attracts one million visitors.

1889 The central railway station is completed. It symbolises the city's (tardy) adaptation to the industrial era.

1890-1948 Reign of **Queen Wilhelmina**.

1900 The city has a population of 511 000.

1902 The Socialists obtain their first seat on the city council.

1914-18 First World War.

1914-18 The Netherlands remain neutral during the First World War. In Amsterdam, food shortages lead to strikes and riots in the Jordaan district.

1915 The Workers Social Democratic Party (SDAP), which holds the majority on the city council, decides to launch an urban redevelopment plan.

Rijksmuseum Amsterdam

Johan Rudolf Thorbecke, Minister of State,
Jan Hendrick Neuman

Amsterdam in modern times

1920 Opening of regular flights between London and Amsterdam Schiphol, the city's future international airport.

1928 The city hosts the 8th Olympic Games of modern times.

1929 Wall Street crashes.

1930 Amsterdam has a population of 750 000.

1932 **The north dike** is completed on the Zuiderzee which then becomes an inland sea.

1934 Riots in the Jordaan district cost the lives of seven people.

1936-39 Spanish Civil War.

1939 The Netherlands declare neutrality.

1940-45 Second World War.

1940 **German invasion** and air raids on the city: the Netherlands capitulate on 15 May after a campaign lasting five days. On 12 May, the Queen and government seek refuge in London.

1941 Numerous incidents in Amsterdam after anti-Semitic violence on the part of the occupying forces. In reprisal, the first deportations of Jews begin. A general strike is organised in the capital in February, mainly by the Communist party.

1942 **Anne Frank** and her family go into hiding.

1945 In May, the allied troops enter Amsterdam.

1948 Abdication of Queen Wilhelmina in favour of her daughter, **Juliana**, who was born in 1909.

1949 Indonesia is the first of the Dutch colonies to be given its independence.

1950 The city, which has a population of 850 000, regains its prosperity.

1952 Opening of the Rhine-Amsterdam canal.

1957 The signature of the Treaty of Rome sets up the EEC.

1963 The town has a population of 868 000. The lack of housing leads to the official organisation of squats.

1965 The ***Provos*** (protest movement) gain representation on the city council.

1966 Marriage in Amsterdam of Princess Beatrix and Claus von Amsberg. The event is upset by the Provos, the forerunners of the hippie movement.

1971 Ajax Amsterdam led by **Johan Cruyff** (a veritable national hero) wins the European Cup.

The signatories of the Treaty of Amsterdam (1997) getting some fresh air

1975	The city celebrates its 700th anniversary.
30 April 1980	Queen Juliana abdicates in favour of her daughter **Beatrix**.
1981	Amsterdam is acknowledged as the capital of the Netherlands.
1986	The architectural complex consisting of the new City Hall and the music theatre is completed despite violent demonstrations.
1989	Fall of the Berlin wall.
1989	Faced with traffic problems, a law is passed to turn the centre of Amsterdam into a pedestrian area.
1991	The centenary of Van Gogh's death is marked by the great success of the exhibition of his works.
1992	The population approves restrictions on motor traffic in the old town centre but only a very low percentage of the population actually casts a vote.
1993	The city has a population of 1 091 000.
1997	The **Treaty of Amsterdam** is signed by the Ministers of Foreign Affairs from the European Union's 15 Member States. By doing so, they give the EU a common foreign policy.
2000	The city has a population of 1 100 000.

G. Geral/GLOBAL PICTURES

Queen Beatrix

Birth of a dynasty: the Orange-Nassau family

THE LOW COUNTRIES IN THE MID 16C

Charles V and territorial unity – After inheriting the Low Countries in 1515, Charles V implemented a fruitful policy of territorial unity: 1523, annexation of Friesland; 1527, receipt of the bishopric of Utrecht; 1528, capture of Overijssel; 1536, incorporation of Groningen and Drenthe. In the following year, the Pragmatic Sanction regulated all 17 provinces in the Low Countries.

Meanwhile, the Emperor of the "States on which the sun never set", took his court to Brussels, the capital of the Brabant. At that time, Brussels functioned as the capital of the Low Countries; it was also the capital of the Habsburg Empire. In order to avoid ruffling feathers, the monarch skilfully granted Amsterdam a monopoly on trade with Denmark in 1544. It was, however, well known that Charles V's empire was just too big. The administration of States in many different areas was becoming problematical. Authority was losing its grip on affairs, despite the competence of **Mary of Hungary**, Charles' sister who governed the Low Countries.

Philip II's Catholic policy – When Emperor Charles V abdicated in 1555, he transferred his Austrian possessions to his brother Ferdinand I and his Spanish possessions, with the Low Countries, to his son Philip II. Unlike his father, who was a cosmopolitan sovereign and inveterate traveller, Philip was born in Spain, brought up in Spain and seldom left the country of his birth. He died in 1598. Politically speaking this king, who has often been described as proud and melancholic, had one major objective: to defend Roman Catholicism in Spain and in his other territories.

Opposition to the Church had already taken root in the misery of the working classes; at this point, it began to spread under the guise of the Reformation. In Spain, the Inquisition led by the monarch waged a pitiless war on the Protestants until, in 1571, the king justifiably claimed to have achieved a unified faith.

Whatever their differences, the 17 provinces in the Low Countries shared the same ideals of freedom. The towns in Flanders enjoyed ancient privileges, each province had its own deputies and the States General sat in Brussels. Indeed, Charles V had shown considerable respect for the specific character of the Low Countries. The religious question was to change everything and modify the destiny of the country as a whole.

The Prince of Orange

The "Holy Office" of the King of Spain – Since Calvinism and Anabaptism had taken hold in the Low Countries, Philip II decided to control this territory in the same way as he controlled Spain. **Margaret of Parma**, the daughter of Charles V, was appointed Governor of the Spanish Low Countries and was required by her brother, shortly before 1560, to apply the measures decreed by him, for example the creation of 14 new bishoprics in order to monitor persecution.

Gradually, resistance began to be organised, resulting in 1566 in the "Compromise of Breda" through which the aristocracy requested the abolition of the Inquisition. That same year, the iconoclast movement, or *Beeldenstorm*, swept through the country, laying waste the monasteries in Flanders and Holland. In 1567, Philip II responded to the rebellion by sending in Alvarez de Toledo, **Duke of Alba**, commander-in-chief of a fearsome force of infantry. As soon as he arrived in Brussels, the Duke set up a Council of Troubles which soon became known as the "Council of Blood" because of the pillaging and numerous executions carried out on his orders.

William "the Silent" – Even before the beginning of what was later to be known as the Eighty Years War, a number of aristocrats had protested against the tyrannical politics of Philip II, among them the Counts of Egmont and Hornes *(see ALKMAAR)* and William of Nassau, Lord of Breda, Marquis of Antwerp, Prince of Orange.

William was born in Dillenburg Castle (in what is now Hessen) in 1533. In 1544, while still a child, he inherited the possessions of his cousin, René de Chalon, namely lands in the Low Countries and Burgundy and the sovereign principality of Orange in the county of the same name (the title of "Prince" had been granted to Bertrand I of Provence by Emperor Frederick I in 1181). Charles V made a proviso with regard to this inheritance which was of major military and political importance – the child, although born German and a Protestant, was to be

Rijksmuseum Amsterdam

William I of Orange,
Adriaan Thomasz.Key

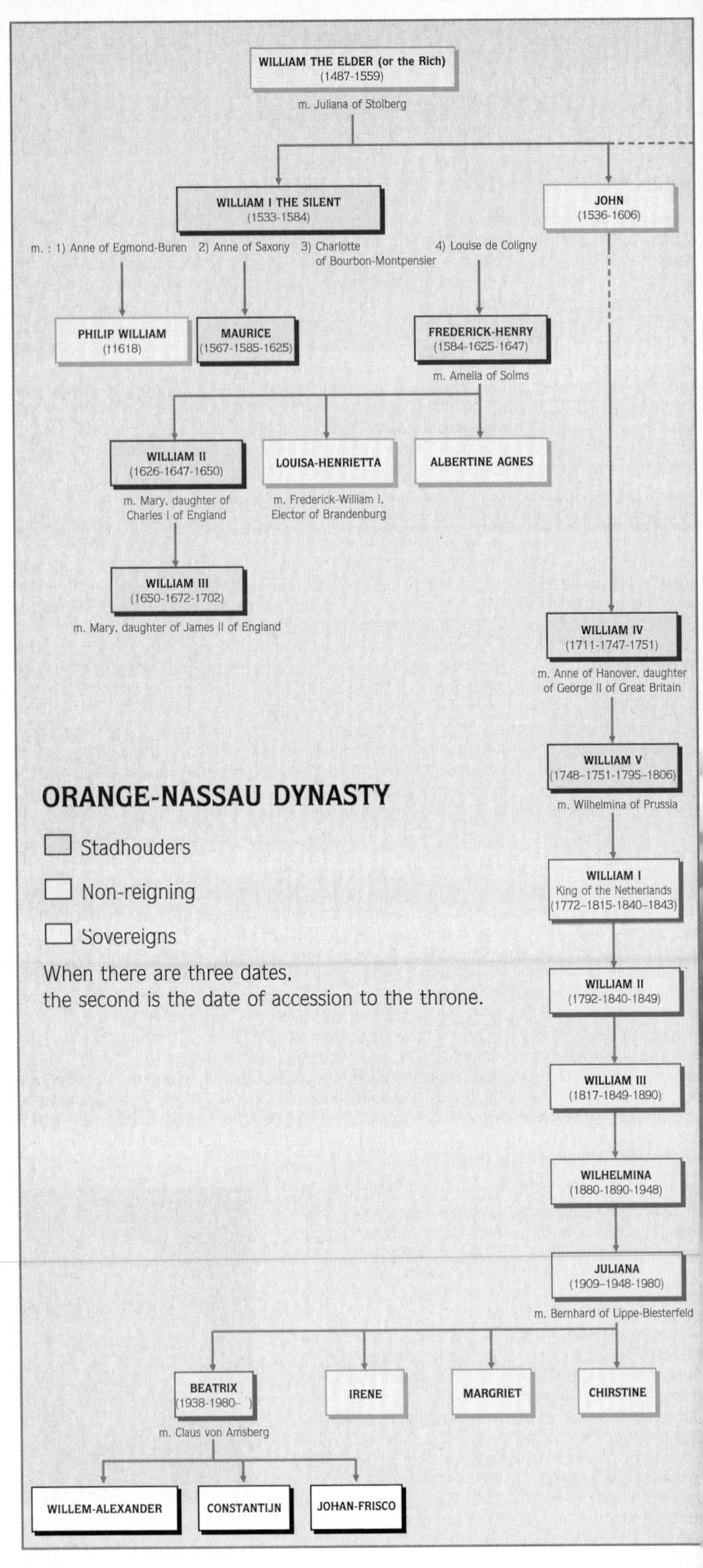
WILLIAM THE ELDER (or the Rich)
(1487-1559)
m. Juliana of Stolberg
WILLIAM I THE SILENT
(1533-1584)
JOHN
(1536-1606)
m. : 1) Anne of Egmond-Buren 2) Anne of Saxony 3) Charlotte of Bourbon-Montpensier 4) Louise de Coligny
PHILIP WILLIAM
(†1618)
MAURICE
(1567-1585-1625)
FREDERICK-HENRY
(1584-1625-1647)
m. Amelia of Solms
WILLIAM II
(1626-1647-1650)
m. Mary, daughter of Charles I of England
LOUISA-HENRIETTA
m. Frederick-William I, Elector of Brandenburg
ALBERTINE AGNES
WILLIAM III
(1650-1672-1702)
m. Mary, daughter of James II of England
WILLIAM IV
(1711-1747-1751)
m. Anne of Hanover, daughter of George II of Great Britain
WILLIAM V
(1748–1751-1795–1806)
m. Wilhelmina of Prussia
ORANGE-NASSAU DYNASTY
Stadhouders
Non-reigning
Sovereigns
When there are three dates,
the second is the date of accession to the throne.
WILLIAM I
King of the Netherlands
(1772–1815-1840–1843)
WILLIAM II
(1792-1840-1849)
WILLIAM III
(1817-1849-1890)
WILHELMINA
(1880-1890-1948)
JULIANA
(1909–1948-1980)
m. Bernhard of Lippe-Biesterfeld
BEATRIX
(1938-1980–)
IRENE
MARGRIET
CHIRSTINE
m. Claus von Amsberg
WILLEM-ALEXANDER
CONSTANTIJN
JOHAN-FRISCO

brought up at the court of Mary of Hungary and become a Roman Catholic. This was why William lived in Breda as a Dutch nobleman and he was very popular with the Emperor. Indeed the latter granted him high-ranking command in 1552.

Before returning to Spain in 1559, Philip II named William Knight of the Order of the Golden Fleece (1556) and member of the Council of State in Brussels (1558). More importantly, he appointed him *stathouder* of Holland, Zeeland and Utrecht (1559), a title that two Counts of Nassau had held before him: Henry III and René de Chalon. Through this position, William soon showed his commitment to tolerance, by a position as far removed as possible from the repression that he was supposed to represent. The prince who was a Protestant by birth and a Catholic by upbringing soon found himself caught between two fires. Which side was he going to support? Moreover, what was the meaning behind his various alliances, both matrimonial and political? Was he a rebel or an ally of his master, the king? It was this smokescreen concealing his true character that led his enemies to nickname him William the Silent.

"Je maintiendrai" (I shall maintain)

The motto of the Netherlands is that of the Princes of Orange. Why is it in French? Firstly because **William I** inherited it from his cousin, René de Chalon, a French prince who died without an heir at the age of 28. Secondly because, despite being born in Germany and brought up in the Low Countries, his usual language was French. This explains why he did not translate the motto which suited him so well. When **William III** became King of England in 1689, he kept it, with "*Dieu et mon droit*".

The trumpet of rebellion

William takes up arms – This takes us to 1568. William no longer believed in reconciliation between the king and his Dutch subjects. After the *Beeldenstorm* and following the crushing defeat of the Calvinists by Margaret of Parma's troops in Antwerp, he travelled to Dillenburg in the spring of 1567 because he felt under threat. At this time, the terrible repression instigated by the Duke of Alba turned into a veritable tragedy for the Low Countries (out of 1 200 found guilty 1 000 were executed). Thereafter the Catholic Prince became openly Lutheran again. He requested assistance from the German princes. He returned to the Low Countries, this time at the head of a mighty army which he had to finance. Resistance was no longer only ideological. The **Eighty Years War** had begun.
For four years, William launched a number of desperate campaigns. On the one hand, he was no longer supported by a population that was terrified; on the other, the Duke of Alba, a born warrior, had no difficulty in countering the attacks. William, though, was intelligent and tenacious; he was soon to experience the heady, bitter taste of victory.

Capture of Brielle by the "Beggars" and assassination of William – On 1 April 1572, the "Maritime Beggars", privateers who were the bearers of the Prince of Orange's letters and who were supported by those in exile, captured Brielle in Zuid-Holland after being driven out of England. William had not directly wanted this success and it had considerable consequences because it coincided with an increase in taxes that the economies of the provinces were too weak to bear. From then on, the rebels took William as their leader and he soon professed the Calvinist religion. Unfortunately, the French aid on which he was counting was swept away on the night of the Feast of St Bartholomew, 24 August, when all the main French Protestant leaders were massacred. Reprisals from the Duke of Alba were merciless. They included the terrible sack of Naarden and the capitulation of Haarlem.
In order to weaken his adversary, Philip II had the Prince's eldest son kidnapped. He also put a price on William's head. The latter proved himself to be an outstanding diplomat and a great statesman. In 1576, by the Pacification of Ghent, the States General appointed him *stathouder* of the 17 Provinces. At that precise moment, he believed he could achieve unity through religious tolerance. Unfortunately for him, **Don Juan of Austria** and **Alessandro Farnese** respectively were to ruin his hopes and, finally, one Balthazar Gerard assassinated him on 10 July 1584 in the Prinsenhof in Delft.
"*I do not need to hope in order to begin an enterprise, nor to succeed in order to persevere*". Even in defeat, William survived. The United Provinces became a reality and thereafter the name of his House was for ever associated with the Netherlands.

The Union of Utrecht

In January 1579, the representatives of the States of Holland, Zeeland, and the territories of Groningen and Utrecht, met with the *stathouder* of Gelderland to sign the Union of Utrecht. By this act, they decided that no separate agreement would be negotiated with Philip II and that only the Protestant religion would be authorised in Holland and Zeeland. Further to the Union of Arras by which Alessandro Farnese had obliged the southern States to submit to the authority of Spain, this treaty led to the separation of the northern and southern Low Countries, the former later becoming the United Provinces.

Independence

Creation of the Republic of United Provinces – On 23 January 1579, the seven Protestant provinces in the north broke away from the Catholic Walloon provinces in the south which had signed the Union of Arras on 6 January. This immediately led the deputies of Friesland, Groningen, Gelderland, Holland, Overijssel, Utrecht and Zeeland to sign the Union of Utrecht. This document was to be the only legal basis for the United Provinces until the end of the 18C. (These seven provinces covered the same area as the Netherlands today with the exception of the territories in the south, previously known as the "Land of the Generality").
The Union of 17 Provinces, then, was a failure. Why? Because two Governors General sent by Philip II succeeded in weakening William of Orange's great project: Don Juan of Austria, first of all, by encouraging rivalry between south and north and Alessandro Farnese thereafter by instigating a policy of moderation aimed at promising a pardon for Catholics in the south and the upholding of local privileges.
In 1581, the seven provinces in the north declared independence and constituted a federal state. The Republic of the United Provinces, a new State with no constitution, then shook off Spanish control and decided to rule from the Binnenhof in The Hague where its States General administered the joint purse and decided on defence and foreign policies.

Maurice of Nassau, defender of the Republic – From the very outset, the new republic appeared particularly weak, even moribund as a result of William's murder. Its survival was ensured within one decade thanks to the second son of the "Father of the Country", Maurice of Nassau (1567-1625).
The defeat of the Invincible Armada in 1588 represented a major turning point in the history of the revolt in the United Provinces. Philip II began to look towards France. In the following year, Maurice became *stathouder* of Utrecht, Gelderland and Overijssel and built up an efficient and effective army while, at the same time, signing treaties with France and England. William's great project to give the question of the Low Countries an international dimension was finally brought to fruition. Maurice won back territories and guaranteed safe borders. Moreover, **Johan van Oldenbarnevelt**, Grand Pensionary of Holland, set his seal in 1596 on the tripartite alliance that finally made the Spanish danger even more remote. When Philip II died in 1598, he left the south part of the Low Countries to Archdukes Albert and Isabella. As to the United Provinces, they could consider themselves, with justification, a new nation if only because Maurice had succeeeded in making the *stathouder* the highest-ranking servant of the State rather than the military collaborator of the States General.

The United Provinces, a great European power

Frederick-Henry of Nassau, an iron hand in a velvet glove – After the signature in Antwerp of the **Twelve Years' Truce** in 1609, which was vital for trade by the Dutch East India Company, and the execution in 1619 of the Grand Pensionary of Holland, the Republic's leading civilian figure, Maurice died in 1625.
War broke out again between the Republic and Spain, not as an extension of older rebellions but as a conflict between two great nations. Frederick-Henry (1584-1647), Grand-General, William the Silent's third son, inflicted violent defeats on Philip V's troops and recaptured a few towns (Bois-le-Duc, Maastricht and Breda). He was quickly appointed *stathouder*, mainly because he was Prince of Orange in command of an army of mercenaries, but the States General were to halt his ambitions of total victory. The Dutch traders who had founded Batavia in 1619 did not support his aspirations to breathe life back into the "Burgundy Circle" created in 1548 by the Imperial Diet (17 provinces in the Low Countries and Franche-Comté) during the reign of Charles V. In their opinion, there was no question of giving the port of Antwerp even the slightest chance of rising from the ashes.
A trial of strength opposed Frederick-Henry and the Dutch bourgeois oligarchy. He declared, "*I have no greater enemy than the town of Amsterdam*". Henri IV of France's godson, however, also had a

Stathouder, a title specific to the Low Countries

In Dutch, *stathouder* means "governor" or "lieutenant". The word, which is of Germanic origin, is related to the German word *Statthalter*, also meaning "governor" or "vicar". The word passed into Dutch *(stathouder or stadhouder)* to describe a provincial governor in the Spanish Low Countries. It can also be the title used by the head of government in the Low Countries.
The office is known to have existed in the Low Countries in the 13C, where the *stathouder* governed a province in the sovereign's name. Charles V passed legislation to give the *stathouder* the right or obligation to sit on the Council of State, chair the College of Justice, and convene meetings of the States General.
The *stathouder* exercised authority in one or more provinces. The office became hereditary in 1674 (despite periods when there was no *stathouder*) and fell into disuse in 1795 with the end of the Republic of the United Provinces.

feeling for dynastic rule. He organised his own succession while the regents won commercial and, notwithstanding, political victories. In 1629, he promoted his son, William, then aged three, to the rank of General of Cavalry and then married him to the daughter of Charles I of England, Henrietta Mary Stuart. Apparently defeated by the trading elite, Frederick-Henry died in 1647, almost certain of having ensured a long life for his House.

William II, or the impetuous stathouder – After Frederick-Henry's death, the burgomaster Andries Bicker, who sold ships to Spain during the conflict, succeeded in having the **Treaty of Münster** signed in January 1648. Spain recognised the Republic which was able to retain all its conquests in the East and West Indies. It also received a guarantee that the Scheldt would remain closed. As to the southern Low Countries, they were brought back under the direct control of Madrid. Thanks to this complete victory, the United Provinces continued to strengthen their position as a great nation.

Having married a woman of royal lineage, the *stathouder* (the function was almost hereditary by that time but the States General waited for the signature of the treaty before confirming the nomination), William II (1626-50), was confronted by strong opposition from the regents. Amsterdam wanted to implement defence cuts that would reduce the armed forces to 30 000. William refused, in particular because he wanted to intervene in the English Civil War. He was obstinate and turbulent, proud of his rank and its power. He marched on the capital to depose what he referred to as the Bicker clique, supported by anti-Dutch feeling in the other provinces. The town put up resistance, opening its sluice-gates. A compromise finally avoided the worst outcome but tension remained high. Suddenly, William was laid low by a fever caused by a cold autumn; he was already suffering from smallpox. His indisposition rapidly became a real illness and soon, at the age of 24, the *stathouder* died.

Accession to the throne after a period of absence

Johan de Witt, Grand Pensionary of Holland – When William II died, his successor was not yet born. In the absence of a *stathouder*, the elite in Amsterdam put forward the Grand Pensionary from their own province. Johan de Witt (1625-72) was none other than the son-in-law of Andries Bicker, the burgomaster. At the age of 25, the new man in power imposed an entirely republican regime. In 1654, he proved his political skill by having the States General agree to the **Act of Seclusion**, a Cromwellian idea which distanced the princes of Orange from the rank of *stathouder*. At the same time, de Witt, a friend of Spinoza, entrusted the education of the young William to the States of Holland and instigated the Veritable Liberty which prevailed until 1672.

Although the regents aspired to a political peace which would be profitable for their commercial interests, the period was nevertheless marked by two wars with England (1652-54 and 1665-67) and one with Norway (1660-66). Moreover, after 1660, France began to attack the Republic's territory. De Witt, meantime, had partly dismantled the army which he deemed to be too supportive of the Orange dynasty. Its weakness stretched the "Veritable Republic" to its limits. William III's hour had come.

The Grand Pensionary

The Pensionary is a man of the robe and Secretary General to the States General in his province. Since Holland was so powerful, its Pensionary was the de facto leader of the federal administration for the seven provinces in the north, hence the title of Grand Pensionary.

William III seizes a royal crown – Having reached his majority, William III (1650-1702) who was born eight days after his father's death, became a member of the States General of Zeeland, just as Johan de Witt was discovering that his pacifist action was fruitless in the face of Louis XIV's expansionist policies. In 1672, the French entered the Low Countries and set up their headquarters in Utrecht. Amsterdam was under direct threat. In 1672, the Act of Seclusion was repealed. In 1672, Johan de Witt was assassinated in The Hague by rioters, probably supporters of the Orange faction. In 1672, in the face of danger from France, William III was appointed admiral and Captain General. Then he was appointed *stathouder*. The Prince immediately removed 10 members of the town council and replaced them by his own men before turning his attention to the disastrous military situation. The French were hesitating, undecided as to whether or not they would attack the capital. William III again ordered the sluice-gates to be opened and took the opportunity to sign an alliance with Spain, Lorraine, Denmark and the Habsburg Empire. He gave the conflict a European dimension, invoking reasons of state in reply to his critics. The French withdrew; William had triumphed.

For six years, Willliam waged war on Louis XIV, an absolute necessity for the Republic. In doing so, he showed a highly-developed sense of tactics in the face of the greatest strategists of the day. He was undoubtedly France's greatest enemy and he took with him all the United Provinces, scandalised by the Revocation of the Edict of Nantes in 1685 and worried by the question of the Spanish Succession.

William's destiny, however, was to take him across the North Sea. Great Britain was being shaken by the **"Glorious Revolution"** (1688-89) created by a conspiracy on the part of aristocrats and bishops. They called on William, James II's son-in-law, who landed on 7 November 1688. James II immediately fled to France and the Parliament interpreted his action as an abdication. **William III** and **Mary II** were proclaimed **King and Queen of England** sharing equal powers.

William I of Orange,
King of the Netherlands, by Acar

The last act

William III died without a direct heir. The country then experienced a second period without a *stathouder* and this caused a serious national crisis between 1672 and 1747. During this time, the Frisian branch of the House of Orange seized power in the provinces of Friesland, Groningen, Gelderland and Drenthe.
The fall of the fortified Bergen op Zoom in 1747 was considered as a humiliation. Streets rang to shouts of *Oranje boven!* (The House of Orange at the top!) and the function of *stathouder* was re-established. The heir of the House of Orange, **William IV** (1711-51), put his dynasty back at the top of the tree of State.

William I, King of the Netherlands – His grandson, William VI (1772-1843), came to the throne on 16 March 1815 under the name of **William I**, King of the Netherlands. The kingdom of Holland had been created in 1806 and the provinces in the south had been reunited with the northern provinces to form a single kingdom in 1814. The Union, which resulted from the Congress of Vienna in 1814, was given its final form after the revolution in Belgium in 1830. The Dutch army invaded Belgium in June 1831, but was soon faced with a French counter-offensive. The Treaty of London (1839) officially ended the conflict, destroying any idea of a larger Netherlands.

A democratic monarchy – **William III** reigned for almost four decades. For many years he resisted the idea of the parliamentary regime, against all logic, but he finally accepted it. The royal family was a symbol of national unity; as such it enjoyed, and continues to enjoy, popular support. **Queen Wilhelmina** was highly respected and frequently showed her determination to maintain national unity, especially during the two world wars.
Following the abdication of her mother, **Queen Juliana**, who was called the "mother of the people", **Beatrix** mounted the throne on 30 April 1980. She is, therefore, the sixth sovereign of the House of Orange and, as queen, she has a character reminiscent of that of her grandmother, Wilhelmina. A smiling but (apparently) authoritarian figure, she is filled with a sense of the dignity of her function and exercises to the full the limited powers at her disposal.

The Golden Age

There can be no finer expression to describe the one hundred years of prosperity enjoyed by the Amsterdam of the 17C. While recession hit almost every country in Europe, a young Republic stood out from the others, further north of the Scheldt, at the mouth of the Rhine. Amsterdam, the main town in the Republic of the United Provinces, cultivated freedom of conscience, freedom of religion and economic freedom. The town's hegemony was such that it was rightfully described as the civilisation of the Golden Age.

THE NORTHERN LOW COUNTRIES IN THE 17C

"The miracle is not a miracle" – There was so much abundance and opulence in the Republic of the United Provinces in the 17C that the admiring **Cardinal Richelieu** spoke of the "Dutch miracle" when summarising the prosperity of this northern land inhabited by, to use his words, "no more than a handful of people". However, the motto of **Simon Stevin**, one of the first people to have worked on the drainage of the Zuiderzee and tutor to Prince Maurice of Nassau-Orange, contradicted the illustrious minister to Louis XIII, "*Wonder is geen wonder*" (the miracle is not a miracle). At the very least the prodigious success of the northern part of the Low Countries had a totally pragmatic reason – economic power and an unrivalled commercial hegemony.

The Province of Holland or the continent's commercial elite – In the late 16C Holland was already highly urbanised and, in the hands of the commercial elite, had greater influence and power than the other provinces. At that time, its population and budgetary contribution to the administration of the States General of the Republic both exceeded 50% of the total. By contrast, Gelderland, a province to the east of that of Utrecht, was mainly rural and dominated by a small aristocratic elite. Although the provinces were independent and sovereign, and despite the fact that the diversity of their component parts ensured a solid basis for the United Provinces, it was obvious that the weight of historical change was soon to concentrate power in the hands of the House of Orange-Nassau and in those of the regents representing the patriarchal group of merchants.

Holland and the Netherlands, two different entities

Holland is the historic soul of the Netherlands. It consists of the provinces of Noord-Holland and Zuid-Holland and includes the country's three main cities: Amsterdam, The Hague and Rotterdam.
In the region, which is the richest and most densely populated in the country (40% of the population and 17% of the territory), are concentrated all the main administrative bodies: the Crown, the government and the Parliament (The Hague), the Stock Exchange and banks (Amsterdam) and insurance companies (Rotterdam).
It is because Holland played such a vital role within the United Provinces that the inhabitants of the Netherlands were often referred to as *Hollanders*.

The action of the stathouders and regents – The interests of the *stathouders* and regents of Holland were radically different. For one, the Republic was to strengthen its new independence acquired as a result of the Treaty of Münster (1648) by means of a policy that was militarily expansionist. For the others, real independence required a pacific economic policy which served the specific interests of the trading elite. The regents, who had succeeded the Roman Catholic oligarchy, headed municipal and provincial bodies and constituted the province's ruling class. The only thing that counted for them was "public tranquillity", not the monarchic ambitions of a princely family.
Despite these opposing views which came to the fore during Frederick-Henry of Nassau's period as *stathouder*, and despite the fact that the Republic remained at war through much of the century, Amsterdam constantly confirmed its increasing power and influence between 1600 and 1650. This power was manifest on land (in war against France) and on sea (the Dutch East India Company was set up in 1602 and the Dutch West India Company in 1621), giving Holland a veritable monopoly in the transport sector.

AMSTERDAM, THE LARGEST CITY IN THE WORLD

The primacy of trade over differences of opinion - Whether they were Walloons seeking refuge in the mid 16C, Jews from Spain and Portugal who arrived c 1600, Poles who had gone into voluntary exile to flee persecution, Mennonites from Friesland, Anabaptists, Remonstrants or Arminians, orthodox Calvinists or Roman Catholics or, later, Huguenots fleeing France following the Revocation of the Edict of Nantes in 1685, they were all welcomed with open arms in Amsterdam.
At the beginning of the 17C, the Dutch nobility was to be found in The Hague, logically around the *stathouder* and his court. Amsterdam, a trading city or, as people these days would impolitely put it, a "city of parvenus", was then a cosmopolitan city. For foreigners trying their luck, the great harbour on the Zuiderzee had an attraction comparable to that of New York for German and Irish immigrants in the mid 19C. The real springboard for the economic might of Amsterdam in the Golden Age was liberty, a freedom guaranteed by Calvinism which, since the Reformation in 1578, was not a state religion but an official religion. This difference in terminology is worth its weight in gold...

Ph. Gajic/MICHELIN

In the 17C, this figure of Atlas bearing the world on his shoulders represented Amsterdam. The statue stands on the roof of the former town hall, now the royal palace

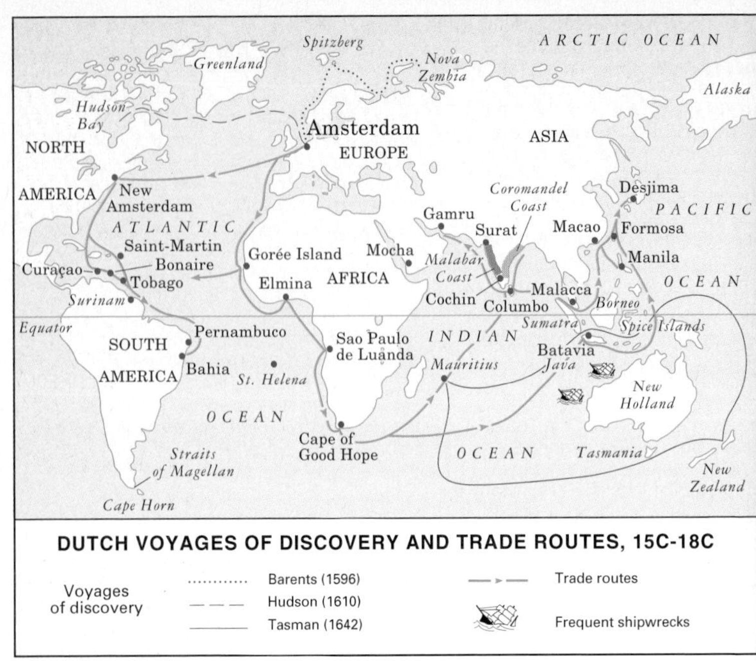

DUTCH VOYAGES OF DISCOVERY AND TRADE ROUTES, 15C-18C

A forest of masts – The success of the two India Companies *(see below)* rapidly took Amsterdam to the centre of a "world economy" to use Fernand Braudel's expression. The Republic had some **15 000 ships**, almost five times more than Great Britain. Two principles differentiated the two great maritime powers: the *mare liberum* of Hugo Grotius and the *mare clausum* of William Monson. In 1651, the Navigation Act required that all goods leaving or entering England had to travel on an English vessel. The principle of an open maritime market developed by the pragmatic Dutch traders revealed the English principle of a closed market for the archaic idea that it was, in commercial terms. The harbour in Amsterdam was packed with masts.

1609: Founding of the Bank of Amsterdam – Capitalism has its rules; Amsterdam applied them as soon as the first signs of its might became apparent. Transactions between merchants and exchange dealers soon led to a chaotic circulation of money. A strict framework was applied: in 1608 the city council required exchange dealers to comply with rates imposed by the council and, in the following year, it set up the **Wisselbank**, an exchange bank which soon became a commercial credit organisation. The availability of money guaranteed by the bank was such that clients poured in from every direction, including foreign countries because the secrecy of banking transactions was already common practice. One sign of the times was the interest rate which was only half as much as the rate levied by British banks (2-4%). This was the start of modern banking.

In 1611 the **Stock Exchange** was opened. Soon agents were negotiating cargoes 24 months in advance! There were risks involved but, no matter, they were covered by the chamber of insurance, and the insurance was even easier to obtain if the ships were chartered with limited liability. Everybody could become involved in the funding of a ship about to leave harbour, for sums equal to no more than 1/64th of the total cost of the voyage.

Trade in its heyday – As Europe's leading city thanks to international exchanges, a melting pot of religious and moral freedoms, and a laboratory experimenting with the capitalism of the future, Amsterdam more or less built itself in 100 years, based on criteria of modernity that were totally unknown at the time. This is evident from its trading elite, people who actually wielded power: **Frans Banningh Cocq**, a rich merchant and member of the council (immortalised in 1642 in *The Night Watch* by Rembrandt van Rijn) was the son of an apothecary; **Nicolaes Tulp**, who was burgomaster four times, was the son of a linen-draper; **Jan Poppen**, burgomaster, was the son of an immigrant who sold herrings. Amsterdam's Golden Age was that of new men for whom frontiers and languages were no longer barriers.

FREEDOM OF THOUGHT

The young Republic of the United Provinces offered ideal conditions for the development of philosophy, as was obvious from the increasing influence of the University of Leyden founded in 1575 by **Prince William I of Nassau**, known as William the Silent. Two 17C figures illustrate the intellectual effervescence of the Golden Age, one a foreigner and the other a native of Amsterdam.

René Descartes (1596-1650) – The most famous and greatest of all French philosophers was born in La Haye, a small village in the Loire Valley. He is thought to have arrived in the Low Countries for the first time at the beginning of 1618. At the time, he was a young, unknown volunteer, accompanied by a valet, who had come to enlist in the army of Prince Maurice de Nassau. He returned to the Low Countries again in 1629, resided in Amsterdam (especially in Kalverstraat and on Westermarkt) and matriculated at the Franeker University as "René Descartes, French national, philosopher". At the beginning of 1636, he settled in Leyden where he published the *Discourse on Method*. He made frequent visits to Amsterdam where a servant girl named Helen gave him a daughter; the child died at the age of five. In 1649 he travelled to Stockholm, where he died.

ROGER-VIOLLET

Spinoza

Baruch Spinoza (1632-77) – Born in Amsterdam in the Portuguese Jewish community, Benedict Spinoza studied in the shadow of the town's Jesuits. Shortly before 1650, he began working with his father and he proved to be an excellent businessman. He spoke Hebrew, Dutch, Spanish, Portuguese, French and Latin. His two-sided culture (Jewish and Latin) encouraged him to move away from dogmatism and, as a result, the Jewish community excommunicated him in 1656. The Christians, however, referred to him throughout his life as the "Jew from Voorburg" (a suburb of The Hague where he settled after 1660). In 1663 he published his first book. His reputation as a liberal thinker became established. He enjoyed the protection of Johan de Witt *(see Birth of a dynasty: the Orange-Nassau family)*, but lived in poverty and developed his philosophy: "*I force myself to travel through life not in sadness and tears but with a still soul, in joy and happiness...*" The author of Ethics was buried in a communal grave.

THE EAST AND WEST INDIA COMPANIES

The beginnings – When the port of Antwerp was closed in 1585, it gave Amsterdam an almost total monopoly of maritime trade between the North Sea and the Baltic (timber and cereals). Moreover, with the herring fishing industry and the export of dairy products and textiles, Amsterdam had become a wealthy city by the end of the 16C. Dutch seafarers had travelled to Asia on behalf of the Portuguese and had brought back information about trade routes and the various commercial trading posts set up along the Asian coast.

On 2 April 1595 four ships, the *Mauritius, Amsterdam, Hollandia* and *Duyfken* left the roadstead at Texel. They were commanded by Cornelis de Houtman and Gerrit van Beuningen, and funded by nine merchants of Amsterdam who set up the Distant Company for the occasion. They arrived in the roadstead at Banten, to the west of Java, 14 months later. Three of the ships returned to Amsterdam early in 1597 (87 of the 240 crew had survived), loaded with spices, mainly pepper. Although the expedition was not a commercial success (only just covering expenses) it proved that, contrary to what had been attempted by other merchants taking the Arctic route, it was possible to sail the Portuguese route via the Cape of Good Hope. The industrious spirit of the Dutch was immediately aroused.

From then on, eight companies chartered a total of 65 ships which sailed to Asia from the ports of Amsterdam, Rotterdam, Hoorn or Enkhuizen. Competition soon led to a lowering of prices despite the fact that the risks remained unchanged, but the idea soon attracted the English, Spanish and Portuguese. Moreover, it appears that Dutch merchants were unwilling to co-operate with each other.

The establishment of the company – Faced with this competition, which risked ruining trade, the government of the United Provinces founded the **East India Company** on 20 March 1602, two years after its English counterpart. The *Verenigde Oost-Indische Compagnie* (VOC for short) not only enjoyed the privilege of having its monopoly confirmed by the government; it was also granted the right to wage war and negotiate treaties with the sovereigns of distant lands. In other words, the Dutch had set up a politico-military commercial company.

The 17 Gentlemen

The governors of the Dutch East India Company were referred to as the *Heren XVII*, ie the 17 Gentlemen. Most of them belonged to the new class of wealthy merchants or came from banking families.
The document founding the VOC, the "grant", indicated the number of ships to be built and the number of members of the board of directors. They were to number 17 and be liable up to the value of their individual investments.

"*On the fourth day of November 1618 arrived at the roadstead in Batavia and dropped anchor, thanks be to God! After having prayed and rendered thanks to God who, in His infinite wisdom, had kept us safe and brought us to our destination, we found two English vessels which paid us homage and gave signs of friendship, but it was a trick.*"
These few lines are signed **Elie Ripon**, Captain-at-Arms to the Company. His memoirs were published under the title *Voyages et aventures aux Grandes Indes* (pub Les Editions de Paris).

A model organisation – The charter founding the company was a model of commercial organisation. The old units in Amsterdam, Zeeland, Rotterdam, Delft, Hoorn and Enkhuizen became "chambers". Their former directors were appointed governors of the chambers. People interested locally became shareholders of the new company. Moreover, staff loyalty was assured. The ships were no longer sold off after each voyage, and it was the company which took liability for any debts rather than the directors themselves.
The chambers funded the company in accordance with their means. Of the 6.5 million florins deposited, the share of the Amsterdam Chamber was 3.7 million, just over half of the total. Although most of the 1 143 shareholders were rich merchants, there were also a few artists, workers and craftsmen and a handful of clerics among them. A servant named Aaltje Gerritsdr even invested 100 florins. This information is not merely a good story; it shows how modern the organisation was. Every level of Dutch society was entitled, albeit without any real power, to take a financial interest in the progress of the East India Company.

Trade routes to Asia and the trading posts of the Far East – The ships left the coasts of Holland during the months of December and January, which meant that they had to withstand cold and difficult sailing conditions, but these dates were chosen so that they crossed the Equator at the right time of year with the wind in their sails. Depending on circumstances, some sailed round Scotland to avoid the French and English warships. After revictualling in South Africa, the ships headed for their main destination, **Batavia**, the general headquarters of the East India Company in Asia. From there, supplies were sent out to other trading posts. The voyage lasted for eight months and if, by chance, it was quicker, the officers received a bonus of 500 florins to be shared among them.
Batavia was founded in 1619 on the island of Java by **Jan Pieterszoon Coen**, a native of Hoorn. It was a small walled town in a central position, which made trade possible with Borneo, Sumatra and the Spice Islands. By c 1700 Batavia had a population of 70 000; it later became Jakarta, the capital of Indonesia.
After establishing itself in **Indonesia** by a combination of military force and mild diplomacy, the Company ventured along the coastlines of Asia. Trade then underwent spectacular expansion, with **India** (Surate in the northwest, the Malabar Coast, Ceylon in the south, the Coromandel Coast, and **Bengal** in the north-east), **China**, **Japan** and **Persia**. In the latter countries, the Company traded directly with the emperor, shogun and shah, obtaining commercial privileges such as the right to set up its own trading posts in the areas concerned: Desjima (in Nagasaki harbour) in Japan, Formosa (Taiwan) in China, and Gamru (Bandar Abbas) in the Persian Gulf. This international trade and

The Harbour at Batavia, Adam Willaerts

Dutch know-how provided the basis for Amsterdam's wealth throughout the 17C. The city's outstanding success and its position as Europe's leading financial centre had their roots in the warm waters of the various tropical seas of the Orient.
Military force combined with mild diplomacy? Not always. The colonisation of the Spice Islands (Ternate, Tidore, Amboine and Banda) was particularly violent. The inhabitants of Banda had been the only people to gather the seed from the fruit of the nutmeg tree, and they traded with Asia, the English, the Spanish and the Portuguese. Jan Pieterszoon Coen, Governor General of the Dutch Indies, decided in 1621 to put a stop to what he considered smuggling. He had the leaders executed, along with many of the population. Those who did not then die of hunger as they fled were deported. After this heroic act, he had Fort Hollandia built, populated the island with slaves and colonials and organised the farming of nutmeg.

Expansion westwards – In 1621, Willem Usselincx set up the *West-Indische Compagnie* (or WIC for short) for the purposes of trade with the west coast of Africa and the Atlantic coastline of America. The **Dutch West India Company** was also granted a commercial monopoly by the government, and was encouraged to pillage Portuguese and Spanish ships. The Company took full advantage of its rights since the truce with Spain was over; it even gained much of its success from this practice. In 1648, the Treaty of Münster put a halt to it by ending the Eighty Years War.
It was this Company which, in 1624, founded **New Amsterdam** on the island now known as Manhattan. The colony was to be renamed New York in 1664. Bonaire, Tobago, Curaçao, St Martin, the Dutch West Indies and today's Suriname became Dutch possessions, as were the trading posts of Bahia and Pernambouc in Brazil. On the coasts of Africa, Goree, Elmina, São Paulo de Loanda and the Cape were, like the island of St Helena, colonised during the 17C. Today, the Dutch West Indies (capital, Willemstadt) still belong to the Kingdom of the Netherlands.
It was, however, for the East India Company that Englishman Henry Hudson discovered the bay that bears his name, while seeking a route to the Pacific in 1609.

The products – The 150 ships built by the Dutch East India Company in its yards in Amsterdam never left the Low Countries with empty holds. Cargoes consisted of precious metals (gold and silver bars), fabrics (linen and worsteds), medicinal products, leathers and hangings, and foodstuffs or drink such as beer and French or Spanish wines. The ships also carried the products required for everyday life at their destinations, as well as passengers (more than one million people travelled on the ships in two centuries). On the return journey, the ships were laden mainly with spices (60% of freight): large quantities of **pepper** from India and Sumatra, **cinnamon** from Ceylon, **cloves** and **nutmeg** from the Spice Islands, **camphor** from Taiwan, **ginger** from Java, and **saffron** from Coromandel. People are sometimes surprised at the commercial importance of such fine spices but it has to be remembered that they were vital for the Europeans, firstly to preserve and season fairly bland foodstuffs and also because salt production was strictly controlled. The remainder of the goods carried reads like a fairy tale inventory: silver from Persia, wild silk and opium from Bengal, pewter from Malacca, bezoars from Borneo, copper and lacquers from Japan, cotton from Surat, porcelain from China, mercury from the Sunda Islands, sugar from Malabar, diamonds from India etc.

A very strange drink

It was c 1606 that the Dutch imported the first leaves of the tea plant having exchanged three measures of **tea** for one of sage.
Thirty years later, tea had become a common drink in Amsterdam. Initially, this strange drink (some people even ate the leaves) was appreciated for its therapeutic values since it treated gout and colds. Later, it enjoyed rapid success, especially among the English.

The western side of the traffic with the Indies was much less poetic. Triangular trade took ships across the seas. The principle was sadly simple. Traders exchanged mediocre products (spirits, tobacco and hardware) for slaves on the African coasts then exchanged the slaves on the coasts of America for tropical products such as timber, lemons, cotton, indigo, salt, sugar, and tobacco for the European market. During the period of monopoly enjoyed by the West India Company, ie until 1738, Amsterdam dominated the national trade in slaves, ahead of Zeeland.

The decline – During the 18C, the network of trading posts in Asia became increasingly difficult to administer. The number of civilian employees and soldiers c 1625 amounted to some 2 500; by 1750, their numbers had risen to 25 000. Costs increased while revenue was beginning to decline. Moreover, the English were gradually replacing the Dutch in trade with America, China and India. The Dutch colonial empire was crumbling away.
Although still powerful, Amsterdam was no longer the centre of world trade. The weakness of the city reflected the decreased power of the United Provinces, which had been greatly diminished by the wars with England and were now being forced to support lesser nations. It was becoming obvious that international competition had overtaken the Golden Age and the extraordinary influence of Dutch culture. The logical result was that both Companies, albeit for different reasons, went bankrupt. They were refloated but no longer had the means to regain their erstwhile magnificence.

The Venice of the North

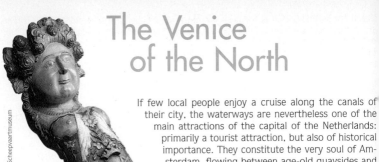

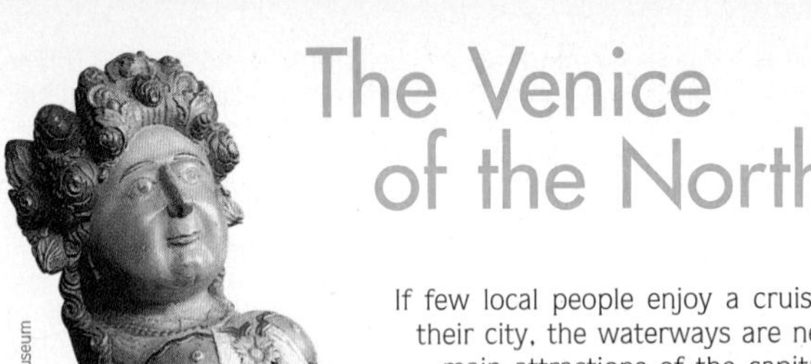

Head of a rudder from a ship belonging to the Dutch India Company

If few local people enjoy a cruise along the canals of their city, the waterways are nevertheless one of the main attractions of the capital of the Netherlands: primarily a tourist attraction, but also of historical importance. They constitute the very soul of Amsterdam, flowing between age-old quaysides and drawing people from all over the world. They are the soul of a city which has been built with and against water, the element that represented a threat while providing the city with its wealth.

A CITY SURROUNDED BY WATER

Birth of a city – The history of the city seems to have begun c 1205, at the confluence of the **Amstel** and **IJ**, when Gijsbrecht van Amstel erected a castle, but where remains a mystery. Then, in 1222, in order to contain the Zuiderzee marshes, the first farming and fishing communities built the first dike (*dam* or *dijk* in Dutch) between the south bank of the River IJ and the River Amstel. The Zeedijk, one of the streets in the old town, serves as a reminder of this event.

Dikes, embankments and sluice-gates – Soon the communities built a further two dikes set at right angles to the first one; they now correspond to streets in the city. On one side is Kalverstraat and Nieuwendijk, and on the other Warmoesstraat. On the embankments, the people who chose to live here built rows of houses made entirely of wood. However the dikes and drainage ditches quickly became obstacles to the navigation that formed the basis of incipient economic growth. The construction of a lock became necessary in order to allow small boats to offload their merchandise on the town's quays, near the shops and processing workshops. The lock was built in the centre of the area, now the Dam, creating a first outer arm to the north, the Damrak (*rak* means "straight section") and a second, inner arm, the Rokin (originally, *Rak-in*).

The "dike on the Amstel" recognised as a town – "Amstelledamme" functioned as a lock enabling the Amstel to flow into the IJ when the latter no longer presented a risk of flooding. In 1275, the site had attracted a large enough population to be termed a "town" since it is known that, at that date, **Count Floris V** of Holland signed an official document exonerating the inhabitants from customs duties on goods carried along the waterways. A town, of course, requires a church – its bell-tower was soon to be seen further south, on the river banks of a small town which still exists today, Ouderkerk aan de Amstel.

CLAIMING BACK ADDITIONAL LAND FOR DEVELOPMENT

Houses by the water – Once the economy had begun to develop, measures had to be taken to cope with the corresponding increase in population. The only solution was to reclaim land by extending the embankments of the first dikes. Moreover, reclaiming land from the water was the major project imposed by Mother Nature on the people of Amsterdam if they were to survive.
During the 14C the local people built houses and warehouses between two embankments along the river. These embankments were known as *burgwal*, a word also used to describe the canals, whether filled in or not, in the historic old town. Oudezijds Achterburgwal *(see OUDE ZIJDE)*, for example, means "the rear bank of earth on the old side". Nieuwezijds Voorburgwal means "the bank of earth in front on the new side". Although unpronounceable for foreigners, the names have a great charm for anybody interested in understanding how the city developed.

The first canals – In 1420 the townspeople still felt cramped, so they began to dig canals parallel to the embankments. The entire 15C was devoted to this project. The town council then decided to build an **outer wall**. In 1540 the town centre was formed and is easy to make out on a modern map. It lies between the central railway station in the north, the Geldersekade and Kloveniersburgwal in the east and the Singel in the south and west. Commissioned c 1538 by Governor **Cornelis Anthoniszoon** (c 1500-60), the oldest map of the town *(illustration, see Introduction, Historical table and notes)* reveals, in reverse perspective, the Damrak and Rokin (cutting the town in half), the Schreierstoren (bottom left), the Oude Kerk and Nieuwe Kerk (the churches on each side of the Damrak), and buildings which have since disappeared, among them the Nieuwebrug (at the mouth of the Damrak). This document is in the Amsterdams Historisch Museum. With a population of almost 14 000, Amsterdam was the largest town in the Low Countries; by 1580, numbers had risen to 30 000. The population was increasing at an extraordinary rate and Amsterdam was overpopulated.

THE CANALS IN THE GOLDEN AGE

First stage in a grandiose urban development project – In 1586 the town council decided to launch the building of the **Grachtengordel** (*gracht* means "canal" and gordel "belt"), a vast ring of four canals which seemed to have been drawn with the aid of a compass to the west and south of the historic town centre. Architect **Hendrick Jacobszoon Staets**, officially the town's carpenter, was commissioned to draw up this particularly ambitious urban development plan which included the widening of the **Singel** (1586) originally created in 1425, and the digging of the **Herengracht** (1586 and 1609), **Keizersgracht** (1612) and **Prinsengracht** (1612) respectively. The work was of Herculean proportions. The town, though it lacked building land, had the determination and funding required to achieve its objective.
Its wealthy traders were a driving force in the young Republic of United Provinces, founded in 1581, and they possessed colossal wealth, as is evident from the setting up of the Bank of Amsterdam in 1609. By 1615, the town had doubled in size!

Second stage in a remarkable expansion – The canals, 25m/81ft wide (28m/91ft in the Keizersgracht) and 2.1m/7ft deep, then stretched from the Brouwersgracht to the current Leidsegracht which was dug in 1664. Four years earlier, the town, still enjoying the wealth produced by the distant but profitable trade of the India Company, began to consider a second stage of development, for the population had now reached more than 220 000. In 1662, the ring of four canals was extended eastwards to the Amstel. By 1665, everything was finished! The town once again doubled in size. As was the case during the first stage of the work, the land was divided into plots, but differently this time. It was subdivided into plots parallel to the canal with the plot overlooking the quay being the most expensive. Houses and warehouses were built on this plot and the rear plot was used for servants' quarters, gardens and workshops. As to the Herengracht, a policy of private sales made it the most prestigious of the four canals in the Grachtengordel.

A new wall dotted with mills – This development led to the town limits being moved further out. The new walls encircled the city beyond the Grachtengordel, along the Singelgracht. They included a series of gates named after neighbouring towns. From north to south, they were Haarlemmerpoort, Leidsepoort, Utrechtsepoort, Weesperpoort and Muiderpoort. The 26 bastions strung out along the wall each had its own mill. Unfortunately none has survived. The De Gooyen Mill now seen to the north of the Muiderpoort dates from the early 18C *(see OOSTERDOK)*. The town retained this layout for the following two centuries.

A. Rossi/ALTITUDE-HOA QUI

Muntplein is more an island than a square

> **Canals with no walls**
>
> In Amsterdam, there are no walls along the quaysides of the canals. Only a low barrier prevents cars from falling into the water. In 1812, the French were astounded by the number of accidents and drownings. They had ropes stretched along the quays but this precaution had absolutely no effect.

THE CANALS TODAY

Cleaning the canals – Before the 17C, the brackish waters of the canals were controlled by locks separating them from the IJ. This meant that the tides cleaned them. From the 18C, the sluice-gates on the Amstel *(Amstelsluizen)* supplied fresh water to clean the water in Amsterdam's canals and gradually remove the deposits that had built up in them. After the opening of the North Sea Canal in the 19C and the building of the sluice-gates *(Oranjesluizen)* in Schellingwoude in 1872, the town was no longer subject to the influence of the tides.

Between 1945 and 1985, the enormous pumping station on the island of Zeeburg to the north east of the city centre took 600 000m³ of water from the Zuiderzee every day to refresh the water in the canals. Since 1985, all the city's houses, except its houseboats, have been connected to mains sewage. The pumps of Zeeburg are less intensively used, functioning twice a week in winter and four times a week in summer. Moreover, ten city council boats sail the canals to pick up any flotsam and three barges are used to dredge the canal beds. The water in the canals of Amsterdam may not be drinkable but it is clean.

★**A canal cruise** – Tourist trap for some, wonderfully relaxing experience for others: whatever one's opinion of a canal cruise, it provides some very interesting and unexpected views because they are quite different to anything one can see from the quayside. The view from water level of the sequence of seven bridges on the Reguliersgracht alone makes this type of tour worth every minute, even if the cruises are sometimes accompanied by a ridiculously stereotyped commentary from some of the tourist guides.

Not all companies offer the same trip but all of them sail the Herengracht and IJ. Some include the Oude Schans and Amstel. Ask for information at ticket offices.

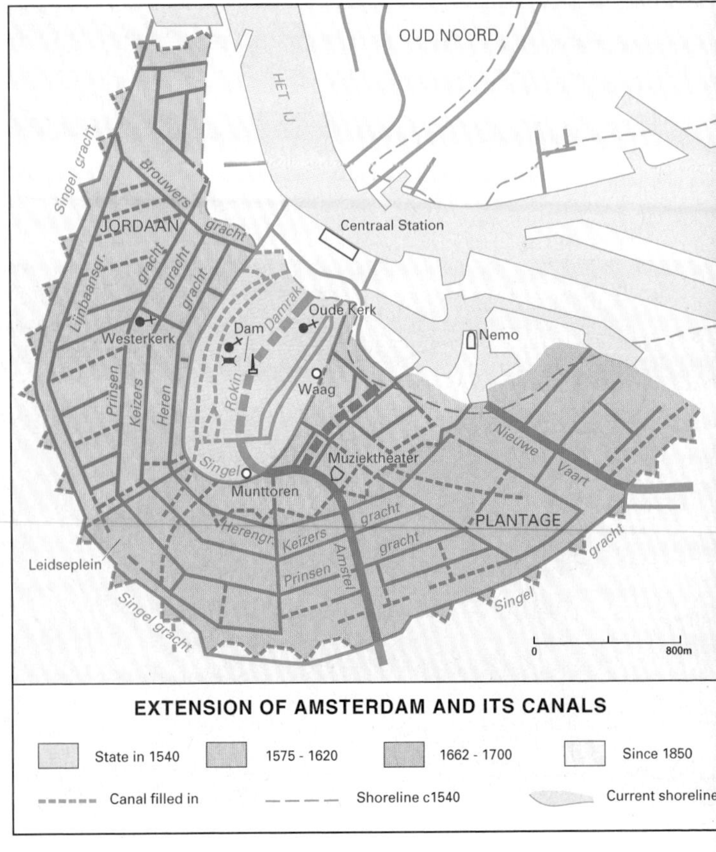

Architecture

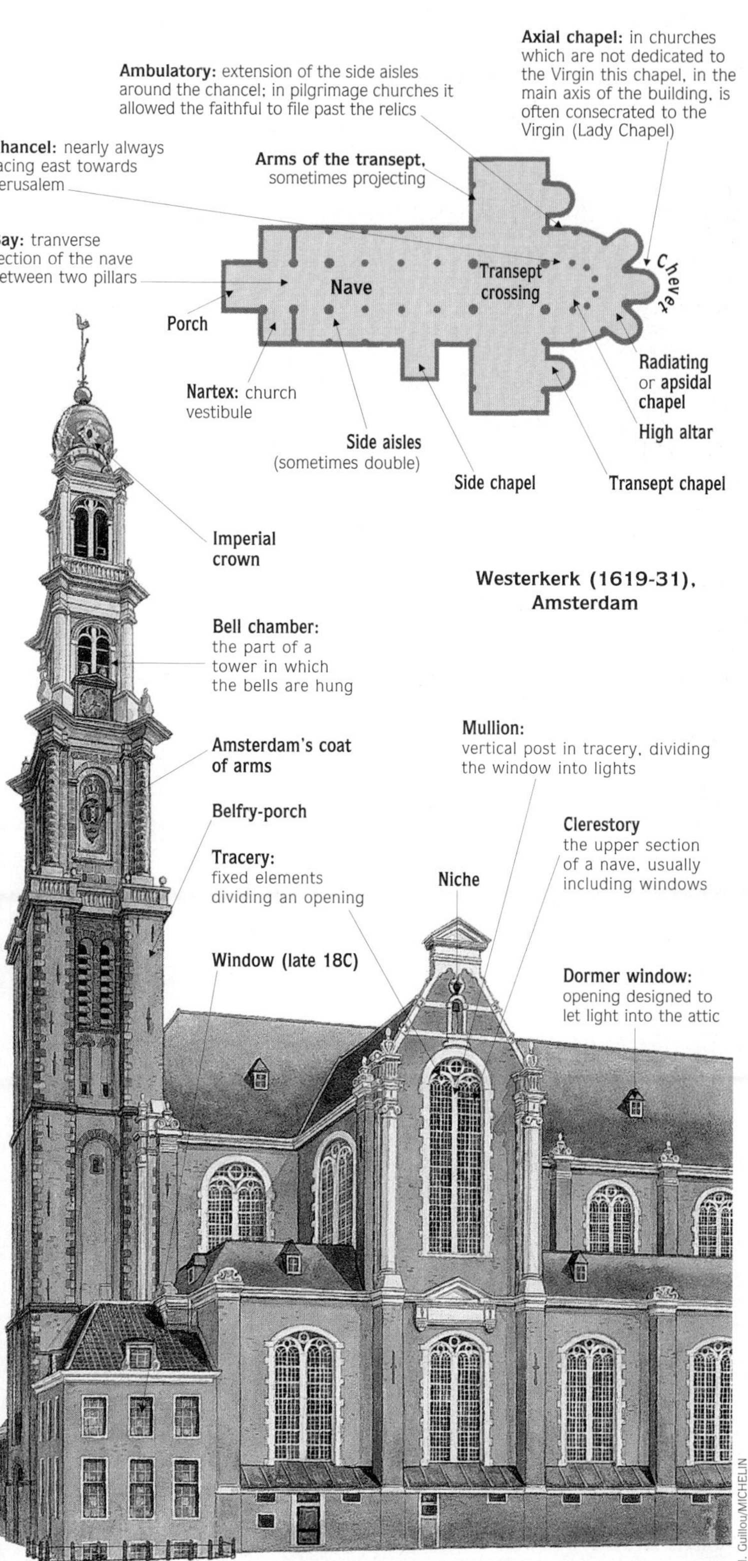

Ambulatory: extension of the side aisles around the chancel; in pilgrimage churches it allowed the faithful to file past the relics
Axial chapel: in churches which are not dedicated to the Virgin this chapel, in the main axis of the building, is often consecrated to the Virgin (Lady Chapel)
Chancel: nearly always facing east towards Jerusalem
Arms of the transept, sometimes projecting
Bay: tranverse section of the nave between two pillars
Nave
Transept crossing
Chevet
Porch
Radiating or apsidal chapel
Nartex: church vestibule
High altar
Side aisles (sometimes double)
Side chapel
Transept chapel
Imperial crown
Westerkerk (1619-31), Amsterdam
Bell chamber: the part of a tower in which the bells are hung
Mullion: vertical post in tracery, dividing the window into lights
Amsterdam's coat of arms
Belfry-porch
Clerestory the upper section of a nave, usually including windows
Tracery: fixed elements dividing an opening
Niche
Window (late 18C)
Dormer window: opening designed to let light into the attic
M. Guillou/MICHELIN

GABLES OVER THE YEARS

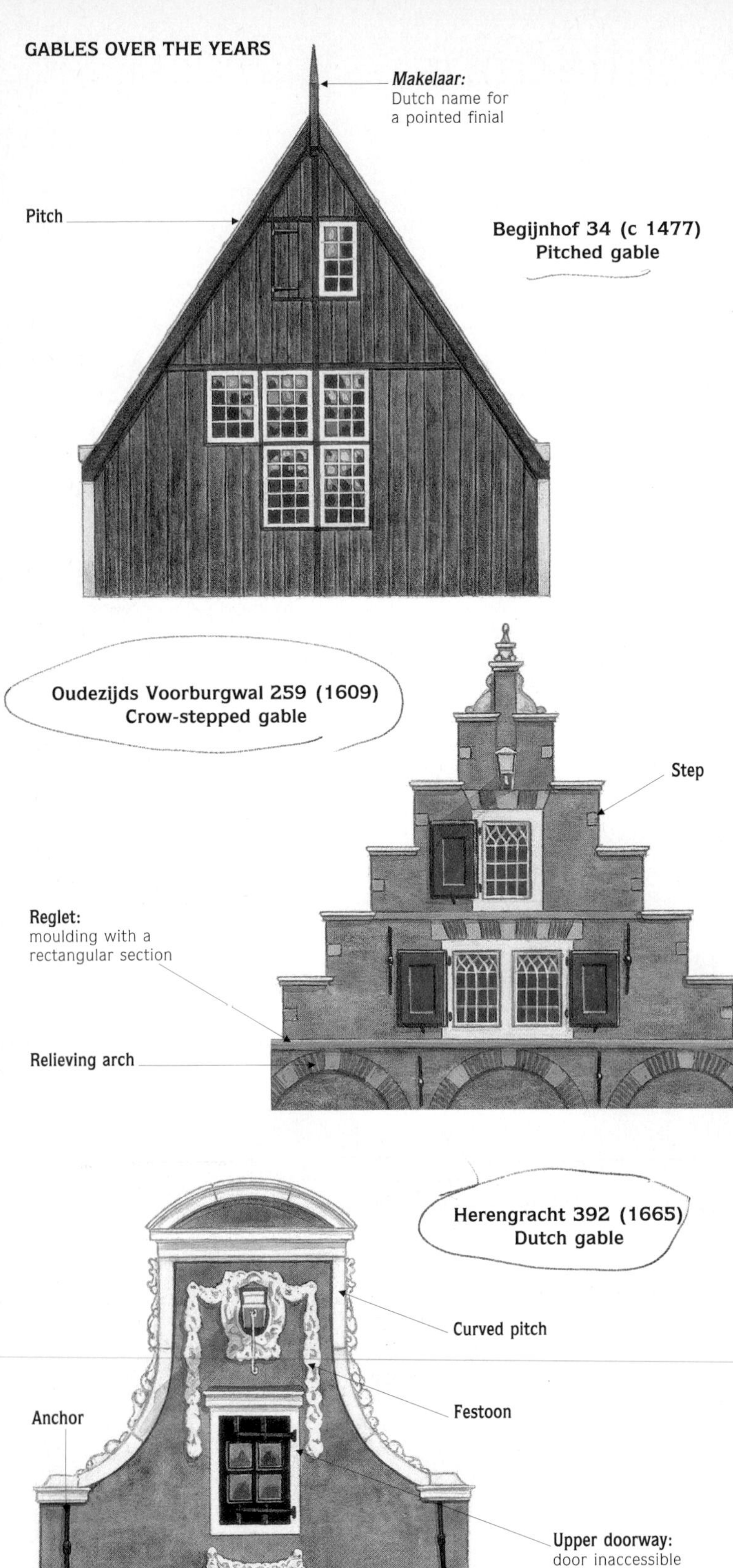

Makelaar:
Dutch name for
a pointed finial
Pitch
Begijnhof 34 (c 1477)
Pitched gable
Oudezijds Voorburgwal 259 (1609)
Crow-stepped gable
Step
Reglet:
moulding with a
rectangular section
Relieving arch
Herengracht 392 (1665)
Dutch gable
Curved pitch
Festoon
Anchor
Upper doorway:
door inaccessible
without a hoist

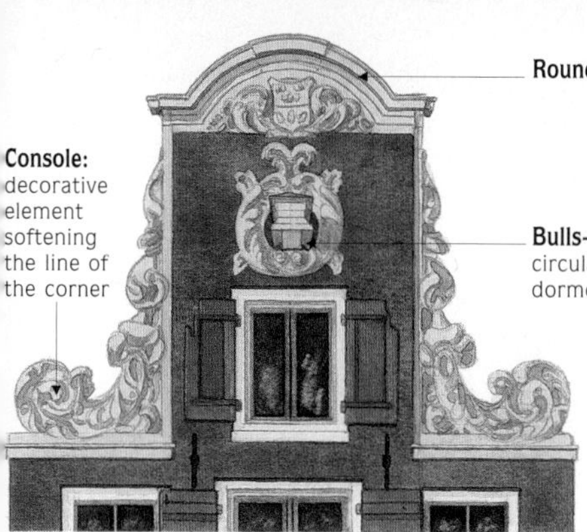

Entablature

Oudezijds Voorburgwal 237
(mid 18C)

Balustrade: in this building, it occupies the attic above the entablature

Frieze: series of decorative elements in a horizontal strip

Façade (1632) of the Westfries Museum, Hoorn

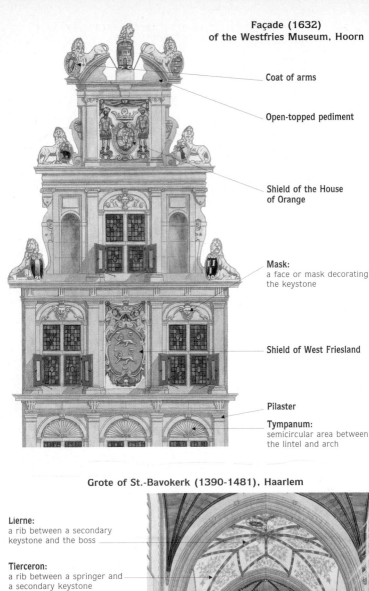

Coat of arms

Open-topped pediment

Shield of the House of Orange

Mask: a face or mask decorating the keystone

Shield of West Friesland

Pilaster

Tympanum: semicircular area between the lintel and arch

Grote of St.-Bavokerk (1390-1481), Haarlem

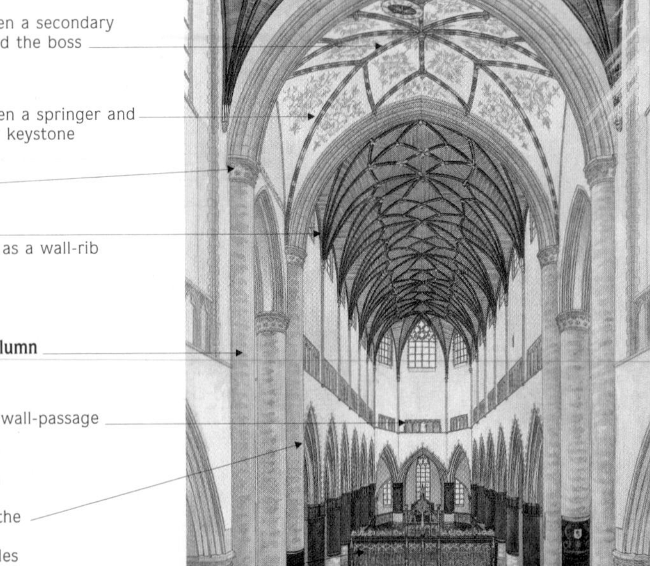

Lierne: a rib between a secondary keystone and the boss

Tierceron: a rib between a springer and a secondary keystone

Capital

Formeret: also known as a wall-rib

Engaged column

Triforium: an arcaded wall-passage

Great arch: separating the nave from the side aisles

Choir screen

Painted floor

Canal house (*Voorhuis* or "front house")

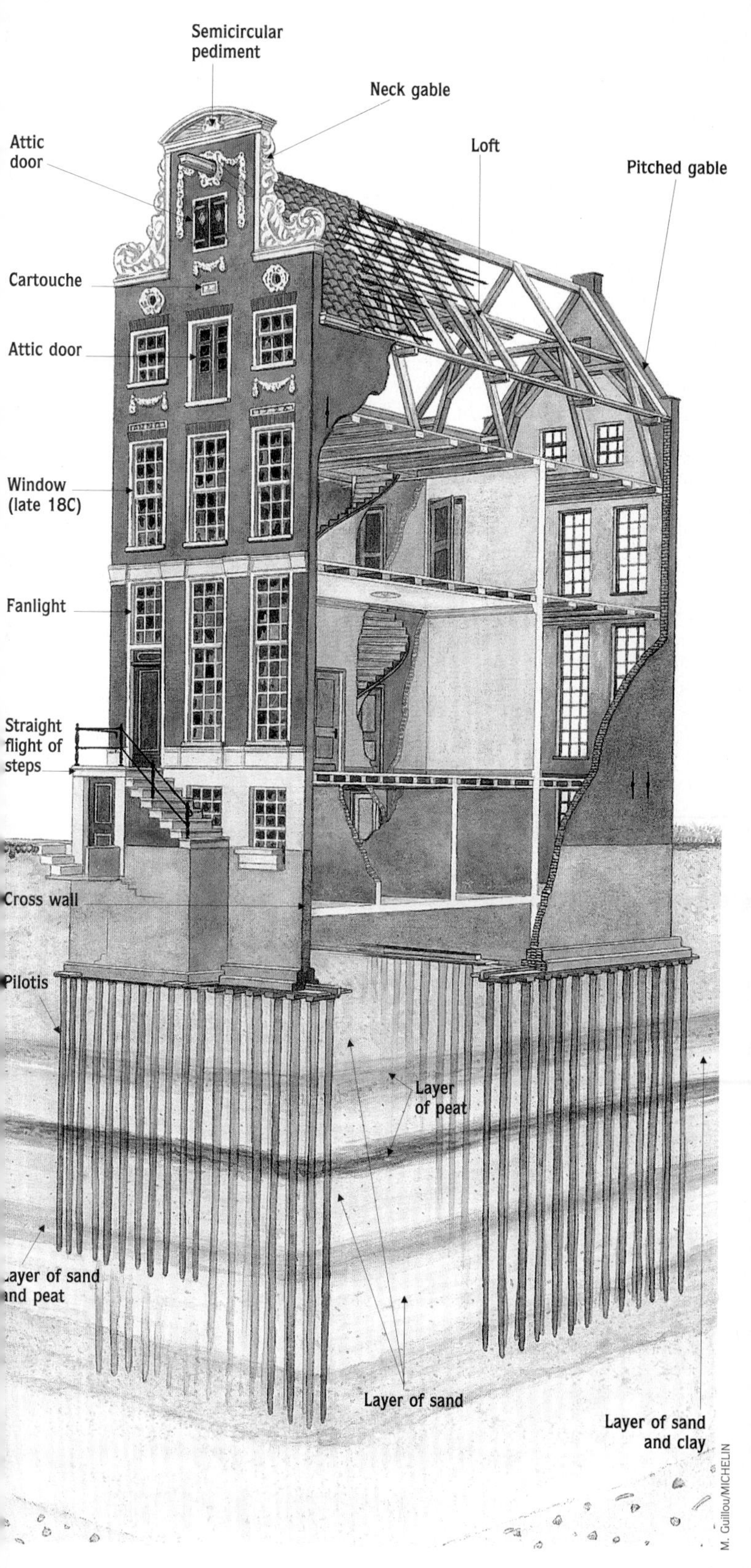

CANAL HOUSES

Well-anchored constructions – As shown in the drawing on the previous page, a canal house has foundations reaching far down into the porous subsoil of the city. In order to provide good foundations, long piles had to be hewn out of strong pine trunks imported from Germany and Scandinavia and sunk to great depths.

A very unstable subsoil – Given the weight of a house, architects had to find the layer of sand in the subsoil; it begins at depths of 13m/42ft. The subsoil below Amsterdam consists of a whole succession of layers: **sand** (0 to -3m/0 to -10ft), **peat** (-3 to -5m/-10 to -16ft), **sand and clay** (-5 to -12m/-16 to -39ft), **peat** (-12 to -13m/-39 to -42ft), **sand** (-13 to -16m/-42 to -52ft), **sand and peat** (-16 to -18m/-52 to -58ft), **sand** (-18 to -21m/-58 to -68ft) etc. Some of the pilotis did not descend below the layer of sand and clay; others, such as the ones supporting the cross walls, could be sunk to the third level of sand and, therefore, be 18m/58ft in length.

A forest of piles – It was no easy matter to sink so many wooden pilotis so deep in the subsoil, even if it was as permeable as the subsoil of Amsterdam. It is true that ordinary houses did not require as many stakes as the royal palace (13 659), but they were nevertheless supported on several hundred.
To sink the pilotis, a pyramid-shaped structure was erected using three beams which held two other vertical beams erected parallel to each other. They were used to guide a metal hammer weighing some 500kg/1 100lbs and known as a *heilblok*. It was the forerunner of the mechanical pile-driver and was hand-operated by between 30 and 40 men pulling on a rope divided into as many strands as there were men. When the hammer reached the top of the pyramid of beams, the foreman gave the signal and all the men released their ropes so that the hammer struck the piloti. Then they began again.

The house – The house was divided into a *voorhuis* or front house and an *achterhuis* or rear house separated by a small courtyard. The front house usually consisted of five storeys topped by a roof of pantiles. The ground floor (or to be more precise the *piano nobile*) was raised above the level of the quayside since the cellar could not be deep. This explains the many flights of steps leading to basements.
The frontage is usually narrow because rates used to be calculated as a function of the width. It is usually built of brick because the law required the use of this building material from the mid-15C onwards, in order to reduce fire risks. Most of the frontages are three bays wide, but over the centuries the decorative features have undergone enormous changes. This is obvious in details such as the shape of the anchors or the types of windows but is most spectacular in the gables.

Changes in gables – A stroll along the canals in the old town of Amsterdam reveals a wide range of different gables. Indeed, it is they, rather than the city's churches and royal palace, which have brought Amsterdam its reputation as a town of artistic and architectural interest. The gables of Amsterdam are absolutely unique. The double page of illustrations on pp 78-9 shows seven typical types of gable and provides a quick means of dating buildings. However it cannot be assumed because the gable dates from the mid 17C that the entire frontage dates from the same period. Many of the gables were erected much later than the frontage below them.
What is a gable? It is the upper section of a frontage, set on a level with the attic. In Amsterdam the attics were used as storehouses, which explains the presence of the hoist used to raise goods to this level. It is part of the wall of the façade and not merely a decorative element like a pediment.
In the Begijnhof, no 34 dates from approximately 1460. It has a timbered frontage with a pitched roof. The gable shows the basic, most elementary shape: a pitch that reflects the triangular shape of the roof. This type of gable was built between 120C and 1550 (approximately). The **neck gables** *(illustration, see above)* on warehouses are of the same type except that they are topped by a small piece of masonry known as a "neck". This type of gable was built between c 1615 and c 1720.
The Three Canals House dates from 1609 and has a **stepped gable** on which the slopes have been replaced by steps. In this case, there is a sandstone shelf on each step to protect the structure from rain. This type of gable was erected between 1600 and 1665 (approximately), then in the second half of the 19C when it again became fashionable to build in the old style.
No 392 Herengracht dates from 1665. Its **bell-shaped gable** has the characteristic shape that has given it its name. This type of gable was built between 1645 and 1790 (approximately). Originally it was wide and topped by a rounded pediment; gradually its bell shape became more pronounced and, influenced by the Louis XV style, it lost its pediment.
No 28 Singel has a **raised neck gable** dating from the early 18C. This type of gable was built between 1640 and 1770 (approximately). Its name is a translation of the Dutch *halsgevel* (*hals* means "neck"), because the base of the gable forms a 90° angle. Since the narrow, vertical structure did not cover the entire width of the rafters, the gable was flanked with a variety of sandstone ornamentation, from scrolled console to intricate carved features.
No 40 Singel, which dates from 1725, has a **fake attic** which is very ornate. The gable itself has disappeared, replaced by a decorative top section. This is also the case on no 237 Oudezijds Voorburgwal which has a more sophisticated construction dating from

the mid 18C, an **entablature** topped by a traceried attic with a **balustrade**. This type of tall construction, which was specific to the 18C, still concealed the ridge of the roof. Finally, no 397 Keizersgracht, which dates from c 1790, has an elegantly traceried entablature and a hipped roof. In this instance, the roof is visible, so there is no gable. The hoist, however, is still in place. This type of construction continued to exist until c 1920.

THE GREAT MEDIEVAL BUILDINGS

Gothic architecture did not appear in the Low Countries until the 14C. The oldest sacred building in the city is the **Oude Kerk**, the "old church", built from 1309 onwards and altered several times thereafter. The influence of Brabant-style Gothic is obvious here. The style was introduced as a result of the power of the Burgundians. It has three aisles and an ambulatory with radiating chapels. The massive tower forms a porch on the west side. The side chapels are topped by triangular gables. There is almost no transept. The more traditional rose window has been replaced by great bays. The **Nieuwe Kerk** or "New Church" was built a century later in the Flamboyant Gothic style. Stone was rare in the Low Countries and, because the subsoil was in any case too light to guarantee the necessary stability, a wooden barrel vault is used, like the one in the Oude Kerk. Outside the capital, the **Grote of St.-Bavokerk** or Great St Bavo's Church in Haarlem was built between the end of the 14C and the end of the 15C. It is one of the most outstanding churches in Holland; its stark interior is typical of the country's Protestant churches.

As far as secular Gothic architecture is concerned, only the **Waag** or public weigh-house has survived. It was built in the late 15C and consists of a fortified gateway flanked by towers and turrets bristling with pepperpot roofs.

Nieuwe Kerk, used for temporary exhibitions

GLOBAL PICTURES

THE DUTCH RENAISSANCE

The Renaissance arrived late in the Low Countries and did not become apparent in architecture until the mid 16C. The style, imported by Italian artists such as Tomas Vincidor of Bologna who designed Breda Castle (Noord-Brabant) from 1536 onwards, was then taken over by local architects.

Renaissance features were used without modifying the architecture itself. The traditional layout was often retained and the new style is evident only in decorative details such as shells on the tympana above windows, dormer windows heavy with pinnacles and arcading, octagonal turrets, pilasters and fake columns, and stepped gables. The combination of red brick and white or pale yellow sandstone was typical of the Dutch Renaissance; it embellished the most luxurious frontages, among them Bartolotti House (on Herengracht) or the House of Heads (on Keizersgracht).

Lieven de Key (c 1560-1627) and **Hendrick de Keyser** (1565-1621) are the two greatest Dutch architects of this period. To them should be added **Hans Vredeman de Vries** (1527-c 1605), although he worked mainly abroad. Lieven de Key designed the meat market or Vleeshal (1602) in the town and the public weigh-house. Hendrick de Keyser, a native of Utrecht, was the leading artist of the Dutch Renaissance period. In Amsterdam alone he designed several churches (Zuiderkerk, Westerkerk, Noorderkerk), private mansions (Bartolotti House, Dolphins House) and a public building (Munttoren), as well as the public weights and measures office in Hoorn in the north of the province. His style was a forerunner of the Baroque.

THE GOLDEN AGE

The mid-17C marked a break with the graceful, ethereal style of the Renaissance. However Dutch Baroque architecture was of outstanding sobriety compared to its effervescence in other countries. It was so restrained that it was described as Dutch Classicism.

One of the most famous architects of the Golden Age was **Jacob van Campen** (1595-1657), who designed the town hall (1648-62) that was later to become the royal palace. Attracted by the designs of Palladio and Mansart, he had a decisive influence on national architecture. However it is the wonderful residential architecture that contains some of the finest examples of Dutch Classicism. **Philip Vingboons** (1607-78) was the best-known exponent of this style. He designed a restrained form of architecture which met the requirements of a Protestant clientele that would never have indulged in the magnificence seen in the *palazzi* of Venice, but nevertheless appreciated sober grandeur. The most austere example of this Classicism was the work of another great architect, **Adriaan Dortsman** (1625-82), who trained as a mathematician and designed the Nieuwe Lutherse Kerk (1671) on Singel.

18C AND 19C

The fashion for all things French and the influx of huge numbers of Huguenots after the Revocation of the Edict of Nantes in 1685 enabled the Louis XIV style (until 1750) and the Rococo Louis XV style (until 1770) to make a subdued appearance in an architecture that otherwise upheld the tenets of the Golden Age. The French architect **Daniël Marot** (1663-1752) who worked on the decoration of great houses in The Hague and Amsterdam (Museum Willet-Holthuysen) introduced greater harmony between interiors and external architecture. The ceilings were decorated with stucco work, windows became longer, and magnificent gardens were laid out at the rear of the most majestic residences.

The 19C was a period of architectural decadence. This can be mainly explained by the commercial and industrial decline of the United Provinces in the aftermath of the Napoleonic Era. A timid form of neo-Classicism was prevalent until 1860 when it was replaced by neo-Gothic and neo-Renaissance styles. **PJH Cuypers** (1827-1921), like Viollet-le-Duc in France, followed the historicist trend that swept through Europe. The Rijksmuseum (1885) is a vast neo-Gothic temple; the central station that he designed with **AL van Gendt** (1835-1901) is a gigantic neo-Renaissance construction.

Ph. Gajic/MICHELIN

The central railway station, impossible to see without a tramway getting in the picture!

20C

This century has seen the revival of architecture in the Netherlands. When he designed the Amsterdam Stock Exchange in 1903, **Hendrik Petrus Berlage** (1856-1934) was the forerunner of an architectural movement that placed the emphasis on simplicity of line and the rational use of building materials. Although inspired by Romanesque architecture, the building marked a profound change. Form met the requirements of certain precise functions and the utilitarian elements were clearly highlighted, resulting in unusual decoration such as the structures bolted onto the roof. HP Berlage was also the architect of the building now occupied by the Nationaal Vakbonds museum and of Amsterdam's "South Plan". This whole district was designed by Berlage who, with the Frenchman Tony Garnier, was the only avant-garde architect in the early years of the century to have brought a town planning project to fruition.

A group of architects influenced by Berlage, while at the same time rejecting his concepts, formed the **Amsterdam School** which favoured less austere architecture. The movement had as its leading members **Michel de Klerk** (1884-1961), **Piet L Kramer** (1881-1961) and **Johan Melchior van der Mey** (1878-1949). Their main designs were the Scheepvaarthuis (1916), "*The Boat*" *(Het Schip)* (1921) and the Dageraad (1922), the latter being to brick buildings what Expressionism is to painting. **KPC de Bazel** (1869-1923) applied the same concepts to the Algemene Bank Nederland *(Vijzelstraat 23, at the corner of Herengracht).*

The Stock Exchange, the best-known of Berlage's designs

Ph. Gajic/MICHELIN

Although the Functionalist movement never directly affected the capital, it swept through Holland at the end of the 1920s and was particularly prolific in Utrecht. Influenced by the German Bauhaus and the theories put forward by Le Corbusier, the movement's followers wanted to impose a less costly form of architecture. In the vicinity of Amsterdam, **Willem Marinus Dudok** (1884-1974) designed the town hall in Hilversum (1932), while in Amsterdam itself **Gerrit Rietveld** (1888-1964) designed the Van Gogh Museum and the alterations to the Metz building on Keizersgracht (1933).

Amsterdam may not be able to compete with Rotterdam, which has some outstanding post-1950 architecture, but it nevertheless boasts a few fine modern designs such as the City Hall designed by **Holzbauer** and **Dam** (1987), the building at no 99 Rokin by Van Schijndel (1990), the Nemo by **Renzo Piano** (1997), and several very promising urban development projects situated mainly on the island of Java and the Zeeburg district.

DUTCH WINDMILLS

Windmills are an integral part of Holland's public image. In days gone by, they were perched on town walls or on dikes overlooking the polders, at the entrances to villages or on the banks of waterways. Noord-Holland still has some 130 windmills, of which nine can be seen in all together in Zaanse Schans *(see ZAANSTREEK)*. Zuid-Holland is somewhat better off in this respect, with 220 surviving mills.

There are two sorts of mills: watermills (which are very rare in Noord-Holland) and windmills. Among these, there are polder mills and industrial mills. The polder mills, a common sight in Noord-Holland, are, or to be more precise, were used to pump water. The second type of mill served to grind corn, extract oil, husk rice and pepper, saw timber etc. A few mills are still in working order.

Polder mills – The earliest windmills appeared in the mid 13C (they are known to have existed in 1274). Unlike the stone-built oriental mills of Persia and Arabia, Dutch mills were built of wood. The earliest type is the **post mill**. Known in Dutch as a *standerdmolen*, its rafters are supported by a vertical post, or *stenderd*, which enables the main section of the construction to be rotated so that the sails turn into the wind. This type of mill is more often to be seen in Zuid-Holland than in Noord-Holland. The earliest windmill used for drainage purposes, c 1350, was therefore a post mill. The **hollow post mill** or *wipmolen*, of which the earliest known example dates from 1513, is a later development. It is more frequent in Zuid-Holland. Its rafters are smaller and its pyramid-shaped support larger.

In Noord-Holland, the mills are often of the **rotating type**, known as *weidemolentje* or *aanbrengertje* in the Netherlands. They are small mills, used for drainage, bearing a resemblance to the hollow post mills. **Smock mills**, often roofed with **thatch**, are the commonest sight in the province; they stand on a **brick** base. Only the **topmost section** (the cap) can rotate to turn into the wind. There were originally several types (hexagonal, octagonal, or round) and many had a gallery. The illustration opposite shows a fine

Sloten Mill, Amsterdam
Smock mill

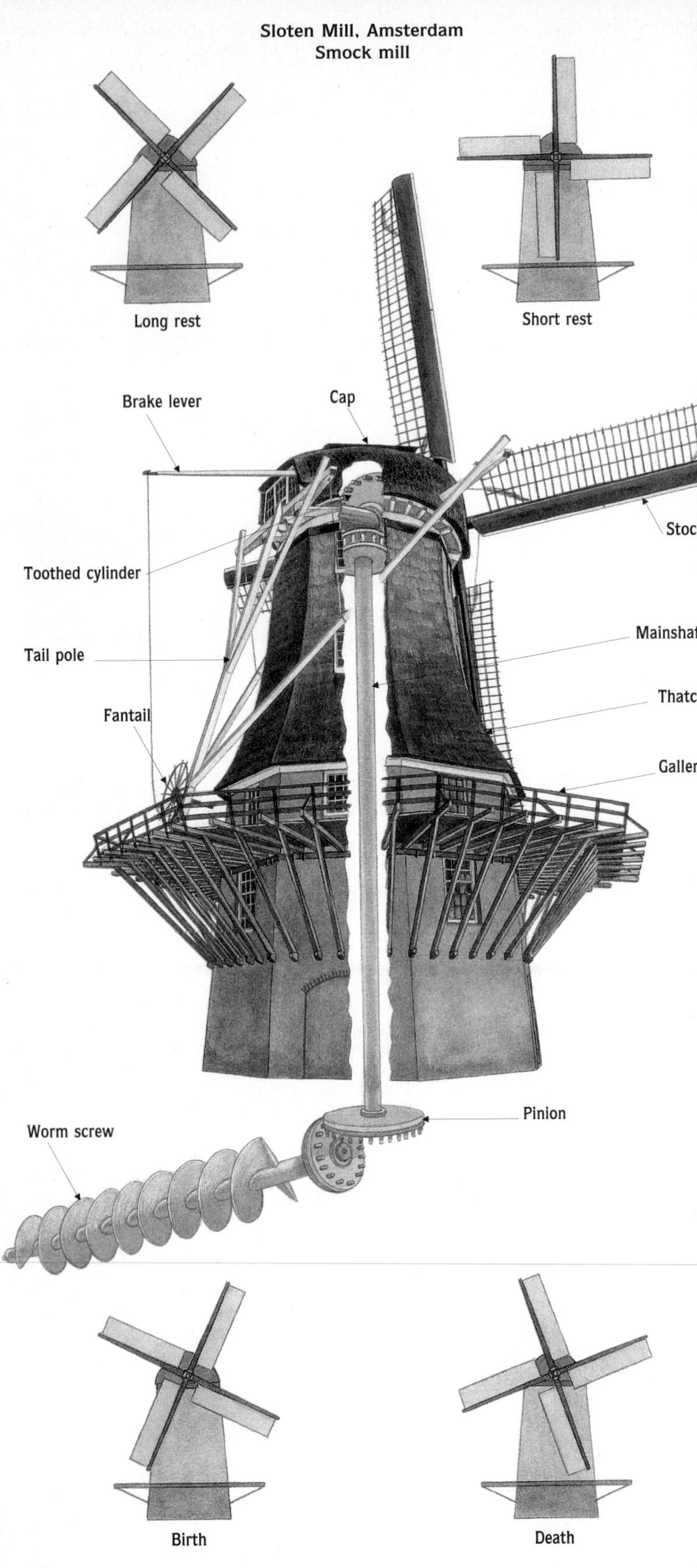

example, currently to be seen in Sloten on the outskirts of Amsterdam *(see SLOTEN)*. The mill is used to draw up water and it operates on the principle of the worm screw. The **screw** (or jack) can be seen, linked by pinions to the central pivot which activates the sails by means of the **toothed cylinder**. On the gallery are the **fantail** and **tail pole** used to move the **cap**. In this position the miller can use a rope to activate the brake control lever which blocks all four arms (consisting of two **stocks**) so that he can mount or remove the sails.

Industrial mills – In 1582, the first oil mill began operation in Alkmaar. Ten years later, Cornelis Corneliszoon of Uitgeest in Noord-Holland built the first sawmill. Once perfected, it became the **paltrok mill** which was totally enclosed on the windward side. It can be seen in Zaanstreek. It gets its name from the word *palzrock* meaning a Mennonite's overcoat. In days gone by, the Zaan area had almost 240 such mills. The **husking mills** date from a later period; the first one was built in 1639 in Koog aan de Zaan. They were used to remove the husks from grain (barley, then rice after the beginning of trade with the Orient) using rotating millstones. **Paper mills** first came into existence c 1600 but developed mainly after 1673 when the French retreated to Zaanstreek, an area in which there were a large number.
There were other types of industrial mill used to grate snuff, manufacture rope from hemp, tan leather, grind spices (especially mustard) and full cloth. Most had a workshop and a gallery. The **galleried mills** or *stellingmolens* could be seen in the polders and on the outskirts of localities where they were taller *(see OOSTERDOK)* because of the houses. When a mill was built on a wall *(wal)*, it was known as a rampart mill or *walmolen.*

The language of mills – The sails turn in a counterclockwise direction. When they stop, their position is important because the mill is sending a message to its neighbours:
– two sails positioned at right angles (+): the windmill is at rest, but ready to be operated again;
– two sails positioned diagonally (X): a polder windmill, at rest for a longer period;
– upper sail just to the right of vertical (ᛡ): a sign of celebration.
– upper sail just to the left of vertical (ᛡ): a symbol of mourning.

THE FARMS OF HOLLAND

The fine farms dotted across the countryside are part of the familiar Dutch landscape, especially in the polders. Often, only their impressive roof is visible; the remainder of the building is concealed by a dike or a curtain of trees.

Pyramid-shaped farm – This type of farm is very common in the north of the Province of Noord-Holland *(beyond the North Sea Canal)* where it is known as a *stolp*. It can also be seen in Friesland where it is called a *stelp*. The vast pyramid-shaped roof with four slopes is reminiscent of a haystack. Inside, the building contains the house, the byre and the barn. One of the roof slopes is covered with tiles instead of thatch; the decorative motif picked out in the tiling is known as a "mirror". Sometimes, in the wealthiest farms, the façade is decorated with a richly ornate brick gable.

Hall Farm – This is the commonest type of farm building in the Netherlands. In Holland, hall farms are to be seen in the south of the province and in the Gooi area around Hilversum. Inside, the rafters are supported by pillars, as they are in hall-churches. The two rows of wooden pillars mark out a sort of wide central aisle and two narrower side passages.

T-shaped farm – It was prosperity that led to the construction of this type of farmstead on the fertile banks of rivers. In Zuid-Holland and in the Gooi district, the house is set at right angles to the barn, hence the name of *T-huis*, or "T-shaped house". From the exterior, the house resembles a veritable transept with two reception rooms, the *pronkkamer* and the *royale opkamer* overlooking the street. In the Gooi district, hay used to be heaped up behind the farmhouse and the doors were on the sides of the building. Later, in the 19C, hay was also stored in an outbuilding. In Zuid-Holland, the cheese-making farms also include a dairy and cheese-making plant in the basement below the house.

The Netherlands have other types of farmhouse which you will see if you travel beyond the area covered by this guide: Frisian farms, "neck" farms, "mixed" farms, Oldambt farms, Drenthe farms, transversal farms etc.

The Arts

PAINTING

In its early days, Dutch painting was very similar to its Flemish counterpart. Later it was influenced by Italian art until, in the 17C, it enjoyed its golden age thanks to the political and economic independence of the United Provinces. Thereafter, its development echoed the increasing wealth of the bourgeois society that it depicted.

Pre-Renaissance

The greatest painter of the Netherlands is undoubtedly **Hieronymus Bosch** (c 1450-1516), but his works are not part of Dutch art since he came from 's-Hertogenbosch in Noord-Brabant.

Among the Dutch artists close to Flemish pre-Renaissance painters were **Geertgen tot Sint Jans** (1460/65 to 1488/93), **Cornelis Engebrechtszoon**, a remarkable colourist, and **Jan Mostaert** (c 1475-c 1556) who produced numerous works influenced by the official artist to the town of Brussels, Rogier van der Weyden.

The Renaissance

The 16C was marked by the arrival of Italian influence. On his return from Rome in 1524, **Jan van Scorel** (1495-1562) introduced Renaissance art into the northern part of the Low Countries. This great portrait artist, whose work bore a resemblance to that of the Flemish painter Quentin Massys, had as his pupil **Maarten van Heemskerck** (1498-1574) who produced refined portraits and religious scenes. **Lucas van Leyden** (1494-1533), a pupil of Cornelis Engebrechtszoon, was also influenced by the Renaissance. **Pieter Aertsen** (c 1509-75), however, was unmoved by the Roman style. The artist from Amsterdam created rustic views or scenes of interiors with a certain delicacy. Another of Van Scorel's pupils, Anthonis Moor van Dashorst (1517-76) was better known under the Spanish name of **Antonio Moro** which he acquired when he became Court painter to Charles V and Philip II.

The Golden Age

Dominated by the great masters, **Rembrandt van Rijn** (1616-69), **Frans Hals** (1581/82-1666) and **Vermeer** (1632-75) *(see biographical inserts in REMBRANDTHUIS, HAARLEM and RIJKSMUSEUM)*, the 17C produced a great number of fine artists. During this century, Amsterdam played the leading role held by Flanders during the reign of the Burgundians in the 15C. The major contribution of Dutch artists was the attention to naturalism, often referred to as "realism", a feature evident in their portraits, genre paintings and paintings of corporations, landscapes, still life or architectural paintings. The artistic effervescence was made possible by the economic success of the United Provinces *(see Introduction: The Golden Age)*, a success which explains the value and wide diversity of artistic creation in 17C Amsterdam.

Many of the works were not designed for churches but for the interiors of fine houses and, because of this, the subject matter was more profane. At the same time, the works constitute outstanding illustrations of everyday life and the aesthetic aspirations of the day.

Rijksmuseum Amsterdam

Woman in Blue Reading a Letter, Johannes Vermeer

Portraits – This topic is much too vast to be covered in just a few lines. However, suffice it to say that the great Dutch masters, unlike their 16C Italian counterparts who

Rijksmuseum Amsterdam

Still Life with Cheese, Floris Van Dijck

produced aristocratic portraits, supplied an inexhaustible range of realistic portraits of wealthy merchants and their families. It is not by chance that this art form became more accessible to a wider range of social classes in Amsterdam than elsewhere. The greatest of the portrait painters were **Rembrandt** and Frans Hals, of course, but other leading artists included **Johannes Corneliszoon Verspronck** (c 1597-1662), **Jan Lievens** (1607-74), **Bartholomeus van der Helst** (1613-70), **Gerard Dou** (1613-75) and **Ferdinand Bol** (1616-80).

Paintings of corporations – Civil guards, government officials, surgeons, and hospital governors all wanted to have themselves put on canvas. These group portraits have no equivalent outside the Netherlands.
The undoubted master of this genre was **Frans Hals** but other artists also supplied excellent works of this type, for example **Nicolaes Pickenoy** (1590/91 to 1654/56), and not forgetting **Rembrandt** with his famous *Night Watch*.

Genre painting – Although often understood to have a wider meaning, genre painting is really an allegory with a moral purpose. Usually the scene shows an aspect of everyday life and has no hesitation in raising a smile or a laugh in the person looking at it, while highlighting a lesson in ethics.
The Flemish painter Jacob Jordaens (1593-1678) was one of the pioneers of this type of work. He was followed by artists from the north of the Low Countries such as **Gerard Terborch** (1617-81), **Gabriël Metsu** (1629-69), **Pieter de Hoogh** (1629-c 1684), and **Frans van Mieris** (1635-81). Vermeer should also be classified in this category of artists. His works draw on scenes from everyday life, but his genius added a timeless dimension to his compositions and, by doing so, make him almost impossible to categorise. It is therefore **Jan Steen** (1626-79) who remains the figurehead of genre painting, and all the great museums in the world display works by this talented, meticulous narrative artist who worked without a studio.

Still life – This type of work had as its source certain 13C religious paintings, but the Dutch still-life paintings are a development of late-16C Flemish art. It is quite understandable that this type of composition could only develop in a region which had embraced the Reformation and its austerity, and which was generally less interested in representations of the human face.
It was, therefore, Flemish artists such as Jan Fyt, Alexander Adrianssen and Frans Sniders who influenced the earliest Dutch still-life painters. The bouquets of flowers painted by **Hans Bollongier** (c 1600-c 1645) are a wonderful example of this transition. The brilliant colours of the Flemish artists were replaced, by the artists of the northern area of the Low Countries, with a monochrome period – colours are still present but there is a predominance of greys. The finest representatives of this type of work in the Dutch provinces were **Pieter Claeszoon** (1597-1661), **Willem Claeszoon Heda** (1594-1680) and **Floris van Schooten**. Their favourite subject was a table covered with the remains of a meal and dotted with various recipients which catch the light. They produced a veritable encyclopedia of period tableware and food! **Floris van Dijck** (c 1575-1651) was the first artist to achieve a compromise between the austerity of his peers and the decorative art form that was soon to replace it.

Still-life paintings

There are three types of still-life works: *memento mori* with skulls, hourglasses and guttering candles to remind people of the transience of life; works referring to the Passion and Trinity in which wine and water are predominant features; and a profane collection of objects designed to demonstrate the skill of the artist.

Reacting against paintings by their elders that were too puritanical and austere, a second generation of still-life artists came into being on the banks of the Amstel. They were virtuoso colourists, using a refined technique for works that were already indicative of the Baroque. They were fond of so-called "scumble" painting which enabled them to achieve delicate opalescent effects, and they took still-life painting to its peak. Among the main artists were **Willem Kalff** (1619-93), **Jan Davidszoon de Heem** (1606-83) and **Abraham van Beyeren** (1620/21-1690).

Architectural painting – A few artists, the spiritual sons of the great Italian masters of perspective, specialised in representing the interiors of churches, especially **Pieter Saenredam** (1597-1665) and **Emmanuel de Witte** (c 1617-92), both of whom were much appreciated in their day. Other artists include the brothers **Job** (1630-93) and **Gerrit Berckheyde** (1636-98), and **Jan van der Heyden** (1637-1712) whose urban landscapes made architectural painting a genre in its own right.

The "Caravaggists" – Many artists who had travelled to Italy returned filled with admiration for Michaelangelo Merisi, alias Caravaggio. They created a series of large paintings, some religious, others profane, but all impregnated with the art of the Italian master of chiaroscuro. The group of artists, which is often associated with the town of Utrecht, includes **Gerrit van Honthorst** (1592-1656), and **Hendrik Terbrugghen** (1588-1629) of whom very few works have survived. The door pushed ajar by the "Caravaggists" in Holland was soon thrown wide open by **Rembrandt van Rijn**, who very quickly became the undisputed master of chiaroscuro.

Landscape artists – It was Jacob Grimmer and Hendrik met de Bies who produced the earliest landscapes in Flanders in the 16C, although the first pure landscape, ie a painting with no human subject matter, was created in Italy in 1521. However, these landscapes were not usually real or identifiable places. With the Dutch this type of composition was subjected to real innovation in the 17C and, by the middle of the century, it had become the commonest and most widely collected form of art.

It was **Hendrick Goltzius** (1558-1617), after his return from Italy where the Venetians used landscapes as a background for their pastoral scenes, who had a profound influence on his compatriots through his series of landscapes drawn without any symbolic or historic content. An artist such as **Hendrick Avercamp** (1585-1634) was still too much part of the 16C as regards technique and subject matter (his skating scenes were particularly archaic). However, two of Avercamp's contemporaries introduced considerable innovation by drawing after nature, with an absolutely new attention to realism. They were **Esaias van de Velde** (1587-1630) from Amsterdam and **Willem Buytewech** (1591/92-1624) from Rotterdam. Important though this stage was, it was in Haarlem that landscape painting finally acquired its pictorial independence. Until c 1630, the landscapes consisted of no more than a succession of details grouped with greater or lesser skill; after this date, a number of artists began to reflect the atmospheric conditions especially the quality of the light. Among them were **Jan van Goyen** (1596-1656), a pupil of Van de Velde, **Hercules Seghers** (c 1590-1638) and **Salomon van Ruysdael** (c 1600-70) who, c 1626, produced views of sand dunes or rivers seen from the side in order to accentuate the depth of field. Wide horizons, peacefully flowing rivers, clouds softening the brightness of the sunshine, light mist, and outlines of trees, churches or mills were the characteristic features of their luminous, serene compositions.

Although **Rembrandt van Rijn** proved to be a landscape painter of the front rank, the leading figure in this genre is undoubtedly **Jacob van Ruysdael** (c 1629-82) whose works have often been described as romantic. In fact, they are perhaps rather more indicative of his determination to transcend the rules of classical composition in order to instill a very pure sense of nature. The art of landscape painting produced other interesting, if less skilled, artists. They included animal painters who used a landscape as a pretext for their works, such as **Paulus Potter** (1625-54) and **Philips Wouwerman** (1619-68), landscape artists rather given to stereotype, such as **Meindert Hobbema** (1638-1709)) and a few artists influenced by the Italians, such as **Nicolaes Berchem** (1620-83) and **Albert Cuyp** (1620-1691), although Cuyp never actually travelled to Italy.

Seascapes – Seascapes may be linked by their very essence to landscapes but they nevertheless form a genre in their own right, born out of great sea battles and trade routes. They were unknown in the north of the Low Countries in the 16C but acquired great popularity over the following century. Although experts still cannot agree who was the first artist to paint this type of composition, there is no doubt that **Hendrik Corneliszoon Vroom** (c 1566-1640) was, with Jan Porcellis from Ghent, one of the earliest real marine artists. They influenced an entire generation of painters, including **Adam Willaerts** (1577-1664), **Willem van de Velde** (1611-93), **Jan van de Capelle** (1624/25-1679) and, more particularly, **Willem van de Velde the Younger** (1633-1707). The first subject treated by these artists was naval battles, a glorious topic which, when official commissions dried up, soon led to more anguished representations of storms and shipwrecks. This second subject, which was more poetic and less organised than the first, enabled artists to develop a much more powerful form of expression. Clouds scud across the sky, the waves are depicted as they really were, and the sea is decidedly rough. In fact, here as in the other genres, realism is the main characteristic of works dating from the middle of the century.

Rijksmuseum Amsterdam

View of Haarlem, Jacob van Ruysdael

From 18C to 20C

The Golden Age of Dutch painting came to an end almost as suddenly as it had started. The first indications of a decline appeared shortly after 1675, just after Louis XIV's troops had invaded the country. The economy collapsed and, where there is no wealth, there is no art. The 18C was, therefore, a period of decline. Despite this, several artists stand out from the general affectation that had taken hold of the arts, beginning with **Cornelis Troost** (1696-1750), an excellent portraitist and genre painter from Amsterdam who has often been compared to the British artist William Hogarth. Another artist from Amsterdam, **Jacob de Witt** (1695-1754), specialised in interior decoration, especially through *trompe-l'œil* works, and he produced some outstanding *grisailles* known as *Witjes*. Finally, although he died very young, **Wouter Johannes van Troostwijk** (1782-1810) may be considered the finest of Amsterdam's artists at the end of the century.

The 19C was dominated by the Hague School *(Haagse School)* directed by Jozef Israëls (1824-1911). Its field of activity covered Amsterdam and the surrounding area. Nature, beaches, sand dunes and the life of fishermen supplied countless subjects for the artists of the school, among them **Anton Mauve** (1838-88). **Johan Barthold Jongkind** (1819-91), a frequent visitor to France and a supporter of Impressionism, sought to depict in his works the quality of the light and a certain transparency in the atmosphere, as did **George Hendrik Breitner** (1857-1923) who was strongly influenced by Gustave Courbet. Finally, **Isaac Lazarus Israëls** (1865-1934), Jozef's son who was born in Amsterdam, succeeded in adding a new dimension to views of beaches and portraits in the Dutch tradition, thanks to the influence of the Impressionists.

At the end of the 19C, **Vincent van Gogh** (1853-90), the century's greatest Dutch painter, began by painting dark works which, as a result of the Impressionism he discovered in Paris, gradually became lighter and more highly-coloured *(see Van Gogh Museum table)*.

After an Impressionist period, **Jan Toorop** (1858-1928), who studied in Amsterdam, turned to Symbolism, a movement in which he held an important place on a European level. He then became interested in Pointillism and Divisionism before producing a large number of Art Nouveau posters.

The 20C saw a major artistic revival in the Netherlands, firstly thanks to **Piet Mondrian** (1872-1944), a teacher at the academy of art in Amsterdam (unfortunately, there are very few of his works in the city's museums). This artist, co-founder in 1917 of the De Stijl movement with **Theo van Doesburg** (1883-1931), was one of the great initiators of Abstract Art with his "neo-plastic" compositions containing lines cutting through each other at right angles and unequal areas of colour.

The interwar years produced **Herman Kruyder** (1881-1935), an artist who worked in Haarlem and succeeded in creating his own personal style filled with mystery, a cross between Expressionism and the early 20C Primitives. Another Dutch artist, **Maurits Cornelis Escher** (1898-1972), enjoyed great popular success after the Second World War with his xylographs representing spatial structures set one into the other so that they could be repeated to infinity.

Donkey Ride on the Beach, Isaac Lazarus Israëls

After 1945, the Cobra movement was founded (**Co**penhagen, **Br**ussels, **A**msterdam) as a reaction against the hegemony of the Paris School. It combined Expressionist, Surrealist and Abstract tendencies. The founders of the movement, which was dissolved in 1951, included Dutchmen **Karel Appel** (b 1921), **Constant** (b 1920) and **Guillaume Corneille** (b 1922).
The **Nul** (Zero) group was founded in 1961 to protest against the partitioning of various artistic activities. It organised international exhibitions in the Stedelijk Museum in 1962 and 1965. Its main representative was **Jan Schoonhoven** (1914-94). In the 1970s an artist from Amsterdam, **Ger van Elk** (b 1941) came to public attention for his works (on a photographic background) bearing a link with Arte Povera and Conceptual Art. In the 1980s **Rob Scholte** (b 1955) and **Marlene Dumas** (b 1953) gained fame in the Netherlands by seeking inspiration in the possibilities provided by the mass media.

DECORATIVE ARTS

Furniture

Every historical period has a style that spreads throughout the country. The Late Gothic era produced carved oak chests, credenzas and dressers decorated with "linen fold" motifs. This was followed after 1550 by a period inspired by the Italian Renaissance. However, as with other art forms, the heyday of furniture design came in the Golden Age.

Golden Age cupboards – Among the wide variety of cupboards, the finest late 16C and 17C Dutch productions are linen presses. The **Dutch Renaissance press** or **"Hollandse kast"** is one of the commonest types. Built of oak, sometimes of walnut, it has a range of ornamentation: lion's heads, caryatids representing the Virtues, friezes of scrolls or grotesques, and flat panelling (later carved with geometric patterns in low relief). It has a wide base, four doors (the lower doors are usually divided into two panels) and is topped by a heavy architectural cornice above a plant frieze. Its uprights consist of fluted pilasters or, later, engaged columns (in this case, it is known as a **column cupboard** or **"kolomkast"**).
From the second half of the 17C, although the cupboard remained a massive piece (this is a characteristic of Dutch furniture), new types of wood were introduced brought back from the distant tropics by the Dutch East India Company vessels. The new woods are most frequently seen in **cushion cupboards** or **"kussenkast"**, so-called because of the pot-bellied shape of their ebony-veneered doors. The cupboard is often flanked by twisted columns and supported on large ball feet *(see illustration)*. Decoration consisting of five Delft vases was often placed on the cornice.
Despite its name, the **Utrecht cupboard** was made in the Province of Holland. Its doors are topped by an arch on which the edges are highlighted with ebony inlays. Certain types found outside Holland are mentioned here because they are displayed in the Rijksmuseum: the **Zeeland cupboard** or **Zeeuwse kast** which is wider than it is tall is unusual for its very finely worked Renaissance decoration. The **Frisian cupboard** with two doors

bearing engraved decoration, has engaged columns and a thick cornice decorated with fine engraving. The **Gueldre cupboard,** which resembles the Utrecht cupboard, has a projecting cornice decorated with gadroons (oval decoration).

From the mid-17C and more particularly in the 18C people acquired a taste for marquetry, especially inlays of ebony, tortoiseshell, metal and ivory. This fashion is evident, as in Flanders, in the writing desks and cabinets full of drawers. The *sterrenkabinet* was a show piece, inlaid with ivory or marquetry representing stars *(sterren)* set in circles or ovals.

18C and 19C cupboards – In the 18C town apartments became increasingly common, hence the enormous change in furniture and the subsequent influence on types and methods of production. The Louis XV style imported by the French Huguenots after the Revocation of the Edict of Nantes (1685) was very fashionable in the 18C, although the style was fairly freely interpreted. The 18C cupboard or *buikkabinet* has two doors and a base containing drawers. From the middle of the century it had a characteristically *bombé* lower section. At the top was an undulating cornice, still with inlays and marquetry.

Towards the end of the century, the more austere, simple and linear Louis XVI style came into fashion and was more faithfully reproduced. In the 19C, the influence of the Empire style was evident as a result of Napoleonic domination and the presence in the country of King Louis Bonaparte and Queen Hortense, both of whom were very fond of Parisian fashions.

Rijksmuseum Amsterdam

Mid-17C Amsterdam press

Amsterdam and its region

NETHERLANDS AND NOORD-HOLLAND

The landscape – The Netherlands had a population of 15 863 950 on 1 January 2000, occupying an area of 41 863km² of which 33 937km² is land. The population is unevenly spread. The most densely-populated provinces are Noord-Holland and Zuid-Holland. With the province of Utrecht, these two areas contain the Randstad Holland, a vast conurbation including the country's four main cities: Amsterdam, Rotterdam, The Hague and Utrecht. **Noord-Holland** is bordered to the west by the North Sea, to the south by Zuid-Holland and the province of Utrecht, to the east by the Markermeer and IJsselmeer and to the north by Friesland.

A "low country" – The country's Dutch name, "*Nederland*", is particularly appropriate. "*Land*" means "country" and "*neder*" means "low". Bordered to the west by a string of sand dunes that form a broken line in Zeeland and Friesland, the "low country" only exceeds an altitude of 5m/16ft in its eastern section along the German border. The highest part of the country lies at its southernmost tip, Drielandenpunt (321m/1 043ft), only a few miles from Aachen. Almost one third of its total area, after an obstinate struggle against the sea, now lies above sea level. Without the protection of dikes and dunes, more than half of the country would be flooded during the highest tides and when the rivers are in spate. The lowest area in the country lies at 6.5m/21ft below sea level, on Alexanderpolder near Rotterdam. The Netherlands correspond to a depression in the Earth's crust which was filled in by alluvium from the Rhine and Meuse, by moraine from huge Scandinavian glaciers and by sand carried in the wind during the Quaternary Era.

Soil and scenery – Noord-Holland is a vast windswept **plain**. The farms are surrounded by rows of poplar trees to provide protection from the wind. The soil consists of **marine clay**, clay from rivers and peat bogs. The peat has been dug out and used for fuel resulting in the formation of lakes which were later drained.
A narrow area of sand runs along the western side, backing a coastal strip running from Noordwijk aan Zee in the south to Den Helder in the north. The **sand dunes** are of vital importance for the province, and for the country as a whole; as such they are carefully monitored by central government departments. Marram grass has been planted to fix them. In certain areas, the public are refused access to the dunes in order to prevent erosion and damage to the protective vegetation. The dunes also act as a sort of water tower, absorbing rainwater which then forms ground water lakes.

Climate – The climate is maritime, which means that it is damp and cool. Average annual rainfall amounts to 750mm, over more than 200 days. Amsterdam enjoys a temperate maritime climate with warm summers and cold, but not rigorous, winters. In January and February, the town sees a few snowfalls and temperatures near freezing. In March and April, the main feature is drizzle. From May to September, the pleasantly fresh climate gives way to sunny days during which the temperature rarely rises above 22°C/72°F. October and November are particularly damp, almost stormy months. With December come the first cold spells, although there are no prolonged periods of frost.

LEVEL OF NORTHERN HOLLAND

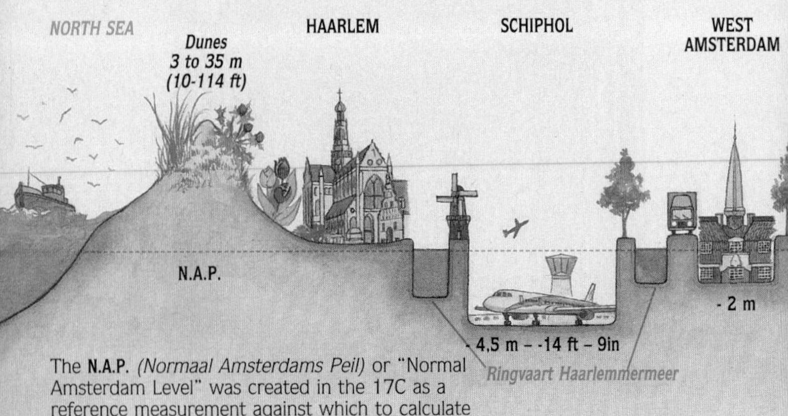

The **N.A.P.** *(Normaal Amsterdams Peil)* or "Normal Amsterdam Level" was created in the 17C as a reference measurement against which to calculate sea level in the Netherlands and Europe.

AN AREA OF POLDERS

The outskirts of Amsterdam consist mainly of polders, land once covered by lakes or the sea. These areas, created as a result of man's determination, give the region its unusual features and create a land to which the light, colours and peaceful atmosphere bring a poetry reflected in the works of the Dutch landscape painters of old.

What is a polder? – In Dutch, the word "*polder*" originally meant "land surrounded by a dike". The word appears in a charter signed in Middleburg (Zeeland) in 1219. A polder then is an area that in its natural state was covered with water and is surrounded by dikes, forming a depression that is artificially enclosed and in which the water level is adjusted by means of its own hydraulic system. A polder is an area of land reclaimed from the sea, from a lake or from a marsh and it lies below sea level. Although polders were known to the Sumerians, it was the Dutch who perfected the technique.

Creating a polder – Despite technical developments, the creation of polders continues to involve the same stages as it did in days of old.
In the peat bogs, along rivers and on the coast, there are single polders (the oldest) protected by a single dike. The names of several towns indicate the presence of these polders, since the word "*dam*" means "dike": Amsterdam, Edam, Volendam, Monnickendam, Uitdam, Durgerdam, Nieuwendam, Zaandam, and Ilpendam were all built to provide protection against high tides and drain a few areas of land, especially after the tidal wave which led to the formation of the Zuiderzee in the 13C. Excess water from the dike polders is directed straight back into the sea or a river by the force of gravity, through sluices at low tide.
The drainage polders are more complex. An embankment dike is built round a lake. Beyond the dike is a circular canal *(ringvaart)* flanked by the encircling dikes from neighbouring polders. The polder is crisscrossed by small canals interlinked by feeder canals. Whenever the desired water level is exceeded, the water is pumped back into the feeder canals then out to the peripheral canal and a whole network of lakes or canals used as temporary reservoirs. In days gone by, the excess water was moved by the windmills. The water then flows into rivers and the sea either by gravity or by pumping. The **Haarlemmermeer** is a perfect example of this system.
The third type is an extension of the second system. It results from the encircling of an area of sea by dikes and subsequent drainage by means of pumping only. This is the Zuiderzee-type polder of which the most impressive example is Flevoland, a group of two polders created with the patience of Job to the east of Noord-Holland. The work began in the 1950s and culminated in the creation of the Province of Flevoland on 1 January 1986.

Windmills to pump water – The drainage of inland areas lying below sea level could not have been achieved without human involvement. The development of drainage techniques is a unique chapter in the history of the Netherlands. Polder windmills were designed to pump water. For the first time, technical resources were successful in controlling a natural element. The sea level was raised and the land was lowered by draining peat bogs.

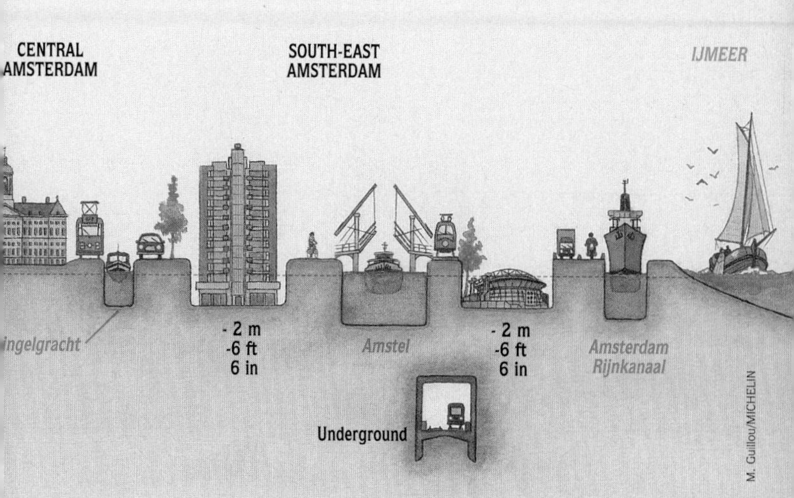

The 17C saw the construction of windmills because, when set out in a row, they could drain inland areas. One name stands out in connection with this vast enterprise: Jan Adriaenszoon Leeghwater (1575-1650), an architect and famous hydraulics engineer whose name literally means "empty of water". Under his direction and with the assistance of 40 windmills, Beemster Lake was drained and the land reclaimed (1612) to the north of Amsterdam. This success encouraged the Dutch to continue their efforts. They created the polders in Purmeer in 1622 and in Wormer in 1626. From 1631 onwards the Alkmaar authorities began draining the Schermer Lake under the direction of Leeghwater, with the assistance of 50 windmills. Four years later the work was finished. The great lakes in the north of Holland then became fertile farmland since the rain washed off the remaining salt. Capital was provided by the wealthy merchants of Amsterdam, who used the fortunes they had built up through maritime trade with the Orient to invest in land.

Major projects – In 1667, Henri Stevin proposed to drain the Zuiderzee in order to "expel the violence and poison of the North Sea". The project was not completed until the 20C.

In the 18C autonomous water management authorities *(waterschappen)* were set up and given responsibility for the maintenance and building of dikes, canals and sluices. They still exist today and have been backed up since 1798 by the Ministry of Water and Public Works *(Waterstraat)*.

Shortly before 1800, steam-powered machinery began to be used to pump the water *(see HAARLEM, Museum De Cruiquius)*. This meant that the work was no longer dependent on wind. The most spectacular period of reclamation began in 1848 with the drainage of the Haarlem Lake or Haarlemmermeer, which was completed in 1852. Then, shortly after the serious flooding of 1916, it was the turn of the Zuiderzee to be turned into a lake, the IJsselmeer, by the construction in 1932 of the huge seaward dike called Afsluitdijk. Several polders were then created on the shores of the lake. The most recent catastrophe struck on the night of 31 January 1953 when, as a result of a strong gale blowing inshore and a particularly high tide, 1 865 people were killed and 260 000ha of land devastated. Since then, the Delta Plan drawn up by a law promulgated by Parliament has guaranteed some far-reaching safety measures including the construction of a whole series of extensive hydraulic engineering projects.

Over the Netherlands as a whole, 7 050km^2 of land have been reclaimed between the 13C and the present day, 4 000km^2 thanks to the construction of coastal dikes. The new European agricultural standards, overproduction in the vegetable and flower-growing sectors, and a critical pollution threshold resulting from intensive pig-farming led the government to adopt a plan in 1993 that aims to return one tenth of farmland to nature. For Noord-Holland this means a return to lakes and marshes.

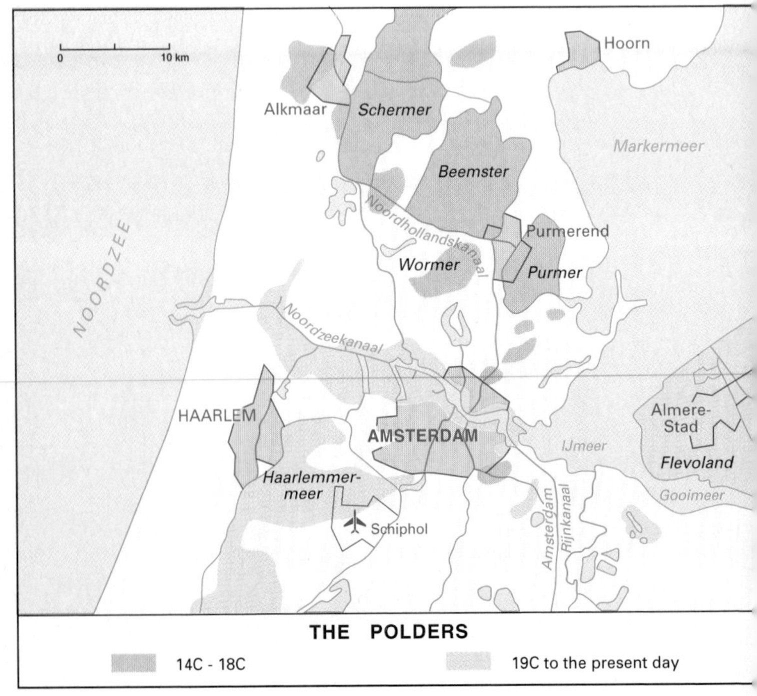

THE POLDERS

At the corner of the Keizersgracht and Reguliersgracht

Zefa - Streicham/HOA QUI

The City of Amsterdam

CYCLING, A RELIGION IN ITS OWN RIGHT

As soon as tourists step out of the central railway station, they are immediately amazed by the number of cycles pedalling past (if they have not been to Amsterdam before). Wherever you look, there is a bicycle. Amsterdam is said to have more than half a million of them. The bike park in the station is a sight worth seeing.
This is an ideal form of transport for a low-lying, flat land where hills are unknown. Cyclists can also take advantage of the many cycle paths, especially since 1978 when politicians had a large number laid out to reduce motor traffic in the capital city.

The Michelin Man had already arrived in the Netherlands by 1916!

Some brief advice – It is useful to draw the attention of a reader who is a potential cyclist to a few specific features of Amsterdam as a city of bike-riders. Firstly, the land may be flat but there is plenty of wind, as you will quickly discover, especially in autumn and winter. Secondly, although the sheer number of cycle paths makes them the envy of all Latin countries where cycles are considered a child's toy or the necessary equipment for a very competitive sport, their use may have a few surprises in store. Mopeds, for example, use them, overtaking cyclists without any regard to where they are going and local cyclists are not accustomed to giving way. It is, one might say, the survival of the fittest. The Dutch are past masters in weaving in and out between cars and pedestrians, a skill not given to everybody. Moreover, those who do not have any trams at home should take extra care; these vehicles are not always separate from the rest of the traffic. Furthermore the tramlines pose a constant danger. Finally, remember that, every day, some 200 bikes are "borrowed" in the city's streets and never returned to their owners. You should ask the cycle hire firm for a good padlock.

Touring the city by bike – These remarks should not dampen your enthusiasm though. A bicycle is undoubtedly the best way of visiting Amsterdam's sights. Unfortunately, tourists usually wait until the end of their stay before realising that they should have used this practical, inexpensive means of getting around a city where car parking is virtually impossible.

The names printed in bold type refer to sights described in this guide. Consult the index at the end of the book. The times indicated do not include any visits or stops. For information on cycle hire, see the Practical Information section.

One last remark before you set off on your bike. In Amsterdam, cyclists are entitled to ride the wrong way along one-way streets. Contrary to appearances, this is actually a very safe method of travel. There is no risk of being surprised by a car driver suddenly opening his door just in front of your wheel and, moreover, the face-to-face system enables everybody to weigh up the situation more accurately.

1 TOUR OF THE HISTORIC OLD TOWN

Tour starting from the central station: 45min

From the central station, take Spuistraat. At the end of this long street, follow the Singel which extends briefly into the Amstel beyond Muntplein. Cross the first bridge on the left (Halvemaansbrug) and turn sharp right into 's-Gravelandseveer. Turn into Groenburgwal and, at the end, turn right and continue along the Raamgracht, then turn into the first street on the right. Cross Zuiderkerkhof and Sint-Antoniesbreestraat then turn into the narrow Snoekjessteeg. Bear left and skirt the Krom Boomssloot at the end of which you should turn right into Recht Boomsloot. Turn left into Oude Schans and return to the station via Binnenkant which runs along the Waalseilandsgracht and the Prins Hendrikkade.

After the long, straight Spuistraat, the road crosses the **Spui** before following the last section of the **Singel**, one side of which is taken up by the **Bloemenmarkt**. The road junction on **Muntplein** in the shadow of the **Munttoren** is a crossroads used by pedestrians, cyclists, trams and cars; it therefore requires care. After this area crowded with tourists, the next section is much less well known and full of many more bends and corners. This is the old town of Amsterdam. The canals are shorter and narrower, and visitors can enjoy a more intimate Amsterdam as they cycle pass the **Zuiderkerk** (South Church) and the **Oude Schans**. The round trip ends with the **Oosterdok** and two of its sights: the **Scheepvaarthuis** and the **Schreierstoren**.

2 WESTERDOK AND THE HARBOUR

Tour starting from the central station: 45min

Cycle round the central station and turn along the De Ruijterkade then right over the bridge to the Westerdoksdijk. Turn left into Barentszplein and Van Diemenstraat. Beyond no 6, follow the narrow passage that runs along the Van Diemenkade warehouses. Pick up the cycle path again and turn into Tasmanstraat beyond the Westerkanaal. Turn right into Stavangerweg and right again into Haparandaweg. Follow Danzigerkade and Minervahavenweg then return to Haparandaweg and left into Archangelweg.

After following the **IJ**, the **Westerdok** (see the delightful row of houses on **Zandhoek**) and **Barentzsplein**, the route takes you past Amsterdam Harbour. Actually, the harbour made famous by Jacques Brel's song is not accessible to non-professionals and is now on the North Sea Canal. The barges on Van Diemenkade and Danzigerkade gradually give way to tugs and huge ships in the "Westpoort" harbour area.

Amsterdam School, Westerpark and Brouwersgracht – *Cross the Spaarndammerdijk and head to the right, then turn left into Zaanstraat. At the end of the street, turn right under the railway bridge (on a level with Zaandijkstraat) and once you reach the park, turn left. At the exit to the park, turn right then left at the traffic lights. On Haarlemmerplein, turn right into Nieuwe Wagenstraat and left along the Brouwersgracht. Return to the station via the Prins Hendrikkade.*

On Zaanstraat stands **"Het Schip"**, one of the main works by the Amsterdam School. On leaving the Westerpark, note the Haarlemmerpoort, a neo-Classical gate built in 1840. The tour ends with the **Brouwersgracht**, a delightful canal whatever the weather and lighting conditions.

3 THE OUTER CANALS

Tour starting from the central station: 1hr 15min

Western outer canals – *From the central station, head for the northern end of the Prinsengracht. Cycle along its banks (even-numbered side) and turn right to the Bloemgracht. Cross the Lijnbaansgracht at the end and turn left into Marnixstraat. This street skirts the Lijnbaansgracht. At Kinkerstraat (on the right), turn left then right to cycle along the other side of the Lijnbaansgracht. Turn left onto the Looiersgracht and, at the end, right onto the banks of the Prinsengracht. Turn right on the Leidsegracht.*

From this section of the **Prinsengracht**, where many houseboats are moored, there is a good view of the bell-tower on the **Westerkerk**. Beyond the delightful **Bloemgracht** is Marnixstraat from which you can see the Singelgracht on the right. This less picturesque route outside the historic town centre is an indication of the extent to which the canals continue to rule the urban geography, even at some distance from the city centre.

Southern outer canals – *At the end of the Leidsegracht, turn left along the Lijnbaansgracht. Cross Leidseplein (look out for trams!) then turn into Plantsoen and Weteringschans. At the Rijksmuseum, turn right then left and cycle along the Stadhouderskade. Opposite the Heineken building, turn left, cross the square and follow the Vijzelgracht, then turn right along the Lijnbaansgracht. At the end, cross the bridge, turn left along the Reguliersgracht then right along the Prinsengracht.*

This tour is a return to the tranquillity of the elegant **Leidsegracht** beyond which is a short stretch of the Lijnbaansgracht. Here you can see **Melkweg** then the bustling **Leidseplein**. Beyond the **Paradiso** is the **Rijksmuseum**, the city's renowned art gallery, and the **Heineken Brouwerij** ⓥ which used to brew the famous beer. This tour ends with one of the most beautiful little canals in the city, the **Reguliersgracht**, and the **Prinsengracht**, the final link in the Grachtengordel.

Eastern outer canals – *At the end of the Prinsengracht turn left then right onto the Magere Brug. Beyond it turn left and right along the Nieuwe Keizersgracht. At the end, turn right into Roetersstraat then left onto Nieuwe Prinsengracht (private road).*

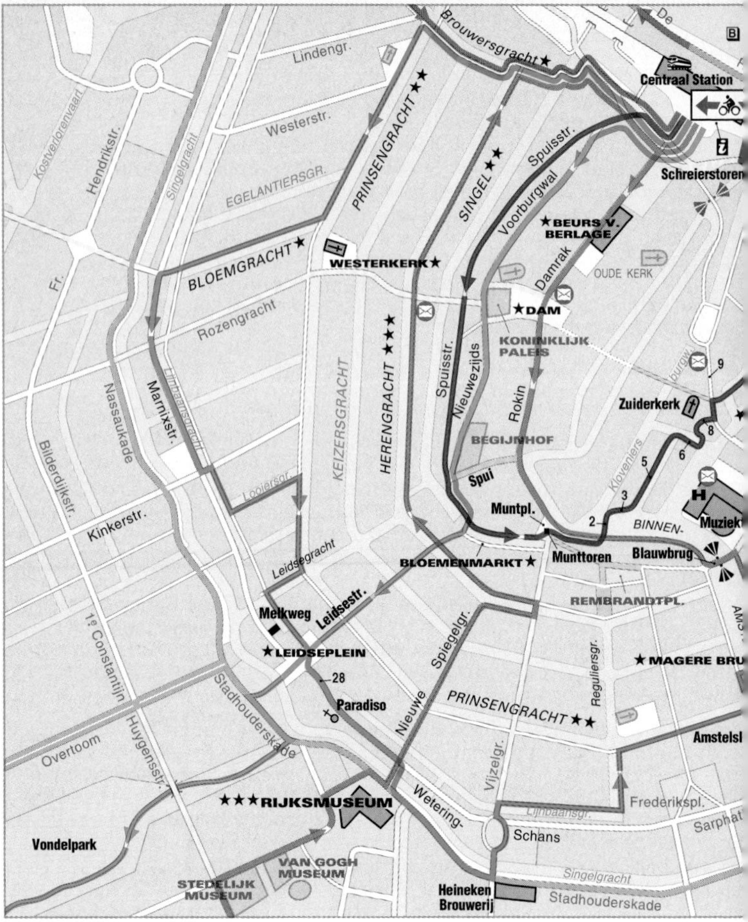

Brouwersgracht ★
Lindengr.
Westerstr.
EGELANTIERSGR.
PRINSENGRACHT ★★
SINGEL ★★
Spuisstr.
Voorburgwal
Centraal Station
Schreierstoren
★ BEURS V. BERLAGE
OUDE KERK
Damrak
★ DAM
KONINKLIJK PALEIS
Kostverlorenvaart
Hendrikstr.
Singelgracht
BLOEMGRACHT ★
WESTERKERK ★
Fr.
Rozengracht
KEIZERSGRACHT
HERENGRACHT ★★★
Spuisstr.
Nieuwezijds
Rokin
Zuiderkerk
BEGIJNHOF
Spui
Muntpl.
Kloveniers
Nassaukade
Marnixstr.
Lijnbaansgracht
Bilderdijkstr.
Kinkerstr.
Looiersgr.
Leidsegracht
BLOEMENMARKT ★
Munttoren
BINNEN-
Blauwbrug
Muziek
REMBRANDTPL.
Melkweg
Leidsestr.
★ LEIDSEPLEIN
1e Constantijn
Huygensstr.
Stadhouderskade
Overtoom
Paradiso
Nieuwe
Spiegelgr.
PRINSENGRACHT ★★
Reguliersgr.
★ MAGERE BRU
Amstelsl
★★★ RIJKSMUSEUM
Vondelpark
STEDELIJK MUSEUM
VAN GOGH MUSEUM
Wetering-
Vijzelgr.
Schans
Lijnbaansgr.
Frederikspl.
Sarphat
Singelgracht
Heineken Brouwerij
Stadhouderskade
2 3 5 6 8 9 28

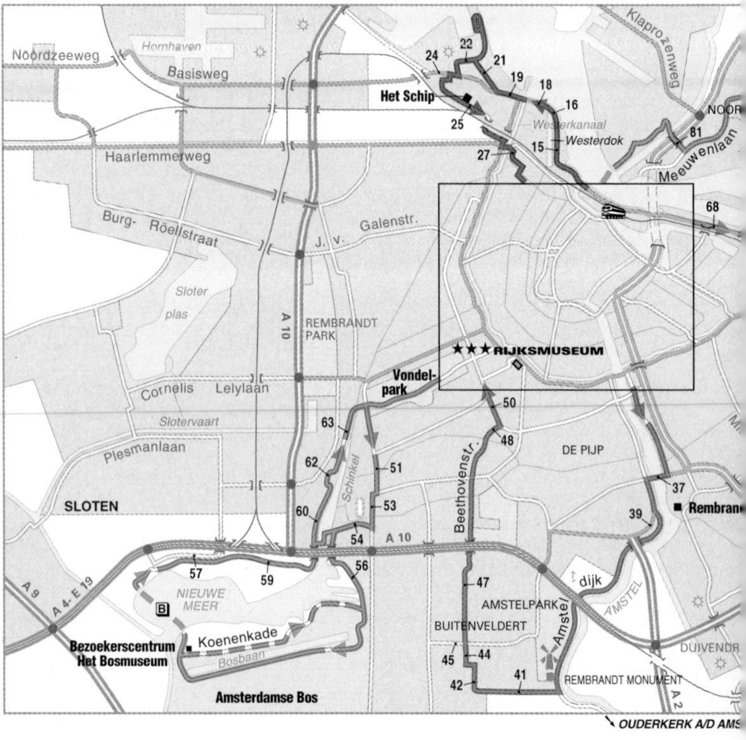

Noordzeeweg
Hornhaven
Basisweg
Haarlemmerweg
Burg- Röellstraat
Galenstr.
J. v.
Sloter plas
A 10
REMBRANDT PARK
Cornelis Lelylaan
Slotervaart
Plesmanlaan
SLOTEN
Klaprozenweg
Het Schip
Westerkanaal
Westerdok
NOOR
Meeuwenlaan
★★★ RIJKSMUSEUM
Vondel- park
Schinkel
Beethovenstr.
DE PIJP
Rembran
A 10
dijk
AMSTEL
AMSTELPARK
BUITENVELDERT
Amstel
NIEUWE MEER
A 9
A 4 - E 19
Bezoekerscentrum Het Bosmuseum
Koenenkade
Bosbaan
Amsterdamse Bos
REMBRANDT MONUMENT
DUIJVENDR
A 2
OUDERKERK A/D AMS
15 16 18 19 21 22 24 25 27 37 39 41 42 44 45 47 48 50 51 53 54 56 57 59 60 62 63 68 81

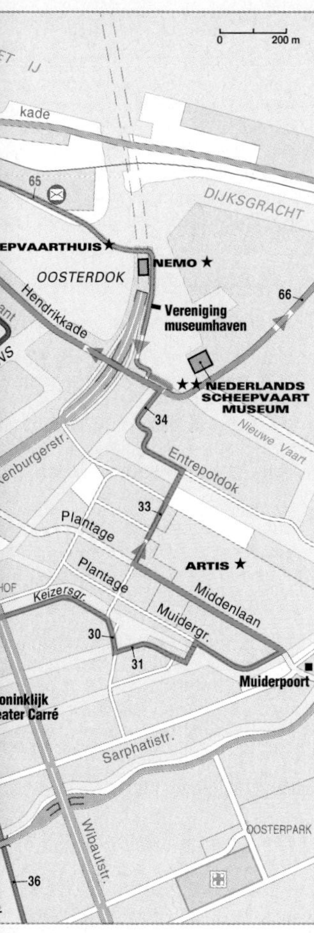

CYCLING IN AMSTERDAM

Index of numbered streets

Tour no 1

2 Halvemaansbrug
3 's-Gravelandseveer
5 Groenburgwal
6 Raamgracht
8 Zuiderkerkhof
9 Sint Antoniesbreestr.
12 Krom Boomssloot
13 Recht Boomssloot

Tour no 2

15 Westerdoksdijk
16 Barentszplein
18 Van Diemenstr.
19 Tasmanstr.
21 Stavangerweg
22 Haparandaweg
24 Spaarndammerdijk
25 Zaanstr.
27 Haarlemmerplein

Tour no 3

28 Kleine-Gartmanplantsoen
30 Roetersstr.
31 Nieuwe Prinsengracht
33 Plantage Kerklaan
34 Kadijksplein

Tour no 4

36 Weesperzijde
37 Berlagebrug
39 President Kennedylaan
41 Kalfjeslaan
42 Reimersbeek
44 Backershagen
45 Van Nijenrodeweg
47 Van Weldammelaan
48 Coenenstr.
50 Van Baerlestr.

Tour no 5

51 Amstelveenseweg
53 Stadionplein
54 IJsbaanpad
56 Jachthavenweg
57 Oude Haagseweg
59 Riekerweg
60 Jaagpad
62 Gen. Vetterstr.
63 Sloterkade

Tour no 6

65 Oosterdokskade
66 Kattenburgerstr.
68 Piet Heinkade
69 Oostelijke Handelskade
71 Verbindingsdam
72 Van Eesterenlaan
74 Cruquiusweg
75 IJburglaan
77 Zeeburgerdijk
78 Schellingwouderdijk
80 Nieuwendammerdijk
81 Havikslaan

Dismount before passing the chicane and crossing the pedestrian bridge spanning the canal. Turn right along the Plantage Muidergracht then left into Plantage Middenlaan. Beyond Artis, turn right into Plantage Kerklaan and head for Entrepotdok. On the Entrepotdok turn left towards Kadijksplein. Return to the station via the Prins Hendrikkade.

The charming **Magere Brug** over the **Amstel** runs past the deaconesses' hospice (Amstelhof) to the new university campus and the Plantage Muidergracht of which the final section provides moorings for barges, not far from the **Muiderpoort**. Beyond **Artis** and its zoo lies the **Entrepotdok** where, weather permitting, you can take a well-earned rest at one of the delightful pavement cafés.

4 ALONG THE AMSTEL TOWARDS AMSTERDAM-ZUID

Tour starting from the central station: 1hr 30min to 1hr 45min

City centre and Binnen-Amstel – *From the central station, follow Damrak and Rokin beyond it. At the end of Rokin, cycle along the banks of the Amstel. Cross the Blauwbrug and turn right along the river banks.*

As you pedal through the city centre, you will see the **Beurs van Berlage**, the **Dam**, then **Muntplein**. Beyond it is the Binnen-Amstel on whose banks stand the **Stadhuis en Muziektheater**. Downstream from the **Magere Brug, Amstelsluizen** and **Koninklijk Theatre Carré**, the river widens out.

Amstel – *Beyond Sarphatistraat, skirt the Amstel Hotel and follow the river bank via Weesperzijde. At the Elvia building, turn right across the bridge (Berlagebrug) and left along Amsteldijk. Further on, at the traffic lights, avoid Pres. Kennedylaan; the Amsteldijk is just on the left. Continue along the Amsteldijk, passing under the A 10 motorway.*

Opposite the 115m/374ft **Rembrandt Tower** (1989-95) is the city's first "skyscraper", in the **De Pijp** district designed by **HP Berlage** *(see De PIJP, Berlage's South Plan)*. A short distance further on, the urban surroundings give way to countryside and the banks of the Amstel soon take on a rustic appearance. Cycle along the road skirting the early 19C Amstelpark (no entrance for bikes) to the mill which once stood in **Sloten**. Not far away is a monument to Rembrandt who so often drew the banks of the river.

If you wish, you can continue to **Ouderkerk aan de Amstel** *(1hr round trip).*

Amsterdam-Zuid – *Beyond the mill, turn right into Kalfjeslaan and right again into Reimersbeek just after the first block of flats. Turn left into Van Boshuizenstraat then right at the traffic lights into Backerhagen. Ignore Van Nijenrodeweg and turn into Van Weldammelaan. At the end of this street turn right at the foot of the ABN/AMRO building. Continue left under the A 10 motorway and enter Beethovenstraat. After the second canal, turn into Coenenstraat and left into Van Baerlestraat. Follow Museumstraat which runs under the Rijksmuseum and return to the railway station via Nieuwe Spiegelstraat and the Herengracht.*

This tour of the southern district of the city shows the extent to which the town planners have worked to maintain parks and gardens. Buitenveldert is a veritable garden city dotted with flowering cherry trees. The return is via the museum district, dominated by the **Rijksmuseum** and by the most prestigious of the city centre canals, the **Herengracht**.

5 THE GREEN CAPITAL

Tour starting from the central station: 1hr 45min to 2hr

City centre and Vondelpark – *From the central station, follow Nieuwezijds Voorburgwal and continue via Leidsestraat leading to Leidseplein (look out for trams!). Cross Leidseplein and turn left onto the Stadhouderskade where you will find the entrance to the Vondelpark.*

After the bustle of the city centre, especially in **Leidsestraat** and **Leidseplein** which are constantly busy, cycling through the **Vondelpark** is a real pleasure.

Olympic district and Amsterdamse Bos – *At the exit to the Vondelpark, turn left into Amstelveenseweg. Beyond Stadionplein, turn right into IJsbaanpad then left into Jachthavenweg. At the roundabout follow the first avenue on the right and skirt the Bosbaan (a long lake). At the end, turn right past the Bezoekerscentrum Het Bosmuseum to the landing-stage: May to September and bank holidays, 11am-7pm, Saturdays 1pm-6pm. Cross the Nieuwe Meer by boat then turn right into Haagseweg and continue along the railway line via Riekerweg. Turn left into Jaagpad which lines the Schinkel. If you do not wish to cross the lake return to the Bezoekerscentrum Het Bosmuseum and turn left onto the Koenenkade. At the end, turn left into Jachthavenweg and left at the end into IJsbaanpad. Cross the sliding bridge over the Schinkel. Both routes rejoin our itinerary here. Continue along Jaagpad and into Gen. Vetterstraat, Spijtellantje, Rijnsburgstraat and along the banks of the Schinkel via the Sloterkade. Turn right at the second bridge to the Vondelpark. From there, return to the station.*

In 1928, the city hosted the eighth Olympic Games of modern times. The route takes you past the old Olympic stadium (now being restored), a red-brick building designed by J Wils and C van Eesteren which has been under threat of demolition over the past few years. Further on is the Schinkel where the houseboats form veritable housing estates on water. The **Amsterdamse Bos** is a gigantic park where you will probably spend more time than suggested by the itinerary. The north side of the park is flanked by the Nieuwe Meer, a huge urban lake lined with reed beds which is a popular haunt with the marsh-dwelling wild life. A wonderful place for a breath of fresh air before returning to the city centre.

6 FROM OOSTERDOK TO AMSTERDAM-NOORD

Tour starting from the central station: 2hr 30min to 3hr

Oostelijke Eilanden and Zeeburg – *Head eastward from the central station via the Oosterdokskade and cross the double metal bridge spanning the Oosterdok basin. Skirt the Nemo building (mind the steps!) and follow the Prins Hendrikkade into Kattenburgerstraat. Cross the Dijksgracht, pass under the bridge and turn right onto the Piet Heinkade and Oostelijke Handelskade. The Verbindingsdam leads to the island of Java. After touring the island, there is no alternative to the Verbindingsdam as a return route. Just beyond the bend in the Oostelijke Handelskade turn left into Van Eesterenlaan and left again into Cruquiusweg. Then turn right into Ijburglaan and left along the Zeeburgerdijk.*

At the beginning of the tour, you will see the **Nemo**, **Vereniging Museumhaven Amsterdam** and the **Nederlands Scheepvaart museum** before crossing the islands in the east. This area once resounded to the clang of shipyards working for the India Company but is now undergoing redevelopment. **Java-eiland**, with its ultramodern buildings, is a stunning example of this transformation. Cross the Zeeburg, noting on the way the Entrepot West, a vast council housing estate built on piles sunk into the waters of Entrepothaven.

Between the IJ and IJmeer – *At the traffic lights, turn left into Zuiderzeeweg. Cross two bridges then turn right towards Durgerdam.*

The first bridge spans the Amsterdam-Rhine Canal opened in 1952 *(see JAVA-EILAND, Het IJ)*; the second overlooks the **IJ** and its Oranjesluizen *(see Introduction: the Venice of the North)* on the left and the IJmeer opening onto the Markermeer on the right.

Durgerdam – *Continue to Durgerdam then return by the same route and pass under the bridge. Follow the Schellingwoude direction.*

Durgerdam bears a certain resemblance to Volendam. It is a fishing and yachting village exactly 1km/0.5mi in length. Opposite the dike providing protection against the IJmeer are a row of brightly-coloured houses and a few cafés with one or two tables outside. A pleasant place to enjoy the sunshine and the breeze that clears the air in the neighbouring polders.

Despite the rustic atmosphere, Durgerdam is part of Amsterdam, as is evident from the presence of the Amsterdammertjes, the small posts decorated with the three St Andrew's crosses that prevent car parking.

Schellingwoude and Amsterdam Noord – *Cycle along the Schellingwouderdijk. Beyond Schellingwoude, continue along Zuiderzeeweg and turn into Nieuwendammerdijk (take care not to turn into Monnickendammerweg by mistake). Turn left after the bridge. At the end of the Nieuwendammerdijk, turn left into Meeuwenlaan and right into Havikslaan. Beyond the bridge, turn left onto the cycle path and take the ferry (no charge) back to the railway station.*

Schellingwoude is best known for the Oranjesluizen, but the village is delightful and it still boasts a few beautiful timbered house fronts. Nieuwendam is a peaceful spot; beyond it is Amsterdam Noord, a mainly working-class district which seems totally unconcerned by the hustle and bustle of the old town on the other bank of the IJ.

R. Dechamps/MICHELIN

Will there be any room for yours?

AMSTELVEEN

Plan p 12, **BR**
Michelin map no 36 U 3 and U 4

Amstelveen is a modern, soulless residential community that is not a district of Amsterdam; it is a town in its own right. However, it has been included with Amsterdam for the purposes of this guide, firstly because it lies in the immediate vicinity of the city and secondly because its principal sight is near Amsterdamse Bos. Amstelveen is one of those towns which, like Zaandam *(see ZAANSTREEK)*, has seen its population rise consistently over the past two or three decades, while during the same period the population figures have remained unchanged in Amsterdam.

★**Cobra Museum voor Moderne Kunst** ⊙ – *Sandbergplein 1. Tram no 5. Alight at the "Binnenhof" terminus.* Between a square opening onto Keizer Karel Weg and a lake that attracts herons and coots, architect Wim Quist built a light, functional museum which was opened in 1995. As its name indicates, the gallery displays many works by the CoBrA movement, but it also includes a wide selection of other post-1945 works.

Recently, the Cobra Museum and the Stedelijk Museum decided to join forces in order to give the public an opportunity to see a wide range of works by this movement, taken from the collections of the two museums. As indicated in the Introduction *(Art, Painting)* the word Cobra comes from the contraction of the first letters of **Co**penhagen, **Br**ussels and **A**msterdam.

The movement which came into being, paradoxically, in Paris in 1948 originally brought together the Danish artist **Asger Jorn** (1914-73), a pseudonym of Asger Oluf Jörgensen, Belgians **Christian Dotremont** and **Joseph Noiret**, and the Dutchmen **Karel Appel** (b 1921), Constant Anton Nieuwenhuys (b 1920) better known under the name **Constant**, and Cornelis van Beverloo (b 1922), alias **Willem Corneille**. Several more artists joined them a short time later, including the Belgian artist Pierre Alechinsky (b 1927).

These artists wanted to break away from the neo-traditional art of the post-war period and used popular art, primitivism and in particular the drawings of children and the mentally ill as sources of inspiration. In so doing they created images that were spontaneous, experimental, colourful and vibrant. The museum shows the works on a rota basis. Also included are works forming part of movements related to Cobra, such as the Netherlands groups known as **Vrij Beelden** and **Creatie**. This body of work gives an excellent overview of the (semi-) abstract art of the Netherlands between 1945 and 1955. The museum also organises contemporary art exhibitions.

The Red Fist (1952), Constant

AMSTERDAMSE BOS

Plan p 12, **AR**
Michelin map no 36 S 6

ocated to the south of Amsterdam not far from the international Schiphol Airport, he vast park known as Amsterdamse Bos (or Amsterdam Woods) attracts numerous isitors for its wide range of amenities.

leisure complex created out of the 1929 stock exchange crash – In October 929, the Wall Street crash sounded the death knell of the illusions that were rife in he 1920s and caused the great depression of the 1930s. The crisis was extraordin-rily sudden and unemployment in Europe immediately rose to considerable roportions, especially in the Netherlands where it quadrupled in 1930, reaching the igure of 500 000 by 1935.

n order to provide some 5 000 unemployed with work, the city council decided to lay ut a vast area of polders as a landscaped park. The future park had to be totally rained before the trees could be planted. The 300km/190mi of pipes laid by the work orce give some idea of the scale of the project.

Amsterdamse Bos – This 800ha park is particularly pleasant. It provides city dwellers and tourists with an opportunity to escape from the disadvantages of urban life. There are, for example, 48km/30mi of cycle paths, 160km/100mi of footpaths, an open-air theatre seating 1 500, a man-made hill which is used for sledging in snowy winters, boating lakes etc. At the end of the Bosbaan, a waterway more than 2km/1mi in length which is an international rowing course, is the **Bezoekerscentrum het Bosmuseum** *(Koenenkade 56)*, a small museum of information including an animal diorama which will enchant younger visitors.

IN THE VICINITY OF AMSTERDAMSE BOS

★**Elektrische Museumtramlijn Amsterdam** – *Amstelveenseweg 264.* Some 70 trams of historic interest from towns and cities in the Netherlands or other countries (The Hague, Groningen, Vienna, Prague, Berlin) add an unusual touch to the line linking Haarlemmermeerstation and Amstelveen via the Amsterdamse Bos. The oldest tramcar dates from 1904, the most recent from 1958.

Kantoorgebouw Van Leers – *Amsterdamseweg 206.* This building, which will be of particular interest to those with a love of architecture, was built in 1958 to designs by American **Marcel Breuer** (1902-81) who was also the designer of the UNESCO headquarters in Paris.

ANNE FRANK HUIS★★

Plan p 10, **KX**
Michelin map no 36 H 9 and H 10

NNE FRANK

orn in 1929 in Frankfurt am Main, Anne Frank was the younger daughter of Otto and dith Frank. In December 1933, 11 months after Adolf Hitler was sworn in as Chancel-r and 9 months after the first oncentration camp was opened Dachau, the family left Frank-urt and moved to Amsterdam here their new address was 37 erwedeplein. During the 930s, almost 25 000 German ews settled in the capital of the etherlands.

he "Secret Annexe" – On her 3th birthday, 12 June 1942, nne received a diary from her ather who began to plan his amily's concealment after the rst Jews were rounded up in ebruary 1941. He finally took he decision on 6 July 1942 ecause Anne's elder sister, argot, had received a call-up otice for forced labour in the ast. He therefore moved, with is family, to 263 Prinsen-racht, or to be more precise, to he unoccupied "Secret nnexe", the "*achterhuis*" at

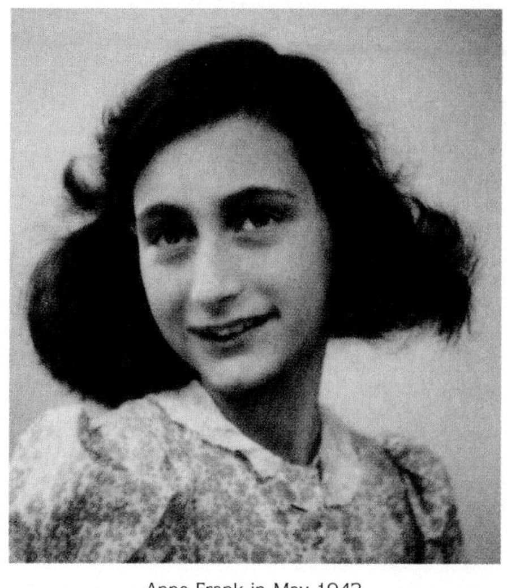

AFF/AFS, Amsterdam

Anne Frank in May 1942

the back of his business premises. This marked the beginning of a long period of concealment and assistance from a few friends. They shared their confinement with the Van Pels (renamed Van Daans in the *Diary*), their son, Peter, and a dentist friend, Albert Dussel (his real name was Fritz Pfeffer).
Day after day, Anne confided in her diary. The young girl carefully recorded everyday events in the life of the small group who were forced to live in a very confined space. She wrote for 25 months, until 1 August 1944. Three days later, after someone had informed on them, a lorry full of German policemen and Dutch auxiliaries dressed in civilian clothes pulled up at the door. The hideaways were arrested and the Diary came to an end.

The first lines of the Diary

"I hope I will be able to confide everything to you, as I have never been able to confide in anyone, and I hope you will be a great source of comfort and support." (Pub by Puffin)

Deportation – The family, and those who had protected them were taken to the Amsterdam headquarters of the SD (*Sicherheitsdienst*, the information, security, espionage and counter-espionage department of the Nazi party and the SS). On 8 August 1944 they were taken from Amsterdam's central railway station to Westerbork in the province of Drenthe, which had been used since the summer of 1942 as a pre-deportation transit camp for Jews; it was guarded by the Dutch police and gendarmerie. On 3 September Anne and her companions were put on board the last convoy to Auschwitz-Birkenau. On 28 October Anne and Margot were transferred to Bergen-Belsen. Both died between 15 and 20 March 1945, victims of typhus and sheer exhaustion. On 15 April the camp was liberated by the British army.

A leading figure of the Second World War – Of the eight occupants of the hideaway behind the office premises, only Otto Frank survived. In 1947, he had his younger daughter's diary published. Mies Gies and Bep Voskuijl, friends of the family, had hidden the exercise books on the day the family was arrested.
The book rapidly became a best-seller. It has been published in more than 50 countries and remains to this day the best-known account of the life and destiny of the Jews during the Second World War. The reason for its success is not only the author's natural style; it is based mainly on the intrinsic value of the diary written by Anne Frank, which is an amazing introspective analysis by a young adolescent who looked beyond everyday life. The book shows a rare degree of sensitivity and is, first and foremost, a message of hope.
The original manuscript (Anne herself had edited her diary with the intention of getting it published after the war) is in the Rijksinstituut voor Oorlogsdocumentatie (the Netherlands State Institute for War Documentation), at no 380 Herengracht. The original diary can be seen at Anne Frank Huis.

OCCUPATION AND DEPORTATION IN AMSTERDAM

On 10 May 1940, the German army entered the Netherlands. After a campaign lasting five days, the Dutch General, Winkelman, capitulated. The surrender, however, did not apply to overseas territories nor to Zeeland (where the national fleet and some French troops were stationed). This meant that, from the legal point of view, hostilities had not ceased. On 12 May **Queen Wilhelmina** and the government sought refuge in Britain. On 18 May Hitler appointed a civilian to run the country, *Reichskommissar* Seyss-Inquart, an Austrian who had played a key role in the *Anschluss* of March 1938. Soon Winkelman was deported and a concentration camp was built at Amersfoort. This marked the beginning of the period of persecution and resistance.
Seyss-Inquart was determined to impose a certain number of discriminatory measures gradually, so as to avoid shocking a population that was deeply attached to its traditions of tolerance. He was, however, a profoundly anti-Semitic man and his objective became clearer from September 1940 onwards, when he prohibited all Jewish newspapers. At the beginning of 1941, serious incidents took place in Amsterdam in response to anti-Semitic violence. The occupying forces took reprisals. On 22 and 23 February the first Jews were deported; 400 of them were assembled on JD Meijerplein and taken away. They were never seen again. On 25 and 26 February the dockers called a major protest strike which spread throughout the capital. The Germans riposted swiftly. They set up the *Joodse Raad*, a Jewish Council responsible for applying the persecutory measures; they also decreed that anybody participating in a strike would be liable to 15 years' imprisonment or even the death sentence.
Jews were forbidden to use public telephones and parks and were obliged to wear a yellow star. Their property was expropriated and they were herded into accommodation in the town's Jewish quarter. They were subject to a curfew. The Resistance movement began to organise itself, without really undertaking any military action. One group, for example destroyed Amsterdam's census registers, making it impossible to carry out a census of the Jews. Unfortunately, from July 1942 to September 1943, the pursuit of Jews had every appearance of a veritable genocide. Of the 140 000 Dutch citizens who died during deportation in the Second World War, 104 000 were Jews.

The last winter of the war was particularly hard in Amsterdam. The population was short of food, water, gas and electricity. Like their compatriots elsewhere in the country, they suffered a serious famine. The "Winter of Hunger" *(Hongerwinter)* killed more than 20 000 people. Moreover, in order to hinder the Canadian advance, the Germans blew up the locks at IJmuiden, causing flooding in the capital and one last problem, an invasion of rats.

★★ ANNE FRANK HUIS ⏲ *Prinsengracht 263*

This house built in 1635 is narrow-fronted but very deep; it includes a "secret annexe" (the "*achterhuis*" which gave the book its original title) that was extended in 1740. It now contains the museum that attracts more than half-a-million visitors every year and has become a memorial to the victims of the Holocaust.

"*M. Kugler thought it would be better to have a bookcase built in front of the entrance [...]. It swings out on its hinges and opens like a door.*" *(Anne Frank, The Diary of a Young Girl*, Puffin Books). This secret passage *(steep staircase)* leads to the rooms where the hideaways lived. They are plain rooms, now devoid of furniture, and they recall the dreadful, claustrophobic conditions: there is the Frank family room, Anne Frank and Fritz Pfeffer's room still containing the photographs that she hung up on the walls, and the rooms used by the Van Pels and their son, Peter.

In addition to an exhibition relating to Anne Frank, there are three audio-visual programmes including a filmed account given by Otto Frank, reminders of the Second World War, National Socialism and anti-Semitism, and temporary exhibitions concerning all these topics in the attic and in the next door house.

The copyright earned from *Anne Frank, The Diary of a Young Girl* is paid to the Anne Frank Foundation which was set up in 1957 to fight racism. The authenticity of the Diary has often been contested, in particular because the exercise books (of which three are on display) included notes written in biro pen (the biro had not been invented at the time). In fact, they were added by the readers contacted by Otto Frank who was not sure of his own ability to notice mistakes in the use of Dutch. There was such confusion that the paper, ink and glue were all analysed by the national legal laboratory. The results put an end to questions that were often raised: the materials did indeed correspond to those used before and during the Second World War and the analyses of the handwriting concluded that everything had been written by a single person, namely Anne Frank.

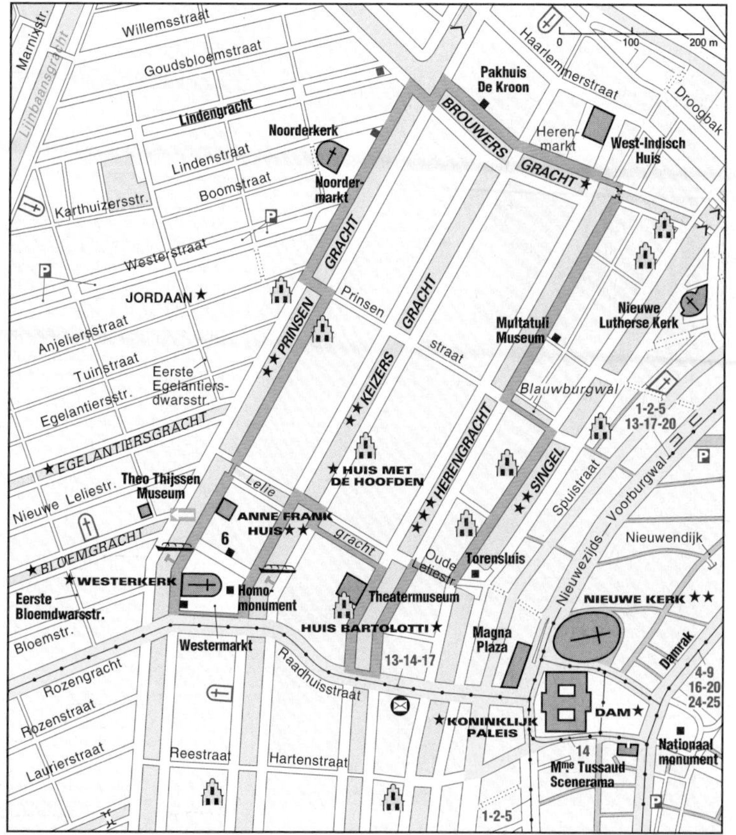

AROUND ANNE FRANK'S HOUSE

★ **Westerkerk** – *See PRINSENGRACHT.*

Westermarkt – Just to the right of the church is a statue of Anne Frank by M Andriessen.
At no 6, the house on the north side of the church, lived **René Descartes** (1596-1650), author of *Discourse on Method*. A wall plaque recalls that the most famous of all French philosophers resided in the house during the summer of 1634. The inscription (in French): "*Quel autre pays où l'on puisse jouir d'une liberté si entière*" ("In what other country can one enjoy such complete freedom") is taken from a letter addressed to J-L G de Balzac in 1631.
On the ground near the east end of the church is the **Homomonument**, a monument to homosexuals consisting of a triangle of which one of the pink marble points (a reference to the symbol that homosexuals were forced to wear in Nazi concentration camps) ends in tiers of seats overlooking the waters of the Keizersgracht.

Leliegracht – The "Canal of Lilies" was once a navigable waterway linking the Jordaan district and the town centre. For many years before the huge project that resulted in the Zuiderzee *(see Introduction, Amsterdam and its region)*, its lock – note the narrowing towards the Prinsengracht – played a vital role in the system that provided water for the town's canals. Unlike the other three parallel canals, the Prinsengracht was linked to the Amstel.
At the corner with the Keizersgracht is an Art Nouveau building that houses the headquarters of Greenpeace *(see KEIZERSGRACHT)*.

Theatermuseum – *See HERENGRACHT.*

★ **Huis Bartolotti** – *See HERENGRACHT.*

★★★ **Herengracht** – Between Oude Leliestraat and Prinsenstraat, the tour deviates slightly to take in the **Singel**★★. Readers might like to consult the chapters on Herengracht and Singel for more information on sights located in this section of the outer canals. In particular, note the Torensluis on the Singel and its memorial to Multatuli *(see below)*.

Blauwbrugwal – A small canal running between the Herengracht and Singel. Known as the "blue bridge wall", it was constructed in 1614. Its strange name comes from the many dyers whose workshops lined the canal in days gone by.

Multatuli Museum ⏲ – *Korsjespoortweg 20.* Eduard Douwes Dekker, better known under his pen-name, **Multatuli** *(see SINGEL)*, was born on 2 March 1820 in this house where there has been a delightful little memorial museum since 1975. The museum houses the sofa on which the writer died as well as his desk, books and funeral urn. This very interesting author's masterpiece is *Max Havelaar* (1860), a work in which the writer opposes what he considers to be the inhuman excess of colonialism in the Dutch East Indies. The language is spontaneous in this book, which has links with both the Romantic and Realist movements, and i brought its author immediate fame. It has been translated into 37 languages. Multatuli disappointed when his nove failed to make a substantia impact on his country's colonial policies, left the Netherlands and died in Nieder Ingelheim (Germany) o 19 February 1887. He wa the first Dutch citizen to b cremated.

X. Richer/HOA QUI

The statue of Multatuli on Torensluis

★ **Brouwersgracht** – This i the most northerly canal i the city centre. It gets it name from the numerou breweries which lined it banks in the 17C and 18C The warehouses were origi nally used to store cereals coffee or sugar and hav heavy wooden shutters an hoists on the gables. The have been wonderfull restored and are now pri vate housing.

There is a very special charm about this peaceful canal with its picturesque bridges. It flows on into the Jordaan district. However, it was undoubtedly one of the most smelly of all the canals in former centuries, for nearly all the industries producing high levels of pollution were situated along its banks (processing of whale oil, tanneries, saltpeter works etc). There are no spectacular sights here, merely the charms of the city and a few houseboats quietly moored one behind the other.

"Short in name but great in stature"

These words come from a song written in honour of **Piet Heyn**, the admiral who captured the Spanish silver fleet in 1628 off Cuba. As soon as he came alongside in Amsterdam, the booty was carried off to be stored in the secret cellars of the Dutch West India Company House.

The **Kroon warehouse** (no 118) has a stone carving on its façade representing a crown *(kroon)*. The building was erected in 1618.

West-Indisch Huis – *Herenmarkt 93-99 and Haarlemmerstraat 75.* This house faces back to front, with the rear overlooking the street. It was here that the **Dutch West India Company**, which was founded in 1621, decided three years later to purchase an island from the Algonquin Indians in order to set up the New Amsterdam trading post. This marked the beginnings of the great city of New York.
The inner courtyard is decorated with a fountain topped by a statue of Peter Stuyvesant (1592-1672), the last governor of the Dutch colony from 1647 to 1664.

Haarlemmerbuurt – Like the vast American metropolis, Amsterdam has a Haarlem. Indeed, it was this town, situated to the west of the Dutch capital city, that gave its name to the famous Harlem district which was named Nieuw Haarlem in 1658 by the Dutch. The Haarlemmerbuurt district in Amsterdam lies between the railway line and the Brouwersgracht.

Noorderkerk – *See PRINSENGRACHT.*

★★ **Prinsengracht** – Between the Brouwersgracht and the Anne Frank Huis the tour runs along the Princes' Canal. See Introduction: The Venice of the North to find out more about this part of the tour. Note the Egelantiersgracht and Bloemgracht *(see JORDAAN)*. Both these canals are part of the nearby Jordaan district.

BEGIJNHOF★★

Plan p 10, **KX**
Michelin map no 36 J 10

The Beguine convent is a haven of tranquillity in the middle of the hustle and bustle of the city. It consists of a group of small houses which were superbly restored in the 1980s. In the centre are a church and a courtyard planted with trees, creating an area of perfect serenity.
Well concealed between Kalverstraat and Nieuwezijds Voorburgwal, which was built in a curve to ensure that the beguine convent lay within the town walls, the finest of Amsterdam's inner courtyards is the only "hofje" *(see JORDAAN, The Hofjes)* officially open to the public. A visit to this courtyard is an opportunity to see a location that resembles a stage set because it is so well tended. It also boasts one of the few timbered houses still existing in Amsterdam.

THE SMALL BEGUINE VILLAGE

Beguines and Beghards belonged to communities that were semi-religious and semi-lay, founded from the end of the 12C onwards, mainly in northern European towns. Their members did not take any religious vows. The great success of the Beguine convents in the 13C was, of course, guaranteed by the piety of those who joined them; it was also (and perhaps more especially) based on general insecurity at a time when single women, whether spinsters or widows, had a particularly hard life.

The first of the Beguine "convents" was founded in Liège (c 1180). It was followed by communities in Tirlemont (1202) and Valenciennes (1220). In the mid-13C, Paris, Cambrai, Brussels and Cologne each had communities with several thousand members, some of whom were high-born women attracted by the contemplative life. The communities were independent of monastic orders, but were nevertheless subservient to the bishop. Beguines lived in poverty despite being frequent recipients of large donations. They also jealously guarded

The etymology of the word "Beguine"

Linguists believe that the word "Beguine" comes from the Middle Dutch "beggaert" which, itself, came from the verb, "beggen" meaning "to say prayers" or "to chat" in Middle Dutch, and "to pray" or "to beg" in Middle High German.

Peace and tranquillity in the Begijnhof

their freedom of thought, and this brought them into conflict with the Church. Indeed, they were condemned by the Council of Vienna in 1311. Threats of excommunication and persecution finally sounded the death knell of the communities in Germany and France, but they survived in the Low Countries and in Belgium. Like the male Beghard order, the Beguines divided their time between prayers, charity work and manual work (wool, and, from the 16C onwards, lace-making).

★★ BEGIJNHOF

The Beguine convent in Amsterdam is one of the few remaining in the Netherlands, with the one in Breda. Like its counterparts in Bruges and Diest in Belgium, it bears witness to the remarkable architectural success of these complexes consisting of individual houses and private gardens. Founded in 1346 (when it was no more than a single building), it resembles the convents in Flemish towns, with a close accessed by two gates. On the outside, above the passageway to the Spui, is a large representation of St Ursula.

The convent seen by visitors today has none of the original buildings; they were destroyed by fire in 1421 and 1452. Among the 17C and 18C house fronts is, however, the city's oldest house, at no 34. It was built of wood c 1460 (as its name indicates – Het Houten Huys means "wooden house") and has a **frontage**★ with a simple double-pitched roof *(see Introduction: Architecture)*. Many stones from the façade are bricked up in the wall to the left of the house. In addition to the various gables and frontage stones used on nos 11, 19 *(The Flight into Egypt)*, 23 and 24, the elegant house at no 26 is also worth a longer look. It was the residence of the Grande Demoiselle, the convent's Mother Superior. At no 29 is the Begijnhofkapel, a Catholic chapel built clandestinely by the women in 1665. For many years, it contained the relics serving as a reminder of the Amsterdam miracle when a dying man spat a communion wafer into the fire. The wafer was not burnt – a miraculous event illustrated in four stained-glass windows. The Beguine convent no longer houses any Beguines; the last one, Sister Antonia, died in 1971.

Engelse Kerk – This early-15C building was used by the Beguines as their place of worship until 1607 when it was taken over by the Anglicans. It is now the city's Presbyterian church.

IN THE VICINITY OF THE BEGUINE CONVENT

Spui – *See BLOEMENMARKT.*

★★ **Amsterdams Historisch Museum** ⓥ – *Enter via Kalverstraat 92, Sint Luciënsteeg 27 and Gedempte Begijnensloot (Schuttersgalerij or the Gallery of Civic Guards)*. Amsterdam's history museum has been laid out in the former Burgerweeshuis orphanage (15C). To the left of the Kalverstraat entrance lies the playground of the orphan boys, whose personal effects were stored in the cubby holes. Opposite, a classical style building houses temporary exhibitions. In **St.-Luciënsteeg** (St Lucy street) a small porch is surmounted by the city's shield and a wall is embellished with numerous picturesque frontage stones **(gevelstenen)** that have been mounted on it.

★ **Gallery of Civic Guards** – A stroll through this covered street-cum-museum (no admission charge) may be an opportunity to appreciate the greatness of **Rembrandt's** *The Night Watch* which is displayed in the Rijksmuseum, but it is also, and more particularly, a chance to understand the purpose of a painting representing the citizens' militia. The works of **Nicolaes Pickenoy** (1588-1650) whose group portraits bear a resemblance to those of Jan Anthoniszoon van Ravesteyn in that they ignore the Mannerist audacity of the painters of Haarlem, are well worth more than a cursory glance from visitors. Among the works is *The Banquet of Militiamen of the Company of Jacob Backer* (1632), a painting of exemplary realism and accuracy. It is interesting to compare this work with *the Banquet of the Officers of the Saint-George Civic Guard (see HAARLEM)* painted by Frans Hals 16 years earlier. The treatment of the standard-bearer suggests that, although Pickenoy was a good artist, Hals was superb.

Museum – The entrance to the museum is situated in the second courtyard which was originally used by the orphans. The building was enlarged several times, notably by **Pieter** and **Hendrick de Keyser** and **Jacob van Campen**. The collections relate the history of the city in a thematic and chronological progression presented in several rooms in the building. (The back of the entrance ticket shows a plan which allows the visitor to follow the various stages of Amsterdam's development).

An **illuminated map** shows the surprising development of the city which was built entirely on sand. Amsterdam rapidly devoted itself to commerce. A **miracle** which took place in 1345 made it a place of pilgrimage. Subsequently the city was under **Spanish rule** and this was also the period of Amsterdam's considerable expansion. Visitors will become aware of the fact that the prosperity of the Golden Age was inseparable from the spirit of enterprise that characterised the India Company. At its peak Amsterdam erected a new town hall (the current royal palace), and attracted many artists who painted portraits and landscapes for the city's wealthy merchants. Other buildings followed, among which were several churches. But as it became rich, the city did not forget its poor, as the proliferation of charitable institutions shows. In the 18C competition from other countries began to be felt but Amsterdam still took the lead in cultural life. The number of painters decreased but the quality of their work was still considerable. In 1795 the French arrived and the cities lost their independence as the country gained national unity. At the end of the 19C the city saw a strong demographic growth. New districts were built and the Rijksmuseum was erected. After the Second World War Amsterdam lifted herself up from the hardships she had endured.

Regents' Chamber – Coming out of the museum, note the Regents' Chamber or **Regentenkamer** on the left. This building, which has retained its 17C style, is where the governors of the orphanage resided.

Amsterdams Historisch Museum

Wiliam VI of Bavaria, Count of Holland (late 15C)

BIJLMERMEER

Plan p 13, **DQ**
Michelin map no 36 T 16

Situated in the southeast of the capital, Bijlmermeer was the scene of massive urban redevelopment programmes in the 1960s and 1970s. Like Slotermeer and Osdorp, the district was annexed to the city to meet the increasing demand for housing. This is the Amsterdam of the late 20C, spreading across the centre of a wide triangle between the motorways leading into the city.

Bijlmermeer is a rather dreary suburb but it became famous thanks to the housing estate designed like a honeycomb by Bijlmer (1973). It was innovative in its day, but it proved to be a social disaster. The suburb was brought to public attention again when an El Al airliner dramatically crashed into it when taking off from Schiphol in 1992. Bijlmermeer, however, has had a claim to glory since 1996, when it became the home of the famous Ajax of Amsterdam football club.

AJAX

Ajax of Amsterdam is renowned throughout the world. Any true football fan will know the true worth of Ajax, and even the least interested of people will have heard of the team with its white and red strip.

A football club quoted on the Stock Exchange – The club, which won its first European Championship in 1971, has become a veritable sporting and financial business enterprise. Since the first half of 1998, the Netherlands' largest football club has been quoted on the Amsterdam Stock Exchange thanks to support from the powerful ABN Amro Bank.
It was the first club on the continent of Europe to become a limited company, following the example of 20 British clubs.

An impressive record – Ajax Amsterdam Football Club was founded in 1900 by a group of friends. Since then, it has won 27 Dutch championships, 13 Dutch cups, four European Championships, one European Cupwinners Cup, one UEFA Cup, three European Supercups and two Intercontinental Cups.
The legendary **Johan Cruyff** was, and has remained, the greatest star Ajax and Dutch football has produced. Other outstanding players include Haan, Rep, Suurbier, the Muhren brothers and, more recently, Van Basten. At the present time, it is the brothers Frank and Ronald De Boer and Dennis Bergkamp (now with Arsenal) who have risen to fame.

Amsterdam ArenA – *Arena Boulevard 3.* This stadium, which has a capacity of 50 000 spectators, was inaugurated in 1996. It was designed to cater for football matches, of course, but also for rock concerts and major popular events. It is already famous for its design and modernity (it is an arena and can be totally roofed over with a sliding roof in 20 minutes). The stadium was designed by a civil engineering firm whose managing director is Rob Schuurman.
The ArenA includes the **Ajax Museum** which traces the club's history (cups, objects, photos). The guided tour *(World of Ajax tour: 1hr 45min)* includes an audio-visual presentation of the building project and a walk across the stands, the field and the press room. A soundtrack recreates for visitors all the atmosphere of a match.

The Amsterdam ArenA

BLOEMENMARKT★★★

Plan p 10, **KY**
Plan Michelin n° 36 K 10

★THE BLOEMENMARKT

At the southern end of the Singel is the flower market, one of the most picturesque sites in Amsterdam. Of the 20 or more markets in the 18C town, two specialised in flowers; only one has survived (it appears to have existed since the 17C). This has been a floating market since 1862, offering passers-by a wide selection of cut flowers (most of the customers are local people who are passionately fond of blooms), bulbs, clogs and other souvenirs (more popular with tourists).
At nos 439-443 a building with a humpbacked roof has an attractive 17C front and elegant doors. At no 496 the *De Berg* (or Mountain) House has a fine bell gable dating from 1739 and a rare double entrance. Further on at nos 516-518 the *D'Eendragt* warehouse (early 17C) is topped by an amazing trapezoidal gable and a dragon.

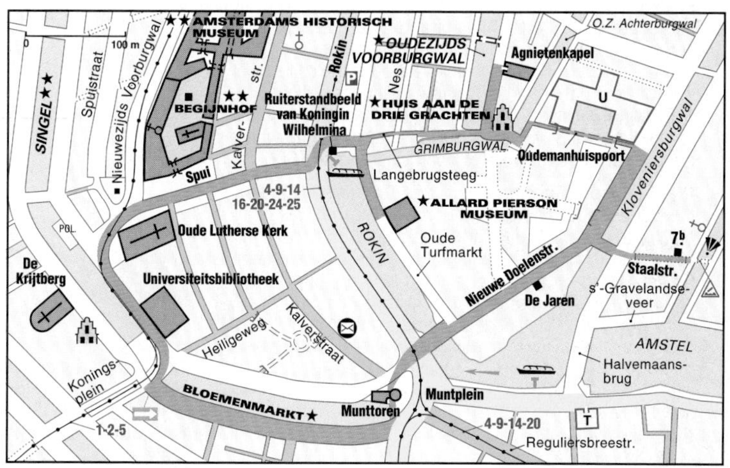

★★IN AND AROUND THE BLOEMENMARKT

Muntplein – Located between the Singel and the River Amstel, the "Mint Square" is a busy road junction filled with pedestrians, cyclists, cars and tramways.

Munttoren – The original "Mint Tower" was built between 1480 and 1490. At that time, it was a corner tower on the old Regulars Gateway. **Hendrick de Keyser** added a Baroque spire two years after it had been partially destroyed by fire, in 1618.
In 1699, the octagonal lantern (36m/117ft) was given a **peal of bells** cast by **François Hemony** (1610-67), a founder who also made the bells for the Oude Kerk and the royal palace in Amsterdam, the Notre-Dame Tower in Amersfoort, the Domtoren in Utrecht and Martinitoren in Groningen. He was born in Lorraine but moved to Holland during the Thirty Years War. With his brother Pierre (1620-80), he opened a workshop on Keizersgracht.
The monument gets its name from the fact that coinage was minted here in 1672 and 1673, during the days when Louis XIV's troops were threatening to overrun the United Provinces.

Nieuwe Doelenstraat – This street boasts a very fashionable coffee shop called De Jaren at no 20. It leads to a metal bridge from which there is a view of the Waag at the end of Kloveniersburgwal.

Staalstraat – At no 7b in this street are the former headquarters of the Drapers' Union immortalised in 1661 by **Rembrandt van Rijn** in a painting on display in the Rijksmuseum (room 230). Further on, there is a delightful **view**★ of the tower of the Zuiderkerk.

Oudemanhuispoort – This passageway (it is closed to the public, theoretically at least) lies between Kloveniersburgwal and Oudezijds Voorburgwal. It is nonetheless very busy, frequented in particular by those in search of bargains in its bookshops. The men's hospice to the right of the entrance of the passageway (the glasses on the Oudezijds Achterburgwal symbolise old age) now forms part of the **University of Amsterdam** which in 1877 succeeded the Ilustrae Athenaeum, an institute of higher education founded in 1632.

Grimburgwal – The canal was dug in the 14C; it marked the southern end of the town. The origin of its name suggests that the area was a marsh. A further two muddy ditches were dug at the end of the same century: the Oudezijds Voorburgwal and the Oudezijds Achterburgwal *(see OUDE ZIJDE)*. At the confluence of these three ditches, which are now delightful canals, stands the beautiful **Three Canals House★ (Huis aan de Drie Grachten)** *(illustration, see Introduction: Architecture)* built in 1609 by Claes Adriaans. After restoration at the beginning of the 20C, it now reveals an attractive combination of brickwork and freestone, as well as two stepped gables that are typical of the Dutch Renaissance period. Note the stained glass in the windows; they are the best designed windows in the city.

Universiteitsmuseum De Agnietenkapel ⓥ – *Oudezijds Voorburgwal 231.* The chapel dedicated to St Agnes was built in about 1470. It is a priceless example of Gothic architecture in Amsterdam. When the Alteratie caused the closure of the convent on which it depended in 1578, the chapel was turned into an admiralty store. It now houses the University Museum (temporary exhibitions on the history of the university from 1632 to the present time).

Rokin – This basin lies at the end of the Amstel. Its extension was filled in in 1936. At the end of the basin is an equestrian statue of **Queen Wilhelmina** by Theresia van der Pant. The mouth of the Amstel has disappeared and been replaced by the wide street extending into the Damrak.
Although modern buildings have spoiled the architectural unity of Rokin, there are still a few frontages designed by **Philip Vingboons** (nos 91 and 141-147). Another notable feature is the elegant Hajenius (nos 92-96), a shop which has been attracting lovers of good cigars since 1826.

★ **Allard Pierson Museum** ⓥ – *Oude Turfmarkt 127*. This museum with its neo-Classical architecture (it was once the Nederlandsche Bank and dates from 1869) contains Amsterdam University's remarkable archeological collection. It bears the name of an eminent professor of the history of fine arts and letters at the university, an erudite, humanist pastor (1831-96).

Since the museum contains a myriad of different objects on two floors, we would draw the reader's attention to just a few of the most representative or most interesting exhibits (the numbers in italics refer to showcases).

Middle East – See the reconstruction of a tomb in Selenkahiyeh, a trading town destroyed c 2000 BC, the cylinder seals (c 2200 BC) which first appeared in Mesopotamia (now Iraq) c 3500 BC *(61, 62)* and the Sassanide silverware *(58b)*.

Egypt – See the 1C mask of a mummy with hair clearly combed behind the ears, a characteristic of the Roman period; the model of the Giza Plateau *(17)*; the collection of ouchebtis or funeral statuettes *(24)*, the limestone head of a man (c 2400 BC) which originally had painted eyes that lit up an already expressive face *(13)*; the model of the Temple of Edfu *(83)*; the sarcophagus of a 2C woman *(94)*; the coptic fabrics *(112, 120, 121)*; a portrait of Le Fayoum *(97a)* and the **series of masks of mummies★** *(86, 87, 88, 93)*. Both children and adults will no doubt enjoy using a computer program to write their names in hieroglyphics.

Allard Pierson Museum

The Amsterdam kouros

Greece – See the so-called **Amsterdam kouros★** (c 590 BC) of a type (a young man) that marked the first attempts at monumental statuary in Ancient Greece, the black-figured ceramics that included the "panathenaic amphora" (c 520 BC) representing Athena and four sprinters taking part in the panathenaic games which were held every four years (227); the **"red-figured ceramic"★** including the Hemelrijk vase (c 480), a krater with a capacity of almost 12 litres decorated with Dionysus, the god of wine (236a).

Etruria and Rome – See the bucchero ware vases. Bucchero ware is a black pottery which came into being c 675 BC; it is obtained in a reducing atmosphere. Note, too, the cinerary urn of a child discovered in Volterra (2C or 1C BC) carved from volcanic rock; the marble sarcophagus of Dionysus decorated with drinking scenes (late 2C) and leonine feet of a later period; the bust of Hermaphrodite (c 100-50 BC); and the sculpture of a woman as Goddess of Fortune (early 1C) which Richelieu placed in the grounds of his château.

Cyprus – On the two male heads (c 500 BC) the smile indicates the influence of Greek statuary from the archaic period *(189a and b)*. The reconstruction of a chariot (c 8C BC) is also of interest.

M. Guillou/MICHELIN

Spui – This bustling square runs from Rokin to the Singel. In the middle of the garden is *Het Lieverdje*, a bronze (1960) by sculptor Carel Kneulman representing a young boy from Amsterdam. During the 1960s, the nonchalantly-posed boy with the rather facetious expression became one of the rallying points for the **Provos**, a youth protest movement led by Robert Grootveld.
Also overlooking the garden, where there are two of the town's busiest cafés in the evening, the Café Hoppe and the Café Luxembourg, is one of the two entrances to the **Beguine convent★★** *(see BEGIJNHOF)*.

Oude Lutherse Kerk – *Spui 29*. The old Lutheran church bears a slight resemblance to a warehouse because the city council requested that the building should look like the *Vergulde Pot* (the Golden Pot), the warehouse located on this site in which Lutherans from Germany used to gather after 1600. The building was completed in 1633 and given its name when the New Lutheran Church *(see SINGEL, Nieuwe Lutherse Kerk)* was built. It now belongs to the University of Amsterdam.

See SINGEL for the buildings located between the church and BLOEMENMARKT.

DAM★

Plan p 10, **KX**
Michelin map no 36 J 10

In Dutch, "*dam*" means "dike". It was this term which gave the city its name, roughly translated as "dike on the Amstel". Dam Square lies on the site of the old dike, making it the geographical centre of the city and the focus of its history.
Laid out in the 13C above a canal lock, the square has always been a particularly busy place. In days gone by, it was the town's central market place; now it lies at the junction of two major city centre thoroughfares, Damrak and Rokin. The Dam is first and foremost a symbol. Not only is it the site of the royal palace; it was also the scene of countless riots and popular demonstrations (from the Anabaptist riot of 1535 to demonstrations against the war in Vietnam at the end of the 1960s). Every year, the square, which is popular with pigeons, is the setting for an open-air draughts competition during which players of all levels of skill pitch their wits against each other on several dozen boards. In summer, the square is rather unfortunately turned into a fairground.
A few centuries ago, the square was flanked by two buildings which have since been demolished: the former town hall and the public weights and measures office. The latter is visible on the right of the painting on the previous page. It was completed in 1566 and was the town's first major Renaissance building. In those days, boats could tie up near the Dam and load their cargoes onto lighters. Any goods weighing more than 23kg/57lb had to be recorded at the Waag, the public weights and measures office. Louis Bonaparte had the building demolished, claiming that it spoilt the view from the royal palace where he was being accommodated!

The Dam in Amsterdam, Gerrit Berckheyde

The royal palace and the Nieuwe Kerk are the two most interesting buildings around the Dam. Note, however, the old house at no 11. Known as **De Wildeman** (The Savage), its red-brick frontage dates from 1632.

IN THE VICINITY OF DAM

★ **Koninklijk Paleis** – The building now known as the royal palace was originally erected between 1648 and 1662 as a town hall. Its late medieval predecessor had been destroyed by fire in 1652 and the town council had commissioned the building of a new one beside the old site.

The architect, **Jacob van Campen** (1595-1657), designed a heavy construction, quadrilateral in form and built on 13 659 wooden piles. It was massive because the new town hall was to symbolise the dominant position of the wealthy trading city. Its architecture was therefore monumental (length: 80m/260ft; width: 56m/182ft). In 1808, the building was damaged by fire. **Louis Bonaparte** had it rebuilt and turned into a royal palace. The town council departments then moved to the Prinsenhof, which they had already occupied from 1652 to 1655. In 1814, when William of Orange became sovereign of the United Provinces, he was granted the palace that had been chosen by Napoleon's brother. The building was the subject of dispute between the town council and the State from 1873 onwards, until the council officially abandoned its claims to recover the building in 1935.

Nowadays, the queen lives in the Huis ten Bosch in The Hague and only makes a few brief visits to the royal palace in Amsterdam.

The east and west walls are topped by tympani decorated with allegorical sculptures by an artist from Antwerp, **Artus Quellin the Elder** (1609-68), who worked in Rome with François Duquesnoy (known to the Italians as Francesco Fiammingo). The pediment on the main façade serves as a reminder of the trading city watched over by Neptune. The carillon was cast by **François Hemony** *(see BLOEMENMARKT)*.

The costly fire of 7 July 1652 – When it was noticed that the old town hall was on fire, the first reaction of the authorities was to call out the bourgeois militia and the army. This was rather a strange thing to do, but the haste with which they sought to protect the building with soldiers is explained by the fact that, in those days, the town hall was the headquarters of the Exchange Bank and there were fears that its reserves might be pillaged.

The Bank of Amsterdam had been founded in 1609 by the town council. Naturally, it required a strong room and the town hall was chosen. On the day after the fire, silver coins to the value of 30 million florins were found in the ruins, melted by the heat. Never were ruins so well guarded.

Tour ⓥ – *A brochure is available free of charge at the entrance.* Quellin the Elder created or directed the work on the decoration between 1650 and 1664; the set of **statues★** is now the subject of great admiration. The most outstanding sights are the wonderful reliefs and caryatids in the Court Room *(Vierschaar)* where death sentences used to be passed; the gigantic and impressive **Citizens Chamber★** with its marble floor inlaid with maps of the eastern and western hemispheres; and the Justice Chamber to which those under sentence of death were brought direct from the Court Room before being executed on a wooden scaffold on the square.

★★ **Nieuwe Kerk** ⓥ – In some ways, the New Church is to the Dutch what Westminster Abbey is to the British. It is used for the coronation of sovereigns. **Queen Wilhelmina** was crowned here on 6 September 1898, **Queen Juliana** was crowned on the same date fifty years later, and her granddaughter, **Beatrix**, became queen here on 30 April 1980. The building gets its name from the fact that it was the second church to be built in the town, with the permission of the Bishop of Utrecht; the first one was the Oude Kerk, the Old Church. Today, after being superbly restored, the Niewe Kerk has become a veritable centre of cultural events. All sorts of activities are organised here, in particular international art exhibitions.

Exterior – The Flamboyant Gothic architecture of the New Church forms an interesting contrast to the rather dull if massive royal palace next to it. The church was destroyed by fire on several occasions and pillaged many times, but the building commissioned in about 1400 by Willem Eggert, Counsellor to William VI, was systematically and patiently rebuilt each time. After the fire of 1645, restoration work was undertaken by **Jacob van Campen**, architect of the town hall *(see Koninklijk Paleis)*, who decided to add a bell-tower. His project, however, was never completed and the building remained unfinished.

★★ **Interior** – Seventy-five windows light up the elegant, luminous interior of the New Church but only one in the lower section is still filled with old stained glass by Gerrit Janszoon Van Bronchorst (c 1650) representing Count William IV presenting the town's coat of arms to the aldermen in 1342 (north transept). The stained glass opposite dates from 1898.

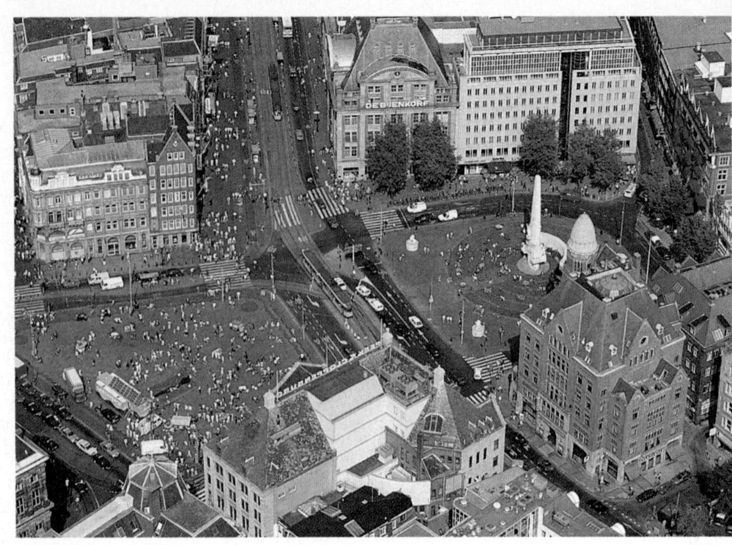

The Dam and its national memorial

The **pulpit★★** (1649) is an outstanding piece of work (and the largest pulpit in Europe); it was carved by **Albert Janszoon Vinckenbrinck** who spent 15 years of his life working on it. The hexagonal pulpit and the enormous sounding board in the shape of a temple show the importance placed by Protestants on sermons. On the pulpit are representations of the virtues and works of mercy.

The Nieuwe Kerk also possesses two organs on which concerts are regularly given. The **loft★★** of the principal **organ★** was made in 1650 after designs by Van Campen, who was also responsible for the interior decoration of the church along with Artus Quellin the Elder. The exterior of the shutters shows the Coronation of David. The painter Gerrit Janszoon van Bronchorst is depicted in the features of the man on the left looking out of the window, the woman on the right being his wife. On the open shutters are depictions of the triumphal entry of David after the killing of Goliath (on the left) and David playing the harp for Saul. The gilded copper **screen★** (c 1650) separating the chancel from the nave is an admirable piece of work by a goldsmith from Amsterdam named **Johannes Lutma**.

The Nieuwe Kerk contains several monuments to Dutch sea heroes. Rombout Verhulst, a sculptor from Mechelen, created the tomb of Jan van Galen and the **mausoleum of Michiel de Ruyter★** *(see NEDERLANDS SCHEEPVAARTMUSEUM)* in the choir (his coffin can be seen in the crypt). **Admiral Van Speijk** *(see EGMOND AAN ZEE)* is also buried in the church, as is a leading national celebrity, the poet and tragic actor **Joost van den Vondel** (1587-1679) who was born in Cologne, although his parents came from Antwerp. Other personalities who have also been laid to rest here include the writer PC Hooft, the **Hemony** brothers *(see BLOEMENMARKT, Munttoren)*, the diplomat Schimmelpenninck and the economist Pieter de la Court.

Madame Tussaud Scenerama ⓘ – *Dam 20.* Thanks to an audio-animatronics system, the scenes are surprisingly realistic, especially the ones relating to the Golden Age. This is a more modest museum than the famous Madame Tussaud's Waxworks in London, but it includes a large number of well-known Dutch or foreign personalities. The **revolving model of Amsterdam** in the 17C is particularly skilful. There is a fine view of the Dam from the large window in the gallery on the fourth Floor.

Nationaal Monument – Inaugurated on 4 May 1956 in honour of Dutch victims of the Second World War, the National Liberation Monument is an obelisk 22m/72ft high, carved by sculptor John Raedecker and designed by architect JJP Oud. To each side of the structure are the two national heraldic lions; inside it is soil from each of the country's 12 provinces and from the former Dutch East Indies.

There is always a crowd around the alabaster obelisk, which underwent restoration in 1998. The locals are invariably drawn by the atmosphere on the Dam, the street musicians or entertainers hoping to earn some money, groups who look more frightening than they really are, and tourists who have tired of walking and who can sit here and watch the world go endlessly by.

Magna Plaza – *Nieuwezijds Voorburgwal 182.* Behind the royal palace is the building designed by CG Peters in 1899 as the central post office. His critics described his style as "postal Gothic". The building was erected on 4 560 piles and has been refurbished. Since 1992 it has housed a shopping complex called Magna Plaza. Forty stores line the elegant arcaded gallery.

HERENGRACHT★★★

Plan pp 10, 11 **KV, KX, KY** and **LY**
Michelin map no 36 H 10, J 10, K 10 and K 11

THE ARISTOCRATS' CANAL

The Herengracht was highly prized by the rich bourgeoisie of the Golden Age. It has existed since 1586, but it was not really dug in its final form until 1609, as part of the Staets plan which included three canals parallel to the Singel which had been widened in 1586. In order to pay for the work as quickly as possible, the Town Council put the land up for sale while the canal was being dug and immediately decided to emphasise the prestigious nature of this new waterway by attracting the wealthiest merchants and traders. To ensure the success of the plan, the plots of land were wider than on the banks of the Singel but purchasers had to pay for the construction of the quayside fronting their residences. It was also decided that plots could not be subdivided and that there would not be any swing bridges on the canal; it would be spanned by fixed bridges built of brick and stone.
The Gentlemen's Canal, which got its name from the *Heren XVII (Introduction, the Golden Age)* of the East India Company, was flanked by luxurious town houses and it has remained, to this day, the most elegant address in the city.

Like the Singel, Prinsengracht and Keizersgracht, houses are numbered from the north end up to the Amstel. The house-by-house description enables visitors to see the sights easily as they stroll through this part of the city. The apparent discrepancy between odd and even numbers is not a mistake. It is designed, as far as possible, to cover houses on the same level but on opposite sides of the canal.

NORTH OF THE GOLDEN CURVE

★ **Brouwersgracht** – *See JORDAAN and ANNE FRANK HUIS.*

No 33 – Standing at the corner of Roomolenstraat, this 17C house has a bell gable topped with cornucopia, the only example of its kind in Amsterdam.

Nos 37-39 – It is very unusual to see warehouses topped with bell gables (mid 18C). The most common form of gable has a single pitch like those at **nos 43-45**, the oldest warehouses on the canal bank (built in about 1590).

No 81 – The house dates from 1590 but its stepped gable was erected 30 years later. The lower section was entirely rebuilt in 1975, the heritage year.

No 115 – It was **Hendrik Petrus Berlage** (1856-1934) who built this large house in 1890, something of a surprise for fans of the great innovator of modern Dutch architecture. With its neo-Renaissance stepped gable, it shows its architect's determination to conform to the style of the buildings along the canal banks.

Leliegracht – *See ANNE FRANK HUIS.*

No 164: Huis Messina – The Messina House (1679) is four bays wide. It has a sandstone frontage topped with an entablature and a traceried attic (1750) with balustrade. The shell in the central shield indicates that the house belonged to a shipowner.

No 168: Theatermuseum ⌚ – The Theatre Museum is part of the Dutch Theatre Institute housed in five buildings (nos 168-174), including the famous Bartolotti House. No 168 has a fine sandstone frontage (c 1638) designed by **Philip Vingboons** (1607-78). The owner at that time, Michael de Pauw, was one of the founder members of the

The elegant Bartolotti House

Ph. Gajic/MICHELIN

M. Guillou/MICHELIN

East India Company. The most outstanding feature of this white house is its gable the **first neck gable★** ever built in Amsterdam. It was altered c 1730 when the triangular pediments that decoratively flanked the windows were removed.
The **interior★★** in the Louis XIV style has retained its luxurious decoration with stucco work, murals and painted ceilings: note the ceiling in the first room where the illustration of the Four Seasons by **Jacob de Witt** (1696-1754) creates a fine impression of depth. Of particular note is the **spiral staircase★** elegantly decorated from cellar to attic (this is highly unusual).
The museum houses posters, accessories and audio-visual archive material in a pleasant layout. Temporary exhibitions are organised on a regular basis.

★ **Nos 170-172: Huis Bartolotti** – This splendid house was designed c 1622 by **Hendrick de Keyser** (1565-1621), the architect who also designed the Munttoren and Westerkerk. The combination of brick and freestone on the **frontage** is typical of what is referred to as the "Dutch Renaissance style" and reminiscent of the House of Heads *(see no 123 Keizersgracht)* and the Dolphins House *(see nos 140-142 Singel)*. The door on no 172 was for daytime use only; the entrance in no 170 was used in the evening.

An elegant Italianate taste – The house is named after Guillelmo Bartolotti, who was in no way Italian; he was a Dutch brewer whose real name was Willem van den Heuvel. He inherited a fortune from his great-uncle, a man from Bologna who had been converted to Calvinism and who was lucky enough to be extremely wealthy. After receiving his legacy, Willem took his benefactor's name and soon became one of the directors of the West India Company as well as the exclusive importer of Russian wheat. The former brewer who was, to say the least, a very wealthy man, was able to commission from the greatest architect of the day a mansion worthy of his status. In two cartouches on the façade he placed an indication of his character which can be taken as the credo of the triumphant 17C bourgeoisie: *Ingenio et assiduo labore* (by ability and hard work); and *Religione et probitate* (religion and rectitude).

No 257 – This beautiful tall **façade** has three orders of pilasters (Doric, Ionic and Corinthian) one above the other. The elegant neck gable dates from 1660 while the fine Louis XV doorway was built in 1770.

Nos 81-283 – Each of these twin houses is 6m/20ft wide and topped by superb **neck gables** (c 1650) that are very ornate. They include decorative garlands on a level with the hoist. The only distinguishing features on these façades are the bull's eye window and the *piano nobile* which was altered in the 18C in the left-hand house.

No 284: Huis Van Brienen – The Van Brienen House and its very elegant sandstone frontage were built in 1728 to designs by **Frédéric Blanchard**, a French Huguenot who was exiled to the Low Countries after the Revocation of the Edict of Nantes in 1685. Johannes van Brienen, a rich merchant, bought the house at a later date. His son, Willem Joseph, was the city's burgomaster and the first Dutchman to be made an imperial baron.

No 314 – An enterprising merchant named Nicolaas Roswinckel owned a trading post in Archangel in the early 18C. That town was equipped with shipyards in 1693 on the orders of Peter the Great and was the only deep-sea Russian harbour until 1703. It was then that Roswinckel was elected Mayor of Moscow. This house, with its rounded cornice, was his residence in Amsterdam.

★ **Nos 361-369** – This row of five houses has a fine succession of gables, all different. The oldest residence, the Sonnenberg House (no 361), has a stepped gable and dates from the mid 17C. The adjacent house to the right (no 363) has a 17C façade with a cornice that was added in the 19C. The next two houses have mid 18C bell gables, although the façade on no 365 (*De Vos* - The Fox) is actually older than this. The last house in the row (no 369) is the tallest construction and this indicates that it was built in the 18C. Its neck gable is decorated with Louis XIV features dating from c 1735.

★ **Nos 364-370: Cromhouthuizen** – **Philip Vingboons** designed this fine row of four houses with neck gables known (nos 364 and 366) as the "Father and Mother" and (nos 368 and 370) as "The Twins". The gracious buildings are Baroque as regards their decoration, commissioned by Catholic artist Jacob Cromhout. Note that no 364 has lost its entrance steps, and that no 362 was given an addition in the Classical style in 1918.
The **Bijbels Museum** ⏲ (Bible Museum) is disappointing apart from a work dated 1477. However it has ceilings painted by Jacob de Witt.

Nos 380-382 – A rich tobacco planter by the name of Jacob Nienhuys commissioned architect A Salm to design this residence in 1889; it has two sections and resembles a small French Renaissance manor house. The luxuriously decorated building is said to have been inspired by the New York residence (then at the corner of 52nd Street and 5th Avenue) of the millionnaire William K Vanderbilt. One thing is certain – this was the first house in Amsterdam to be lit by electricity. In those days, the generator filled an entire room.

Beulingsloot – The smallest and narrowest of the city's canals is also one of the few to recall Venice, because its houses are built in the water.

★ **Nos 386-394** – This is another fine row of houses, beginning with another of **Philip Vingboons'** designs, a noble residence with a Classical frontage decorated with pilasters that was one of the first to occupy a double plot of land. The house is five bays wide and dates from 1663. Until then, architects had to produce designs that took account of the narrowness of the plots. After the pediment on no 386 come three superb neck gables dating from 1655 (no 388) and 1665 (nos 390-392). At the corner of Leidsegracht (no 394) stands a narrow house topped with a bell gable dating from 1672. The **stonework on the front** illustrates the legend of the four Aymon sons (Renaut, Alart, Guichart and Richart, barons who rebelled against Charlemagne). They were the subject of a *chanson de geste* which enjoyed great success in France as well as in 13C Spain and 14C Italy.

Leidsegracht – *See LEIDSEPLEIN.*

THE GOLDEN CURVE

This part of the Herengracht, situated between Leidsestraat and Vijzelstraat, owes its name to the immense wealth of the ship owners and merchants who came to live here in the most vast and luxurious mansions of the Golden Age. The frontages, in the Louis XIV, Louis XV and Louis XVI styles, recall the fashionable influence of France and all things French in high society at that time.

An urban elite – The members of the elite in Amsterdam, merchants and traders, congregated on the banks of the Herengracht and Keizersgracht for practical reasons: the wealthy upper middle classes of Amsterdam had to be near the Stock Exchange and the offices of the India Company, but more importantly they had to remain within easy reach of the town hall because the economic wellbeing of this class was largely dependent on city politics. Influencing policies to favour trade was commonplace. In the 17C it seemed quite natural to consider politics as a source of profit, quite simply because politics also caused many to run into financial ruin.

★ **No 475** – This is undoubtedly one of the finest houses on the banks of the Herengracht. It was built between 1668 and 1672 for Denys Nuyst. In those days it had a mansard roof. In 1731, Petronelle van Lennep had this altered, probably by **Daniël Marot** *(see No 605: Museum Willet-Holthuysen)*. The frontage was then ornately decorated with flowers, acanthus leaves, a balustrade, decorated chimney stacks etc. The central caryatids on the first floor were carved by **Jan van Logteren** (1709-1745).

No 450, opposite, forms a contrast with its much more austere sandstone façade. It was built in 1663 for banker Willem G Deutz to plans by **Philip Vingboons**. The attic was added in 1922.

De Appel – *Nieuwe Spiegelstraat 10*. For lovers of modern art, "The Apple" hosts temporary exhibitions of the latest works.

At the end of Nieuwe Spiegelstraat is the impressive Rijksmuseum.

No 495 – The son of the famous Jan Six *(see REMBRANDTPLEIN)* who held 16 successive mandates as burgomaster of Amsterdam had this house built in 1739 by the French architect Jean Coulon. He designed a balcony above the front door, a very unusual sight in Amsterdam.

Next door, at no 497, is the **Kattenkabinet**, the only house in the Golden Curve that is open to the public. The Cat Museum contains a delightful collection of objects relating to our feline companions.

M. Guillou/MICHELIN

A much admired forger

During the Second World War, a German art dealer bought the house at no 468. He also purchased a painting by Vermeer of Delft from one **Hans van Meegeren**, and exchanged it, with Goering, for stolen works that were valued at approximately 12 million florins. In 1938, Van Meegeren had already sold a painting by the great artist from Delft, *The Disciples on the Road to Emmaus*, which can be seen in the Boijmans Van Beuningen Museum in Rotterdam. Actually the art dealer was a superb forger and the painting dated from 1937! He was suspected of collaborating with the Nazis and had to prove that all the paintings he had sold were really fakes. He was so talented that he was only sentenced to one year's imprisonment.

★ **No 476** – This splendid private mansion was built c 1740. Its façade is a magnificent construction divided by six Corinthian pilasters marking out five bays decorated with elegant garlands. Above the entablature is an attic with traceried balustrade decorated with the coat of arms of the owner. At the very top is an eagle. The garden dates back to the early 18C.

ABN-AMRO Bank – *Entrance on Vijzelstraat.* The last section of the Golden Curve is disfigured or embellished, according to your personal taste, by the lateral façade of the ABN-AMRO bank. This gigantic building (100m/328ft wide) was built in 1923 by the Nederlandsche Handel Maatschappij, a trading company, the successor to the East and West India Companies. This brick construction, designed by the architect **KPC Bazel**, does at least provide a very different element among the majestic, patrician residences surrounding it.

SOUTH OF THE GOLDEN CURVE

No 502: Huis met de Kolommen (The burgomaster's residence) – This 17C house, which was altered in 1791 to designs by Abraham van der Hart, City Architect, has been the official residence of the city's mayor since 1927.

No 527 – The Classical features of this house give it a French appearance. It is built of sandstone with Ionic pilasters. It was purchased by **Louis Bonaparte**, then King of Holland, as accommodation for his Field Marshal. His brother, Napoleon, is said to have stayed here in 1811 (the eagle on the front is older than this). Czar **Peter the Great** stayed here in 1717 *(see ZAANSTREEK)*.

Ph. Gajic/MICHELIN

A sea god riding a dolphin, Herengracht 510

Nos 508 and 510 – These two elegant **neck gables**★ date from the end of the 17C. They are supported by marine divinities (no 510) and tritons (no 508). The gods are sitting on dolphins; the tritons, half man and half fish, are blowing conch shells to calm the waves.

No 539 – This fine frontage dating from c 1720 has a double flight of steps and a balcony both of which are more recent (c 1830). In Amsterdam, as in all towns and cities built over the water or on very unstable land the cellars are higher than in other towns. This is why there are so many houses here with first floors raised above street level and why there are so many flights of steps above a door down to the cellar.

No 514 – *"A delightful house, isn't it? The two heads that you can see there belong to negro slaves [...] The house belonged to a slave trader."* (*La Chute*, Editions Gallimard) **Albert Camus** was wrong; the owner was not a slave trader and the two bust were designed to represent trade with distant lands.

Reguliersgracht – *See REMBRANDTPLEIN.*

★ **No 605: Museum Willet-Holthuysen** ⓥ – Housed in a luxurious mansion buil between 1685 and 1690, with a superb mid 18C doorway, this museum has a interesting succession of elegantly furnished rooms giving an idea of the lifestyle o wealthy merchants of the day.

In the basement kitchen and scullery are graceful **tiles**★ decorated with bird cage (late 17C) on each side of the fireplace. On the *piano nobile*, the blue room wa originally the men's smoking room; the ceiling and front of the canopy above th fireplace are the work of **Jacob de Witt**. They are *grisailles* known as *Witjes*, afte their creator. On the upper floor, the bedroom used by Mr and Mrs Willet has bee turned into a curio cabinet (bronze, ceramics and porcelain from Weesp and Loos drecht). As to the antiques cabinet, so named because it was here that Abrahan Willet displayed his most valuable acquisitions, it provides a wonderful view of th garden.

The **garden**★ *(also visible from Amstelstraat)* has regained its original layout designe by Frenchman **Daniël Marot** (1663-1752), a Huguenot who had sought refuge i Amsterdam after the Revocation of the Edict of Nantes. He introduced the Loui XIV style into the Low Countries. He was architect to William of Orange, even whe William mounted the throne of England under the title of King William III.

JAVA-EILAND

Plan p 13, **CN**
Michelin map no 36 H 13 and H 14

The northern end of the Eastern Islands *(Oostelijke Eilanden)*, reclaimed from the I by the use of dikes, has been the object of intense architectural activity over the pas few years. This is particularly obvious on the **Island of Java** to the north of the Zeeburg The long, thin island lies parallel to the Oostelijke Handelskade where cruise liners ti up. The quayside has literally begun to bristle with ultramodern apartment blocks sinc the 1980s when it was decided to use this area to build low-rental housing. It is th new wave of Amsterdam architects who have given vent to their creative expressio here: the PRO workshop (Entrepot-West in the south of the island), W Arets, J Coener H Kolihoff, F and P Wintermans etc.

Ph. Gajic/MICHELIN

The poetry of large apartment blocks

The IJ – The IJ is an arm of the former Zuiderzee. It was this river which gave rise to the founding of Amsterdam when its south bank was dammed in the 13C by farming communities. In the early 19C it began to silt up, and a canal was dug along a distance of 79km/49mi between Amsterdam and the coast. It was refurbished and shortened in 1876 to become the **North Sea Canal**. The building of the **Amsterdam-Rhine Canal** in 1952 cleared the maritime congestion and today, with almost 100 000 ships arriving annually, harbour traffic represents some 35 to 40 million tonnes.

Open Haven Museum ⓥ – *KNSM-laan 311.* At the entrance to the KNSM-eiland (the eastern part of Java-eiland, named after the Dutch Royal Navigation Company) stands this small museum in which the exhibits refer to the history of the harbour. It also hosts temporary exhibitions. Visitors with special interest in the merchant navy will appreciate the authentic KNSM embarkation room on the first floor.

JORDAAN★

Plan p 10, **KV**
Michelin map no 36 J 9, H 9 and G 9

The district is a logical conclusion to the digging of the four central canals. It was built in the early 17C around old drainage ditches. At that time it was a district of workers and craftsmen, an area of noisy, evil-smelling activities which were prohibited in the town centre. Since the Second World War, though, the Jordaan district has gradually been improved and is no longer the scene of abject poverty. Its picturesque atmosphere and eternally working-class soul have attracted students and artists, as well as a comfortably-off population, who form a sharp contrast to those who were born and brought up here. The etymology of the word "Jordaan" remains a mystery. Originally, the district was called Nieuwe Werck ("New Work"). One explanation of this 18C name is that it comes from the French "*jardin*" ("garden"), a term thought appropriate given the many vegetable gardens dotted across the area and the large number of French Huguenots who lived here. It is tempting to agree given that many of Jordaan's canals and streets are named after flowers or trees: Lindengracht (Linden Canal, now filled in), Egelantiersgracht (Eglantine Canal), Palmgracht (Palm Tree Canal), Goudsbloemstraat (Marigold Street), Anjeliersstraat (Carnation Street) etc.

A GUIDED TOUR OF JORDAAN

The tour begins with the Elandsgracht and continues northwards to the Brouwersgracht, the northern edge of the Jordaan district.

Elandsgracht – In 1891 the canal was filled in and has unfortunately been turned into a car park. Set in the heart of the old tanning district, it gets its name from the elk hides that were sold here. At the eastern end, only a few yards from the Woonbootmuseum *(see PRINSENGRACHT)*, is a statue of **Johnny Jordaan** whose real name was Jan van Musscher (1924-89). He was a singer of romantic ballads who rose to fame in the 1950s. He was well known throughout the country and often performed with Tante Leen, who also has a statue. Note the fine carved wooden shop front at the corner of Eerste Looiersdwarsstraat.

Looier Kunst- en Antiekcentrum ⓥ – *Elandsgracht 109.* The covered market was inaugurated some twenty years ago. It is one gigantic flea market where time will fly past for anybody with an interest in antiques and bric-à-brac.

Hazenstraat – At no 62 (1765) one of the stones on the frontage represents a bul on a stone bridge called a "*sluis*" in Amsterdam *(see SINGEL, Torensluis)*. This unexpected scene can be explained by the name of the first owner: Jan van de Sluys. No 56 is a housing unit designed by architect **Herman Zeinstra** during the 1970s There are several small flats grouped around communal areas and rooms including the lounge.

Lauriergracht – The "Laurel Canal" had a famous resident, **George Hendrik Breitner** (1857-1923), a painter and photographer. Several of his canvases are displayed in the Rijksmuseum (Room 20). He lived at no 8. The most famous resident of the canal banks, though, was Mr Droogstoppel, the hero of **Multatuli**'s best-known nove *(see ANNE FRANK HUIS, Multatuli Museum)* and one of Dutch literature's leading characters. The first chapter of the novel *Max Havelaar* begins with the words, " *am a coffee trader and I live at 37 Lauriergracht*".

At no 23 stands one of the oldest neck gables in the city (1658). It is an elegant construction decorated with a garland and topped by a rounded pediment flanked by lions. This elegance is understandable given the proximity of the Prinsengracht.

At the end of the Lauriergracht, turn left into the Prinsengracht. For descriptions of the houses at no 242 and no 349, see PRINSENGRACHT. Turn left into the Rozengracht then right into Eerste Bloemdwarsstraat.

Eerste Bloemdwarsstraat – As you cross Bloemstraat, note the delightful view o the Westerkerk. Further on, to the right, the house at no 3 (1787) used to be a stables, as indicated by the stone on the frontage decorated with a galloping horse and the words "*IJder zijn zin*" (each to his own).

★ **Bloemgracht** – Ironically nicknamed the "Herengracht of the Jordaan district" the peaceful "Canal of Flowers" fortunately escaped the project that resulted in the drainage of several canals in the district for health reasons. In days gone by dyers and paint makers had their shops here. Now it enjoys a certain prestige because many of the houses are listed buildings. They indicate that the craftsmen who used to live on the banks of the Canal of Flowers were fairly wealthy.
The three houses with stepped gables (1645) at **nos 87 to 91** have regained thei original beauty thanks to restoration work carried out in 1947. The houses are, in order, *De Steeman* (The Farmer's), *De Landman* (The Peasant's) and *De Zeeman* (The Seaman's). At the corner of Tweede Leliedwarsstraat, at no 29, is the house that was once the home of the Blaeu dynasty, famous as publishers of geographical maps *(see NEDERLANDS SCHEEPVAARTMUSEUM)*.
A large number of **frontage stones** (*gevelsteen* in Dutch) decorate the houses in the Bloemgracht. At no 19, for example, there is a pelican; at no 23 a unicorn; at no 34 a trout; and at no 77 a sower. The stone decorating the front of no 34 is accompanied by a line from Schubert's famous *Trout Quintet*; it was set in place in 199 in homage to Jan Huck riede, the founder of Amsterdam's Philharmoni Orchestra.

Turn into Eerste Lelied warsstraat. There is a wonderful view of the bell tower on the Westerkerk.

Theo Thijssen Museum – *Eerste Leliedwarsstraa 16.* This small museum occupies the birthplace o the writer and contain exhibits relating to hi works.

The Jordaan cult book – **Theo Thijssen** (1879-1943) wa a primary teacher *(hi statue stands on the Lindengracht)*, a Socialist politician and a writer. In 1923 he published Kees de Jongen, a work in which he described his youth with th Jordaan district as the setting. The book made him very popular with th general public in Amsterdam.

Before the introduction of house numbers

After the gigantic fire that swept through the town in 1452, house owners were required by law to use brick and stones in their building projects. In the absence of any number on the houses, **frontage stones** were used; they were decorated with a carving in relief illustrating the owner's profession or identity. When the French introduced the numbering system, the use of frontage stones rapidly died out; it has come back into fashion over the past few years.

Ph. Gajic/MICHELIN

A well-earned rest on the banks of the Egelantiersgracht

★**Egelantiersgracht** – With its splendid 17C and 18C frontages, the Eglantine Canal has retained most of its erstwhile charm. Like the Bloemgracht, it has become a sought-after address and is no longer the home of the workers who once crowded along the quaysides.

The Hofjes – The *hofjes* are inner courtyards or former hospices, noticeable for the many numbers at their single entrances. When the Reformed Religion was adopted in 1578, the Roman Catholic Church could no longer take care of old, destitute people. The task was taken over by rich citizens or Protestant charities who built small almshouses set out around an inner courtyard.
The Jordaan had more than 100 such enclosures at one time; now there are only 75 left in Amsterdam as a whole. Some of them uphold tradition; others have become havens of peace, usually with very well-tended gardens.

Sint-Andrieshofje – *Egelantiersgracht 107-145.* It was a donation from Jeff Gerritsz, a cattle breeder, which enabled this enclosure to be built; it was completed in 1617. The entrance is particularly attractive, located at the end of a corridor lined with Delft ceramic tiles.

Follow Eerste Egelantiersdwarsstraat.

Claes Claeszhofje – *Eerste Egelantiersdwarsstraat 3 (entrance opposite no 4).* This enclosure (1616) was also known as Anslohofje. It consists of three courtyards (the fourth one is a later addition) and includes the "Lion" fountain. The accommodation is reserved for students at the academy of music. Claes Claesz. Anslo was an Anabaptist linen draper.

Leave the Claes Claeszhofje by the blue door in the corridor on the right-hand side. In Egelantiersstraat, turn right and right again into Eerste Egelantiersdwarsstraat. Continue along this street until you reach Westerstraat, a wide but uninteresting thoroughfare (once the Carnation Canal, filled in in 1861). Go straight along Tweede Boomdwarsstraat and turn left into Karthuizersstraat.

Karthuizerhofje – *Karthuizersstraat 169-171 (entrance at no 173 or beyond 85).* The façade, some 70m/228ft long, conceals the largest of all the *hofjes* in Amsterdam, the Carthusian enclosure. The hospice was built in 1650 by Daniël Stalpaert, the town's architect, on the site of a Carthusian monastery which had been destroyed in the 16C. It was reserved for widows, hence its name, *Huyszitten-Weduwenhof* (Non-Working Widows Enclosure). The second name of the institution indicates that food was supplied here and that the old women living alone in their houses also received rations of peat. The pediments visible in the courtyard bear the city's coat of arms (three St Andrew's crosses) and a cog (former emblem of the city, *see Introduction, Amsterdam's coat of arms*).
On Karthuizersplantsoen ("Carthusian square"), there is an interesting succession of four stepped gables (nos 11-19) known as the "Four Seasons".

Go along Lindenstraat to Noordermarkt.

Noordermarkt – *See PRINSENGRACHT.*

Lindengracht 167

FRONTAGE STONES, ANCESTORS OF NUMBERED ADDRESSES

Zandhoek

Lindengracht 55a, 57a

Prinsengracht 175

Lindengracht 53

The 1934 riots – The 1930s were a dark decade for the world as a whole, and like other countries the Netherlands experienced the Depression. In 1930 unemployment quadrupled. Farm prices dropped by 30%, as did industrial production. In July 1934 the Dutch government decided to reduce unemployment benefit by more than 10% despite the fact that it was already very low. A demonstration was immediately organised in the Jordaan district and it soon degenerated into a riot, causing the army to be called in to support the forces of law and order which could no longer contain it.

The district lived through a veritable state of war. Lamp standards were knocked down to deprive the police of lighting at night, bridges were raised like shields, barricades were erected using beams and various pieces of furniture and the army charged, to be met by a hail of cobblestones. The unemployment benefit was suspended and soon the district was starving.

On 9 July 1934 seven dead and more than 30 injured were reported. And the city council had the streets of the Jordaan district covered in tarmac.

Lindengracht – This canal was also filled in at the end of the 19C, but it has retained traces of its modest working-class housing, especially at nos 206-220. This group of two-roomed flats was built in 1896 to designs by J E van der Pek (1865-1919) to provide housing for the poorest members of society by guaranteeing an extremely low rent. The system continued to operate until 1971. On the house fronts, it is still possible to read the names of crafts: no 206 reads *Steenhouwer* (Stonecutter) and no 220 *Metselaar* (Mason).

At the end of the Lindengracht, or Linden Canal, is a statue of **Theo Thijssen** (1879-1943), a primary teacher and writer who published *Kees de Jongen* in 1923 *(see above)*.

The Eel Revolt – The Jordaan has a long tradition as a district of social misfits, extending into the 1960s with the *Provos* movement which had its roots in this district.

On 25 July 1886, during popular festivities known as "eel shooting" *(palingtrekken)* which consisted of catching hold of a live eel attached to a rope strung across the canal, the police intervened, reminding people that the event was forbidden. One policeman cut the rope and, by mistake, the eel struck one of the contestants in the face. Since the population of the Jordaan district is by nature rebellious, the incident caused a battle royal which eventually degenerated into a riot. The public disorder had a dramatic side: 26 people lost their lives! The tragi-comic episode has gone down in history as the "*Paling-Oproer*", the "Eel Revolt".

Turn into Tweede Goudsbloemdwarsstraat which extends into Palmdwarsstraat.

M. Guillou/MICHELIN

Oranjebrug, Brouwersgracht

Driehoeksstraat – "Triangle Street" is built over marshland that was drained in 1650. At no 10 it boasts the last gin distillery still operating in the Jordaan district, owned by the firm of **Van Wees**. The drink (*genever* in Dutch) is a 40% proof spirit which was reputed to be excellent protection against seasickness. This explains why it was so popular with sailors.

★ **Brouwersgracht** – *See also ANNE FRANK HUIS.* This canal, named after the breweries that lined its banks in the 17C and 18C, is now flanked by an almost unbroken row of renovated warehouses (especially between nos 172 and 212). Several of them proudly bear the city's coat of arms because the city council used to store guns on the ground floor and corn on the upper floors. Some of them are named after distant towns or islands (for example, Danzig and Spitzbergen), reminders of the varied and difficult voyages undertaken by Amsterdam's navigators that brought Amsterdam some of its wealth.

KEIZERSGRACHT★★

Map pp 10 and 11, **KV**, **KX**, **KY** and **LY**
Michelin map no 36 H 10, H 9, J 9, K 9, K 10 and K 11

THE EMPEROR'S CANAL

The canal, part of the Grachtengordel, was given this name in honour of Maximilian I, future emperor of the Holy Roman Empire who, in 1489, authorised the town to add his crown to the municipal coat of arms. The privilege was granted in return for a loan given by Amsterdam to the man whom the Italians had nicknamed "Maximilian the Penniless" *(see also Introduction, Amsterdam's Coat of arms)*.
The Keizersgracht (1612) is 4km/almost 3mi long and is spanned by 14 bridges. With houseboats at each end, the canal is one of the finest in Amsterdam.

Like the other three parallel canals, house numbers begin at the north end and continue up to the Amstel. The house-by-house description ensures that you will see all the sights as you stroll through this part of the city. The change from odd to even numbers is quite intentional. The order of the numbers is designed to ensure that you look at both sides of the street as you progress along it.

★ **Brouwersgracht** – *See JORDAAN and ANNE FRANK HUIS.*

No 22 – The *De Zayer* (The Sower) building has had various uses. It was initially a warehouse; now it is an architect's office. At one time it was a Jesuit church (c 1633) and even a sports hall (during the 1930s). The date of 1836 visible on the façade shows when it was converted into a Classical-style church.

Nos 40-44 – In days gone by, the north end of the Keizersgracht was highly industrialised, as was the Brouwersgracht set at right angles to it. The Groenland warehouses belonged to the **Northern Company** which was set up in 1614 after the Dutch, who were seeking a northern route to the Indies, had discovered schools of whales. The route did not lead to the warm waters of the Indian Ocean, but the mammals represented a ready supply of the oil (a sperm whale contains 5 tonnes of oil) used for lighting, soap and tar making, the treatment of wool, tanning, and even paint making. After a bitter struggle with fishermen from the Basque Country the Company acquired the monopoly of whale-hunting until 1642 when they lost their dominant position to the fishermen of Zaandam.
The ground floor in each warehouse was equipped with five tanks that could contain up to 100 000 litres of the precious liquid. The upper floors were used to store barrels and whale bones used in the production of knives. Small bones were used to make corsets.

No 101 – This splendid sandstone façade rises to a wonderfully ornate attic (c 1715) which bears great resemblance to the one at Singel 40 *(illustration, see Introduction: Architecture)* built at almost the same time.

No 105 – The façade of the *D'Bruynvis* building (the "brown fish", see above the door) is five bays wide. It is actually a combination of fragments of several different frontages. Note the superb doorway dating from c 1760.

No 104: De Rode Hoed – The "Red Hat" *(see the cartouche)* dates from the early 17C, but the bell gable was rebuilt in the 19C. It gets its name from a hatter who lived next door at no 102. The two-storey façade on the latter building is fairly banal; it dates from 1876. In earlier times the address concealed an almost clandestine church attended by Remonstrants or Arminians, followers of **Arminius**, the Latin name of Hermann Armenszoon (1560-1609), one of Amsterdam's pastors. In 1610, they drew up a "Remonstrance" by which they requested from the *stathouder* greater flexibility in the Calvinist doctrine. They opposed the Gomarists who were recruited in rural areas whereas the Arminians came from the ruling bourgeoisie. They highlighted the importance of the tolerance that is still a marked feature of Dutch culture to this day.

No 118-120 – This was the home of **Hendrik Petrus Berlage** (1856-1934), the architect who designed the Stock Exchange. The wide house with its humpbacked roof (19C) is flanked on the left by a neck gable (no 122, c 1720) and on the right by a tall house rising to a bell gable (no 116, 1745).

No 117 – This double house built c 1620 has retained its original height, except for the stepped brick gable which was replaced by a dormer window framed between wooden scrolls. The **door** is a fine example of the Louis XV style (c 1760).

No 119 – The frontage on this house (c 1735) rises to a fine attic over a traceried entablature.

Ph. Gajic/MICHELIN

One of the noble effigies on the House of Heads, Keizersgracht 123

★**No 123: Huis met de Hoofden** – The spectacular **façade** on the House of Heads was built in 1622. It is easy to understand the name: six heads decorate the wonderful combination of red brick and white stone topped by a stepped gable with pinnacles. The gable has been attributed to **Hendrick de Keyser** (1596-1676), but this is not certain. However, the attribution is confirmed by the fact that the owner, Nicolaas Sohier, was a friend of the Bartolottis *(see HERENGRACHT: nos 170-172, Huis Bartolotti)* whose house, built during the same period in a very similar style, was designed by this architect. He entrusted the construction of the building to his son Pieter de Keyser.

Stop, Thief! – The heads are resolutely Roman and are said to represent six thieves who were beheaded by the servant one night while she was alone in her masters' residence. She is said to have picked up a sword to defend herself and surprised the intruders just as they put their heads through a window that they had forced open. This is possible, albeit difficult to believe. What is certain, however, is that the heads depict divinities: Apollo, Ceres, Mars, Minerva, Bacchus and Diana.

A pedagogical philosopher – Jan Amos Komensky (1592-1670), a Czech Humanist better known as **Comenius**, lived in this house from 1656 to 1670 *(see NAARDEN)*.

No 157 – This charming house at the corner of Leliegracht dates from the 17C, as is obvious from the horizontal beam above the ground floor and the height of the building. The rough-cast is a 19C addition, as is the **gable** in the shape of an upturned hull, a very unusual sight (there are only about 20 of them in Amsterdam).

Leliegracht – *See ANNE FRANK HUIS.*

Nos 174-176 – At the corner opposite no 157 stands the headquarters of Greenpeace Nederland. It is a rather massive freestone Art Nouveau construction designed by Gerrit van Arkel and HH Baanders in 1905 for a life insurance company. In this respect, the mosaic of an angel selling an insurance policy is in decidedly doubtful taste. There are very few Art Nouveau buildings in Amsterdam; there are many more in The Hague.

Greenpeace

Greenpeace is a non-governmental organisation founded in Vancouver (Canada) in 1971. It opposes nuclear energy and supports disarmament as well as the saving of the world's oceans and the protection of the tropical rain forests. At the same time, it fights atmospheric pollution and toxic products.

Westermarkt – *See ANNE FRANK HUIS.*

★**Nos 244-246** – These twin houses are each 5.5m/17ft wide and passers-by can therefore study in detail the decorative system used in the mid-18C *(illustration, see Introduction: Art)*. Both houses rise to an identical entablature with a traceried attic and balustrade, a style typical of the period. Above the attic is a vase immediately above the hoist. The entablature flanked by purely ornamental scrolls has been rounded to allow for an opening through which the goods lifted up to this level by the hoist can be brought in. It is therefore understandable that excessive decoration (in this case in the Louis XV style) was never allowed here, even though this is a canal house.

De Groote Keijser – The "great Keijser is everywhere" was the slogan of the **squatters** who occupied the five houses nicknamed *De Groote Keijser* between nos 242 and 252 from November 1978 onwards. One year later, despite an expulsion order, the police were unable to remove them. Indeed, spurred on by the annulment of the decision, they set up a pirate radio station, the *Vrije Keijser* which picked up the frequencies used by the police. They had no hesitation in inciting others to disrupt Queen Beatrix's coronation in the Nieuwe Kerk on 30 April 1980.

The "Proletarian Shopping Spree" – The major demonstration organised by the squatters (they were less ideological but more highly motivated than their predecessors, the *Provos*) quickly degenerated. The disorder reached such a pitch that, on the following day, the national vocabulary acquired a new expression to describe the concept of pillage. The squatters soon lost the support of their fellow citizens and the movement returned underground from 1985 onwards.

No 324: Felix Meritis Huis – In Latin, *felix* means "happy" and *meritis* means "through merit". This was the name of an association which was seeking to promote the ideals of the Age of Enlightenment. Since 1788, when this building was erected by Jacob Otten Husly, it has also been the name of the theatre which has an unusual neo-Classical façade reminiscent of a small palace. It is unusual in the city, but its design inspired that of the Concertgebouw. Brahms, Schumann, Grieg and Saint-Saëns performed here. It became the headquarters of the Dutch Communist party after the Second World War, but the building re-established a cultural role and now houses the Meritis Foundation for the promotion of European artists, as well as the Amsterdam Summer University.

Almost opposite, at **no 317**, is a fine façade dating from the early 18C. The building accommodated Czar **Peter the Great** in 1697 *(insert, see ZAANSTREEK)*. Note, too, no 319, a wonderful building designed by **Philip Vingboons** (1639).

No 454 – The Emperor's Canal has few warehouses. Located at the corner of Molenpad, this one dates from approximately 1680. Its façade has undergone almost no changes since then. The warehouse has the neck gable that is traditional on this type of building.

Leidsegracht – *See LEIDSEPLEIN.*

No 464 – This house at the corner of Leidsegracht is topped by a bell gable with scrolls but dates only from 1936. It is a reconstruction of a canal house, built with materials from several other houses which had been demolished. The bell gable and shop front are therefore originals.

No 455: Metz & Co – **Gerrit Rietveld** (1888-1964) holds a very important place in the history of 20C architecture, yet he designed only one building in Amsterdam, the Van Gogh Museum. However he had a link with this building (1891) with its decorative caryatids, erected by J van Looy for the New York Life Insurance Company whose emblem (an eagle) can still be seen today. With a height of 26m/85ft, it was the city's tallest commercial building in its day. It was purchased in 1908 by the owners of the Metz store, suppliers of the royal family since 1740, and was altered by Rietveld at their request. In 1933 he added to the top floor a circular glass and metal gallery. It was a showroom, initially designed to display functional furniture, from which there is an interesting **view** of the surrounding area.

ABN-AMRO Bank – *See HERENGRACHT.*

Nos 606-608 – This set of two **neck gables**★ (c 1730) is quite outstanding. Not only are they the tallest two in the city (see the supporting beams at the rear) but they are also the most elegant. The ornamentation is in the Louis XIV style.

★**No 672: Museum Van Loon** ⌚ – In Amsterdam there are very few luxury residences open to the public, and almost none provide an opportunity to admire their gardens. The Van Loon Museum, therefore, is a happy exception.

The architecture – In 1671, a Flemish trader by the name of Jeremias van Raey must have warmly thanked **Adriaan Dortsman** (1625-82) for the magnificence of the twin mansions that he had commissioned. They are veritable mini-palaces within the urban landscape, overlooking a canal which had recently been extended to flow into the Amstel. Each of the houses has a similar façade built of sandstone imported from Germany. Above is a balustrade broken up by statues which are supposed to symbolise the owner's trading activities (Mars, Minerva, Vulcan and Ceres). The frontage itself is elegantly topped by a Doric entablature with alternating triglyphs and blind meteops. Together, the buildings form a wonderful design that is both luxurious yet unostentatious.
Van Raey lived at no 674 (his initials can be seen below the balcony); no 672 had as its first tenant the artist **Ferdinand Bol**, one of Rembrandt's students. As a portrait artist, he was very popular with the urban bourgeoisie in the great Dutch city.

The tour – The house was turned into a museum by the Van Loon family (owners since 1884) and has undergone several alterations. Visitors are mainly impressed by the decoration (post-1750) and by some of the paintings in the family's large collection.
The staircase is decorated with stucco work and has a superb **handrail★** (second half of the 18C) made of interlacing copper. Visitors may be able to pick out "V HAGEN" between the ground floor and the landing and "TRIP" between the landing and the first floor. The graceful piece of ironwork was commissioned by Abraham van Hagen who married Catharina Trip. The Chamber of Paintings on the first floor is decorated with wallpaper depicting imaginary Mediterranean landscapes. The corridor contains four fine *grisailles* inspired by engravings by Jean de Lairesse, depicting Alexander the Great and Julius Caesar *(left)*, and Ninus and Cyrus *(right)*. Finally the master bedroom conceals two amusing decorative artifices: the rosettes formed by eight stylised S's (the monogramme of Hendrik Sander), and a real door hidden amid the wainscoting in order to blend in with the symmetry of the corridor and a fake door opposite the fireplace to blend in with the symmetry of the bedroom. *The Four Ages of Life* is an allegory painted in 1630 by Jan Miense Molenaer (c 1610-68) who specialised in domestic interiors and small genre paintings. *Willem van Loon* (1636) by Dirck Santvoort shows the family ancestor at the age of 30 months; it was used as the subject matter of a stamp issued in 1955.
The formal **garden★** was relaid during the 1970s in accordance with a bird's-eye view in a 17C map; it has all the appearance of a miniature park. The neo-Classical pavilion (1758) closing off the view is a *koetshuis*, a coach house with an entrance on Kerkstraat. Despite appearances, this is a rear façade. The coachman lived over the stables and the architect, in an effort to preserve the privacy of the owners, intended to include fake windows with *trompe-l'œil* curtains. The pediment is decorated with Apollo's quiver and lyre; the bust of the god can be seen over the door, between statues of Silena and Flora.

Ph. Gajic/MICHELIN

Museum Van Loon: The room looking out onto the garden

Reguliersgracht – *See REMBRANDTPLEIN.*

No 716 – At the corner of the delightful Reguliersgracht is what one might be tempted to call a doll's house, a tiny dwelling built in 1671 and topped by one of the city's bell gables. The unusual frontage has been rather well preserved.

No 778-790 – This is an interesting row of five identical neck gables dating from 1688. The rounded pediments bear a carving of a shell. Nos 784 and 786 have lost their vases, and only no 780 has retained its flight of steps and original door.

No 822 – The bell gable on this elegant façade (1672) was built only one year after the one on no 716, although its garlands show a degree of decorative refinement that would suggest a much later building.

LEIDSEPLEIN★

Plan p 10, **KY**
Michelin map no 36 K 9

NEVER-ENDING HUSTLE AND BUSTLE

This square is one of the city's nerve centres, by day and by night. The elegant early 20C meeting-place has been overtaken by a continuous flow of pedestrians and tramways with, in their midst, street entertainers doing juggling tricks or playing music. In winter, part of the square is turned into an ice rink.

American Hotel – *Leidseplein 28.* This hotel, a survivor of the end of the 19C, is one of Amsterdam's institutions.
Designed by **Willem Kromhout** (1864-1940) and CJ Jansen, the building was completed in 1902. It is an outstanding combination of Art Nouveau and the style of the Amsterdam School. It got its name from the building erected in 1882 on the same site, given by its promoter, W Steinigeweg, after a long stay on the other side of the Atlantic. The café is attractively Art Deco, with stained-glass windows and Tiffany lampshades; it is one of the most select venues in the city.

Stadsschouwburg – *Leidseplein 26.* The neo-Renaissance style municipal theatre has been famous throughout the country since 1894 for the quality of its performances (drama, concerts, dancing). Yet its balcony is equally famous as a rallying point for the players and supporters of **Ajax** when they have won a major victory.

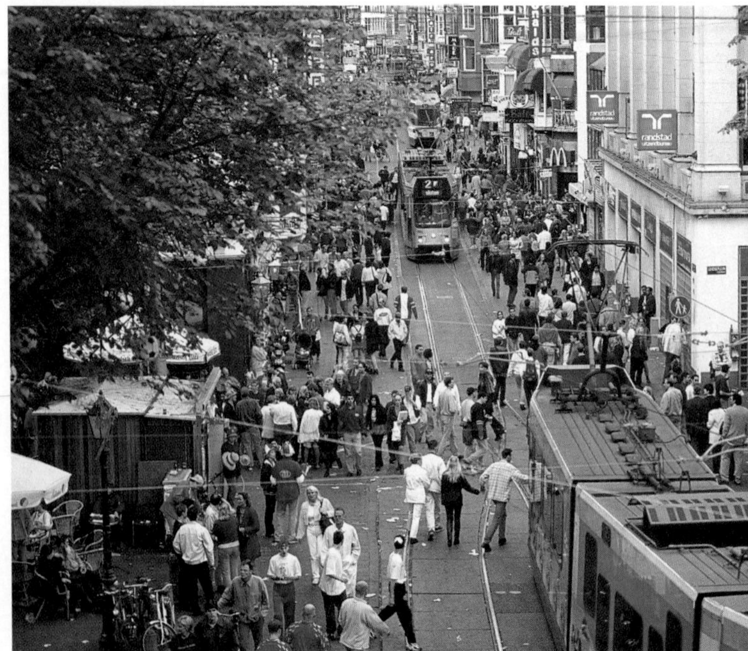

Leidsestraat and the never-ending movement of the trams

Melkweg – *Lijnbaansgracht 234a.* During the 1970s, the "Milky Way" was a temple of the avant-garde movement and so-called "alternative" culture. Visitors come to the former dairy with a name that is evocative of the hippie culture to discover the works of artists from all over the world. The high point of the centre's year is the *World Roots Festival* in June.

Leidsegracht – This charming canal, which was dug in 1664, owes its name to the town of Leyde to which flat-bottomed boats called *kagen* used to sail. This is now a very sought-after address, which is understandable given that it leads into the Lijnbaansgracht, a small, quiet canal that cuts across the famous three canals encircling the city centre: Prinsengracht, Keizersgracht and Herengracht.

Leidsestraat – The narrowness of the street running from Leidseplein to Koningsplein does not prevent it being one of the city centre's main thoroughfares (trams and cyclists only). It is so narrow that the many tramways travelling through it can only pass each other on the bridges, which are wider.
The shopping street is as busy as the Leidsegracht is quiet; it is the kingdom of fast-food outlets and bargain shops.

Max Euwe-Centrum ⓥ – *Max Euweplein 30a1 (entrance at 24/26).* Max Euwe (1901-81) was the Netherlands' only world chess champion (1935-37). In addition to a small exhibition concerning the champion, the centre is a meeting place for players who can enjoy a game here in quiet surroundings.

Paradiso – *Weteringschans 6-8.* This disused church is not a tourist venue; it is a temple of music created as a result of the action of the Provos protest movement. The large empty nave echoes to the sounds of international stars such as David Bowie or to the music of young local artists.

MUSEUMPLEIN

Plan p 10, **KZ**
Plan Michelin n° 36 L 9

his immense esplanade, situated between Amsterdam Zuid and the central canals, has ways been subject to controversy. Its entire expanse has been the setting for all sorts f cultural events. In the 19C World Fairs and sporting activities took place on the site nd for a long time Amsterdam's Skating Club had an ice rink here. In 1953 the notorway from The Hague and Schipol ended in a cul-de-sac here and it became known s the "shortest motorway in the Netherlands". Its development, based on a project y the Danish landscape gardener Sven-Ingvar Andersson, seems to have brought conoversy to an end. Museumplein, bordered as its name suggests by the Rijksmuseum, ne Van Gogh Museum, the Stedelijk Museum and the Concertgebouw, now constiutes the cultural heart of the city. The green "donkey's ear" above the entrance to ne car park as well as the two pavilions opposite the Rijksmuseum give it a touch of riginality.

★**Rijksmuseum** – *See RIJKSMUSEUM.*

★**Van Gogh Museum** – *See VAN GOGH MUSEUM.*

Coster Diamonds ⓥ – *Paulus Potterstraat 2-6.* It was in Amsterdam (in Coster's) that the famous Koh-i-Noor diamond (108.93 carats) was polished. The diamond belongs to the British Crown. The rough stone was discovered in India in 1304. Unfortunately for Amsterdam, the city is no longer the capital of the diamond industry *(insert, see PLANTAGE).*
Visitors, who usually come here to buy, can also find out about the various stages required to produce, for example, an 8/8 diamond from a rough stone – cleaving, sawing, rough-cutting and polishing, followed by the various operations involved in mounting the stone in jewellery.

★**Stedelijk Museum** – *See STEDELIJK MUSEUM.*

Concertgebouw – *Concertgebouwplein 2-6.* Like the Tonhalle in Zurich or the Gürzenich in Cologne, the name of this building erected in 1888 has gradually become confused with the name of the eminent orchestra which has its home here. To mark its centenary, it was given the title "Royal" by Queen Beatrix.

The best acoustics in the world – When the marshland to the south of the city centre was drained *(see RIJKSMUSEUM, Geographical Location)* during the last three decades of the 19C, patrons of the arts came forward and offered to pay for the construction of an auditorium seating an audience of 2 000 in order to remedy the lack of musical amenities in the city. **AL van Gendt** (1835-1901) was the engineer and architect who won the competition organised in 1881 by Cuypers, the architect of the Rijksmuseum.

Behind the austere neo-Classical façade is an auditorium that has become a legend for music lovers throughout the world. As soon as the first concert had been held, on 3 November 1888, it was obvious that the main auditorium (Grote Zaal) provided extraordinary acoustics and would become a temple of classical music.

A prestigious orchestra – It was undoubtedly **Willem Mengelberg** (1871-1951) who was, and remains, the most significant figure in the history of the *Concertgebouworkest* even if his predecessor, Willem Kes, laid down the standards for modern concerts by requiring that the audience remain silent during the performance. Mengelberg based his mandate on a repertoire of Romantic and post-Romantic works and was a great exponent of the symphonies composed by his friend, Gustav Mahler. Mengelberg was dictatorial during rehearsals but full of ardour when conducting performances and he brought the orchestra worldwide reputation. In 1988 **Riccardo Chailly** succeeded **Bernard Haitink**, who had brought the Concertgebouw Orchestra wider popularity through numerous recordings. Riccardo Chailly became the fifth permanent conductor of this orchestra, famous for its extraordinary sensitivity. Four conductors in 100 years: Proof indeed of the unusual stability of this institution. Thanks to the smaller additional auditorium used for recitals, the people of Amsterdam were able to enjoy more than 600 concerts in 1997.

NEDERLANDS SCHEEPVAART MUSEUM★★

DUTCH MUSEUM OF MARITIME HISTORY

Plan p 11, **MX**
Michelin map no 36 J 12

'his is one of the world's largest maritime museums. It is visible from some distance ɔecause of the ship *Amsterdam* moored in the Oosterdok. The vessel is actually the eplica of a 43m/141ft three-master, the *Batavia*, which sailed the seas in the 18C ınder the flag of the Dutch East India Company.

THE BUILDING *Kattenburgerplein 1*

Since 1973, the Museum of Maritime History has been housed in the building once used by the Admiralty as its main store; in those days, it stood near the Dutch naval dockyard. The building dates from 1656 and was designed by **Daniël Stalpaert**. It stands on 18 000 piles sunk into the bed of the Oosterdok.

It used to store all the supplies necessary for the rigging of the ships built in the shipyards of the Dutch East India Company. The yards covered almost the entire area of Oostenburg, one of the three "eastern islands" (Oostelijke Eilanden) created in the IJ as a result of land reclamation. Today, the islands of Oostenburg, Wittenburg and Kattenburg are connected to the town centre by the two bridges set at each end of the Nieuwevaart.

THE COLLECTION ⓥ

The exhibition, set out in more than 30 rooms, presents the maritime history of the Netherlands in chronological order. The displays present a fairly comprehensive view of mercantile shipping, the Navy and the Dutch fishing fleet through scale models, paintings, atlases, globes, weapons, instruments and supplies, textual sound documents etc illustrating the great moments in the history of seafaring. A 30min film *(with Dutch commentary)* narrates in fascinating detail the expeditions to the Indies (multimedia room, first floor).

The finest exhibits in the collection – *A map of the museum is supplied with the admission ticket. Begin on the first floor.*

Votive offering: model of a three-master – *Room 1.* This superb votive offering dating from 1560 is in the form of a three-master given in thanks for a safe arrival after a dangerous sea voyage. Like all such objects, it bears an expression of gratitude.

Model of a store ship – *Room 1.* This type of large cargo vessel was probably the greatest naval innovation in the 16C and 17C. It was fairly inexpensive and was the commonest merchant vessel in use in Europe in the 17C.

Chart on parchment – *Room 1.* This amazing document was created in Naples in 1515 by Vesconte de Maggioli. It represents the Mediterranean Sea starting with the eastern part of the Atlantic Ocean.

Deed of sale for New-Amsterdam – *Room 1.* This document (facsimile) dated 1631 serves as a reminder that, in 1624, Dutchman Pieter Minuit purchased the island now known as Manhattan from the Algonquin Indians for the equivalent of 24 dollars.

★ **Atlas Blaeu** – *Room 2.* Printed in Amsterdam in 1663 by cartographers Willem Janszoon and Johannes Blaeu (1598-1673), this is a unique copy. It consists of 16 volumes, poetically entitled *Le Théâtre du monde.*

Scene from the Battle between the Dutch and British fleets and a ship in the King of Spain's Invincible Armada – *Room 3.* This blazing seascape (1588) by Hendrick Vroom (1566-1640) illustrates the end of Philip II's naval power.

Naval Battle off Gibraltar – *Room 3.* On 25 April 1607, the Spaniards and Dutch engaged in battle off Gibraltar. This painting (1622) by Cornelis van Wieringen is a spectacular reminder of the furious combat which led to the death of Admiral Jan van Heemskerk.

Admiralty Lion – *Room 3.* Like the eagle, the lion is a symbol of domination, hence its considerable role in heraldry. Here, it bears the letters PPP, meaning *Pugno Pro Patria*, "I fight for my country"; it dates from the 17C.

The Blaeu family's famous wall maps

In the 17C the Netherlands was the main centre of cartography. Amsterdam had three large publishing houses specialising in atlases and wall maps: Hondius, Visscher and Blaeu. Willem Janszoon Blaeu and his son, Johannes, enjoyed an international reputation which lasted thanks to certain paintings by Vermeer in which their wall maps constitute the background to the main subject. This is the case, most notably, in *The Artist's Studio*, displayed in the Kunsthistorisches Museum in Vienna, and in *Woman in Blue reading a Letter*, which hangs in the Rijksmuseum.

A great seafarer

Michiel de Ruyter (1607-76) was born in Flushing. He took part in various maritime campaigns, defeating the English Admiral George Aiscue in 1652. In 1672, after being appointed lieutenant-admiral, he opposed the naval coalition between France and England. Four years later, he was ordered to fight Admiral Duquesne off Messina, because the United Provinces supported Spain in its struggle against France following the revolt of the townspeople against Charles II in this Sicilian community. Despite the fact that his legs had been smashed by a cannon ball, De Ruyter supervised the retreat of his fleet in good order until he drew his last breath. When Louis XIV was informed of his death, he declared, "This man was an honour to the human race."

Admiral De Ruyter – *Room 3.* This painting (1667) by Ferdinand Bol (1616-80) is a portrait of the man who joined the Navy as a mere cabin boy in 1618 and eventually became the country's most famous admiral.

★ **Canal barge** – *Room 5.* This 18C barge was drawn by horses. It was originally known as a *treckschuit*, and was used to carry passengers along canals. It took almost 12 hours to reach Rotterdam from Amsterdam.

Rudder heads – *Rooms 5 and 6.* In maritime parlance, the head is the top section of the rudder. Some of them, like this one, combined the aesthetic with the functional and were shaped like a Turk wearing a turban, the head of Flora the goddess, the head of an oriental woman etc.

Bronze cannon – *Room 7.* Cast in 1695 by Claude Fremery for the Dutch East India Company, this gun fired six pound cannon balls. It was found in the wreck of the ship *Hollandia* which sank in 1743. The gun mounting has been rebuilt.

★ **Boarding weapons** – *Room 8.* Muskets (for long-distance fire), bombards (also known as hand cannons), pistols (for close combat), cannon primers, axes, crows' feet, grappling hooks, defensive pikes etc.

Chronometer – *Room 9.* Made by Ferdinand Berthoud in 1788, this chronometer was used to calculate longitude. Berthoud was one of the most distinguished clockmakers able to put into practice the progress made by physicists.

Dutch East India Company shipyards – *Room 10. See also Introduction, The Golden Age.* This anonymous 18C engraving illustrates the East India Company's shipyards in which some 1 300 men (in 1791) built an average of five ships per year.

The Amsterdam, a replica of the *Batavia*

Model of the *'D'Keulse Galy'* – *Room 12.* This ship sailed the West Indian route. It belonged to the Middelburg Company in Zeeland, which accounted for 20% of the Low Countries' triangular trade (slave trade).

Model of the *Europa* – *Room 17.* This steel frigate weighing more than 3 000t was the last of the great sailing vessels to be launched by the shipyards in Amsterdam, in 1898. The three-masted warship was sold to a foreign country in 1908.

Model of a double-keeled barge – *Room 20.* The double keel enabled suitably equipped vessels to be beached at high tide. This meant that they could land in places with no harbour.

Furniture from a liner – *Room 22.* Designed c 1930 by a specialist in this field, CA Lion Cachet, this pewter-encrusted lounge furniture was placed on board a liner sailing to the Dutch Indies.

★ **Royal barge** – *Room 14.* This superb vessel 17m/55ft in length for a weight of 6t was built in Rotterdam in 1818 to designs by Glavimans. It was last used on the occasion of the 25th anniversary of **Queen Juliana** in 1962.

Flying Dutchman – *Room 28.* The *Flying Dutchman* was the first single-hulled racing yacht equipped with a trapeze and it enjoyed huge success. The boat was designed in 1951 and is almost legendary.

★★ **Replica of the *Batavia*** – *Pontoon. See drawing below.* The three-masted *Amsterdam* is a replica of the *Batavia*, a ship fitted with 32 cannons which sank off Australia in 1629. It is particularly interesting to tour this vessel which is typical of the merchant ships used by the Dutch East India Company. In addition to a number of animated figures *(at the entrance)* which will delight children, the vessel shows the living conditions endured by the crew. In so little space, it is difficult to imagine that approximately 350 people travelled on the *Batavia*.

NIEUWE ZIJDE★★

Plan p 11, **LV**
Michelin map no 36 H 10

The "new side" or Nieuwe Zijde, together with the Oude Zijde, now form the heart of historic Amsterdam. These two districts are both more or less the same age, in other words as old as the city itself. The Nieuwe Zijde corresponds to the western section of the city centre and the Oude Zijde to the eastern section. They were given their names for reasons relating to parish boundaries, when the Nieuwe Kerk was built early in the 15C. Bordered by the Spui, Spuistraat (formerly Nieuwezijds Achterburgwal) on one side and by the Damrak and Rokin on the other, the Nieuwe Zijde is crisscrossed by narrow alleyways and streets that recall its original layout. Today, however, tourism and the resultant commercial activity have made this layout less visible.

★★ **Begijnhof** – *See BEGIJNHOF.*

★★ **Amsterdams Historisch Museum** – *See BEGIJNHOF.*

Rokin – *See BLOEMENMARKT.*

★ **Dam** – *See DAM.*

Damrak – This street is constantly crowded with people heading to and from the central railway station. Originally, it was a canal flowing into the Dam and leading to the public weights and measures office. In the 13C, this was a basin covered with sailing boats from the Baltic. A distant reminder of this can be seen north of the Stock Exchange where the pleasure boats tie up.
Today Damrak is lined with cafés, exchange bureaux, hotels and souvenir shops making it impossible to try and imagine that this was historically the city's harbour. The building of the central station sounded the death knell for its maritime soul.

★ **Beurs van Berlage** – *Damrak 277.* This is a vital building in the history of the city and in the history of 20C architecture. The Stock Exchange is the main masterpiece of **Hendrik Petrus Berlage** (1856-1934). For a fuller appreciation of the contribution of the red-brick building to modern architecture, bear in mind that it was completed in 1903. At the beginning of the 20C, the Stock Exchange indicated new ideas in the treatment of external architecture – simple materials and the end of historicism.
Berlage's Stock Exchange laid the foundations for rationalist architecture in the Netherlands. The building was designed to fulfil precise functions and drawn to strict geometric proportions. The external result of this creative approach is the harmony that is the outstanding feature of the long façade stretching along Damrak. Since 1984 when the Stock Exchange left the building, it has fulfilled other functions in the three areas provided by the architect. An exhibition and conference centre now occupies the central foyer and the former commodity exchange. The other two smaller areas house a concert hall in what was once the stock exchange itself, and a rehearsal room in the former grain exchange. The 48 offices in the galleries overlooking the main foyer are used by companies working in the cultural sector and the main entrance has been turned into a café. The restoration and refurbishment of the building were brilliantly undertaken by architect Pieter Zaanen.
The original decoration of the Exchange has been left untouched and remains clearly visible. The sculptures are by Lambertus Zijl and Mendes da Costa, the murals by Jan Toorop and Roland Holst, and the stained glass by Derkinderen. The mottos on the sundials "Duur Uw Uur" (Last out your time) and "Beidt Uw Tyd" (Bide your time) are by the Symbolist poet Albert Verwey, co-founder of the review, *De Nieuwe Gids*, in 1885.
The **Beurs van Berlage Museum** ⌚ contains a small permanent exhibition relating to the construction itself. It reveals that 4 880 piles were necessary to support the nine million bricks used for the 141m/458ft long building. The tour includes th

Mercury, god of business

Mercury, known in Greek as Hermes, was the son of Jove, or Jupiter. In the world of the Ancient Romans and Greeks, he was the god of business and industry. He is shown as a young man, fleet of foot, usually holding a stick around which two entwined snakes are curved. He symbolises trade and prosperity.

He was, needless to say, a pagan god who was also the god of thieves. Makes you think, doesn't it?

Ph. Gajic/MICHELIN

Mercury no longer stands guard over the quotations on the Stock Exchange

austere but elegant Chamber of Commerce meeting room (decorated throughout by Berlage) and the magnificent **exchange hall** (area 1 665m^2) in which the balcony is decorated with a statue of Mercury.

The tour ends with the viewing platform at the top of the clock tower rising to a height of 39m/127ft (95 steep steps). From the platform there is one of the most interesting **views**★★ of the city centre, encompassing the IJ and central railway station to the north; the chimneys of the blast-furnaces to the west; the royal palace and Nieuwe Kerk to the south west; the Rembrandt Tower to the south east; and the Oude Kerk and Scheepvaarthuis to the east.

Sexmuseum Amsterdam Venustempel – *Damrak 18.* The objects and documents on display are mainly in bad taste and the term "museum" is frankly a distortion of the truth. The unpleasant realism of certain photographs is, in some cases, nothing short of sinister.

Centraal Station – When it was decided to build Amsterdam's railway station, just after the development of the railways, there was lively discussion as to its location. Despite the contrary view of the City Council which preferred the Leidsepoort area (now Leidseplein), the government accepted the proposal put forward by the State Engineer. It was therefore decided, much to the displeasure of the local people and those who felt deeply about the "Venice of the North", to close off Amsterdam's opening onto the IJ, in other words to close off the city's seaboard. It was to be a decision with huge consequences.
It took seven years to build the central station on three manmade islands and 8 700 piles. **PJH Cuypers** (1827-1921), the architect of the Rijksmuseum, and **AL van Gendt** (1835-1901), the architect of the Concertgebouw, completed a gigantic neo-Renaissance building in 1889. The red and white brick façade visible from Damrak has now become one of the best-known buildings in the city centre. It has two square towers bearing a clock *(right)* and a weathervane *(left)*.
Tradition has it that Tokyo's central station is a replica of the building designed by Cuypers and Van Gendt.

Sint-Nicolaaskerk – Nicholas is the patron saint of seafarers, which explains why the capital of the Netherlands, very much a maritime city until the building of the central railway station, has several churches dedicated to the saint. He is equally famous in Nordic countries, as a bringer of gifts. Indeed *Sinterklaas*, which has become "Santa Claus" in Britain and the USA, gave rise to the Father Christmas we know today. On the evening of 5 December, children used to put their wooden clogs in front of the fireplace, filled with hay to feed the saint's horse. The next morning, they found their clogs full of sweets.
The Roman Catholic church was consecrated in 1888, having been commissioned by the congregation of *Ons' Lieve Heer op Solder* (Our Lord in the Attic) from AC Bleys (1842-1912). He designed a neo-Renaissance building in which the main features are the black marble columns and the wooden vaulting.

OOSTERDOK

Plan p 11, **MX**
Michelin map no 36 J 12

The Oosterdok is the basin running along the Prins Hendrikkade. The boats tied up here bring a maritime atmosphere to the city centre, a reminder of the Amsterdam of old. Around the Oosterdok are basins and narrow canals marking out the tiny islets claimed back from the sea during the glorious days of the India Company. Today, the tang of the ocean and memories of sea voyages still fill the air even though the building of the central station and its railway lines has unfortunately, and permanently, isolated the historic city centre from the IJ which flows down to the North Sea.

Schreierstoren – Tradition has it that it was near this semi-circular tower (late 15C), part of the old town walls, that sailors' wives used to come and say goodbye to their husbands, hence its name ("Weepers' Tower"). A bas-relief dating from 1569 illustrates the scene.

A bronze plaque mounted here in 1927 by the Greenwich Historical Society recalls the voyage of the English navigator **Henry Hudson** (c 1550-1611), who set sail westwards in 1609 in the name of the Dutch East India Company and sailed up the North American river which now bears his name. His ship was called *Halve Maen* meaning "half-moon". One year later, commissioned by merchants from London, he crossed the ocean on board the *Discovery* and entered the bay that was later given his name, but the crew mutinied and abandoned him on land without any weapons or food.

Behind the tower, at 8 Geldersekade, is a former warehouse. The stone frontage indicates that it was used for the tobacco trade.

★ **Scheepvaarthuis** – *Prins Hendrikkade 108-114.* The House of Navigation is generally considered by historians to be the first real building designed by the Amsterdam School. It was completed in 1916 to house the offices of six shipping companies. Its main architect was **Johan Melchior van der Mey** (1878-1949) who was assisted by Piet L Kramer and Michel de Klerk, three followers of Berlage who designed the Stock Exchange *(see NIEUWE ZIJDE, BEURS VAN BERLAGE)*.

The building is full of vertical lines and is noticeable for its truly unusual style, emphasised from close up by a multitude of simplified decorative details reminiscent of Art Deco (whales, mermaids, waves, ships). The sculptures adorning the frontage are by Hendrik Albertus van den Eijnde (1869-1939).

No 131 Prins Hendrikkade was the home of Admiral **Michiel de Ruyter** *(see NEDERLANDS SCHEEPVAARTMUSEUM)* who is depicted in a stone medallion on the façade.

Follow Binnenkant and continue along the Waals Eilandsgracht, a canal crossed by a bridge designed by J-M van der Mey.

★ **Oude Schans** – The old St Anthony's Dike was turned into a canal in the decade following 1510 after Gelderland's troops were attacked. The canal still has its erstwhile charm, thanks to the simple beauty of the architecture of the houses lining its banks. The ceaseless toing and froing of barges add life to the waterway. There are some fine cartouches on the house fronts (for example, no 171), barges and house boats are tied up here, and people out walking seem to be in less of a hurry. The real charm of this canal, however, is impossible to describe. Admiring nightfall from the banks of Oude Schans after a wonderful day is one of the unforgettable memories of a visit to Amsterdam.

At no 39 is the Pepper House recognisable for its heavy bars closing off the central window. In the 17C pepper was as valuable as gold.

Montelbaanstoren – *Oude Schans 2.* This delightful fortified tower (1512) used to be part of the town walls, like the St Anthony Gate. The origin of its name remains open to doubt although there are those who believe that it is a distortion of the French word "Montauban" either in homage to the town in Aquitaine in the south west of France, which was a former Protestant stronghold, or in honour of Renaut de Montauban, one of the four Aymon sons.

The Baroque spire was added by Hendrik de Keyser in 1606 and is reminiscent of the bell tower on the Oude Kerk built some 40 years earlier. The tower, which used to afford protection for the St Anthony Dike, is now the headquarters of the city's water department.

★ **Nemo** ⌚ – *Oosterdok.* This museum is subtitled Science and Technology Center. Its massive green bulk resembles a ship ready for launch. It was the Genoese architect **Renzo Piano**, designer of the Centre Pompidou in Paris (with Rogers) who designed the enormous hull facing in the direction of the IJ. To enjoy the **view**★ use the upper entrance via the long ramp.

Its attractive, hands-on display makes it a good introduction for young children to the development of science and technology

The centre is divided into sections called "districts". They enable visitors to learn while enjoying themselves. The museum has been designed so that visitors can touch and handle equipment and attend demonstrations *(in Dutch)*. Children can, for example, use interactive equipment to experience the effervescence of a virtual stock exchange (Level 1), imagine themselves at the wheel of a tanker (Level 2) or carry out scientific experiments (Level 3). The Actua terminals provide information about the day's events (click on *vandaag* or "today").

Vereniging Museumhaven Amsterdam – *Oosterdok.* Opposite the replica of the *Batavia* belonging to the Nederlands Scheepvaart museum are a dozen boats forming a small open-air museum. Among them, note the *Stern*, an attractive clipper 25.7m/83ft long which was launched in 1910.

What is a clipper?

A clipper was a large ship with an elongated hull and enormous sails, designed to take full advantage of prevailing winds. Between 1820 and 1870, they were admired by people all over the world for their speed. They get their name from the verb "to clip", in the American sense of "move fast". The first clippers were built in the USA. By the end of the 19C, they were gradually being replaced by gigantic steel-hulled vessels with five, six or even seven masts.

★★ **Nederlands Scheepvaart Museum** – *See NEDERLANDS SCHEEPVAART MUSEUM.*

Werf 't Kromhout – *Hoogte Kadijk 147.* This shipyard is part of the Nederlands Scheepvaart museum; it has been operating since the mid 18C. Its small museum (the opening times are fairly arbitrary) contains a number of ship's engines in working order, illustrating the development of maritime technology since sailing ships were replaced by steam, ie since the second half of the 19C.

Entrepotdok – Along the banks of this canal are 84 warehouses constructed between 1708 and 1829; they were turned into offices, cafés and council housing from 1985 to 1988. It goes without saying that these council houses are fairly sought after, a credit to the architects (AJ and J van Stigt) who were responsible for their redevelopment. When the warehouses stretching over a distance of 500m/542yd were first completed in 1829, they formed the largest set of storage buildings in Europe.

This magnificent example of urban renovation has retained its old neo-Classical gate (1830) opening onto Kadijksplein. In order to prevent smuggling, the gate used to be well guarded; it was the only entrance to the warehouses. If you study a town plan, you will see that it stood in the immediate vicinity of the canal's only opening onto Oosterdok and the harbour.

M. Guillou/MICHELIN

Pelikaanbrug, Nieuwevaart

Ph. Gajic/MICHELIN

De Gooyer Mill

In fine weather, the pavement cafés of Entrepotdok provide quiet, unusual surroundings for visitors wishing to get away from the crowds of the city centre.

Molen de Gooyer – *Funenkade 5.* Amsterdam still has six windmills within the city boundaries. This one is said to have been the country's first flour mill to have aerodynamic sails. It is thought to date from 1725. Originally, this rotating cap mill, also known as Funenmolen, stood further west near the Nieuwevaart basin. It was moved after the building of the Orange-Nassau barracks (1814) on Sarphatistraat, a building which had deprived it of the wind.
The superb octagonal **gallery** was fully restored in 1925. The lower section of the mill is now a private house. The brick base comes from an old pumping mill which used to stand on this site; it was demolished in 1812.

OUDE ZIJDE★★

Plan p 11, **LX**
Michelin map no 36 H 10, J 10 and J 11

The "old side" is part of the historic city centre. It got its name in the early 15C *(see NIEUWE ZIJDE)*. Originally it centred on the Oude Kerk; later it spread eastwards with the arrival of Jewish refugees from Portugal and Spain in the late 16C.
Today, the Oude Zijde includes the famous "red light district" whose outlandishness should not conceal from visitors the more architectural and historical charms of the "old side" of the city.

A close-up of the organ in the Oude Kerk

★★ RED LIGHT DISTRICT OR THE WALLETJES

Set within a dense network of canals and narrow streets and flanked to the west by Warmoesstraat, to the south by Damstraat and Oude Doelenstraat, to the east by Kloveniersburgwal, Nieuwmarkt and Geldersekade, this district is famous throughout Europe. Reactions may be varied but the district never leaves anybody indifferent. Moreover, much of the historic old town can only be seen by entering or crossing this district, where organised prostitution is rife.
Centring on Oudezijds Achterburgwal, the first features of the red light district to attract visitors' attention are the shop windows lit with pink neon lights in which prostitutes pose, wearing very little. This is almost a tourist attraction in itself, a fact that is confirmed in the early evening when crowds of tourists bustle along the streets, with facial expressions that combine amazement and a rather embarrassed smile.
The locals use the word "Walletjes" to describe this district frequented by seafarers from the 14C onwards. The word means "small walls" and refers to the fact that the shop windows displaying the ladies' charms are sometimes ensconced in old, particularly narrow streets (especially south of the Oude Kerk, between the Warmoesstraat and the Oudezijds Voorburgwal). Unfortunately, the days of the seafarers and distilleries have now gone. The attraction is now used as the basis for an industry that is equally colourful but much less light-hearted, full of sex shops and stores selling pornographic videos. Visitors will not be surprised to see a great deal of distress and unhappiness in this district, and groups of drug addicts trying to deal in some illegal substance or other. The district is not dangerous, but visitors should nevertheless be on their guard as the area is well known for its pickpockets and bag-snatchers.

J.-P. Lescourret/PIX

★ Oudezijds Voorburgwal

Huis Leeuwenburg – *Oudezijds Voorburgwal 14.* This picturesque façade of rustred brick topped by a stepped gable (17C) decorated with lead-mounted tiles is adorned with a carved stone representing a fortress containing a lion.

★ **Museum Amstelkring Ons' Lieve Heer op Solder** ⌚ – *Oudezijds Voorburgwal 40.* After 1578 Roman Catholics were forced by the Reformation to abandon their churches, and they therefore celebrated Mass in private homes. Although Catholic worship was officially forbidden, it was nevertheless tolerated (an example, as far back as the 17C, of the spirit of tolerance so dear to the people of Amsterdam).
The **Secret Chapel**, "God in the Attic", was laid out in the lofts of two houses and used for worship from 1663 until the building of the new church dedicated to St Nicholas in 1887 *(see NIEUWE ZIJDE)*. Certain ceremonies are still held here and concerts are sometimes performed in the chapel.
The stairway to the second floor passes in front of the "drawing room", an authentic Dutch 17C interior, and the vicar's bedroom with its box bed. The **church**, in which the two rows of galleries correspond to the third and fourth storeys, contains interesting 18C furnishings, including a Baroque fake marble **altar** backed by an altarpiece by Jacob de Witt, known as *The Baptism of Christ*, and a small organ. There is also an interesting collection of silver liturgical objects

The astonishing clandestine chapel, Ons' Lieve Heer op Solder or "God in the Attic"

★ **Oude Kerk** ⓥ – *Oudekerksplein 23.* The Old Church, constructed in brick, was built in 1306 and dedicated to St Nicholas. Its date of construction makes it the oldest church in the city. The building was miraculously spared by the fires that took hold of the city in 1421 and 1452. To each side of the east end of the church are the baptistery, a former vestry and 17C and 18C houses. The Old Church was so named after the building of the New Church *(see DAM, Nieuwe Kerk)*; it juts up from the red light district. The shop-window displays opposite the north side of the church are a surprising, and slightly anachronistic, sight. The octagonal wooden steeple (31m/102ft) rising above the bell-tower was once a landmark for sailors; it is 36m/118ft high. The **view**★★ from the top, particularly of the complex construction of the roof, is breathtaking. The tower was added in 1565 by Joost Janzoon Bilhamer. It contains a peal of 47 bells, some of which were cast in 1658 by **François Hemony**.

Interior – The interior was badly damaged by iconoclasts in 1578. It consists of a nave and side aisles with wooden vaulting. The general impression is one of austerity, an impression that is further heightened by the horizontal beams spanning each double bay. The vaulted side aisles regained their elegant 15C paintings in 1955 when a coat of 18C distemper was removed. Above the entrance to the nave is the **organ loft**★ built in 1724 by Jan Westerman. The pipes made by C Vader and J Casper-Müller produce a sound that is highly acclaimed by music lovers. Note the biblical figures and, beneath the organ loft, the imitation marble panels restored in 1978 by Henk Dogger.

The Lady Chapel (north aisle) contains three **stained-glass windows**★ (1555) designed by Pieter Aertsen (1509-75). They represent the Immaculate Conception, the Visitation of the Virgin Mary and the Dormition of the Virgin Mary.

Numerous famous people have been buried in the Old Church, as can be seen in the layout of tombstones. These include Saskia, the wife of Rembrandt van Rijn; artist Pieter Aertsen; writer Roemer Visscher; composer Jan Pietersz. Sweelinck; architects Justus and **Philip Vingboons**; and several admirals, among them Jacob van Heemskerck (1567-1607), who was killed by the Spaniards off Gibraltar after seeking a passage to the Indies via the Arctic Ocean, and Abraham van der Hulst (1619-66) who was killed in the "Four Day" Battle.

The church is used for a range of events such as organ concerts, exhibitions, and drama productions.

Prinsenhof – *Oudezijds Voorburgwal 197.* The "Princes' Court" was once the residence of princes before being used by the Admiralty for meetings. It housed local authority offices in 1808 when the City Hall was turned into the royal palace on the orders of Louis Bonaparte (the building had already housed the departments from 1652 to 1655).

After the building of the Stadhuis en Muziektheater in 1987, the Prinsenhof was turned into a luxury hotel, *The Grand*. The Café Roux housed in the former canteen is decorated with a wall painting by **Karel Appel** called *Vragende Kinderen* (Children Asking Questions).

Universiteitsmuseum De Agnietenkapel – *Oudezijds Voorburgwal 231.* *See BLOEMENMARKT.*

Oudezijds Achterburgwal

Hasj Marihuana Museum ⓥ – *Oudezijds Achterburgwal 148.* This is the only museum of its kind in Europe, retracing the history of cannabis which was already being grown in China in 2800 BC.

Waalsekerk – The Walloon church is all that remains of the monastery of the Brothers of St Paul. In 1586, the city council gave the church to French-speaking members of the Reformed Religion who came from the Low Countries to seek refuge in Amsterdam in the mid-16C, so that they could continue worshipping in French.

Kloveniersburgwal

Nieuwmarkt – Despite its name the "New Market" is the oldest in the city. This huge cobbled square, which separates two canals (Kloveniersburgwal and Geldersekade), has become a colourful venue at the junction of the tiny **Chinese district** and the red light district.

Waag – The public weigh-house in the centre of the square is the oldest civil building still visible in Amsterdam. It is, in fact, St Anthony's Gate dating from 1488, once part of the city walls. In 1617, the impressive fortified gate flanked by towers and turrets was turned into the public weigh-house because the moat that had once surrounded it had been filled in, thereby removing the gate's original purpose. People came here to weigh butter and cheese before it was put on sale. The massive building was restored in 1996; it now houses a restaurant and a café.

The Anatomy Lesson – The surgeons' guild had a dissection laboratory in the octagonal tower in the centre of the public weights and measures office. Housing the Anatomisch Theater (anatomy room), the room is of interest because the guild asked **Rembrandt** to come here to prepare the sketches for his famous paintings of the anatomy lessons given by Dr Tulp and Dr Deijman. The first of these works (1632), painted when the artist was 26 years old, can be seen in the Mauritshuis in The Hague; the second (1656) is displayed in the Amsterdams Historisch Museum. The later work gives a more accurate picture of an anatomy lesson than the work painted in Rembrandt's youth and now in The Hague.
In 1723, fire irremediably damaged three-quarters of the painting, which was undoubtedly influenced by Borgianni's work, *The Dead Christ*, and by Mantegna's painting of which Rembrandt is known to have owned an engraving. As a result of the fire, the face of Dr Deijman and seven spectators are missing. This means that, in its original form, the work is one of the group portraits that made Dutch painting so famous. The man to the left of the cadaver is the assistant, Gysbrecht Matthyszoon Calckoen. It was created to pay homage to Deijman who succeeded Tulp as inspector of the College of Medicine in Amsterdam.

Trippenhuis – *Kloveniersburgwal 29*. When the brothers Lodewijk and Hendrik Trip had made their fortune from trade in metals and weapons, they commissioned **Justus Vingboons** to design them a residence. He drew a façade that was very much in the French style (1662) built of grey stone (now blackened) with a Classical triangular pediment. The eight fluted pilasters with Corinthian capitals are equally Classical in design. The single façade conceals the owners' mansions. Note the chimney stacks in the form of mortars.
In the 19C the house accommodated the collections from the Rijksmuseum ie the "National Museum", including Rembrandt's famous *Night Watch*.

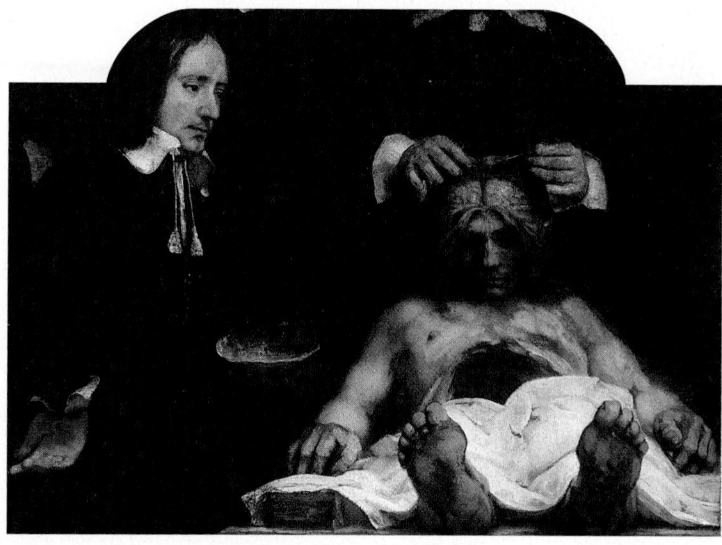

Amsterdams Historisch Museum

The Anatomy Lesson of Dr Deijman, Rembrandt

Ambiguous freedom

Holland is a traditionally tolerant country and has been since the days when Portuguese Jews, British Protestants and French Huguenots poured across its borders. The Roman Catholic Church even survived here despite being a symbol of Spanish oppression and despite the adoption of the Reformed Religion in 1578. Not only did it survive; it flourished, as indicated by the poet Vondel, a literary figure who is an emblem of the Golden Age and who had no hesitation in converting to Roman Catholicism.

Freedom of conscience has been a rule in Amsterdam, cultivated over the centuries as much by ideal as by personal interest. Throughout its history, the city has succeeded in encouraging economic liberalism based on private initiative and free competition. It was within the "hermitage", as Descartes called it, that social liberalism developed. There can be nothing more natural in a town in which merchants and philosophers shared the same ideal, namely to avoid prohibition of any kind.

The city is also a harbour and here, as in all the world's great ports, the arrival of merchandise from many different countries led to a mixing of cultures, and a relatively indulgent attitude to minorities. In the area now known as the "red light district", seafarers found the distractions appropriate to the hard life they led and the isolation lasting several months during long sea voyages. In 1850, Amsterdam had some 20 000 prostitutes.

More recently, in the 1960s, the *Provos* protest movement came into being; it was typically Dutch in style, being both happy-go-lucky and somewhat violent. The decade also saw the national pastoral council refuse to condemn married priests, a position which went against that of the Vatican II council that ended in 1965. Without wishing to form an amalgam of these events, they revealed a division in Dutch society at large and aspirations for change held by many of the population. These aspirations were founded on both **liberty** and **tolerance**.

It was from the 1970s onwards that the Netherlands in general, and Amsterdam in particular, began to protect individual liberties, even if this meant breaking away from what many referred to as collective security. Brothels were officially recognised in 1990 despite the fact that prostitution on the streets was against the law, and this led to the legalisation of shop-window displays. Homosexuality became legal above the minimum age of 16. The consumption of cannabis is accepted in coffee shops but nowhere else.

This brings us to the crucial question of **drugs**. Cannabis is illegal in Amsterdam but the authorities have distinguished between the so-called "soft drugs" (marijuana, hash) and "hard drugs" (LSD, heroin, crack, medicines, cocaine, ecstasy or "E"). The city council tolerates 5g of soft drugs for personal use (the quantity was reduced from 30g to 5g at the request of France) and these drugs are on sale in the hundred or more registered coffee shops where customers are not allowed in unless they have reached the age of majority. These coffee shops also have "cakes" on the menu. Do not let this mislead you – they, too, contain pot or hash and eating them can cause you a few very unpleasant surprises.

Although Amsterdam was one of the first cities in Europe to launch methadone programmes (there are fewer heroin addicts in the Netherlands than in France, Spain and Italy), there still remains a problem which will be visible to observant visitors. It is very easy to obtain soft drugs by walking around the streets and alleyways of the red light district. There are countless pushers here, and there are also *drugspanden* (places, often empty apartment blocks, in which drugs are sold illegally). The pushers are also users, often selling poor quality drugs. This has led the city to set up a foundation that checks the quality of the substance *(Stichting Adviesburo Drugs)*. The borders of tolerance become very difficult to distinguish because it has to be said that many tourists come here solely because they are attracted by drugs and that, for every harmless joint, there is a whole forest of hard drugs.

Kleine Trippenhuis – *Kloveniersburgwal 26.* The stones not required by Justus Vingboons (see above) are said to have been used to build this small house for the Trip brothers' coachman. Although by no means a patrician residence, it is nevertheless very picturesque.

Oost Indisch Huis – *Corner of Kloveniersburgwal and Oude Hoogstraat 24.* This large house (1605) was once the seat of the **Dutch East India Company** *(see Introduction: The Golden Age)*. Ships returning from the Far East laden with various spices and fine porcelain tied up in front of this building, said to have been designed by **Hendrick de Keyser** (1565-1621).

The interior, now the home of the Faculty of Political Sciences, has not retained any of its erstwhile splendour. However, note the elegant yellow sandstone window surrounds in the inner courtyard, and, on the south wall, a wide balustraded gable.

In the vicinity of the three canals

Warmoesstraat – Around 1550, this street, which corresponds to an ancient town dike, was the main trading street. It is difficult to imagine that it was the home of leading traders and merchants prior to the building of Herengracht. Now it is lined with cheap hotels and sex shops.

Koffie- en Theemuseum ⓥ – *Warmoesstraat 67.* Geels & Co has belonged to the same family for more than a century. On the first floor it has opened a small tea and coffee museum.

Zeedijk – Over the past few years the "Sea Wall" has lost its overpowering shop windows and regained something of its natural charm. It is a historic place because it was probably the city's first dike, from which it got its name, "Dike on the Amstel". At the beginning of the street is one of the only two surviving timber houses in the city; the other one is in the beguine convent *(see BEGIJNHOF)*. It dates from the mid-15C. Note the astonishing presence of the **Buddhist temple**, opened by Queen Beatrix in September 2000.

See BLOEMENMARKT. The tour follows and crosses Kloveniersburgwal, Oudezijds Achterburgwal and Oudezijds Voorburgwal.

OUDERKERK AAN DE AMSTEL

Plan p 13, **CR**
Michelin map no 36 V 11

Ouderkerk aan de Amstel to the south of the city is older than Amsterdam itself. It lies at the confluence of the Bullewijk and Amstel, the river to which it owes part of its name. The river banks are lined with delightful cafés in this picturesque little village which is popular with the people of Amsterdam on a Sunday. The trip is an old custom because Amsterdam's citizens had no church until the early 14C; before then, they used to travel out to the church built on the banks of the Amstel in the 11C. The old church ("*Oude Kerk*" in Dutch) was destroyed by a storm in 1674.

Sint-Urbanuskerk – The church dedicated to St Urban was consecrated in 1867; it was built to designs by **PJH Cuypers** (1827-1921), the architect responsible for the Rijksmuseum and Amsterdam's central station. Its spire rises to a height of 50m/162ft.

Oudheidkamer ⓥ – *Kerkstraat 4-6.* This small local history museum occupies three early 18C houses built for deaconesses.

Portugees-Israëlitische Begraafplaats – The Jewish cemetery dates from 1614 and is an unexpected site. It contains more than 1 000 tombstones inscribed in Portuguese and Hebrew, surrounded by luxuriant foliage and shrubs that have grown up over the years.

De PIJP

Plan p 12, **BP**
Michelin map no 36 L 10

This district lies to the south of the city centre, flanked by the Amstel to the east, Singelgracht to the north, Boerenwetering to the west and the Amstel Canal to the south. It is, therefore, an island, linked to the surrounding areas by 16 bridges.
Where does its surprising name ("The Pipe") come from? Some people believe that it is a reminder of the chimneys on the Heineken brewery whose outlines resembled pipes; others refer to the long, narrow ditches that ran through the district before they were filled in.
De Pijp has always been a working-class district, but its population is now mainly made up of immigrants. Indeed, its heterogeneous character has earned it the nickname of "Amsterdam's Latin Quarter".

P. Van Riel/EXPLORER

The old stills in the Heineken brewery

Heineken Brouwerij – *Stadhouderskade 78.* In 1864 Gerard Adriaan Heineken founded the brewery that is now world famous among beer drinkers. It was closed in 1988 when it became too small, and the massive brick building (built in 1934 by BJ and WB Ouerdag) has been used for a quite different purpose since two more modern production plants were opened in Zoeterwoude (near Leyden) and 's Hertogenbosch.
Visitors are required to take a guided tour. Using audio-visual programmes, the tour retraces the history of beer and brewing and the story of the famous brand name Heineken. Visitors are also shown the brewing rooms themselves with the enormous copper stills, and are taken through the stables, a reminder that in days gone by beer was delivered by drays. The tour ends with a chance to taste the product (theoretically this is reserved for visitors over 18 years old).

A product typical of Amsterdam

In the mid-14C, Amsterdam was at the centre of the export trade in Dutch beers for the Baltic. Hop-growing was, and still is, very widely developed in Flanders and the Netherlands. Indeed, the middle Dutch word *bier* gave rise to the words *bière* (French), *birra* (Italian), *beer* (English) and *bier* (German). The distant origin of the word can be found in the Latin verb bibere whose meaning ("to drink") brings us back to the basic function of beer.

★ **Albert Cuypmarkt** – *Albert Cuypstraat.* This multi-racial market, described by certain locals as the "best-known market in the world" has occupied this long street since 1904. The street was named after Albert Cuyp (1620-91), a landscape painter from Dordrecht. The market sells absolutely everything from fruit to clothing, from every country in the world, but mind out – it is also a paradise for pickpockets.

Sarphati Park – Laid out at the end of the 19C, the park pays homage to Samuel Sarphati (1813-66) who funded many social projects in the district. One of them was a bank which financed housing; another was a bakery producing cheap bread.

Gemeentearchief Amsterdam ⓥ – *Amsteldijk 67.* Anybody in Amsterdam wishing to trace their family tree or interested in the city's history can consult the municipal archives.

The department has been housed since 1914 in the former neo-Renaissance City Hall in Nieuwer Amstel, a district founded in the 12C which was not annexed to Amsterdam until 1869. The archives contain the official document dated 27 October 1275 by which **Floris V**, Count of Holland, exempted the local people from customs and excise duty. Temporary exhibitions are held here; some of them are extremely interesting.

★DE DAGERAAD

North of the Amstel Canal is a housing estate with 350 working-class homes built between 1919 and 1922 by a housing association. De Dageraad means "Dawn". The association was part of the cooperative of socialist diamond workers which bore the same name.
De Dageraad was included in the list of historic monuments in 1970 and is now a small urban district centring on Pieter Lodewijk Takstraat and widening out to include Burg. Tellegenstraat, Pastoorsstraat, Talmastraat, Thérèse Schwartzestraat, Thérèse Schwartzeplein, Henriette Ronnerstraat and Henriette Ronnerplein.

The Amsterdam School at its peak – A short stroll through De Dageraad enables visitors to understand the extent to which **Michel de Klerk** (1884-1923), the School's most important architect, and **Piet L Kramer** (1881-1961) designed one of the most amazing working-class housing estates of the inter-war years. There is no doubt that the dynamic, organic designs represent, together with "The Boat" *(see WESTERDOK, Het Schip)*, the heyday of the Amsterdam School or, to be more precise, represent the heyday of the "Second" Amsterdam School embodied by these two architects and by **Johan Melchior van der Mey** (1878-1949) who designed the Scheepvaarthuis *(see OOSTERDOK)*. The name refers to the movement's Expressionist period.
The forms used in the houses are unusual, to say the least. Orange-tiled roofs form undulating waves, the beige brick walls are rounded and a totally static symmetry characterises the buildings. Curving lines rise up out of the great straight blocks thrusting skywards and every detail is treated decoratively. This architecture, although designed with a strong sense of social awareness, also has dreamlike quality that cannot fail to touch visitors. Yet within an estate where every building is different from its neighbour, all the windows have been standardised.

BERLAGE'S SOUTH PLAN

To the south of the Amstel Canal is the area known as **"Berlage's South Plan"**, an exemplary design in the opinion of many of the world's town planners. **Hendrik Petrus Berlage** (1856-1934), the architect of Amsterdam's famous Stock Exchange *(see NIEUWE ZIJDE, Beurs Van Berlage)*, created this urban development between 1915 and 1917. The South Plan was a vast project, much more important than De Klerk and Kramer's Dageraad estate designed several years later. By the end of the 19C it had become obvious that the expansion of the city in concentric circles was reaching its limits and, with the dawn of the 20C, the city council approached Berlage and asked him to look into the possibility of an urban development to the south. The commission could not fail to delight an architect with socialist convictions who had created a rationalist style of architecture.
The heart of Berlage's South Plan is shaped like a triangle on the banks of the Amstel. A town plan shows Churchilllaan and Rooseveltlaan meeting at Victorieplein and continuing together into Vrijheidslaan ("Liberty

R. Dechamps/MICHELIN

An unusual outline, Burg. Tellegenstraat 66-76

Street") lying at right angles to the river which is spanned by the Berlagebrug Berlage's greatest source of inspiration was the Austrian town planner and archi tect **Camillo Sitte** (1843-1903), who made an enormous contribution to the urba culture of his day by demanding that towns and cities should be laid out to a for mal plan. The result is a dense, uniform district consisting of groups of houses com bined geometrically, but in such a way as to avoid the banality of the traditiona checkerboard layout.

On **Victorieplein** is a statue of Berlage by Hildo Krop, at the foot of a small towe block which, in its day (1931), was nicknamed the "skyscraper" ("*wolkenkrabber* in Dutch). The building is 40m/130ft high. It was designed by **JF Staal** (1879-1940 and when it was first built it offered every modern convenience – lift, rubbis chute, hot water, electric doorbells and speaking tube.

PLANTAGE★

Plan p 11, **MY**
Michelin map no 36 K 12

Situated to the east of the town centre, the Plantage district was, for many years, th home of the wealthiest members of the Jewish community. It was developed in th late 19C and is now a residential area. Plantage gets its name, of French origin, fror the space allocated to parks and gardens (the Wertheimpark, the botanic garden c Artis and its zoo).

Hortus Botanicus ⓥ – *Plantage Middenlaan 2a.* At the request of the town's pharma cists and doctors, the University of Amsterdam laid out its botanic garden in 168 in order to grow medicinal plants which were, in many cases, supplied by the Dutc East India Company.

In addition to the outdoor gardens, there are two large glasshouses. The first i an attractive palm grove, restored in 1997; the second, known as the "House c Three Climates" has contained numerous tropical plants, among them members c the water lily family, since 1993. The desert section (Africa and South America boasts a very rare cactus, the *Soehrensia bruchii.*

Tradition has it that the first coffee plants to have grown outside Africa, producin arabica, were germinated here.

Hollandsche Schouwburg ⓥ – *Plantage Middenlaan 24.* From the summer c 1942 onwards, during the German Occupation, this theatre, which was opened i 1893, was used as a Jewish transit camp. Between 60 000 and 80 000 Jew passed through here. The theatre has been a memorial since 1962; on the firs floor, there is an exhibition recalling these dramatic events.

Nationaal Vakbondsmuseum ⓥ – *Henri Polaklaan 9.* In 1894, after a major strik by workers in the diamond industry, Henri Polak co-founded the general union c diamond workers (*Algemene Nederlandse Diamantbewerks-bond* or ANDB). I 1900 **Hendrik Petrus Berlage** (1856-1934) completed the building that Polak ha commissioned as the headquarters of the trade union. The outline of the buildin earned it the nickname "*de Burcht*", the Fortress.

Inside, there is a superb **staircase★**, an outstanding example of the architect's dec orative ideas. He used almost nothing but brick, a traditional building material i the Netherlands. Although a rationalist, Berlage had no hesitation in using glaze brickwork to create forms that combined the stark austerity of these man-mac building materials with the rather heavy, severe masses of an almost nec Romanesque style of architecture. *(See also NIEUWE ZIJDE, Beurs van Berlage.*

There could be no better address for the Dutch Trades Unions Museum. The ANDE which was founded in the same year that saw the setting up of the Social Demc crat Workers Party (SDAP), had a historic dimension for the country at large.

Amsterdam, the diamond city?

There are those who refer to Amsterdam as the "diamond city" and it is true that the city boasts more than 200 skilled diamond workers. Today, however, the diamonds produced in the Dutch capital are destined mainly for tourists.

Although Amsterdam has had a diamond industry since the late 16C, since the inter-war years it has not been the main centre for these gems (as it was some 100 years ago when fabulous diamonds were discovered in South Africa). Indeed, the ANDB (union of diamond workers) was dissolved in 1958. Thanks to more flexible legislation and lighter taxation, Antwerp began taking away the Dutch diamond business and, since the end of the 1930s, it has been the world's real "city of diamonds".

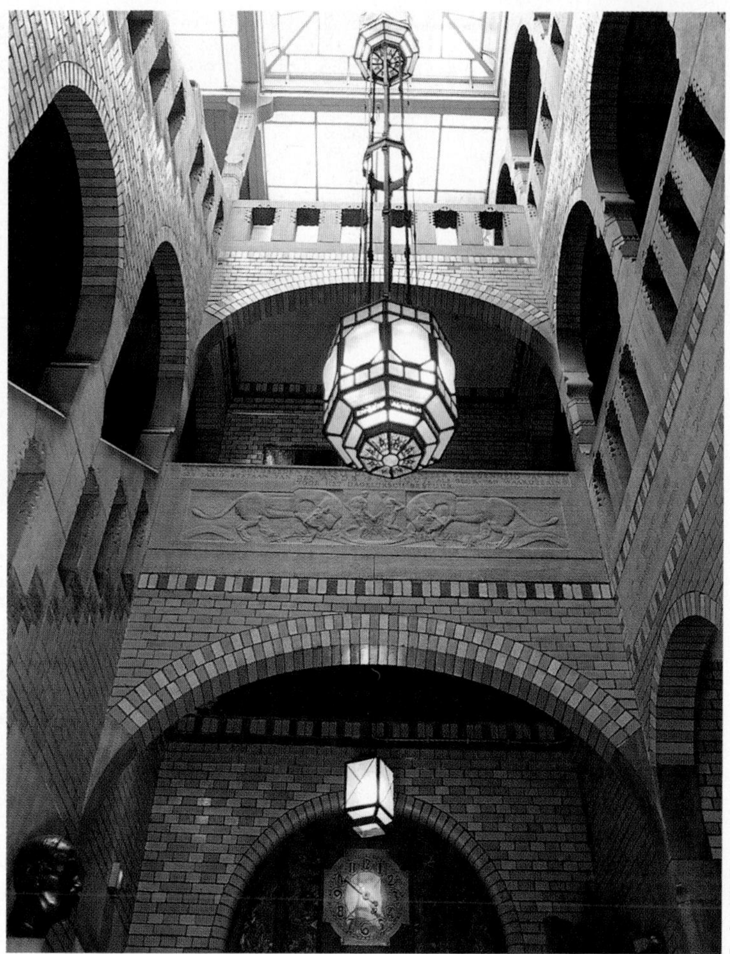

Ph. Gajic/MICHELIN

A forerunner of the Art Deco style: the staircase (1900) in the Nationaal Vakbondsmuseum

this respect the **Art Deco chandelier★** in the staircase, which immediately attracts visitors' attention for its elegance, is equally interesting for its inscriptions in honour of the trades union movement: *offervaardigheid* (spirit of sacrifice), *eenheid* (unity), *bewustheid* (conscience), *standvastigheid* (tenacity). Designed by Jan Eisenloeffel, the triple chandelier was a gift to the trade union in 1919, marking its 25th anniversary.

The permanent exhibition is of special interest to English or Dutch-speaking visitors. It is housed in the Council Chamber (once the diamond industry's "parliament") and in H Polak's former office where the murals are by Richard Roland Holst. The President's chair was a gift from the American Federation of Diamond Workers Unions.

★ **Artis** ⊙ – *Plantage Kerklaan 38-40.* In 1838, the Natura Artis Magistra society, whose Latin name means "Nature, Mistress of Art", opened a vast park commonly known as Artis. This is one of the oldest zoos in Europe as can be seen in the hotchpotch of neo-Classical and modern buildings which house more than 6 000 animals (about 1 200 species). Note the **monkey** pavilion with its astonishing array of orang-outangs, capucin monkeys and mandrills who all show interest in passers-by, and the noisy and colourful **aviary**. Visitors cannot fail to be captivated by the **reptiles** *(the crocodiles' Sunday feed can be seen at 2.30pm)*, the **carnivores** (lions, Siberian tigers), the recently installed **African savannah**, the insectarium, the **gorilla pavilion**, the **seal and sea-lion pool** as well as the powerful white bears. **Jungle by Night** houses nocturnal animals.

The neo-Classical buildings situated on the Plantage Middenlaan form the most interesting part of Artis. The fine **aquarium★**, inaugurated in 1882 and completely restored in 1997, gives an opportunity not only to discover the world of coral reefs but also to get a glimpse of the forms of life present in Amsterdam's canals.

The mandrill

Its basins contain one million litres of water and house some 2 000 species of fish silent actors in a show full of ceaseless, multi-coloured movement. The buildin also contains a zoological museum **(Zoölogisch Museum)** which organises temporar exhibitions. The circular amphitheatre contains the **Diorama Heimans** (lasts 15min which presents the diurnal and nocturnal cycles of the flora and fauna of the dunes Artis also houses a geological museum **(Geologisch Museum)** with exhibitions on th earth's formation and a collection of minerals, precious stones and crystals. Ther is also a **Planetarium** with special sittings for children.

★**Verzetsmuseum** – *Plantage Kerklaan 61.* The Plancius building, constructed i 1876 for a Jewish choir, has housed the interactive Resistance Museum sinc 1999. Film extracts, fragments of sound, life-size photographs and various perio objects evoke occupied Holland at the time of the Second World War. As well a showing the horrors endured in this period, the museum also illustrates daily lif in wartime. What to do in the event of an air raid warning? What were the clan destine newspapers and radio stations at the time? How did Nazi Germany carr out propaganda? How did Resistance fighters send messages? Why did som people not want to hide fugitives? How were false documents produced and hov could one tell if they were false? All these questions are answered by following th museum's itinerary that leads through reconstructed streets and houses of th period. Farewell letters thrown out of train windows by deported prisoners, Star of David and numerous testimonies recall the deportation of more than 100 00 Jews. Other objects such as makeshift radio sets (made in books, matchboxes an cigar boxes), paper toys made by people in hiding, chessboards and Christma trees made in prison, all testaments to human ingenuity in times of adversity Books, magazines and Internet sites can be consulted in the information area.

Muiderpoort – This old gate dating from the early 18C underwent extensive alter ation in 1771 in accordance with plans drawn up by Cornelis Rauws. Forty year later, it was by this gate that Napoleon entered Amsterdam. The town's coat c arms can be seen in the centre of the pediment; the reliefs were carved by Ziesenis.

The Muiden Gate now houses the inland revenue's library.

★**Tropenmuseum** – *Entrance: Linnaeusstraat 2.* It was the father of writer Fred erik van Eeden, co-founder in 1885 of the literary review *De Nieuwe Gids*, wh first mooted the idea of the Tropics Museum. He was an enthusiastic botanist wh created a curio cabinet "as much for the instruction as for the entertainment" c the Dutch people; the collection was registered as a museum collection in 1864 Initially housed in a luxurious villa in Haarlem, the Van Eeden collection was late added to that of the Colonial Museum. In 1910, when the Colonial Institute Foun dation (the forerunner of the Tropics Institute) added these collections to thos belonging to the Natura Artis Magistra Society, it became urgent to erect build ings that reflected the wealth of the Dutch colonies. The museum was bui between 1916 and 1923 to designs by JJ and AM van Nieukerken. The architec ture has a certain majesty; its eclectic style combines exotic features symbolisin the culture of the former colonies, for example the weathervanes in the shape c mythological figures from Garuda (a kite) or Makara (a man who is half-crocodil and half-elephant).

Today the museum is an excellent source of information on the cultures of the tropical and subtropical regions of Africa, Asia, the Middle East, the Pacific and Latin America. The three floors house temporary exhibitions and permanent collections. They cover both art and everyday life (see the picturesque reconstructions of street scenes). Although the layout is sometimes old-fashioned, this should not be allowed to detract from exhibits such as the **Bis masts★** (New Guinea, c 1950) carved out of mango trees and depicting a community of ancestors who were killed by their enemies *(illustration, see Admission Times And Charges)*; the **ceremonial dug-out canoes★** (New Guinea) on which the faces of the deceased are mixed with tortoises, the symbol of fertility; or the set of **animal masks** from West Africa which grant the wearer supernatural powers.

Kindermuseum – The Museum of Childhood is designed especially for children between the ages of 6 and 12. The exhibition is changed every two years and is designed to introduce them to distant cultures in a hands-on display. They can also ask their guide questions *(in Dutch or English)*.

PRINSENGRACHT★★

Map pp 10 and 11, **KV**, **KX**, **KY** and **LY**
Michelin map no 36 H 10, H 9, J 9, K 9, K 10 and K 11

THE PRINCE'S CANAL

The longest and outermost of the four canals encircling the city centre gets its name from William of Nassau, Prince of Orange, the hero of the national uprising against the Spaniards *(see Introduction, Birth of a Dynasty: the Orange-Nassau family)*. The Prinsengracht was dug in 1612, like its neighbour the Keizersgracht, and is arguably less ornate than its three illustrious brothers, at least as regards its domestic architecture. However, the large number of old workshops and warehouses here (this was a less affluent area), the many old churches, the countless houseboats, the absence of any head offices from the banking sector, and the proximity of the Jordaan undoubtedly make this canal the most charming of all the city's waterways.

Like the Singel, Herengracht and Keizersgracht, houses are numbered from the north end up to the Amstel. The house-by-house description enables visitors to see the sights easily as they stroll through this part of the city. The apparent discrepancy between odd and even numbers is not a mistake. It is designed, as far as possible, to cover houses on the same level but on opposite sides of the canal.

★ **Brouwersgracht** – *See JORDAAN and ANNE FRANK HUIS.*

Nos 2-4 – Standing at the corner of the Brouwersgracht, this wonderful house (1641) with its double stepped gable (rebuilt in 1955) used to contain a dwelling and a shop; it is now the *Papeneiland Café*. Its name means "Papists' Island". Its original purpose explains its height and width, both of which were unusual in its day. The windows have lost their traverses over the years. They decrease in size towards the top of the house, a typical feature of old canal houses.
The small house at **no 4** is only one bay wide and is one of the narrowest in the city.

Noordermarkt – The "North Market" has existed since 1627. The organic produce market *(Boerenmarkt, Saturdays)* and the traditional market *(Warenmarkt)* of today uphold tradition here.

Noorderkerk – The church was designed by **Hendrick de Keyser** (1565-1621), the architect of two other main buildings in the city (Westerkerk and Zuiderkerk). He died two years before the work was completed. Building was completed under the direction of his son Pieter de Keyser and the municipal carpenter Hendrick Jacobszoon Staets.
The "North Church" was designed with a central layout and influenced many Protestant churches built in the country because the "Word of God" preached from the central pulpit can be heard all round the church. Note the octagonal layout and the superstructure in the form of a Greek cross. The interior is otherwise of no particular interest.

Nos 89-113: Starhofje – A ***hofje*** *(see JORDAAN)* can be an inner courtyard or a hospice where it has given its name to the buildings round about or the hospice buildings themselves. This one was a hospice, built in

> **The Hofjes along the Prinsengracht**
>
> There were several inner courtyards along the "Princes' Canal": Starhofje (1804) at nos 89-113; Zon's hofje (1765) at nos 159-171 named after a former secret church; Nieuwe Suykerhofje (no longer in existence) at nos 365-369; a nameless courtyard at no 497; and Deutzenhofje (1695) at nos 855-899.

1804. Its precise name is *Van Brienens Gesticht de Star*, a reminder of the *De Sta* brewery which previously stood on the site. It was founded by a wealthy merchant Aernout van Brienen, as a result of a vow made when he was accidentally shut ir his strongroom. Designed by the city architect, Abraham van der Hart, it has a Catholic chapel with a small steeple on the side facing the canal and, hidden within a delightful, well-maintained garden.

No 151 – This large pink-fronted house is strange, amazing, and impossible tc miss. It is topped by a fake balustrade that is particularly dramatic and is an amus ingly quirky piece of architecture. It was erected in the 19C and later underwen some spectacular alterations especially around the windows.

★ **No 36** – This tall, narrow, elegant **façade** dates from 1650. It is very ornate wit a triangular pediment above a neck gable, Ionic pilasters, a festoon beneath the loft door, scrolls, attractively ornate sandstone bull's-eye windows, and flora motifs. The house has been called *De Veersack* ("Sack of Feathers") after the design on the frontage stone.
The façade slopes outward. There are several explanations for this strange propensit on the part of the houses lining canal banks. The houses, say some, are designed fo visual, aesthetic effect; others say that the angle provides protection against snow and rain. More seriously, the design made it easier to hoist goods up to the door in the loft without their becoming snagged on the windows. In 1565, a law limited the slope to 1.25m/3.5ft in order to prevent the collapse of the building as a whole.

No 175 – The façade of this house with a stepped gable dates from 1661. It ha three **decorative frontage stones** depicting two sheep and a cow *(for more informatio on decorative stones, see JORDAAN).*

Nos 187-195 – The row of five **warehouses** has a delightful succession of raised-nec gables. This type of gable is specific to warehouses; it consists of a double pitch and is usually topped by a small, straight gable with rounded cornice. The warehouses a nos 189 to 193 were built in the mid-18C and have undergone very little alteratio since then, apart from the replacing of the loft doors by windows when the building were turned into apartment blocks. There is one eye-catching detail: the doors are no more than 1.80m high (under 6ft), but it has to be said that no goods were take in through the ground floor. The ground floor in no 195 is much higher; it was altered in the early 20C.

★ **Nos 211-217** – The four identical **warehouses** (late 17C) here have typical frontages with small windows and a central loft door on which the shutters are often three-quarters open. This type of building is commonplace at the northern end of the Prinsengracht and along the Brouwersgracht because, in the 17C, this was an industrial area which also provided storage for merchandise.

Nos 235-237: Nieuwezijds Huiszittenhuis – The city's poor knew that they would always be able to find bread and herrings at the "House of the Peripatetic Poor" (1645). Rebuilt in 1850 in a palatial style, no 237 was later used as a harbour workshop then, after 1871, as a fire station. Now it is a hall of residence for students. The tympanum on no 235 illustrates the legend of the founding of Amsterdam by a Norwegian prince and a Frisian fisherman sailing on board their cog with a dog *(see Introduction: Amsterdam's coat of arms)*. The current façade dates from the 19C. The tympanum dates from 1649 and was brought here from another house.

No 126 – The very ornate semi-circular wooden cornice dates from about 1755. The asymmetrical decoration is in the Louis XV style. This type of ornamentation is more commonplace along the banks of the other city centre canals, especially the Herengracht.

Most of the city's warehouses have been turned into flats

Leliegracht – *See ANNE FRANK HUIS.*

★★ **No 263: Anne Frank's House** – *See ANNE FRANK HUIS.*

No 156 – The house stands opposite the Westerkerk. It is topped by a delightfully ornate neck gable (early 18C). The façade is not in line with the house but set at a slight angle in relation to its site in order to respect the alignment of the Prinsengracht (see the line of the hoist). The same feature is perhaps even more noticeable at **no 162**, the house known as "Morning Star" (see the cartouche bearing the word "*Morgensther*"). The T-shaped windows are typical of the mid-19C.

★ **No 281: Westerkerk** ⏱ – The tower on the "West Church" rises so majestically above the Amsterdam skyline that it has become one of the city's landmarks and one of its most appropriate symbols.

Exterior – The church was built between 1620 and 1631 under **Pieter de Keyser** (1595-1676) but was designed by his father, **Hendrick**. From 1985 to 1990, an extensive restoration project gave the original colours back to its brick and stone, building materials that were typical of the Renaissance period in the Low Countries *(illustration, see Introduction: Architecture)*. This is the largest Protestant church in the city.
The **bell-tower**★★ or Westertoren (1638) rises to a height of 85m/276ft and is the tallest in the city. The instability of the soil did not allow the structure to be constructed entirely in stone, which explains why the two upper levels were built in wood faced with lead. The tower contains a remarkable peal of 47 bells (they are rung on Tuesdays, noon-1pm) cast by **François Hemony** *(see BLOEMENMARKT, Munttoren)*. The bell which rings out the hours weighs more than 7t and is the heaviest in the city. The magnificent bell-tower, which features in many of Rembrandt's sketches, is topped by the **Austrian imperial crown** which **Maximilian I** authorised to be included in the city's coat of arms in 1489. After climbing the steps, which will present a major difficulty for the less energetic visitor, there is a splendid **view**★ of the Jordaan.
Left of the entrance is a plaque in memory of Carel Verbrugge (1926-85), better known under the name of **Willy Alberti**, *"Onze Amsterdamse tenore napolitano"* (our Neapolitan tenor from Amsterdam). The realist singer from the Jordaan district celebrated the bell-tower in one of his songs, "*O mooie Westertoren, hoog in tie blauwe lucht*" (Oh, beautiful bell-tower on the Westerkerk, pointing up into the blue sky).

Ph. Gajic/MICHELIN

Interior – The interior is very austere, a characteristic of the Protestant faith as is the fact that the church bears the name of its geographical location rather than that of a saint. This is the largest Protestant church in the country. The nave has barrel vaulting made of wood so as not to add weight to the general structure built on fairly unstable soil. The **shutters** on the organ loft were painted by Gérard de Lairesse (1640-1711) from Liège who introduced to Amsterdam the style developed by Charles Le Brun and Simon Vouet. These are the only paintings in the Westerkerk. The paintings on the upper shutters represent King David dancing in front of the Ark of the Covenant and the Queen of Sheba facing King Solomon, while the lower shutters depict various ancient musical instruments.
It was in this church that in 1669, just one year after his son Titus, **Rembrandt van Rijn** was buried. The exact site of his grave is not known.

No 242 – The frontage is a clear illustration of the main feature of many canal houses: the juxtaposition of styles and historical periods. The house was built in the 17C as is obvious from its height and the timbered shop-front, but the remainder of the frontage is 100 years younger, dating from about 1770. The bell gable is decorated with features in the Louis XV style, an example of which is the assymetry of the finial.

No 349 – A **warehouse** topped by a bell gable is unusual. Such buildings usually sport raised-neck gables. This exception dates from the mid-17C. The warehouse extends 30m/98ft back from the canal, as was usual in Amsterdam, and has undergone very little alteration.

Woonbootmuseum – *Opposite Elandsgracht.* Built in Amsterdam in 1914, the *Hendrika-Maria* is an old industrial sailing boat which has been turned into a houseboat museum. The tour is, of course, short *(mind the companionway at the entrance; it is very steep)*, but it provides an opportunity for a pleasant rest *(drinks are available)*.

Houseboats

Some 2 500 barges and houseboats connected to the gas, electricity and sewage systems line the banks of the city's waterways. Most of them are to be seen on the Prinsengracht and Amstel. In all, they accommodate almost 6 000 people. This type of accommodation became popular in the 1950s when Amsterdam suffered an acute housing shortage. Current regulations prohibit people from mooring their own barges alongside one of the city's quaysides so the only solution open to anybody wishing to live in a barge or houseboat is to buy one that is already in place.
Every three years, the houseboats, one of the city's main attractions, are taken to a boatyard where the hulls are thoroughly cleaned.

★ **No 300** – The attractively decorated **neck gable** flanked by scrolls is undoubtedly one of the finest in the city. It has been remarkably well preserved and dates from approximately 1760. The **timbered shop** front on the ground floor is also eye-catching because of its ornate "frontage beam" ("*puibalk*" in Dutch, the beam that runs across the frontage horizontally and supports the brick masonry above). Such ornamentation is unusual. Above the double doors, the beam is decorated with a fox holding a bird in its mouth; immediately above this, there is decoration in the Louis XV style.

Leidsegracht – *see LEIDSEPLEIN.*

Nos 581-583 – The piano manufacturer **Cristofori** occupies these two warehouses. The pleasant rooms regularly provide the setting for piano and jazz recitals.

★ **Nos 681-693** – This unique row of seven **neck gables** (c 1715) paid homage to the creation and independence of the Republic of the United Provinces, a federation of the seven northern provinces whose names can be seen on the façades: (left to right) Overijssel, Utrecht, Holland, Gelderland, Zeeland, Friesland, and Groningen. Their independence was not actually recognised until 1713 in the Treaty of Utrecht. The house in the centre *(Gelderland)* has a double flight of steps at the entrance; this is a very unusual feature on a frontage that is only three bays wide.

No 436: Paleis van Justitie – The august, wide, neo-Classical façade of the Law Courts is an exception in a city which builds rows of tall, narrow houses along its canal banks. The former orphanage (1665) underwent extensive alterations between 1825 and 1829 and was turned into a building with Corinthian pilasters by Jan de Greef, the city architect. It now houses the Court of Appeal.

Nos 504-506 – It was in this house (the frontage dates from 1860) that **Pietro Antonio Locatelli** (1695-1764) died. He was a virtuoso violinist, a pupil of Corelli and a precursor of Paganini, who settled in Amsterdam in 1729 and became involved in the great movement which aimed to spread Italian music. He was also a composer and publisher and was very popular with Amsterdam's elite to whom he gave lessons.

Nos 771 and 773 – These two **warehouses** *(Elseneur and Frankfort)* were built c 1655 and turned into housing and offices in 1975. Elseneur is named after the Danish port of Helsingør (Elsinore).

No 556 – A **gable in the shape of a ship's hull** is a rarity in Amsterdam (there are only some 20 of them in all). This one was erected in the 19C at the top of a façade built in 1669. It is topped by a triangular pediment.

Nos 855-899 – These three wide houses form the façade of the former **Deutzenhofje** hospice which cared for poor women with no special skills. It was built in 1695 to designs by Agneta Deutz and has undergone very little alteration.

Reguliersgracht – *See REMBRANDTPLEIN.*

Amstelkerk – *Amstelveld 10.* During the building of the church on the Amstel by **Daniël Stalpaert** in 1670, it was understood to be a temporary centre of preaching until such time as a church could be built on Amstelveld on the banks of the Prinsengracht. This explains why the church was built of wood, a building material that is not usually seen on the banks of the city's canals. Part of the building now houses a restaurant.

No 756: De Duif – "The Dove" is a neo-Classical church opposite Amstelveld. This, though, is not the church that was supposed to replace the Amstelkerk. It is a Roman Catholic church whereas the Amstelkerk belongs to the Protestants. It was designed by T Molkenboer in 1857.

RAI

Plan p 12, **BQ**
Michelin map no 36 N 10

ver the past few years, part of the southern end of the capital has become a major usiness centre. There are two railway stations in this area – the Station Zuid, near ıe "World Trade Center" and the Station RAI near the historic "RAI" site.

Amsterdam RAI – *Europaplein.* With a total of some 2.5 million visitors every year, Amsterdam's exhibition centre is one of the world's largest. The origins of its success date back to 1893, the date of Amsterdam's first exhibition, specialising in cycles and cars, hence the name "RAI", the abbreviation for *Rijwiel Automobiel Industrie.*

The exhibition centre has been regularly extended. It now consists of three sections with 11 halls, 22 conference centres, seven restaurants and more than 6 000 car parking spaces. The centre is a veritable hive of business, with numerous agents in foreign countries (USA, South Africa, Thailand etc). It also hosts cultural events (concerts, operas etc).

Peter Stuyvesant Stichting ⌚ – *Drentestraat 21.* This foundation, set up in 1960, has an extensive collection of modern art (sculpture and painting) of which only a selection is on display. The buildings surround a garden laid out by Mien Ruys. All of them (including the gallery) were given their dimensions using the Modulor measurement system that was so popular with Le Corbusier. They belong to a tobacco company.

REMBRANDTHUIS*

Plan p 11, **LX**
Michelin map no 36 J 11

EMBRANDT'S HOUSE

y the time, in 1639, the artist purchased this beautiful, wide-fronted house built in 606, it had already lost its original double stepped gable. **Jacob van Campen** (1595-657), future architect of the royal palace, had altered the frontage just before 1630 y adding an extra storey and erecting a triangular pediment at the top. Rembrandt aid 13 000 florins for the house, payable over six years; in 1658, it was sold to reimurse his creditors. Rembrandt lived and worked here, producing large numbers of orks in his studio on the first floor. Indeed, most of his greatest masterpieces were ainted here.

ıe initial address of the house was Sint-Antoniesbreestraat, meaning "wide St nthony's Street"; it was later renamed Jodenbreestraat in honour of Amsterdam's ewish community.

★ **Museum Het Rembrandthuis** ⌚ – *Jodenbreestraat 4-6.* In 1906, the tricentenary of the artist's birth, Amsterdam city council purchased the house and had it restored. In 1999 the interior of the house was faithfully brought back to its original state thanks to an inventory drawn up when Rembrandt went bankrupt. The various rooms give a good idea of the layout of Rembrandt's lodgings, from the room where he received his clients and sold his pictures (the inspiration behind the "Kunst Caemer" or Art Room) to the room where he taught his pupils the art of painting and engraving.

Woman holding an Arrow (1661) by Rembrandt

The museum's new wing ha a permanent exhibition c etchings by Rembrandt an a few paintings by contem poraries (Dirck Sandvoor Ferdinand Bol and Piete Lastman); it also house temporary exhibitions shed ding light on his work.

The rooms open to the pub lic will convince even th most hardened detractor c etchings that Rembrand was not only a master c chiaroscuro; he was also a outstanding engraver. Nc only did he have stupendou technical skill at every stag of the etching process; h also produced an impressiv range of different subjects There are biblical scenes portraits and self-portraits nudes and genre scenes and scenes from everyda life, some depicted wit complete realism.

The few etchings describe here are, in our opinior both the most representa tive and the most remark able of his works. ***The Thre Crosses***★★ (1653): this serie reveals the various ways i which the artist treated ligh within a single compos ition, in this case Christ a Golgotha. Stage I is much more luminous than Stage IV. ***Self-portrait with a Surprise Expression***★ (1630) is one of the many compositions in which the artist took him self as the subject matter; it is amazing for its spontaneity. ***Woman with an Arrow*** (1661) is an admirable example of Rembrandt's mastery. The shadows in the back ground are represented by very fine hatchring. Is this Venus holding Cupid's arrov or Cleopatra awaiting the arrival of Mark Anthony? There is no documentary answe to this question. *Beggar with a Wooden Leg* (c 1630), a common sight in the street of the Middle Ages and Renaissance, shows that, in this type of subject, Rembranc concentrated his attention on the hands and the facial expression. *Small Dog Sleep ing* (c 1640) will move many visitors because of its finesse and inherent tende ness, but we prefer to draw attention to ***The Three Trees***★★ (1643), a superb piec of work produced with dry-point needle and chisel which shows a technical eas far beyond that of most engravers. The soft shading of the clouds was worke while the plate was being inked; it is then the palm of the hand which decide whether or not the work is ready for printing.

Etching? Child's play!

Cut out a metal plate to the required size (Rembrandt preferred a thin copper plate). Coat with a ground then make your drawing using an etching needle. The lines should cut through the ground and reveal the plate beneath. Once the drawing is finished, place the plate in a bath of nitric acid diluted with water. The acid eats away at the metal. Remove the plate from the bath when you think that it is time to do so. Then remove the ground and coat the plate in ink (NB: only the grooves should remain inked). Dampen a sheet of paper and press the plate down onto it (using a printing press if necessary). The result is what is known as "Stage One".

IN THE VICINITY OF REMBRANDT'S HOUSE

This is the **Jodenbuurt**, c old Jewish quarter, c which only memorie remain *(see ANNE FRAN HUIS)*. It used to stretc from Nieuwmarkt to J Meijerplein. Rembranc saw most of his mode here, people from Spair Portugal, Germany an Central Europe whom h used to personify th heroes of his biblica works. The destruction c the area and removal of i inhabitants both durin and after the Second World War, as well as the increase in car traffic, have resulted in the almost total disappearance of the old buildings. Only a few buildings evoke the Jewish origin of this once prosperous quarter.

Holland Experience ⏱ – *Waterlooplein 17. Also accessible from the Rembrandthuis.* Only its proximity to the Rembrandthuis justifies its inclusion in these pages as there is a surprisingly expensive entrance charge to see a promotional film, even if there is also an "odorama" and a rotating platform.

Zuiderkerk ⏱ – *Zuiderkerkhof 72.* The "South Church" was built between 1603 and 1611 to designs by **Hendrick de Keyser** (1565-1621), hence the resemblance between the **bell-tower★** here (height 70m/228ft) and the one on the Westerkerk (the bells are rung on Thursdays, noon-1pm). This was the first Protestant church to be built in Amsterdam, and it was also the last resting place of its architect. Since 1988 it has been used as a municipal housing and development service. From the bell-tower, there is a superb **view★** of the city centre.

The square, Zuiderkerkhof, was once a graveyard, hence the skull above the gate opening onto Sint Antoniesbreestraat. At no 69 in this street is the beautiful **Huis De Pinto** built c 1680 for the banker Isaäc De Pinto. This is one of the very few survivors of the former Jewish quarter razed to the ground by the Germans and further damaged by recent urban redevelopment projects.

Rembrandt van Rijn

His father was called Harmen Gerritszoon van Rijn; his mother Cornelia Willemszoon van Zuytbroeck. He was a miller, grinding malt for the town's breweries. He was a Calvinist; she was a Roman Catholic. Their eighth child (they had nine in all) was called Rembrandt and he was born in Leiden on 15 July 1606.

In 1620, Rembrandt matriculated at the Protestant University of Leiden, the great rival of the Catholic university in Lieuwen. However, he soon abandoned his study of humanities because he "*showed neither liking nor inclination for them, his natural preferences being for painting and the art of drawing*" as Johannes Orlers wrote in 1641. He immediately began work in the studio of Jacob Isaacszoon van Swanenburgh, remaining there for three years. Then, in 1624, he joined the artist **Pieter Lastman** in Amsterdam. The following year, Rembrandt moved to Leiden as a freelance artist. He was not yet 19 years old.

Museum Het Rembrandthuis

Self-Portrait with a Surprised Expression (1630)

Rembrandt was friendly with the artist **Jan Lievens** with whom he shared a studio until 1631. They were so close that their contemporaries frequently confused their works which were, it is true, inspired by the same themes although Rembrandt's works were smaller in size. Their talent came to the attention of the Prince of Orange, **Frederick-Henry of Nassau**, who soon commissioned works from them. In 1631, Rembrandt moved to Amsterdam where he became a member of the Guild of St Luke in 1634, the year in which he married Saskia Uylenburgh.

There followed a decade of luxury and success. Rembrandt trained his first students, including **Gerard Dou**, who came to work in the master's studio at the age of 15. Rembrandt began selling many of his works, and he moved several times until he finally purchased the beautiful large house in Sint Antoniesbreestraat now occupied by the museum that bears his name. He was rich, he was famous to the point of adulation, and followers came in large numbers, among them **Ferdinand Bol**. He worked, he made purchases, he seemed to be avid to learn about everything except Italy, which he never visited, unlike all the other great artists with the exception of Vermeer. In 1642 he painted his great masterpiece, *The Night Watch*.

Drama struck that same year. Saskia died, probably of tuberculosis. Rembrandt suffered the pain of loss just as his genius was being recognised, bringing glory with it. He soon discouraged his models. He delivered his works late, produced increasing numbers of "stages" when making etchings. He promised works that were never completed, built up debts, became insolvent, and saw his property sold off by auction. Still passing on his great expertise his know-how without paying any heed to material things. the master of *chiaroscuro* died in 1669, one year after the death of his son, Titus.

REMBRANDTPLEIN★

Plan p 11, **LY**
Michelin map no 36 K 10

Even though this square has been spoilt by neon signs, it is still a pleasant place fo
a stroll and a popular meeting place. It is one of the points where the potency of Am
sterdam's night-life can be felt at its most intense. Around the former butter marke
which was the town's first public weights and measures office *(see DAM)* are a numbe
of large cafés and grill-rooms. The square was originally called Reguliersmarkt an
was renamed in 1876. In the centre stands a statue of Rembrandt by Royer (1852

IN AND AROUND REMBRANDTPLEIN

Tuschinskitheater – *Reguliersbreestraat 26-28.* It would be worth going to thi
cinema just to be able to see the luxury of the **Art Deco auditorium★** (Tuschinski 1
in which all-time greats such as Marlene Dietrich and Edith Piaf performed.
The building was funded by Abraham Tuschinski (he died in Auschwitz in 1942
and built in 1921 by HL De Jong. It was originally a theatre. Study the **frontage**;
is a masterpiece in its own right. Step into the foyer to see the magnificent **carpe**
which had to be totally rewoven by hand in accordance with the original cartoon
after being subjected to cigarette and cigar burns for more than half a century!
Opposite, the building that was once the Cineac cinema (J Duiker, 1934) is a goo
example of the differences between Art Deco and Functionalism.

Muntplein – *See BLOEMENMARKT.*

Amstel – In days gone by, the Amstel flowed into the IJ via what is now the Roki
Basin. That was before the building of the dike (or dam) which was to give th
town its name – dam on the Amstel.
Beyond the Halvemaansbrug, on the other bank, is the spire of the Zuiderkerk a
the end of Groenburgwal. Further to the right is the marble and brick façade c
the opera house.

Blauwbrug – Built for the International Exhibition of 1883 by Springer and Gree
the "blue bridge" was said to have been inspired by the Alexander III Bridge i
Paris. It is decorated with sculptures on a maritime theme. At the top of the lam
standards is Maximilian's crown *(see WESTERKERK).*

Museum Willet-Holthuysen – *See HERENGRACHT.*

Colectie Six – *Amstel 218.* Most tourists will find it difficult to get to see this col
lection, but it is included here for the most persevering visitors. Housed in a super
mansion designed by Adriaan Dortsman, the collection has some very fine work
by artists such Thomas de Keyser, Frans Hals, Gerard Terborch and Rembrandt
The latter was a personal friend and a client of Jan Six I, a rich merchant who wa
also the town's burgomaster. The artist painted his portrait in 1654. A descend
ant of the Six dynasty still lives in the house.

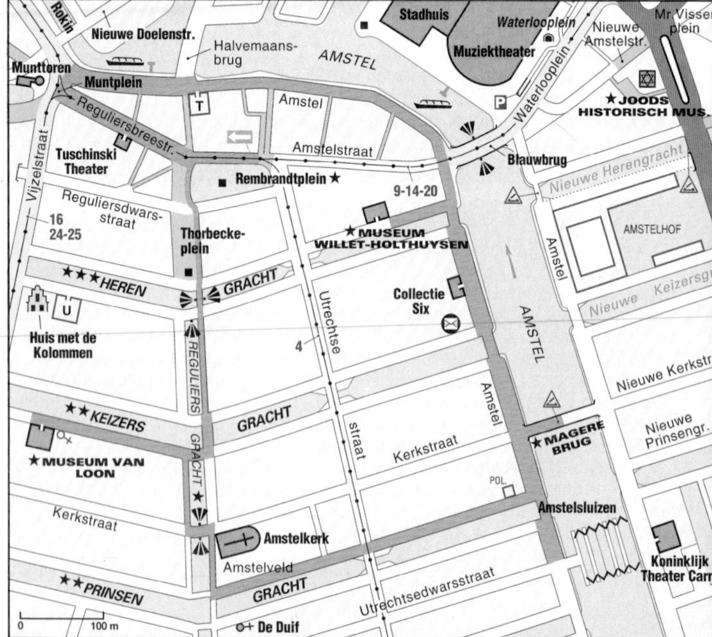

M. Guillou/MICHELIN

The Magere Brug on the Amstel

Opposite, on the other side of the Amstel, are the replica of the Magere Brug opening onto the Nieuwe Herengracht, and the deaconesses' almshouse *(Amstelhof)* built in 1683. The hospice still operates today. For many years, it was the capital's largest building in terms of area.

★ **Magere Brug** – The "Thin Bridge" is a fragile wooden construction, arguably the best-known in the capital. Built in the late 17C, the double-leaf bascule bridge has undergone renovation on many occasions but has remained manually operated. It often features on photographs used to promote the city's tourist attractions, and is a particularly romantic sight when it is floodlit (April to September).

Amstelsluizen – These wooden locks date from the 18C. They are the sluices for the gigantic pumping system that takes fresh water into Amsterdam's canals. They were automated in 1994 and are operated four times a week in summer; in winter the system operates only twice a week.

Koninklijk Theater Carré – *Amstel 115-125.* Built at unbelievable speed in 1887 as a home for the Oscar Carré circus, this neo-Renaissance building now offers a very wide range of entertainments (circus, opera, concerts, musicals, and variety shows).

★★ **Prinsengracht** – The section of the Prince's Canal (Prisengracht) which is flanked by the Amstel and the Reguliersgracht makes an interesting journey for visitors interested in looking at the numerous houseboats and barges which line this route. *(See PRINSENGRACHT for further information on the area included in the itinerary.)*

★ **Reguliersgracht** – This delightful canal built in 1664 was named after the former convent of regular nuns. The idea of enclosing the canal in order to build a tram line was dropped and the canal was then covered by a conservation order. It provides one of the most attractive **views**★★ of any of Amsterdam's waterways. From the bridge spanning the canal beside Kerkstraat, the view encompasses the seven bridges across the Reguliersgracht.

Amstelkerk – *See PRINSENGRACHT.*

★ **Museum Van Loon** – *See KEIZERGRACHT.*

Thorbeckeplein – Like its neighbour, the former butter market is a shady square with a statue (1874, by E Leenhoff) at one end. It represents **Johan Thorbecke** (1798-1872), an eminent figure in the political history of the Netherlands, famous because he was the first editor of the 1848 Constitution. It is a pity that the square is lined with so many restaurants and strip-tease clubs.

RIJKSMUSEUM★★★

Plan p 10, **KZ**
Michelin map no 36 L 9

The museum is one of the city's main tourist attractions, along with the Van Gogh Museum and the canals. It is best known for its outstanding collection of 15C to 17C Dutch paintings, in particular its series of works by **Rembrandt van Rijn** and **Vermeer of Delft**. This collection, brought together under a single roof, is so extensive that the Rijksmuseum, the temple of Dutch painting, should be considered as one of the greatest museums in the world.

THE ORIGINS OF THE COLLECTIONS AND THE HISTORY OF THE BUILDING

Founding by Louis Bonaparte – On 21 April 1808, Louis Bonaparte, brother of Napoleon, signed a decree ordering the setting up of a great national museum in Amsterdam.

By that time, Louis Bonaparte had been King of Holland for two years and he was doing his utmost to serve the interests of his subjects. The founding of the Rijksmuseum was one of the things that Napoleon's brother had time to do before the Emperor annexed the northern Low Countries to France, in 1810. He decided to transfer to the capital city the collection set up in 1798 in The Hague by the French. The collection of 225 paintings was housed in the royal palace which became the "Royal Museum"; it was renamed "Rijksmuseum" (national museum) in 1815.

Geographical location – After being housed in the royal palace for some time, the museum was moved to the Trippenhuis. Over the years, donations, bequests and purchases expanded the collection which soon began to lack space in the Trip brothers' house. Gradually, it became essential to erect a building worthy of the treasures contained in the Rijksmuseum.

When, in 1872, central government announced that it would cover the building and running costs of the future museum, the City Council gave the site free of charge. It lay to the south of the town, outside the ring of canals, near a new area that had recently been reclaimed from the surrounding marshland, now the vast Museumplein. This explains why Museumstraat runs under the museum. It linked the historic city centre to the residential district that was about to be built, beginning with the Concertgebouw.

A "Gothic conspiracy" – In 1875, the plans presented by **Petrus Josephus Hubertus Cuypers** (1827-1921) were awarded first prize in the competition organised by the government. Ten years later, he delivered a building that immediately aroused strong criticism.

It is true that the building does not include the neo-Renaissance ornamentation found in the award-winning designs. The pilasters on the first floor, for example have disappeared and been replaced by purely neo-Gothic designs. This was far from the "Old Dutch style" demanded by the competition rules. However, although the controversy was bitter, it was not based solely on aesthetic considerations. It had quite another reason. Cuypers was considered to be a Symbolist architect, and if he made use of Gothic features, this meant that he had used the Catholic style. Roman Catholics, however, had not really regained freedom of worship until the mid 19C and there were many Protestants who were careful to ensure that a tight rein was kept on their liberties. When the museum was inuagurated on 13 July 1885, it was compared to an episcopal palace and a Gothic cathedral, and it was understood to have resulted from a veritable Roman Catholic conspiracy.

The building and its decoration – The red-brick building has many ornamental features to offer passers-by, too many in fact to be able to describe in detail here. The theme of the decorative features on the façades is the role of the Netherlands in the history of fine arts. The ornamentation was produced by two sculptors, Bart van Hove and François Vermeylen. In the 19C, the leading figure in national art was Rembrandt, which explains why he is represented several times and in life size carvings. The 20C would also have included Vermeer and Hals, but they were not yet recognised as they are today, hence their more discreet presence.

In the centre of the façade, above the Museumstraat passage, is a relief illustrating the Glory of Dutch Art. Flanked by allegories of Wisdom and Justice, the Virgin of the Netherlands (centre) is surrounded by Lucas van Leyden, Claus Sluter, Rembrandt, Jan Steen and Adriaen van der Werff, an artist who has practically fallen into oblivion at the present time. Further up, to each side of the central window, are Art (left) and History (right). Above them is an owl, Athena's bird symbolising Knowledge.

THE COLLECTIONS ⏲

As is often the case in large museums, some of the works are put into storage from time to time, others travel to exhibitions held outside the museum, and the works in store are displayed on a rota basis. Our selection cannot take account of these changes and it is therefore likely that some of the works mentioned will not be on show during your visit.

★★ DUTCH PAINTING (15C-17C)

East wing: first floor

Outstanding works – Even visitors who are confirmed art lovers may not have time to see everything in a museum like this one, with its countless rooms. It would be a pity to miss works that are important in the art history of the Netherlands. The aim of our selection is to present the quintessential works in an art gallery that is remarkably representative of Dutch art production, especially during the period known as the Golden Age. Remember, too, that it is better to appreciate to the full a selection of works than to attempt a marathon tour that will leave few memories other than exhaustion.

The artists are described here in alphabetical order so that you can find them easily in these pages if the exhibition layout has been changed since our visit to the Rijksmuseum. The numbers in brackets correspond to the numbers of the rooms.

Begin in room 201.

Master of ALKMAAR (first half of the 16C) – As his name suggests, very little is known about this anonymous painter except that he seems to have lived mainly in Haarlem rather than in Alkmaar.

★★ ***Seven Works of Misericord*** (1504) *(202)* – This work, still in its original frame, represents the six actions listed during the Day of Judgement and according to which men would be placed to the right or left of Christ. The hierarchy indicated in the Gospels is as follows: Giving food to the hungry; Giving drink to the thirsty; Giving hospitality to strangers; Giving clothes to those who are naked; Caring for the sick; and Visiting prisoners.

Jan ASSELIJN (c 1615-52) – This Dutch artist was probably born in Dieppe. He spent a long period in Italy between 1640 and 1650. He enjoyed an excellent reputation as an animal painter.

The Swan in Danger (c 1652) *(221)* – The words below the swan can be read as "The Grand Pensionary of Holland"; the ones above the lion indicate "The Enemy of the State". They were added by the owner of the work in homage to **Johan de Witt**.

Hendrick AVERCAMP (1585-1634) – The artist, born in Amsterdam, was one of the earliest landscape painters in the Dutch School. He provides a transition between the still archaic Flemish ideas and the aspirations of Dutch realism.

Winter Landscape with Skaters (c 1608) *(209)* – This work, painted on a wooden panel, is reminiscent of the works of Pieter Bruegel the Elder, who died in 1569. The artist shows an acute sense of detail.

Abraham BLOEMAERT (1564-1651) – The artist was born in Dordrecht and died in Utrecht. He lived in Amsterdam from 1592 to 1600. From 1621 onwards, he began creating works that were influenced by the Caravaggists of Utrecht.

The Sermon of St John the Baptist (c 1600) *(208)* – This large painting belongs to the artist's Mannerist period. Note the secondary role of the saint; he is placed under a tree, in the shadows.

Ferdinand BOL (1616-80) – The artist was born in Dordrecht and died in Amsterdam. He was a pupil of **Rembrandt van Rijn**. His realist portraits brought him favour with the elite of Amsterdam.

Maria Rey (1650) and ***Self-Portrait*** (c 1669) *(232)* – A portrait artist had to paint his own portrait. This one shows the artist at the age of 53 (the painting is still in its original frame).

Hans BOLLONGIER (c 1600-c 1645) – The artist was born in Haarlem to Flemish parents. He was influenced by **Adriaen Brouwer**, another Flemish artist known to have been working in Haarlem in 1626. He painted a few "conversation pieces" then specialised in still-life works.

Still Life with Flowers (1639) *(214)* – The variations in the colours of the tulips, anemones, roses, carnations and primulas, and their careful display above the vase are two of the characteristic elements of works created between 1620 and 1640.

Adriaen COORTE (known to be working between 1685 and 1707) – Little is known about this artist who specialised in still-life canvases. Technically, he should be associated with the pupils of a great master of this genre, **Willem van Aalst**.

Still life with Asparagus (1697) *(219)* – Set against a black background is a simple bunch of asparagus, its tips attractively tinged with green and purple. The small work (paper on wood) is created with a wonderful transparent glaze. The companion work is in the Hermitage Museum in St Petersburg.

RIJKSMUSEUM

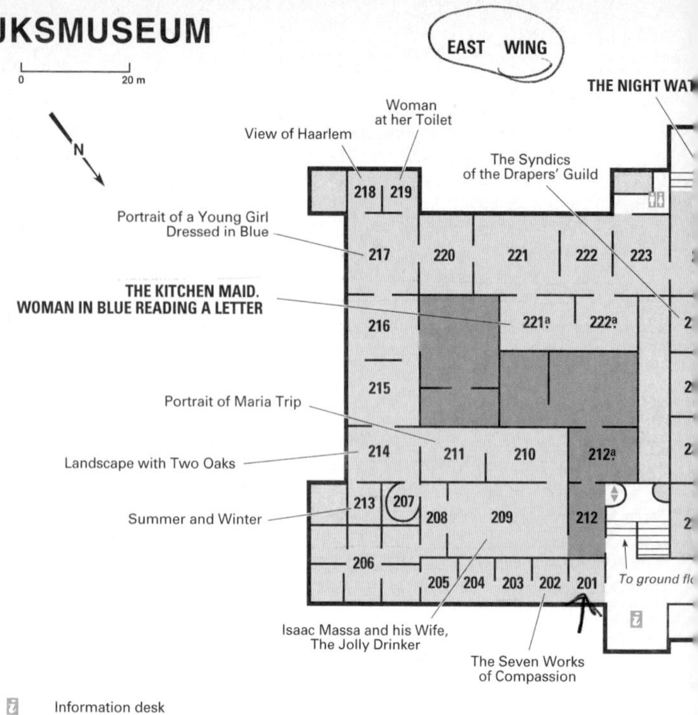

0
20 m
N
EAST WING
THE NIGHT WAT
Woman
at her Toilet
View of Haarlem
The Syndics
of the Drapers' Guild
Portrait of a Young Girl
Dressed in Blue
THE KITCHEN MAID.
WOMAN IN BLUE READING A LETTER
Portrait of Maria Trip
Landscape with Two Oaks
Summer and Winter
218
219
217
220
221
222
223
216
221ª
222ª
215
214
211
210
212ª
213
207
208
209
212
206
205
204
203
202
201
To ground fl
Isaac Massa and his Wife,
The Jolly Drinker
The Seven Works
of Compassion
Information desk
Shop
Audio guide
Telephone
Cloakroom
Lift
Toilets
Restaurant
Disabled access

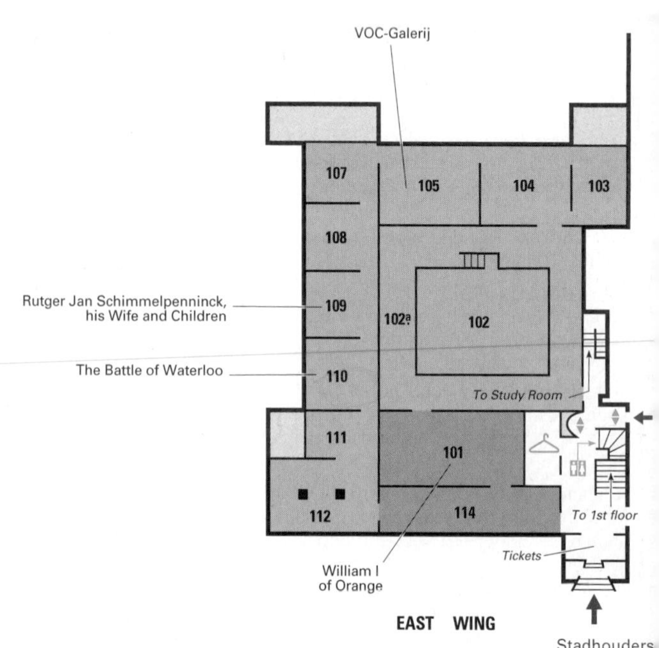

VOC-Galerij
107
105
104
103
108
Rutger Jan Schimmelpenninck,
his Wife and Children
109
102ª
102
The Battle of Waterloo
110
To Study Room
111
101
112
114
To 1st floor
Tickets
William I
of Orange
EAST WING
Stadhouders

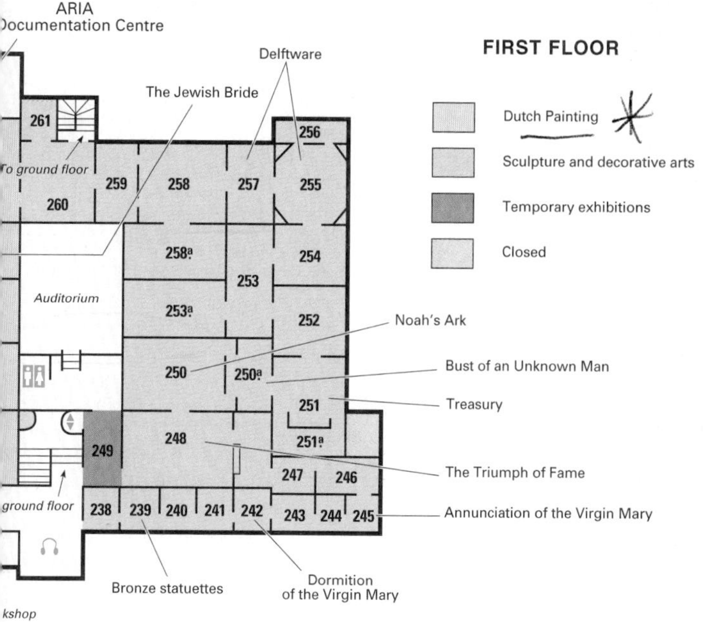

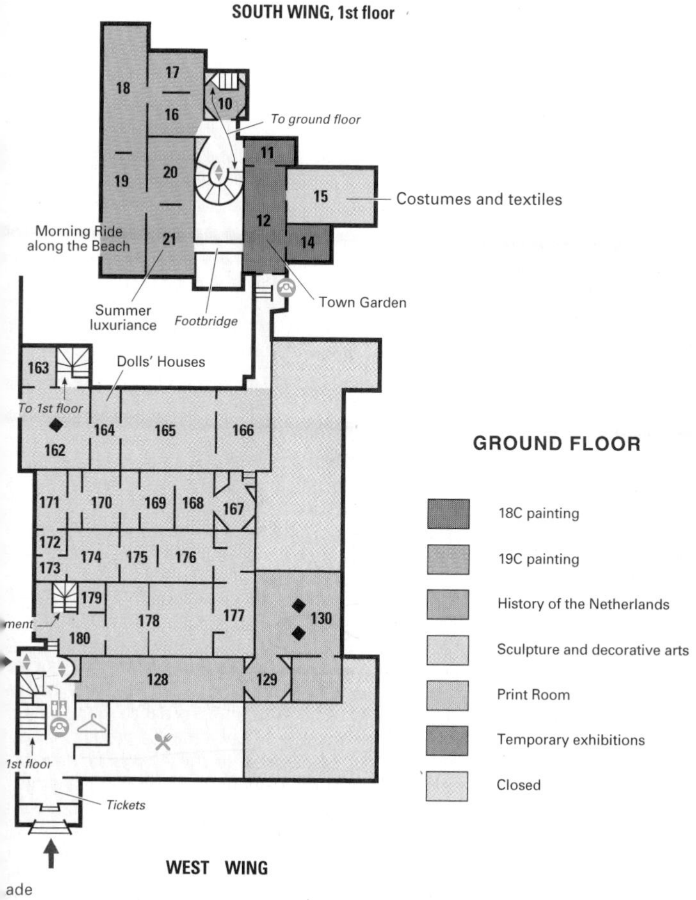

SOUTH WING, 1st floor

18
17
16
10
To ground floor
11
19
20
15
Costumes and textiles
12
Morning Ride along the Beach
21
14
Town Garden
Summer luxuriance
Footbridge
163
Dolls' Houses
To 1st floor
164
165
166
162
171
170
169
168
167
172
173
174
175
176
179
178
177
130
ment
180
128
129
1st floor
Tickets

WEST WING

ade

GROUND FLOOR

18C painting
19C painting
History of the Netherlands
Sculpture and decorative arts
Print Room
Temporary exhibitions
Closed

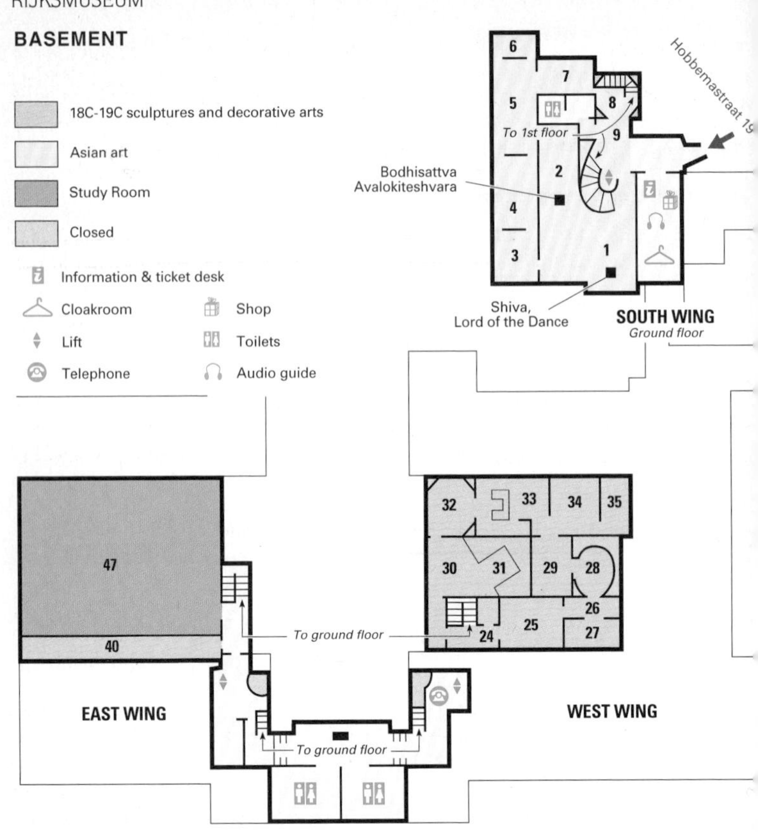

Gerard DOU (1613-75) – The artist was born, and died, in Leiden. He was pupil of **Rembrandt van Rijn** and a great specialist in small works and artificia light. He is a master of "fine" painting and enjoyed success during his own life time.

★ ***Old Woman Reading a Lectionary*** (c 1630) (211) – This oil on wood is a work from the artist's youth but it is a wonderful example of his delicate brushwork which is especially obvious in the treatment of matter such as fur, fabric, paper and skin The woman (perhaps Rembrandt's mother) is reading an extract from the Gospel according to St Luke telling the story of Jesus' entry into Jericho, an episode which strengthened the Protestant idea that sinners are saved by faith.

Hendrick GOLTZIUS (1558-1617) – In 1585, Goltzius founded the Haarlem Academy with **Karel van Mander**. He was a follower of the Venetians who had considerable influence on the landscape painters of his own country.

Lot and his Daughters (1616) (208) – This episode from Genesis is typical of the stories of impropriety that interested the painters of the Renaissance and the Counter-Reformation. Artists such as Il Guercino, Rubens and Simon Vouet a depicted this tale of the unwittingly incestuous father whose daughters gave birth to Moab and Ammon, Lot's sons and grandsons!

Frans HALS (1581/82-1666) – *See HAARLEM.*

★★★ ***Portrait of the Massa Marriage*** (c 1622) (209) – This is the only double portrait produced by this artist. It shows a man and his wife and is steeped in seeming unalterable affection. The composition was daring at the time because the subjec are placed sideways and not centred as was customary. However the artist wa careful to place the husband to the right of his wife, in accordance with tradition Several details show that this is a married couple. The woman is proudly showin off two rings on the same finger (it was fashionable in those days to wear bot the engagement and the wedding ring) and the painting includes pampas grass symbol of the Eucharist and of fertility), ivy (an emblem of fidelity) and a thist (the emblem of austerity and, therefore, of long-lasting love). Finally, there almost absolute certainty as to the identity of the two figures who seem to b really happy. They are Isaac Abraham Massa, a merchant, and Beatrix van der Lae the daughter of a burgomaster.

★ ***The Jolly Drinker*** (1628/30) *(209)* – The main features of this work, which critics have always found difficult to classify, are the limited number of colours and the rapid brush strokes. It is described as a genre painting rather than a portrait. It was a work that broke away from the traditions and tenets of its day.

★★ ***The Company of Captain Reynier Reael*** (1637) *(208)* – This painting was begun by Hals, the great specialist in the painting of companies of civic guards *(see insert below and HAARLEM)* and completed by **Pieter Codde**. The work, then, combines two very different talents. Hals used wide, sure brush strokes while Codde was a meticulous artist. It was a disagreement between the artist from Haarlem and the people who commissioned the work, because of his lack of speed, that resulted in two artists working on the same painting.

Willem Claeszoon HEDA (1594-1680) – The artist was born, and died, in Haarlem. He gained his reputation from a series of monochrome "luncheons".

till Life with Gilded Jar (1635) *(209)* – The elements in the painting resemble the leftovers of a luxurious meal; they are actually designed to highlight the artist's dexterity. It is an exercise in style, in which Heda excelled.

Meindert HOBBEMA (1638-1709) – This artist from Amsterdam (he was the town's gauger) was a friend and student of **Jacob van Ruysdael**. He was a landscape artist who produced very few works, most of them depicting eastern Gelderland.

Watermill (1655) *(220)* – At this time, Van Ruisdael's influence is not yet totally obvious. The watermill was Hobbema's favourite subject – he painted 40 of them in all.

Dirck JACOBSZOON (c 1497-1567) – The artist was brought up, lived and died in Amsterdam (his place of birth remains unknown). He was, at one time, said to be the **Master of Alkmaar** and is one of the earliest Dutch painters to show an interest in portraits.

Pompeius Occo (1531) *(203)* – This type of composition is known as a "memento mori". The skull and carnation show that the subject, a banker, is aware of the ephemeral nature of life.

Gabriël METSU (1629-69) – He is thought to have been a pupil of **Gerrit Dou** and he was certainly influenced by Gerard Terborch in his early works. He is famous for his genre paintings. He left some 150 works.

★ ***The Sick Child*** (c 1662) *(222a)* – From 1660 onwards, Metsu began a period of Vermeer-like works characterised by static scenes with a light background and use of cold colours. This painting, which may be an allegory of charity, and the *Woman with Dropsy* (National Gallery, London) were new subjects, and absolutely unique in the history of 17C Dutch painting. There are those who attribute the fame of the work to the novelty aspect, but this is an unfair judgement. The emotion that seizes those who see the work is not due solely to the choice of subject matter. All the artist's pictorial simplicity is used here in the treatment of a particularly difficult theme.

Jan MOSTAERT (c 1475-c 1556) – The artist is thought to have been born in Haarlem and to have died in Hoorn. He is a direct descendant of the Flemish Pre-Renaissance painters. He worked as court painter to Margaret of Austria, Regent of the Low Countries in Mechelen.

★ ***The Adoration of the Magi*** (c 1510) *(202)* – *See below.*

REMBRANDT VAN RIJN (1606-69) – *See insert.*

Rijksmuseum Amsterdam

The Adoration of the Magi (c 1510) by Jan Mostaert

The Adoration of the Magi

Several of the paintings displayed in the Rijksmuseum illustrate the legend and cult of the Three Wise Men.
Everybody knows the story of the kings from the East who arrived in Jerusalem seeking the King of the Jews whose birth had been revealed to them by a star. It is less well-known that only St Matthew's Gospel mentions it, and that their names are not given until the 9C: **Gaspar**, **Melchior** and **Balthazar**. Not until the 11C was it decided that the Persian astrologers (Magi) should exchange their Phrygian caps for royal crowns, and not until the 12C did they become the subject of widespread veneration.
In pictorial terms, the subject always includes five figures: the Virgin Mary, the Infant Jesus, and the three Kings. A close look at the various paintings hanging in successive rooms reveals the changes in the scene, for example, one of the Kings may be positioned in the background to comply with the rules of symmetry in artistic compositions, and the kiss given by the oldest of the Magi may be treated differently.

★ ***Tobias Accusing Anne of Stealing a Young Kid*** (1626) *(211)* – This scene from the Ol[d] Testament should, if tradition is strictly adhered to, be called *Tobias being scolde[d] by his wife whom he suspects of having stolen a young kid.* Tobias was a rich ma[n] who had been ruined by God and he is shown, in this work, repenting his sin rather than accusing his wife.

★★ ***Self-Portrait at a Young Age*** (1628) *(211)* – The artist was aged only 22, yet h[e] had already achieved near perfection in this unusual concept of a self-portrai[t] which plunges the face into darkness. Rembrandt's chiaroscuro technique is i[n] its earliest form here, in this image of himself which should be regarded as [a] study.

★ ***Anna the Prophetess*** (1631) *(211)* – Based on 16C engravings in which th[e] prophetess was shown seated at a church door with Bible in hand, Rembrand[t] depicts a very biblical figure with a scarf that resembles a tallith (prayer shaw[l]) and a text in Hebraic writing.

★ ***The Stone Bridge*** (c 1638) *(211)* – This landscape on wood (Rembrandt usually use[d] etchings for landscape scenes) shows his mastery as a landscape artist. The intens[e] light diffused by the setting sun over the opaque vault of clouds above the rive[r] landscape is absolutely magnificent.

★★ ***Portrait of Maria Trip*** (1639) *(211)* – The young woman in her 20s is the daughte[r] of a business man who earned his wealth in the trade and production of arms. She is therefore rich, as is obvious from the jewellery and the elegance of he[r] clothes. The artist excelled in his painting of her silky hair and fine lace. Almos[t] every aspect of the work translates the dignity and reserve imposed upon th[e] subject by her high social rank. Almost every aspect? Yes, because Rembrand[t] could not be content with this polished image. He placed a vague smile on Mari[a] Trip's face, and it is this smile that turns the work into a masterpiece.

★★★ ***The Night Watch*** (1642) *(224)* – This is the most outstanding work in the artist' biography, a gigantic canvas (3.63m/12ft by 4.37m/14ft) which was originall[y] called *The Company of Captain Frans Banningh Cocq and Lieutenant Willem va[n] Ruytenburch.* It was indeed, the captain wh[o] commissioned the work t[o] immortalise his company which had had the privileg[e] of serving as guard [o]f honour to Marie de Medici during her visit in 1638.
The aesthetic qualities [of] the painting are now universally known. They wer[e] recognised when Rembrandt delivered the painting, in particular by one [of] his pupils, **Samuel va[n] Hoogstraten**: *"This work whatever the criticisms [it] arouses, will outlive a[ll] those which claim to equa[l]*

Rembrandt and self-portraits

In the western world, the first self-portraits were painted at the end of the Middle Ages when mirror glass became available, in the late 14C. The first examples were "situated" self-portraits (figures were lost in a crowd), followed by "hidden" self-portraits (in the reflection of armour) and "natural" self-portraits (with no pictorial support). Psychoanalysts will no doubt frown to hear that Rembrandt painted 55 self-portraits (not counting the engravings), a ferocious series of works showing the slow disfiguration that time caused to his own image.

The Night Watch (1642) by Rembrandt

it because it is designed in such a pictorial manner, enlivened with such power and so mightily painted that all the other works present look like playing cards by comparison." This, then, was a moment of glory for Rembrandt, but it was a glory tinged with sadness for, in the same year 1642, his wife died of tuberculosis.

★★ ***Titus as a Monk*** (1660) *(229)* – Titus was Rembrandt's son, shown here at the age of 19 as a Capuchin or Franciscan friar. The artist created several works of this type, the only difference being that the subjects were older and wrinkled like the countless paintings of apostles and evangelists left by the artists of the 16C and 17C. However, this work shares with the others the same background imprecisely brushed in with brown tones in order to concentrate the light on the face.

★★ ***The Staalmeesters of the Drapers Guild*** (1661) *(230)* – This group painting shows the management committee of the drapers' guild which was responsible for monitoring the quality of fabrics. The men come from various religious backgrounds but this is ignored in the face of their joint responsibilities. They seem to have been disturbed by Rembrandt in the middle of a meeting. The Chairman, Willem van Doyenburgh, has his sample book open; Volckert Janszoon *(left)* is rising to his feet while Aert van der Mije *(right)* is picking up his gloves. Spectators have the impression of entering the canvas, as if stepping into the committee room. In order to heighten this feeling, the artist used rising perspective: the five men dressed in black (and the servant) look down on the spectators.

★ ***Self-Portrait as Paul the Apostle*** (1661) *(222)* – "Become like me, since I have become like you", ordered the saint. There is no other written document explaining this choice.

★★ ***The Jewish Bride*** (1667) *(229)* – Once referred to as *Isaac and Rebecca*, this painting seems to be based on a bible story, that of Isaac and Rebecca surprised by Abimelech in the land of the Philistines, a subject already depicted by Rembrandt who had sought inspiration in a fresco by **Raphael** in one of the lodges in the Vatican. Here, though, the artist has separated the figures from their historic background (Abimelech is absent) and has illustrated a gesture on the part of the man (his right hand lies on the woman's breast) which has caused entire rivers of ink to flow ever since art works were first the subject of commentaries. There are those who, naively, saw this as a father taking leave of his daughter. Most, however, basing their appreciation on the carnal qualities of the work, see this as a couple from Amsterdam who asked to be depicted in the tender pose of the biblical heroes. The identity of the models is a total mystery.

Pieter SAENREDAM (1597-1665) – This artist, who worked in Haarlem, specialised from 1628 onwards in architectural paintings, in particular church interiors. His works are recognisable for their rigorous perspective.

The militias of Amsterdam...

In 1578 the Calvinists seized power in Amsterdam, assisted by the Gueux ("Beggars") and supported by a majority of the population and a handful of merchants. Three years later, the Republic of the United Provinces was created and it became urgent, and essential, to strengthen the town's defences. This led to the setting up of the civic guards whose role was to provide back-up for the existing companies of armed men. The combination of these groups resulted in the *schutterijen* or "citizens' militias".
Each district had its own company, each divided into four korporaalschappen or brigades which were themselves subdivided into three sections. The brigades were commanded by sergeants and the companies by captains assisted by lieutenants.
The companies were organised into five regiments, each with its own colour recognisable by the scarves (green, orange, blue, yellow and white). The five regiments were initially placed under the control of two colonels. Later, there were up to five colonels for each regiment.
For comparison's sake, it is interesting to note that the town was divided into 11 districts in 1580 and that it therefore had 11 companies. By 1672, the number had risen to 60. At that time, some 10 000 militiamen were responsible (in theory at least) for the protection of Amsterdam.
The numerous paintings of citizens' militiamen *(a visit to the gallery of civic guards in the Amsterdams Historisch Museum is worthwhile in this respect)* were designed to portray the majesty of the regiments, transmit their sense of collective responsibility, define their operational hierarchy, and represent the doelen, the place in which the men trained and held banquets.

...and the "Night Watch"

As Eugène Fromentin, an artist more famous for his writings about art, put it, *The Night Watch* has its merits but, more importantly, it has a meaning which he found in the *chiaroscuro* technique used here on such a large scale. It is true that, if Rembrandt's legacy had to be summed up in a single term, it would be *chiaroscuro*. However it is important to leave on one side for a moment the purely artistic dimension and see this painting for what it is, a painting of a citizens' militia and not just another painting by Rembrandt, albeit transcended by the treatment of light and shade. Let's make no mistake about it, this represents the last word on this type of work. Why? None of the people depicted here recognised themselves (the archives are absolutely clear on this point), the proportions are inaccurate (the lieutenant is too small), the presence of a small girl is strange to say the least (this is a nonsense in this type of painting) and there is apparent chaos (in a situation that should be imbued with a sense of order). There is no doubt that Rembrandt made fun of the vanity of his models who, as time passed, fulfilled an official function that was totally devoid of danger.

The Night Watch (detail), Rembrandt

★ ***Interior of St Bavo's Church in Haarlem*** (1637) ***and Interior of the Mariakerk in Utrecht*** (1641) *(214)* – These two paintings are fine examples of the extremely meticulous attitude of the artist whose works bear the mark of his training as draughtsman in their pure lines. However, just because he was a draughtsman does not mean that his talent was limited or any less worthy of the acclaim enjoyed more generally by other painters, for, in the 16C and 17C, those who had mastered the techniques of perspective considered themselves high-class artists.

Jan STEEN (1626-79) – This artist from Leiden, a pupil of **Knüpfer** in Utrecht, is an outstanding genre painter. He had an eventful life but it was probably less pagan than suggested by his works.

The Happy Family (1668) *(215)* – Steen's ironic view of life often found enjoyment in minor family dramas or slightly cheeky drinking sessions. However, he was equally capable of being a moralist, as in this work where he denounces the bad example set by drinking, an example that was quickly followed by children.

★ ***Woman at her Toilet*** (date unknown) *(219)* – In the 17C, a woman wearing red stockings was considered as a prostitute. The chamber pot on the floor confirmed this opinion because a "*pisseuse*" was a tart. It is obvious that Steen had a sharp sense of humour which he no doubt also put to good and extensive use in his other profession, that of innkeeper in Warmond, Delft and Leiden. **Sir Joshua Reynolds** admired his "firm, virile" technique which, if lacking in the elaborate features of many of his contemporaries, was nevertheless that of a virtuoso painter, a genius who created many canvases while working very little.

The Interior of the Mariakerk in Utrecht,
by Pieter Saenredam

Gerard TERBORCH (1617-81) – His earliest drawing still in existence was executed when he was eight years old. His was a precocious talent. Gerard travelled throughout Europe perfecting his art and became one of the best genre painters of his day.

★★ ***Gallant Conversation*** (c 1654) *(222a)* – Once entitled *The Paternal Reprimand,* this canvas is a fine example of the series of paintings of interiors showing facets of everyday life created by the artist during the 1650s. Do not seek any trace of a reprimand or a father in this work. The man is a soldier and his gesture is one of a customer seated beside the owner of a brothel as suggested by the red bed in the background and the candle – it is not only writers who use candles to symbolise night-time labours. The reproduction of the fabric of the young woman's dress is absolutely superb.

Geertgen TOT SINT JANS (1460/65-1488/93) – Geertgen Tot Sint Jans was born in Leiden and died in Haarlem. He was a pupil of **Van Ouwater**. He was a Dutch Primitive who was strongly influenced by **Hugo van der Goes**.

★ ***Adoration of the Magi*** (c 1490) *(201)* – *See insert.*

Jan VAN DE CAPELLE (1626-79) – By profession, he was a fabric dyer; by inclination, he was an art collector. He revealed himself as a talented artist late on in life. Although a dilettante because he was not working to earn a living, he achieved a strange precision that nears perfection.

Winter Landscape (date unknown) *(220)* – The subject is depicted with awesome accuracy. Because of this, spectators are tempted to allow their eyes to wander up to the sky which the artist illustrated with a lighter or, in a word, more poetic touch.

Esaias VAN DE VELDE (1587-1630) – He worked in Haarlem from 1610 onwards. One of his pupils there was **Jan van Goyen**. He then moved to The Hague in 1618. He is best known for his landscapes.

The Ferry (1622) *(209)* – This painting on wood is one of the first great success stories of Dutch landscape painting, although it is still one of those landscapes painted in the artist's studio and not in situ.

Willem VAN DE VELDE the Younger (1633-1707) – The artist was born in Leiden and died in London, where he was court painter to King Charles II. He was a marine artist and, as such, was present at all the great naval battles so that he could depict them on canvas.

The Storm (c 1680) *(220)* – The atmosphere and skilful spatial layout of this composition proves the artist's virtuosity – if proof were necessary.

Floris VAN DIJCK (c 1575-1651) – The artist is very little known outside the Netherlands; indeed his reputation is limited within his own country because of the very small number of works produced by this still-life artist. He was born and died in Haarlem. He studied in Italy under **Cavalier d'Arpin**.

★ ***Still Life with Cheese*** (c 1615/20) *(Illustration, see Introduction: Art)* – This remarkably well-balanced composition is meticulously painted and can be considered as the archetypal Dutch "luncheon" scene, consisting here of crockery and food on a damask tablecloth. Speaking of the subjects painted by this artist, one of his contemporaries said, "It could attract and take in joyous little women and even birds": no comment.

Jan VAN GOYEN (1596-1656) – Van Goyen was born in Leiden and died in The Hague. He is one of the small band of artists who brought Dutch landscapes their reputation for excellence by abandoning Mannerism in favour of a more modern Naturalism.

★ ***Summer and Winter*** (c 1625) *(213)* – These charming circular paintings represent landscapes although they are still genre paintings. They reveal the legacy of the artist's teacher, Esaias van de Velde.

★★ ***Landscape with Two Oaks*** (1641) *(214)* – The muted colours, touches of gold and monochrome scumbles are all typical of the artist. This work reveals his anxious, almost romantic temperament (knotty trees and leaden sky). After 1630, landscapes became preponderant in the artist's works in which he brushed in a wide sky while making the human figures smaller. The great spatial unity of the composition shows his exceptional talent. In short, the real subject of this painting is its atmosphere and this is a veritable artistic feat.

Cornelis VAN HAARLEM (1562-1638) – This Mannerist painter was steeped in the art of the Fontainebleau School and influenced by **Hendrick Goltzius**. With **Karel van Mander** he founded the Haarlem Academy.

The Massacre of the Holy Innocents (1580) *(206)* – The academy inaugurated the study of nudes in Holland, as is exemplified in this painting which was probably commissioned by Prince **Maurice von Nassau**.

Maarten VAN HEEMSKERK (1498-1574) – Van Heemskerk was a pupil of **Jan van Scorel**. He travelled in Italy where he was greatly impressed by the faces of **Michelangelo**.

Portrait of Anna Codde (1529) *(205)* – When it was painted, this work on wood was innovative because of the foreshortening of the arm. The other painting in the pair, of *Pieter Bicker*, Anna's husband, also hangs in this room.

Gerrit VAN HONTHORST (1590-1656) – The Italians nicknamed this painter from Utrecht Gherardo delle Notte (Gerard of the Night-scenes) because of his many night paintings He stayed in Rome from 1610 to 1620 and was influenced by the genius of **Caravaggio**.

★ ***The Joyous Minstrel*** (1623) *(209)* – This painting is not really representative of the night scenes discussed above but it shows the great sense of space enjoyed by the artist. The composition is almost a trompe-l'œil but is resolutely caravaggist in its style and subject matter.

Lucas VAN LEYDEN (1494-1533) – This artist was influenced by the Flemish masters, and he showed a constant preference for popular details which he treats with great realistic energy.

Triptych of the Adoration of the Golden Calf (c 1530) *(204)* – This very technical work is unusual for its plasticity. It is one of a series of Italianate paintings.

Jacob Corneliszoon VAN OOSTSANEN (c 1470-1533) – This painter and engraver, who settled in Amsterdam in 1500, marked the transition between Late Gothic and the northern Renaissance.

★ ***Adoration of the Magi*** (1517) *(203)* – *See insert.*

Jacob VAN RUYSDAEL (c 1629-82) – He studied under his uncle, Salomon, and worked in Haarlem and Amsterdam. He is undeniably one of the greatest landscape painters in the history of Dutch art.

★★ ***View of Haarlem*** (c 1670) *(218)* – *(Illustration, see Introduction: Art)*. This painting is part of a panoramic series entitled "Little View of Haarlem". Here, the town and its church dedicated to St Bavo are seen from the village of Overveen, consisting of the laundries visible in the meadow in front of the houses. The single source of light used by the artist in this work, which is veiled by the clouds, makes this an undisputed masterpiece.

Jan VAN SCOREL (1493-1562) – This knowledgeable canon worked in the Vatican as one of the protegees of Adrian VI, former Bishop of Utrecht, the town of his birth. He was a portrait artist but also produced a large number of historical works.

Mary Magdalen (date unknown) *(205)* – This powerful face is typical of the artist's works. It is reminiscent of the strong, sculptural representations of the Virgin Mary which he painted on his return from Rome.

Johannes VERMEER (1632-75) – The Rijksmuseum has four paintings by the great master from Delft, who only produced some 30 works in all. Room 221a is therefore something of a shrine for the painter's many admirers *(see insert below)*.

Johannes Vermeer

Times have changed for Vermeer of Delft or, to be more precise, for his admirers in the knowledgeable world of art experts. He was frequently confused, at the time of the early exhibitions of old masters organised in the late 19C, with the artist of the same name from Haarlem (1628-91), a landscape artist now consigned to limbo by art history.

Born in Delft in 1632, the town which had "as many bridges as there are days in the year", Johannes Vermeer was the second child of Reynier Jansz, a weaver, and his wife Digna Baltens. His father was not only a weaver of silk cloth; he was also registered as an art dealer with the Guild of St Luke in Delft. It was, then, almost inevitable that Johannes should begin a career as a painter in December 1653 when he was accepted as a member of the same guild.

There are very few documents about his life and his reputation as an artist is based on a relatively small number of works. Nothing is known about his training and nobody knows whether he travelled outside his national borders to learn the techniques used by German, French or Italian artists. However, an indication in the archives reveals that, in April 1653, the man who was to become one of the most outstanding artists of the 17C married Catharina Boines, daughter of a wealthy Catholic family, and that the couple had 11 children. There is no doubt that he knew his colleague **Gerard Terborch**, and it is presumed that he was acquainted with **Pieter de Hooch** since the latter was active in Delft in 1652, and with **Jan Steen** who is known to have lived in the town between 1650 and 1660.

Kunsthistorisches Museum, Wien

Vermeer showed himself from behind in *The Artist's Studio*

His biographers have been able to do no more than interpret a few scant documents. They indicate that he was elected a member of the Council of his guild in 1663, and this meant that Vermeer enjoyed a reputation as a serious, important artist. A French amateur by the name of Balthasar de Monconys considered Vermeer's works to be too expensive when he visited the artist's studio that same year. Three years before his death, Vermeer was elected Dean of the guild and he was consulted as an expert on Italian paintings, a detail that is of particular importance for those who comment on his works. However, 1672 was a disastrous year for the United Provinces, confronted by the ambitions of Louis XIV. Vermeer sold no paintings at all and was forced to rent out his house. Like many of his contemporaries, he was up to his ears in debt. He died in 1675, leaving his wife and 10 under-age children to face his creditors.

★ ***The Street*** (c 1657/58) *(221a)* – *The View of Delft* (c 1660/61, Mauritshuis in The Hague) and this painting are the only exteriors painted by Vermeer. The format (53.5cm/21.5in by 43.5cm/17.5in), subject matter which is more centred and the absence of architecture revealing the geographical location make this a totally intimist work. There are those who believe that Vermeer was influenced here by **Pieter de Hooch**, a great specialist in this type of composition. It is possible, of course, but why should de Hooch have suddenly changed his style when he arrived in Delft where Vermeer was already working?

★ ***The Milkmaid*** (c 1658/60) *(221a)* – If anybody needed a reason to go to Amsterdam, it would be this Milkmaid. A reproduction of the painting is not sufficient to understand its incredible magic. The canvas measures only 45.4cm/18in by 40.6cm/16in, but it is striking for the almost hyper-realism it exudes.

How many visitors expect the serving girl to move and finish pouring the milk into the earthenware basin? How many have been in quiet ecstasy as they contemplated the intensity of colour and light? When Vermeer created this work, he had already delivered four genre paintings, including his famous *Officer and a Young Woman Laughing*, now part of the Frick Collection in New York.

These works all show the extent to which the artist had become a master of perspective. Here, although he has placed his subject in the optimum position, he has also, and more importantly, created a wonderful sense of harmony between the

The Milkmaid, by Johannes Vermeer

rough serving girl and the simplicity of the room (note the broken window). Th light and the contrasting colours visually accentuate the physical presence of th subject and heighten the realism of this scene from everyday life.

★★★ ***Woman in Blue reading a Letter*** (c 1663/64) *(221a)* – *(Illustration, see Introduction: Art,* Vermeer's elegant technique is such that there is a temptation to wax lyrical to expres the intensity of his works. This oil painting is particularly moving for its subject an its plasticity. This is one of the few paradoxes in Vermeer's art for, although he ha transcended the art of painting by giving a timeless quality to his scenes from everyda life, he did not revolutionise art by introducing a new style as did most of the ver great artists. This, though, cannot conceal one absolute certainty: Vermeer is a geniu one of a very small number in the history of painting. The woman betrays no feeling yet the scene is steeped in emotion and, in order to underline and balance the sens tive nature of his subject, the artist was careful to reduce his composition to th essential and to use almost exclusively blue tones to rest the spectator's eye. Quit apart from its outstanding technical quality, the strength of this work lies in its conte or, to put it another way, its theatrical layout.

★★ ***The Love Letter*** (c 1669/70) *(221a)* – It is more than likely that this compositio was created under the influence of **Pieter de Hooch** who has been mentioned abov in relation to *The Street*. He painted several genre scenes through open doorway whereas Vermeer almost never attempted such a setting. However, although th view here is similar to those of de Hooch's works, as is the inclusion of the mis tress and servant, the atmosphere is very much Vermeer's own. On one hand, h emphasised the psychological dimension of his work and, on the other, he wa very interested in the camera obscura, an optical instrument which provided ne means of expression, especially the halo effect found in all his works.

Johannes Corneliszoon VERSPRONCK (c 1597-1662) – This artist was born and die in Haarlem. Approximately 100 works have been listed to date, most of them portrait He worked in the studio of **Frans Hals** but did not adopt the master's techniques.

★ ***Portrait of a Young Girl in Blue*** (1641) *(217)* – This portrait of a child seen half-lengt is his best-known painting. The subject is dressed like an adult and the feathe fan, lace, gold braid and jewellery are designed to confirm that she comes from wealthy family. Only the absence of a bust and her bored and vaguely facetious expres sion reveal her age, thought to be 10. Her secret smile is much more attractive than the disdainful sneer on the face of another child, the young Andries Bicker, son of a very rich business man (see B van der Helst's painting in the same room).

★★ SCULPTURE AND DECORATIVE ARTS

West wing: first floor, ground floor and basement

This is an extensive department occupying several rooms. The following description covers the most outstanding works.

First floor

Room 238 – The oliphant (an ivory horn carved out of an elephant's tusk) comes from southern Italy (late 11C). For many years it belonged to the church dedicated to St Mary in Utrecht, which has now been demolished with the exception of the cloister. Among the exhibits in Limoges enamel made using the champlevé technique are a 13C reliquary and two 13C bishops' croziers. The **aquamanile** (water container) shaped like a horseman (first half of the 13C) comes from Hildesheim; it is a delightful item made of bronze using the lost wax technique. The hole visible on the horse's breast marks the position of the spout.

Room 239 – The St Frederick reliquary (Utrecht, 1326) was made of silver gilt by goldsmith Elias Scerpswert. The series of 10 **bronze statuettes★** (Brabant, 1476) used to decorate the tomb of Isabelle de Bourbon in the Abbey of St Michael in Antwerp. They represent the mourning family of the deceased.

Room 240 – *The Descent into Limbo* is a fine polychrome work on oak (southern Low Countries, c 1440) showing Christ before the Resurrection.

Room 241 – The **two oak panels** (Nativity, Meeting of the Magi) were carved by Adriaen van Wesel (c 1417-90), a sculptor who worked in Utrecht. These remarkably expressive pieces were originally part of an altarpiece depicting the Life of the Virgin Mary.

Room 242 – The ***Dormition*★★** (c 1475) by the same sculptor represents the death of the Virgin Mary. The Holy Scriptures remain totally silent on this subject and nobody actually knows how Christ's Mother died. However, the Roman Catholic Church declares that she "really died" since she was human.

Room 243 – The superb ***Entombment*★** by Arnt van Kalkar (c 1460-1492) illustrates a topic that was particularly popular with artists because the Gospels remained fairly vague on the subject and artists could give free rein to their imagination. Note also the oak press (Low Countries, c 1525), a Gothic design attractively decorated with linenfold carving. The front panels are carved like the tracery used with stained glass.

Room 245 – The ***Annunciation of the Virgin Mary*★** (c 1480) carved by Tilman Riemenschneider (c 1460-1531), who specialised in painted alabaster, is a fine example of Late German Gothic. The Annunciation shows two or three figures (the Virgin Mary, the angel bringing the message and the Holy Spirit), but has been subject to various pictorial interpretations depending on the denomination of the artist.

Room 248 – The tapestry known as the ***Triumph of Fame*★★** (1515-25) was woven in Brussels, one of Europe's leading centres of this art form until the end of the 16C. The first quarter of the century was marked by a characteristic style inspired by the Italian Renaissance, thanks to the influence of the Humanists: monumental composition, effects of depth, figures with clothing draped like sculpture and meticulously reproduced plants. The tapestry is part of a series of six panels based on Petrarch's *Triumphs*. Note the carved wooden roodscreen from the church in Hevloirt (c 1500, Noord-Brabant) and the altarpiece showing *The Virgin Mary between St Jerome and Nicolas de Myre* (1502) by Benedetto Buglioni (1459/60-1521), a piece of majolica that is reminiscent of the works of the Della Robbias.

Portrait of a Young Girl in Blue (1641), Johannes Corneliszoon Verspronk

Room 250 – The tapestry known as ***Noah's Ark***★ was produced in Brussels c 1565 in the workshop of Willem de Pannemaker, a member of a talented family o tapestry weavers. See also the tapestry of the *Triumph of Scipio the African*, alsc made in Brussels c 1550.

Room 250a – The ***Bust of an Unknown Man***★ shows the extent to which the great architect **Hendrick de Keyse** (1565-1621), the designer of the Zuiderkerk, Westerkerk and many other buildings, was also a very talented sculptor. This bust (1606) is made of terracotta; it denotes a marked sense of realism heightened by the meticulous attention to detail in the face and doublet.

Maiolica was introduced into the Low Countries in the 16C. The **panel of tiles** representing soldiers (c 1600) was designed as a mural Take a close look at the figures depicted on the tiles – they are quite amusing.

Room 251 – The **treasure**★★★ contains some superb **nautilus and coconut cups** as well as goblets, platters, enamels and jewels. Note the **map of the Iberian peninsula** (Nuremberg, before 1549) presented to Philip II, and the astonishing German chessboard made of boxwood in about 1550.

Room 254 – The **cabinet** (Antwerp, first hal of the 17C) in this room is decorated with paintings by Frans Francken II (1581-1642) an artist from Antwerp who was famous in his day for his carefully executed genre paintings. The small works on the shutters and drawers of this cabinet represent scenes from Genesis (Adam and Eve, Cain and Abel).

Rijksmuseum Amsterdam

Bust of an Unknown Man, Hendrick de Keyser

Room 258a – The superb Boulle marquetry on the ***table top***★★ made in Antwerp in 1689 is by Michiel Verbiest and Peter de Loose. The extraordinary design includes mother-of-pearl foliage laden with fruit and flowers.

Also note the Renaissance cupboard *(252)*, the etched glass *(253)*, the colonial ebony bed *(253a)*, the **Delft ceramics** *(255-257)*, the "cushioned" cupboard *(260)* and the lacquer sideboard *(261)*.

Ground floor – Note the intricately designed **dolls' houses** *(164)*, the 18C four poster bed *(165/169)*, the 1730 **apothecary's cupboard**, probably made in Delft *(168)* the **Dresden porcelain** *(170/1)*, the fine marquetry secretaire *(176)* and the enamel snuffboxes *(179)*.

Basement – Etched glass *(24)*, 18c furniture *(25/27)*, Art Nouveau jewellery *(34)* a 1909 Art Nouveau drawing room *(35)* as well as Weesp and Loosdrecht Dutch porcelain *(32)*.

A table top, Michiel Verbiest and Peter de Loose

A Ride along the Beach (1876) by Anton Mauve

★★ HISTORY OF THE NETHERLANDS

East wing: ground floor

Developments in Dutch art are attractively highlighted here in order to trace the main events in the country's history, from the Eighty Years War to the Second World War. Room 102, with its model ships, paintings and weapons, is devoted to the Golden Age. The **Gallery of the East India Company** *(102a)* recreates daily life on board the Company's ships. The Netherlands owed their great naval power to admirals such as Marten Tromp and Michiel de Ruyter *(104)*. The objects displayed in room 107, among which are a painted Japanese parchment depicting cannibals and Dutch naval officers, show the presence of the Dutch in the East Indies. The painting of Rutger Jan Schimmelpenninck with his Wife and Children *(109)* is by the French painter Prud'hon. Schimmelpenninck was the Ambassador in Paris of the Batavian Republic of which he was Grand Pensionary, in other words President. The monumental painting by J.W. Pieneman *(110)* depicts the illustrious victory over Napoleon at the Battle of Waterloo, 18 June 1815. The seat on which William III was enthroned in the Nieuwe Kerke in 1849 is on display in room 112.

★★ PRINT ROOM

South wing: first floor.

This vast national collection of engravings and drawings has grown out of the collection of Pieter Cornelis, Baron van Leyden, which was purchased in 1807 by the King of Holland, Louis Bonaparte. The fragility of the works prevents prolonged public display; the museum therefore organises **temporary thematic exhibitions**. Because of this it is impossible to suggest a selection of works here.

The collection includes more than one million drawings and engravings. It has the largest collection of etchings by **Rembrandt van Rijn** and is the fortunate owner of engravings by **Hercules Segers**. However, the collection is not limited to works by Dutch artists. Depending on the exhibition, visitors can see prints by Watteau, Dürer or Boucher and oriental works, in particular xylographs and Japanese surinomos. Visitors are strongly recommended to ask about the current exhibition during their visit to the Rijksmuseum.

★ 18C and 19C DUTCH PAINTING

South wing: first floor.

The 18C paintings are hung up the full height of the walls, as was usual at the time and can be seen in the painting by Adriaan de Lelie, *The Art Collection of Brentano in his House on the Herengracht.* Note among the paintings of dignified and sumptuously dressed people the works of **Cornelis Troost**. The **Pastel room** *(14)* displays works of the Swiss painter Jean-Etienne Liotard as well as miniature portraits.

The rooms devoted to 19C art *(16-21)* bring to life the Napoleonic era (PG van Os), Dutch Romanticism (BC Koekkoek; WJJ Nuyen with *Shipwreck on a Rocky Coast)* and The Hague school (H Weissenbruch, J Maris with *Feeding the Chickens,* J Israëls, Anton, Mauve with *A Ride along the Beach)*. The main exponents of Dutch Impressionism are George Breitner, Isaac Israëls and Jacobus van Looy *(Summer Luxury)*.

COSTUMES AND TEXTILES

South wing: first floor (room 15).

The collection is presented on a rota basis. It includes mainly 18C and 19C Dutch costumes, oriental carpets, lace and damask fabrics.

★ASIAN ART

South wing: ground floor. Direct entrance from 19 Hobbemastraat.

The nine rooms in this particularly interesting section display more than 500 objects (some of them are exhibited on a rota basis) from the Indian subcontinent, Cambodia, Indonesia, Japan and China.
India is represented by **Shiva, Lord of the Dance★★** (12C) *(1)*, a magnificent bronze from southern India (Chola dynasty). Shiva is the god of creation and destruction; he combines the visible and the invisible, the transcendent and the immanent, the masculine and the feminine. This is a processional sculpture (see the slots in the base where the carrying poles would be placed) showing the god as the king of the cosmic dance. This is why he is encircled in flames.

Rijksmuseum Amsterdam

Shiva, Lord of the Dance (12C), India

Among the statues note the *Shakyamuni Buddha* (7C or 8C) which was found in Indonesia. There are also some elegant funerary statues from China, some magnificent porcelain Buddhas whose sitting position is executed with great naturalism. The **Bodhisattva Avalokiteshvara★★** (12C) *(2)* known as the Merciful, is a wooden statue with traces of paint and gilding. The Bodhisattva is a being *(sattva)* on the path to awakening *(bodhi)*. He is, therefore, a future Buddha. The very intense expression fulfils a religious function, a ritual aiming to "open up to the light". The statue, shown crouched down, has a relaxed attitude "of the great sovereign".
In the Japanese collection note the ceramic wares used for tea ceremonies, the lacquer objects and the refined screens.

SINGEL★★

Map pp 10 and 11, **LV**, **KX** and **KY**
Michelin map no 36 H 10, J 10 and K 10

THE ENCIRCLING CANAL

The Singel (in Dutch, the "canal" or to be more precise the "street running along a canal") was once a moat skirting the town walls; it constitutes the geographical boundary between medieval Amsterdam and the urban expansion implemented at the turn of the 16C and 17C. On older maps it was referred to as a "belt". It surrounds the western section of the historic city centre, completing the characteristic shape of the Grachtengordel, an almost complete ring of four canals which were instrumental in making the city famous.
It was in 1586 that the town council decided to widen the moat and build another quay on its outer bank. The quay was to result in the Herengracht. Initially designed for the transport of goods, the Singel gradually acquired the residential appearance it has today. Like the canals lying parallel to it, it boasts a fine set of warehouses, churches and canal houses.

Like the Herengracht, Keizersgracht and Prinsengracht, houses are numbered from the north end up to the Amstel. The house-by-house description enables visitors to see the sights easily as they stroll through this part of the city. The apparent discrepancy between odd and even numbers is not a mistake. It is designed, as far as possible, to cover houses on the same level but on opposite sides of the canal.

Ph. Gajic/MICHELIN

The old frontage on Singel 2-2a

★**Nos 2-2a** – Most of the stepped gables were built between 1600 and 1665 (approximately). The double-frontage house on this site dates from about 1603 which means that this is one of the oldest gables of its type. It is also one of the widest since the building included both a warehouse and a private home. This is clearly visible from the façade where five central warehouse doors come between the mullioned windows. The façade is, then, an outstanding reminder of 17C architecture even if the windows were widened in the 19C. The frontage stone contains a wheelbarrow because the first owner was called Cruywagen (in Dutch, "*Kruiwagen*" means "wheelbarrow"). The premises are now occupied by *De Spaanse Gevel* (The Spanish Façade).

★**Brouwersgracht** – *See JORDAAN and ANNE FRANK HUIS.*

No 7 – This is reputed to be the smallest house in the city (it is one door wide). In fact, it is the rear passageway from a house on Jeroenensteeg *(see no 166 below)*.

No 36 – The façade dates from 1763 and has asymmetrical decorative features that are characteristic of the Louis XV style. The inscription *ZEEVRUGT* means "seafood".

No 40 – This house was built in 1725. It has a very elegant fake attic decorated in the Louis XIV style and flanked by decoration in the shape of vases *(Illustration, see Introduction: Architecture)*. The original steps have disappeared. Note, to the right, the attic on **no 36**: it has a balustrade and a Louis XV finial. It dates from a slightly later period (1763).

No 11: Nieuwe of Ronde Lutherse Kerk – Consecrated in 1671, the New Lutheran Church (also known as Koepelkerk or Dome Church) was designed by **Adriaan Dortsman** (1652-82). The restrained Classical dome is unusual in the Netherlands, a country more accustomed to bell-towers. The presence of this dome is explained when one learns that Lutherans were not allowed to build churches with bell-towers, a privilege that was only bestowed on the Reformed Church. It would be more exact to call it the old Lutheran church since it is now used for conferences and concerts organised by the hotel to which it belongs, but that would make the situation too complicated because it actually replaced the existing Old Lutheran Church *(see BLOEMENMARKT)*.

Nos 19-21 – This house is wider than it is deep. It has a very elegant entrance (late 17C). Beneath the bell gable (1760) it bears the following inscription: *Vita hominum (left) similis Naviganti (right)* meaning "The life of man is like that of seafarers".

Nos 62 and 64 – On the left is a house with a stepped gable dating from 1638 and on the right a house with a stepped gable dating from the 19C. Their juxtaposition provides an opportunity to see what distinguishes an authentic design from a copy.

Nos 104-106 – These semi-detached houses date from approximately 1740. They have the largest bell gables in the city. Towards the top of the façade, the windows decrease in size, a typical feature of old canal houses. These two houses are identical. The fanlight above the door on no 106 is not original; it dates from the 19C.

No 83-85: Huis De Swaen – Almost opposite, at the corner of Lijnbaansteeg, stands "Swan House" *(note the frontaqe stone in the alleyway)* which gets its name from its first owner, Nicolaas Swaen. This elegant construction (1652) has Ionic pilasters and is decorated with festoons. It still has the wonderful shop front on the ground floor.

★ **Nos 140-142: House of the Captain of the "Night Watch"** – This magnificent house with very ornate double stepped gable is better known as the **Dolphins' House**. The name pays homage to its first owner, HL Spieghel (1549-1612), author of the first Dutch grammar in which one of the texts concerned dolphins.
The house was built c 1600 to designs by **Hendrick de Keyser** (1565-1621), the architect responsible for the Bartolotti house and the House of Heads. His plans were found in 1967 and this enabled the reconstruction of the façade on the right of the house, which had been demolished in the 19C to make room for a building totally devoid of interest.
Captain **Frans Banningh Cocq** (1605-55) was immortalised in 1642 in Rembrandt van Rijn's famous masterpiece. He lived here from 1630 to 1655. He was a wealthy man, a doctor of law by profession and member of the Council.

No 166: The narrowest house front in the city – This façade (1634) is only 1.80m/6ft in width. Behind it is a house which widens out to the rear. The smallest house in the city (2.02m/6.5ft wide and 6m/20ft deep) stands at no 22 Oude Hoogstraat (near the Zuiderkerk) *(see also no 7)*.

Torensluis – In Amsterdam, the stone and brick bridges are referred to as sluices (sluis), even though they were not designed to retain or release the water in the canals. In this case, the word refers to the building techniques used. The "Tower Lock" gets its name from the Jan Rodenpoortstoren, a 17C tower-cum-prison which once stood on this spot. It was demolished in 1829. The demolition of the tower left room for the widest bridge in the city (42m/136ft). As soon as the weather turns mild, it becomes a pavement café almost from one end to the other. This provides an opportunity to enjoy a delightful view of the neighbouring houses while having a drink beside the **Multatuli** statue.

No 210 – At the corner of Driekoningenstraat, from which there is a superb view of the Bartolotti House and the Westerkerk, stands the *De' Theeboom* warehouse dating from the early 18C (most of the city's warehouses were built in the 17C).

No 288 – This mid-18C house has a wonderful sandstone façade, a building material rarely used for such a narrow house. However, the interest of this particular building lies elsewhere – in its **attic★** decorated in the Louis XIV style. A careful study reveals that the hoist beneath the finial is covered by a projecting sculpture representing the mouth of a dolphin. This decorative subtlety is fairly uncommon, even very uncommon; we found only one other such ornament at no 59 Prins Hendrikkade where the hoist is concealed by the mouth of a lion.

No 370 – The frontage stone of this house topped with a bell gable is decorated with an ostrich (in Dutch "*struisvogel*") because the first owners were called Vogelstruys. The CCTV camera and fortified glass in the windows dates from the time of the expulsion of squatters on three occasions and the punitive police raids that followed.

Nos 377-379 – These small semi-detached houses date from 1730. Their attractive Rococo neck gables are identical but only the house on the left still has its original windows (one wide bay in the centre flanked by two smaller lights). Both have their shop fronts on the ground floor, and a third, communal door (in the centre) leading to the upper floors.

No 411: Oude Lutherse Kerk – *See BLOEMENMARKT.*

No 446: De Krijtberg – The "mountain of chalk" is a neo-Gothic church (1881) officially called the Church of St Francis Xavier. The Jesuit church (St Francis Xavier was one of the order's founders) was built by Alfred Tepe on the site of three houses, one of which was occupied by a chalk merchant.

"I have endured much"

This sentence is the Latin translation of the pen name taken by Eduard Douwes Dekker (1820-87), a figure who is difficult to classify in Dutch literature. **Multatuli** chose it in October 1859 when he was in Brussels.
He was brought up in a Mennonite family in Amsterdam. Later, he became a civil servant in Indonesia; here he was appointed Vice-Resident in a poor region in the west of Java where civil unrest was rife. He fought against the exploitation of the islanders, and this inspired his famous novel *Max Havelaar* which he wrote in Brussels after having resigned his position. Multatuli was something of an adventurer, certainly not averse to taking risks, a literary visionary in some people's opinion, and a Christ-like prophet for others; his works are certainly worth reading *(see also the nearby Multatuli Museum)*.

The interior immediately surprises visitors simply because its decorative richness is unusual in a city filled with austere Protestant churches. The fine **sculpture** of the Immaculate Conception dates from the 18C. It used to decorate the clandestine Jesuit chapel that stood beside the chalk merchant's shop.

No 423 – This house belongs to the library of the **University of Amsterdam (Universiteitsbibliotheek)**. It has a superb **façade** which is fairly surprising given its date of construction (1606). At the top is a plethora of decorative features. Note, too, the load-bearing arches over the windows. In 1972 renovation work resulted in the removal of the front door since nos 421 to 425 are all occupied by the University library, which has more than one million books and a collection of 50 000 maps. Originally, this house was used as an armaments depot and a meeting place for the **citizens' militia**. The meadow at the rear, which stretched to Kalverstraat, was used as a firing range. Handbookstraat and Voetboogstraat which cross this area today are named after militia groups.

No 460: Odeon – This beautiful tall façade decorated with festoons was designed by **Philip Vingboons** (1607-78) in 1662. It has a strange neck gable on which the hoist protrudes from an elegantly sculpted bull's-eye window.

From Nuremberg to Odeon – In the late 18C, this house, which originally belonged to a rich brewer, accommodated the second President of the United States, **John Adams**, who had come to negotiate a loan from the young Batavian Republic. At that time, the frontage stone bore the inscription "Nurenberg" but this was removed c 1830 and replaced by "Odeon" in an effort to provide the newly-opened imperial concert hall with an evocative name. After being a cinema and a gay club, the premises suffered fire damage in 1990. They have been restored but in the form of a café and a nightclub.

★★ **Bloemenmarkt** – *See BLOEMENMARKT.*

SLOTEN

Plan p 12, **AQ**
Michelin map no 36 N2

This locality dates back to the 11C (1063) and is now covered mainly with houses from the 19C. It was annexed to Amsterdam in 1921. In the centre of the district is *Terminus proscriptionis* or "Banishment Stone", an obelisk dating from 1559 (and rebuilt in 1794) which, with four others, marked the boundary beyond which those sentenced to banishment were not allowed to come.

Molen van Sloten – *Akersluis 10.* In days gone by, a mill built in 1636 used to stand on this spot on the Slotermeerpolder that leads to the nearby Sloterplas lake. It was relocated in Buitenveldert on the banks of the Amstel in 1956 *(see CYCLING IN AMSTERDAM, tour no 4)* and the people of Sloten, who missed the mill of which they had fond memories, joined forces and showed themselves to be both patient and determined. In 1991 they could not conceal their joy when they attended the inauguration by Princess Juliana of this windmill with gallery; the upper section comes from the Watergraafsmeer and dates from 1847.

Although there are several more windmills around Amsterdam and in Zaanse Schans *(see ZAANSTREEK)*, it is here that tourists have an opportunity to find out how a **polder mill** actually worked *(Illustration, see Introduction: Architecture)*.

When the wind blows across the flat Dutch landscape, the hydraulic jack operated by the main shaft pumps water up from the lower of the two small neighbouring canals. It has a capacity of up to 60 000 litres per minute, depending on the wind of course, for a rise of some 1.5m/4.5ft. Depending on the wind direction and strength, the miller then has to rotate the cap (it weighs 12t) to the correct position and mount the sails. Both of these operations are spectacular sights for tourists on a one-day visit.

Today, the first loft is used for wedding ceremonies and is very popular with Amsterdam's future brides and grooms. The second loft, the "*stellingzolder*" opens onto the gallery where the miller activates the brake lever and the wheel that rotates the cap into the wind. The third loft *(no entrance for unaccompanied children because of the possible danger)* contains the wheel, pivot and brake. The cog wheels are regularly coated with beeswax; the pivot is greased with pork fat.

STEDELIJK MUSEUM★★★

Plan p 10, **JZ**
Michelin map no 36 L9

THE "HOUSE OF MUSEUMS" *Paulus Potterstraat 13*

Ever since it first opened its doors to the public in 1895, the municipal museum has been collecting works of contemporary art and organising exhibitions of works of art from 1850 to the present day. There are works by artists who have now become a traditional part of modern art, such as Manet, Picasso or Mondrian, and some of the most recent examples of present-day art such as Minimalist creations or industria design.

The building – The Stedelijk Museum (1895) was built slightly later than the Rijks-museum and the Concertgebouw. It was designed by **AW Weissman** (1858-1923), the municipal architect. Built of stone and brick, it has a neo-Renaissance façade over-looking Paulus Potterstraat. The niches in the façade contain sculptures of artists from the Renaissance period: *(left to right)* Hendrick de Keyser, Jacob Corneliszoon var Ostsanen, Joost Janszoon Bilhamer, Jan van der Heyden, Thomas de Keyser and Jacob van Campen.
The architectural "shell" is something of an anachronism given that it is supposed tc symbolise collections that do not pre-date the 1850s. It was extended by a wing con-sisting of bay windows (1954) after the foyer was whitewashed to remove any traces of historicism (1938). The building is now too small but an additional wing is under construction.

The collections ⓥ – The Stedelijk Museum was originally built with a legacy from Sophia Augusta de Bruyn whose husband, Lopez Suasso, had bequeathed his prop erty to the city. Originally, the municipal museum contained the collection of the Sophia-Augusta Foundation and a collection of modern art consisting of 19C works It is this latter collection that provided the works by French artists and others by the Hague School. The collection was then constantly extended and the distinctior between the two collections was dropped.
It was, however, **Willem Sandberg** (1897-1984), Curator from 1945 to 1962, who made the museum world famous. Under his leadership, it abandoned old-fashioned museum layouts and launched a vast programme of international exhibitions. His purchasinc policy was particularly enlightened as is obvious from the purchase of works by the CoBrA group or by German Expressionists and, most of all, his purchase of a collec tion of works by Kasimir Malevich which are absolutely outstanding. His policy wa continued by successive curators, so that the Stedelijk Museum, which is open to a forms of art, fully deserves the name "House of Museums".
At the present time, the museum has 4 000 paintings, 1 000 sculptures, 17 00(prints and drawings, 16 000 posters and 3 000 photographs, plus Art Deco and indus trial exhibits.

IN HONOUR OF MODERN ART

Temporary exhibitions – One of the great attractions of this museum is the larg number and the quality of its temporary exhibitions which always echo news an trends in contemporary art. The exhibitions of the CoBrA group in 1949, Ameri can Pop Art in 1964 or Nam June Paik's video art in 1976 are excellent example of this policy. The corollary to this policy, which was developed by successive cur ators, is the temporary absence of certain works. It is, therefore, worth knowin that the Stedelijk Museum sets aside the summer months for an exhibition of it collections.

"A museum of contemporary art starts from the present and returns, one step a a time, to the past." (Willem Sandberg).

The 1980s and 1990s – The museum draws on the main trends in "conceptua attitudes" which gained strength during the 1980s (Minimalism, Arte Povera Italian Trans-Avant-Garde, New Subjectivity etc). Among its purchases are work by Dutch artists such as Jan Dibbets, Ger van Elk (*Kinselermeer*, 1985) or Fran van den Broek and by foreign artists including Americans Donald Judd, Walter d Maria (*17 Sided Open Polygon*, 1984), Robert Ryman, Julian Schnabel, Phili Guston and Jeff Koons (*Ushering in Banality*, 1988), Germans Anselm Kieffe (*Innenraum*, 1981) and Sigmar Polke *(Farbtafeln)*, the Italian Enzo Cucchi *(La Fior tura dei galli neri)*, the Greek Jannis Kounellis or the Frenchman Roland Topor. A is obvious from the large number of works produced in the United Kingdom a the end of the 20C, it is becoming increasingly difficult to label the trends of th 1990s. However, there is no doubt that the Stedelijk Museum will soon be dis playing a judicious selection.

1945-80 – It is difficult, in just a few lines, to describe the diversity and richnes of the works since all the main trends are well represented here (Pop Art, paintin of matter, Kinetic Art, Paris School, Op Art, New Realism, Dutch Lyricism

Expressionism, Art and Language etc). The museum boasts an admirable **collection of works by the CoBrA group**★ *(see AMSTELVEEN)*, a movement whose greatest national exponent was **Karel Appel** (his murals can be seen in the restaurant and in the *Appelbar* in room 15c).

The most outstanding of all the museum's exhibits, however, is the dazzling **collection of American Abstract Expressionists**★★ with works by Willem de Kooning, Barnett Newman (*Cathedra*, 1951), Morris Louis (*Gamma Mu*, 1960), Ellsworth Kelly and Kenneth Noland. The museum also has works by Americans Robert Rauschenberg (*Charlene*, 1954), Jasper Johns, Roy Lichtenstein (*As I opened Fire...*, 1964), Claes Oldenburg, Frank Stella and Andy Warhol, by French artists Jean Dubuffet (*Personnage hilare*, 1947), Germaine Richier and Martial Raysse, by the Italian Lucio Fontana, by Swiss painters Daniel Spoerri and Jean Tingueley, by the Spaniard Antonio Tapiés, and by Dutchmen Jan Schoonhoven, Wessel Couzijn and Ad Dekkers.

1920-45 – Numerous artists represent the interwar years, a period which saw recognition for Abstract Art and Expressionism while Realism enjoyed a new upsurge of creativity. A list of works would be too long and tedious; we shall therefore restrict ourselves to an indication of just a few artists. It should also be emphasised that the museum has almost no Surrealist works. The room contains paintings by Mexican mural artist Diego Rivera, Frenchmen Jean Pougny, Fernand Léger (*Les Trois Camarades*, 1920), and Russian-born Chaïm Soutane, the Swiss artist Paul Klee, Germans Max Ernst, Max Beckmann and Willy Baumeister, Belgians Constant Permeke and Jean Brusselmans, Spaniards Julio Gonzáles and Joan Miró, and Dutchmen Bram van Velde and Herman Kruyder.

Room 7 contains ***La Perruche et la sirène***★★ (1952) by Henri Matisse, a masterpiece purchased in 1967 consisting of paper cut-outs. It had an enormous influence on American artists in the Colourfield movement of the late 1960s.

Stedelijk Museum

Head of a Peasant Woman, Kazimir Malevich

1900-20 – In 1958, the museum purchased 29 paintings, seven gouaches, 15 drawings and 17 diagrams by **Kazimir Malevich**. In doing so, it created an absolutely unique **collection of Malevich's works**★★★, enabling visitors to see the artist's progression from Figurative to Abstract between 1911 to 1915, ie from paintings of Ukrainian peasants to Suprematist works. The progression is spectacular, especially as regards colours which are almost Fauvist in the density to be seen in the series of paintings of peasants. An analysis of the construction of his compositions is the best way to appreciate his rapid development. The forms are pre-Cubic in their robustness in this series, elementary in the *Head of a Peasant Woman* and geometric in *Supremus Nr. 50* (1915).

The museum presents many other works from this period when artists were freeing themselves from the constraints of visible reality. Among the many paintings are compositions by Dutch artists Jan Toorop, Christ Beekman, Kees van Dongen (*Old Clown*, 1910), Theo van Doesburg, the editor of the review *De Stijl*, and Piet Mondrian, a major artist who began by painting academic landscapes before creating the analytical compositions that are well known to all those with a love of modern and contemporary art, and that are well represented in *Tableau III, Composition dans l'ovale* (1914). Equally well represented are German Expressionists in works by Franz Marc (***Blue Ponies***★, 1912), Heinrich Campendonck, August Macke and Ernst Kirchner (*Young Girl Nude behind a Curtain*, 1910), French artists such as Georges Braque (*Still Life with Pot and Bottles*, 1909), Marc Chagall (*Self-Portrait with Seven Fingers*, 1913), Pierre Bonnard, Maurice de Vlaminck, Edouard Vuillard and Robert Delaunay, Belgians Rik Wouters (*Woman with a Plait*, 1912) and James Ensor, Spaniard Pablo Picasso, Italians Gino Severini and Filippo de Pisis and Russian Wassily Kandinsky (*Improvisation 33*, 1913).

Harvesting Rye, Kasimir Malevich

The 19C – The collection of works produced between 1850 and the end of the 19C consists of paintings by Dutch and French artists, displayed on a rota basis. The Stedelijk Museum has 30 canvases by **George Hendrik Breitner** who, at the end of the 19C, was much better known in Amsterdam than Van Gogh, and who was often regarded, wrongly, as the leader of the Dutch Impressionists. Although his views of towns illustrate the distance that separated them, they are nevertheless of great interest, especially *Le Dam* (1898). Note too the works by Isaac Israëls (*The Sand Dealer*, c 1895), Anton Mauve, Willem Roelofs, Matthijs Maris, Jacob Maris (*Polders after the Rain*, 1892), Johann Barthold Jongkind, Willem Witsen and Vincent van Gogh.

Great French artists are not forgotten. There are paintings by Auguste Renoir, Charles Daubigny, Claude Monet, Paul Cézanne (*La Montagne Sainte-Victoire*, c 1888), Edouard Manet (study for *A Bar at the Folies-Bergères*, 1881), Gustave Courbet, Edgar Degas and Odilon Redon (*Apollo's Chariot of the Sun*, c 1900).

VAN GOGH MUSEUM***

Plan p 10, **JZ** and **KZ**
Michelin map no 36 L 9

THE MUSEUM ARCHITECTURE *Paulus Potterstraat 7*

The Van Gogh museum was opened in 1973. Its outline recalls the trends introduced by the De Stijl movement, (literally, "the Style"); the main concept behind the movement's designs was that only mathematical structures could express the real essence of things. The architect of this building was **Gerrit Rietveld** (1888-1964), who, although not one of the movement's founders, remains one of its leading personalities. His greatest work was the Schröder House (1924) in Utrecht, a concrete construction consisting of a juxtaposition of cubes. The principle is recognisable here, but it has been adapted to suit the proposed use of the building as a museum. Indeed, the adaptation is so remarkable that visitors are invariably amazed at the light pouring into a building which looks from the outside like a totally enclosed block of concrete.

Vincent van Gogh

Born on 30 March 1853 in the village of Zundert in Noord-Brabant, Vincent van Gogh was the eldest of six children. His father was a minister; three of his uncles were art dealers. He began to work at the age of 16 as an employee with the Goupil art gallery in The Hague before being sent by the firm to Brussels, London and, finally, Paris in 1875. A visit to the Louvre brought him face to face with the works of Corot, Millet and Delacroix.

He was dismissed in the following year and decided to study theology in Amsterdam in order to be ordained. In 1878 he abandoned his studies and travelled to the Borinage mining area of Belgium where he looked after the poor. Vincent was disavowed by the Church because he was considered to have little aptitude for preaching and a tendency towards the mystical. In 1880 he decided to become an artist. "*I cannot tell you how happy I am to have begun drawing again.*" (*Letters to Theo*, 24 September 1880, Éditions Gallimard)

From 1881 to 1886 Vincent lived in the Netherlands. Funded by Anton Mauve, he studied painting, worked at his art and began producing his paintings of country life, while still living with his parents in **Nuenen**. This was not only the beginning of his artistic life; it was also the period of unhappy love affairs. In 1886, he set off to join his brother Theo in **Paris** where Theo managed the Montmartre branch of the Goupil gallery. He met several artists and his first experience of Impressionism was like a religious revelation.

Van Gogh Museum

Self-Portrait in a Grey Hat

Exhausted by life in Paris and/or disturbed by his brother's forthcoming marriage, Vincent moved to **Arles** in 1888 where he lived in the "yellow house". The dazzling Provençal sunshine transformed his painting, in which he began to distance himself from Impressionism. On 23 December, after a period of work with Paul Gauguin and temperamental outbursts from both artists, he cut off one of his ear lobes; he was taken into hospital. This unfortunate incident took him back into a life of solitude.

In January 1889 he was again placed in an asylum, at the request of the local people in Arles. In May he asked to be admitted to the asylum in **Saint-Rémy** because he was suffering from constant ideas of suicide. Yet the early part of 1890 was more favourable; an article by Albert Aurier praised his painting and he sold his first (and last) work, to a Belgian artist named Anna Boch. In May, probably on the advice of Pissaro, he travelled to **Auvers-sur-Oise** to receive treatment from Dr Gachet. Overwhelmed by his feeling of mental isolation and convinced that he was going insane, he shot himself in the chest. Vincent van Gogh died two days later, on 29 July 1890, with Theo at his bedside. His brother died the following year.

There are plans to extend the museum built by Van Dillen and Van Tricht from 1963 to 1973. A semicircular pavilion designed by the Japanese architect Kisho Kurokawa has already been added to the rear of the building.

The museum built by Van Dillen and Van Tricht from 1963 to 1973 has recently been enlarged. An oval-shaped pavilion designed by the Japanese architect Kisho Kurokawa was added at the back of the building in 1999.

THE COLLECTIONS

Seven sketchpads, 200 paintings, 580 drawings and some 750 letters written by Vincent van Gogh, plus works by contemporary artists bought by Vincent or his brother, constitute the museum's unusual collection. Several years ago the museum instigated a different purchasing policy so that it could present more works from the second half of the 19C.

The new, oval-shaped wing of the museum organises temporary exhibitions devoted to 19C art, allowing a better understanding of art in Van Gogh's era.

Contemporary works – *Ground floor and third floor.*

Even if it contained only the admirable paintings purchased by Theo van Gogh or the museum's curators, the collection would still be outstanding. The only disadvantage for visitors who can come only once is the system of display on a rota basis. The paintings described below are not, therefore, all displayed at the same time: *Tulip Fields and Mills near Leyden* (1886) by Claude Monet; **"Rice Powder", Young Woman at a Table★** (1887) by Henri de Toulouse-Lautrec; *Portrait of the Artist's Grandmother* (1887) by Émile Bernard; **Landscape in Martinique★★** (c 1887) and *Self-portrait* (1888) by Charles Laval; *Les Misérables, self-portrait with portrait of Bernard* (1888) and **Portrait of Vincent van Gogh Painting Sunflowers★** (1888) by Paul Gauguin; **The Two Sisters★** (1891) by Maurice Denis; **The Boat★** (1897) by Odilon Redon; Rue de l'Épicerie, Rouen (1898) by Camille Pissaro; **Still Life with Flowers★** (c 1901) by Pablo Picasso.

> **Extract from the last letter sent by Vincent to Theo van Gogh**
>
> *"As far as I am concerned, I am working assiduously on my canvases and am trying to paint as well as certain artists whom I have loved and admired so much."* (*Letters to Theo*, 23 July 1890, Éditions Gallimard)

Among the sculptures, note *Solidarity* (1898) by George Minne; *The Tall Peasant* (1902) by Jules Dalou; *Maternity* (1902) by Constantin Meunier.

Charles Laval (1862-94) – There are those who will probably be surprised to see the name and works of Charles Laval mentioned here, for the artist was almost totally unknown to the general public. He became friendly with Gauguin in Pont-Aven in 1886 and went with him to Martinique and Panama the following year. Although he produced only a small number of works, his paintings were often attributed to Gauguin, a tribute (albeit an unfortunate one) to the quality of his painting.

Vincent van Gogh: life and work

The Dutch period (1880-85) – This period produced a large number of drawings and watercolours in predominantly dark hues. Vincent was moved by the "man-machine", to use the phrase coined by Michelet whose work *Le Peuple* he had read. He was also influenced by the works of Millet which he had seen and admired in Paris in 1875. During this period, Vincent depicted the misery that surrounded him.

He painted numerous portraits and canvases such as his *Autumn Landscape with Poplar Trees* (1884), *The Cottage* (1885), **The Potato Eaters★** (1885), a painting which linked the artist to the great Realist traditions of Dutch painting through the subject matter and through the brutal contrasts in the chiaroscuro.

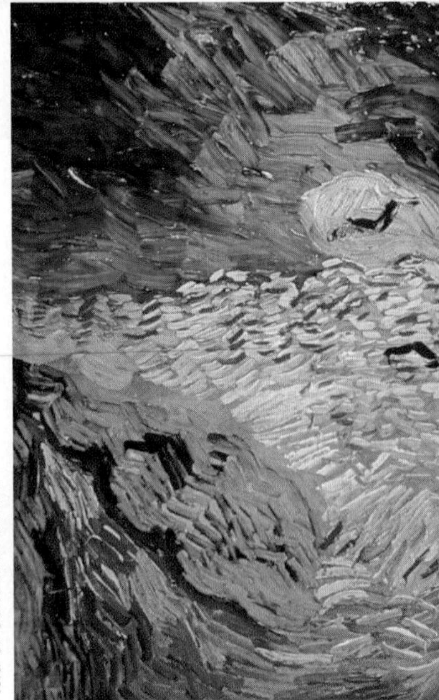

Field of Corn with Crows

Van Gogh Museum

Fishing Boats on the Beach at Les Saintes-Maries-de-la-Mer

On 26 March 1885 his father died. Van Gogh travelled to Antwerp (from November 1885 to February 1886) where he studied at the city's academy of art and saw Japanese prints for the first time. He then went on to Paris.

The Parisian period (1886-88) – Van Gogh discovered the Impressionists. He became friendly with Émile Bernard, Paul Signac and Henri de Toulouse-Lautrec. His artistic vision was immediately renewed and his style underwent a profound change. He used lighter colours and his compositions rapidly became less tortured. Because he could not pay for models, Van Gogh decided to use his own image, and this marked the beginning of a long series of self-portraits.
The Montmartre paintings from the period Vincent spent with Theo at 54 rue Lepic are part of a series of works that are often reminiscent of the canvases produced by the painters of the Barbizon School – *View of the Rooftops of Paris* (1886),

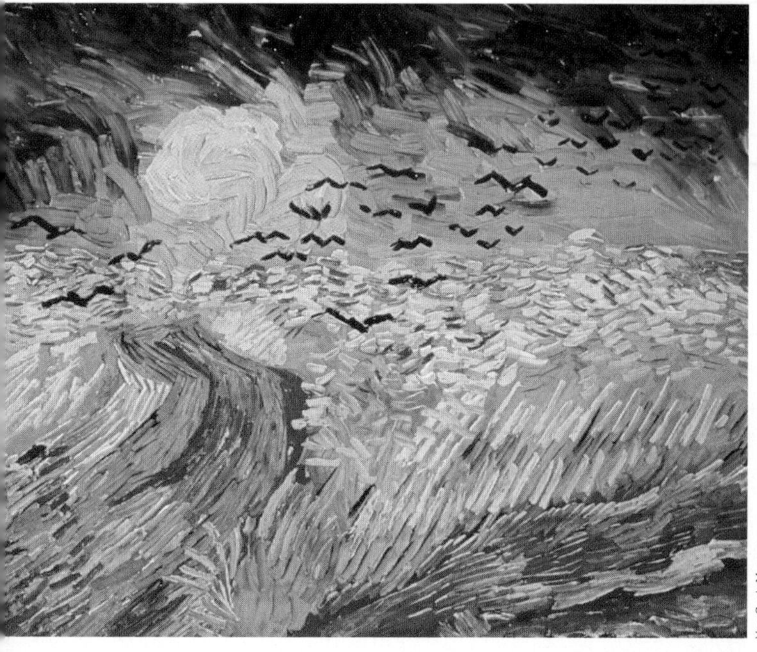
Van Gogh Museum

The Irises (1890)

Woman Sitting in the Café du Tambourin (1887), *Boulevard de Clichy* (1887), *View of Paris from Theo's Apartment, rue Lepic* (1887).

Still-life works gave the artist an opportunity to study colour. Many of them are not signed and depict flowers given to him by friends. Gradually, he began to paint still-life works with fruit, for example the *Still Life with Jug and Lemons* (1887) and more importantly ***Still Life with Quinces and Lemons***★★ (1887), in which the frame is painted in the same colouring as the canvas in order to heighten the effect of the composition. This process had already been used by Georges Seurat.

Most of the 18 self-portraits in the museum were painted during Van Gogh's time in Paris. ***Self-Portrait in front of an Easel***★ (1888) and ***Self-Portrait in a Grey Hat***★★ (1887/1888) are among the most introspective works of this period. In the latter, the Pointillist technique serves a pictorial dynamism that was particular to Van Gogh. The artist's face is surrounded by something akin to a halo. His ***Self-Portrait in a Straw Hat***★ (1887), an oil on cardboard, illustrates the artist's visits to the country. They became increasingly frequent as he attempted to flee the ever-present noise of Paris, even in the still rustic Montmartre. *Cornfield with a Lark* (1887) and *Woodland* (1887) are forerunners of the future works painted in the open air, both in their subject matter and in their simplicity.

Arles (1888-89) – Although there seem to be many reasons for this departure, the letters written by the artist shed light on the context of his decision: *"Success takes ambition, and ambition seems absurd to me. [...] And then I am going to retire somewhere to the south of France where I shall not see so many artists who disgust me in human terms."* (*Letters to Theo*, summer 1887, Éditions Gallimard) Influenced by the southern sunshine, he began using more luminous colours an his paintings acquired a new chromatic power. It was here that Vincent produced his most serene works, an indication of the major canvases of the future. Unfortunately, a form of hereditary epilepsy was to destroy his dream of creating an artistic community in Arles (the "yellow house") and drag him down into the depths of despair. He painted countless landscapes, several of which were in the style of Japanese prints: *The Pink Orchard* (1888), *Peach Trees in Bloom* (1888), *Pear Tree in Bloom* (1888), ***Fishing Boats on the Beach at Les Saintes-Maries-de-la-Mer***★★ (1888), also known as the *Still Life with Four Boats* since the artists stylised the boats to such an extent that they made him think of flowers. *La Rue* (1888) depicts the house that he hoped to turn into an "artists' centre". The amazing ***Vincent's Room***★ (1888) is steeped in the peace and sleep that are so attractive to an artist exhausted with working so much outside. During the summer of 1888, Van Gogh completed several versions of a theme of which he had become particularly fond after seeing a certain work by Millet and deciding to devote himself to Art. None of the canvases really satisfied him until, towards the end of the year, he created a small but outstanding painting, ***The Sower***★★★. In 1889, he painted ***The Sunflowers***★★, flowers which, in his eyes, symbolised gratitude. The painting is a replica of one of those that used to decorate Gauguin's room in the "yellow house".

Saint-Rémy (1889-90) – After happiness followed by tension in his relationship with Gauguin, and after having cut off his ear and been hospitalised, Van Gogh suffered from increasingly violent hallucinations and he went of his own accord to the lunatic asylum in Saint-Paul-de-Mausole. This, though, did not prevent him from working; indeed he experienced a period of intense activity. Soon he was given permission to go outside the asylum, and he again began painting nature before suffering from further hallucinations. His style reflected the difficulties of his existence. The lemon yellow colours of the Arles period were replaced by a range of more muted colours. Nevertheless the compositions remained admirable, showing a magnificent, captivating graphic skill.

A close look at *The Garden of the Hospital in Saint-Paul* (1889) reveals Vincent's suffering. Although reminiscent of the Arles period in its colouring, ***The Irises***★★ (1890) is part and parcel of his internal torment. Everything in the work is based on the principle of opposition, of "the effect of terrifying, disparate complementary elements". The total anguish of the artist, though, is best seen in the *Pietà* (1889) after Delacroix and *The Resurrection of Lazarus* (1890) after Rembrandt. Indeed, numerous critics commenting on the works of Van Gogh suggest that the figures of Christ and the saint are in fact self-portraits, and that the *mater dolorosa* and the women removing the linen from the face of the resurrected Lazarus are two of Vincent's friends from Arles.
One of the few paintings instilled with an optimistic note is the ***Cornfield with Reaper***★ (1889), although it is known that the artist saw the figure as a representation of Death and that the corn was humanity being cut down.

Auvers-sur-Oise (1890) – As a result of an article published in the *Mercure de France*, Van Gogh was no longer anonymous. One of the six canvases hung at the eighth Salon des XX in Brussels was sold. By that time, he was some 30km/19 miles north of Paris, in an artists' village in "the care" of Dr Gachet, a lover of modern art who taught Van Gogh the basic techniques of etching. The tranquillity of the surroundings and the visits from Theo encouraged him to continue producing works despite the despair eating away at him. His touch is turbulent, expressive, sometimes confused, but the colours have again become vivid, even denser than before, more sonorous. Although hindsight now makes it possible to see in these last works all the tragedy of imminent death, they should first and foremost be appreciated for their immense creative value and the contribution made by a man who must be considered as one of the fathers of modern art.
The final paintings constitute a fascinating and constantly moving series, including **Cornfield with Crows**★★★ (1890), a highly dramatic work both in its subject matter and treatment; ***Cornfield under a Stormy Sky***★★ (1890), outstanding for the depth of the large expanses of two colours; and ***The Château d'Auvers***★ (1890) with its melancholy atmosphere.
Among the last thoughts written by Vincent for Theo (although he did not send the letter) is this: "*Well! Really we cannot make our paintings talk. [...] I tell you again [...] you have a share in the production of certain canvases which retain their calm even in the midst of disaster.*" (*Letters to Theo*, no date, Éditions Gallimard.)

VONDELPARK

Plan p 10, **JZ**
Michelin map no 36 L 8

Laid out originally in 1864 by DJ Zocher and extended in 1874 by his son, LP Zocher, in the style of English gardens, the Vondel Park was the second stage in the project to create a green belt around the city centre. It was first known as the Nieuwe Park, but was renamed after Joost van den Vondel when a statue of the great poet, a leading light in the Golden Age, was erected here in 1867.
Covering a distance of almost 1.5km/1mi and an area of 48ha, this delightful park boasts a number of particularly fine trees of more than 120 varieties including sweet chestnuts, oaks, poplars and Louisiana cypress. Lawns, a rose garden, sinuous lakes and fountains create surroundings that are much appreciated by people out for a stroll or a cycle ride and, over the past few years, by roller-skaters. It is not uncommon to see some of them gliding along the tarmac of the pathways with the same wide swinging movement used by speed skaters on ice, speed skating being a traditional sport in the Netherlands whose champions are national heroes, ready to outshine the competition at every Winter Olympics.
As soon as the weather turns mild and the sun shines, the park's lawns attract large numbers of visitors and crowds of (neo-)hippies, delighted to set the world to rights while sitting on the banks of the ponds. During the 1970s the park became a vast open-air dormitory. Free concerts are given in the open-air theatre *(Openluchttheater)*. Although the park remains open throughout the night, the large houses flanking the Vondelpark now constitute Amsterdam's most expensive urban distict (as is obvious from the shops in PC Hoofstraat). The streets in the vicinity of the park have the same atmosphere as those in Chelsea in London.

Filmmuseum ⓥ – *Vondelpark 3.* This huge pavilion located in the northeast of the park was originally designed by PJ Hamer to house a restaurant which opened in 1881. The building was restored just after the Second World War and, since 1991, has housed a film library which shows some 1 000 films every year. Free open-air film shows are organised in the summer.

The ever-relaxed atmosphere in the Vondelpark

Hollandsche Manege – *Vondelstraat 140.* The Dutch indoor ring is resolutely Viennese in inspiration. However, although the building designed by **AL van Gendt** *(see MUSEUMPLEIN, Concertgebouw)* in 1882 was magnificently restored in 1986 under the direction of Prince Bernhardt, it cannot compete with the superb Winterreitschule in Vienna where visitors can watch the famous Spanish Riding School at work.

Vondelkerk – *Vondelstraat 120.* **PJH Cuypers** *(see RIJKSMUSEUM)* designed and built his largest neo-Gothic church here in 1880. It was almost totally destroyed by fire in 1904 and it was his son, Joseph Cuypers, who was responsible for the reconstruction of the tower. The building was deconsecrated in 1979 and is now used as offices.

WATERLOOPLEIN

Plan p 11, **LY**
Michelin Map no° 36 J 11

This vast square is home to an animated market selling furniture, second-hand clothing, ethnic jewellery and fabrics. With the exception of the Church of Moses and Aaron, the buildings bordering the square are modern.

Mozes en Aäronkerk – *Waterlooplein 205.* If the Church of Moses and Aaron bears a surprising name for a building devoted to Roman Catholic worship, it is because it stands on the former site of the house a Jewish merchant who had decorated the frontage with statues of Moses and Aaron. The building was then purchased by a priest who wanted his congregation to be able to practise their religion in a secret church.
The current neo-Classical style building was built between 1837 and 1841 to the designs of the architect TF Suys. The stone statues on the rear façade depicting Moses and Aaron were salvaged from the demolished houses. Restored in 1990 the building is now the setting for exhibitions and concerts.

Stadhuis en Muziektheater – *Waterlooplein.* This building, along with the Rijksmuseum and the central station, has caused more controversy than any other among the inhabitants of Amsterdam. This is partly because of the architecture of the building itself, but also because the old Jewish quarter that used to surround Waterlooplein was demolished to make way for its construction.
Designed by the Viennese architect **Wilhelm Holzbauer** and the Dutch architect **Cees Dam**, the building houses a town hall and an opera house that is also used for concerts. It was nicknamed "Stopera", on the one hand as a contraction of *Stadhuis* and *Opera* but also to signify "stop opera", and the name has stuck. Completed in 1987, this imposing building bordering the Amstel river has a modernity that inevitably seems rather brutal in the context of a city that has so carefully preserved its traditional architecture. But then again contemporary architecture is rarely well received by critics.
The Muziektheater is the seat of the National opera (De Nederlandse Opera) and the National Ballet Company (Het Nationale Ballet). The auditorium seats 1 689 people.

The NAP – In the passageway that separates the two sections of the building there are three glass columns filled with water. Two of the columns show the sea level at IJmuiden and Vlissingen; the third shows the level reached in 1953 when

Zealand was flooded. Descending the stairs one can see a pile driven in to the second layer of sand under the city: a bronze marker indicates what is known as the **NAP**, that is to say the normal sea level of Amsterdam. This level is used as the standard all over Europe for the sea level.

In front of the building, at the corner of the Amstel and the Zwanenburgwal, an austere black marble **monument** serves as a reminder of the resistance by the Jewish civilians who were killed between 1940 and 1945.

★ **Joods Historisch Museum** ⓥ – *Jonas Daniël Meijerplein 2-4.* Opened in 1987, the Jewish historical museum occupies four Ashkenazi synagogues. The first, known as the Great Synagogue, was built in 1671 to designs by **Daniël Stalpaert**. The building was too small so the Obbene (1685), the Dritt (1700) and the New Synagogue (1752) were added subsequently. The New Synagogue is easily recognisable by its Ionic columns at the entrance and its dome.

The exhibition covers five aspects of Jewish identity: religion; Israel and Zionism; war; persecution and survival; history and the mixing of cultures.

In the **New Synagogue** the holy arch dates from 1791 and comes from Enkhuizen. Note the **Haggadah manuscript**, a collection of illuminated manuscripts created in 1734 by Joseph de Leipnik.

The **Great Synagogue**★ still has the white marble holy arch which was presented in 1671 by the Rabbi Abraham Auerbach. The displays cover various themes such as the Jewish year and its feasts and Bar Mitzvah. Also on display are ceremonial and ritual objects including silverware, lamps, robes and Torah ornaments. The galleries are devoted to the socio-economic history of the Jews in the Netherlands. On display in a side room is a **mikwe**★, a rare example of a ritual bath that women immersed themselves in on certain specific occasions in their lives, such as before getting married. It was used from 1671 to c 1820.

Dokwerker – *Mr Visserplein.* A work by Mari Andriessen, the statue of a docker commemorates the strike launched by the dockers in protest against the deportation of the Jews of Amsterdam on 25 January 1941.

★ **Portugees-Israëlitische Synagoge** ⓥ – *Mr Visserplein 3.* This massive building was constructed by Elias Bouwman between 17 April 1671 (or 6 Iyar 5431 in the Jewish calendar) and 2 August 1675 (10 Menachem 5435). It was destined for the three congregations of Portuguese Sephardic Jews who had just merged into one group known as the *Talmud Torah.* The immense building is made of red brick with light provided by tall windows

As can be seen from Emmanuel de Witte's painting in the Rijksmuseum, the interior has remained unchanged since the 17C, with its wide wooden barrel vaults, its very tall columns and its galleries for women only. There is no parochet (curtain), which is unknown in the Hispano-Portuguese Jewish tradition. Note instead the Parnassim pew reserved for dignitaries, the Hechal or Ark of the Covenant made of jacaranda wood imported from Brazil and the large **copper chandeliers** bristling with a thousand candles.

Sand is regularly laid on the floor to absorb humidity and muffle the sound of footsteps. As in the 17C there is no electricity or heating. This place of worship also possesses one of the most important Judaic libraries in the world.

Ph. Gajic/MICHELIN

Portuguese-Israelite Synagoge

WESTERDOK

Plan p 12, **BN**
Michelin map no 36 G 10

The Westerdok is the most westerly harbour basin in the city centre. On many town plans, it is referred to as *Gouden Reael* (the Golden Reael, after Realeneiland – see below).
To the north of Haarlemmerbuurt *(see ANNE FRANK HUIS, West-Indisch Huis)* and the canals forming the Grachtengordel (Prinsengracht, Keizersgracht, Herengracht and Singel) are three man-made islands built in the early 17C *(Westelijke Eilanden)*, the western islands in the IJ. They were built to make room for hemp and linen warehouses and boatyards filled with the clamour of ships' carpenters and caulkers. Paradoxically isolated by the railway line from the hustle and bustle of the central railway station nearby and almost totally devoid of any of the traditional tourist attractions, this area has retained the authentic charms of Amsterdam's age-old maritime harbour.

Bickerseiland – This island lined with boats and houseboats has become residential. It was purchased in 1631 by Jan Bicker, a very wealthy businessman whose brother, Andries, became mayor of the town.
Jan Bicker, who lived in Keizersgracht, moved to a house at the corner of Grote Bickersstraat and Minnemoersstraat (the house was demolished in the late 17C). In the Rijksmuseum there is a painting by B van der Helst depicting Andries' son as an obese child who is apparently very satisfied with his social rank.
There are still some small boatyards on the first of the islands, successors to the famous *DE WALVIS* ("the whale") whose sign has survived the passing years.

Zandhoek and its unchanging maritime atmosphere

Realeneiland – **Laurens Jacobszoon Reaal** (1588-1648) was one of the merchants who had the first houses built on the island, in particular on **Zandhoek**, a delightful quay opposite Westerdok. Its name (*zand* means sand and *hoek* means corner) is a reminder that a sand merchant once worked here selling sand for use as ballast in ships. A row of 17C merchants' houses with gables and façades delightfully decorated with carved stones has been magnificently restored. Note the two-storey shopfronts on nos 2 to 7. No 6 (1657) has a frontage stone representing a white horse on a red background. No 11 has a frontage stone depicting an anchor; this indicated that the house was a seamen's hostel. Zandhoek is undoubtedly one of the most photographed places in Amsterdam because of its elegant houses and because of the old boats and barges *(tjalken)* tied up here. Yet this charming little corner of the city owes its survival to a novel by **Jan Mens** (1897-1967), *De Gouden Reael* (1940) whose title was directly inspired by the sign hanging outside the restaurant at no 14. The book's success saved from demolition a district that was then the home of the unemployed and dockers.
The quays lining the Realengracht are still backed by warehouses such as, at no 22-38, the perfectly restored **De Lepelaar** (the Spatula) and others at the corner of Taandwarsstraat which are awaiting renovation.
The **Drieharingenbrug** (Three Herring Bridge) links Realeneiland to Prinseneiland. The narrow bridge is reserved for pedestrians and cyclists; it replaced a wooden pontoon which swung back against the bank to enable boats to pass through. For an explanation of the strange name of this bridge, see the frontage stone on the house with three chimney stacks in the tiny Vierwindenstraat.

Prinseneiland – Prince's Island, the smallest of the three islands in the west of the city, has some fine groups of warehouses which have been renovated and turned into flats. **George Hendrik Breitner** (1857-1923), several of whose paintings hang in the Rijksmuseum, had his studio at no 24. Nos 49-51 have an amusing frontage stone (*LACHEN*, meaning "laugh") on which the face is highly expressive.

The street running centrally across the island, Galgenstraat (Gibbet Street), owes its sinister name to the fact that the view used to extend as far as the gibbets placed on the other bank of the IJ until the end of the 18C, on a strip of sand which later became Amsterdam Noord.

M. Guillou/MICHELIN

Drieharingenbrug, Realengracht

IN THE VICINITY OF THE THREE ISLANDS

Barentzplein – Although it is a historic monument, the huge corn silo (1895) projecting into the IJ remained abandoned for many years. Until recently, it was occupied by squatters. Renovation work began on the building in 1998.

Haarlemmerpoort – *Haarlemmerplein*. The Haarlem Gate is officially called Willemspoort because it was built in 1840 to mark the coronation of William II or, to be more precise, to serve as the setting for his triumphant entrance into the city. The neo-Classical construction was designed by Cornelis Alewijn (1788-1839).

★ **Het "Schip"** – *Corner of Zaanstraat and Oostzaanstraat*. "The Boat" (1921) was a leading creation of the Amsterdam School and, with De Dageraad *(see De PIJP)* was one of the major works of **Michel de Klerk** (1884-1923).

The building centres on a courtyard and includes 15 different types of housing. In addition to the strong curves on the façade, note the Expressionist **steeple** (Expressionist because it served no purpose) overlooking Hembrugstraat. The building was criticised after its inauguration on the grounds that the external appearance was given greater importance than the housing within. This fault was inherent to the movement which was, by its very essence, highly individualistic.

Amsterdam and the Hanseatic League

There have been four Hanseatic Leagues in history, but the best known is the **Teutonic Hanseatic League**. It was formed from regional leagues whose aim was to protect their merchandise. It was not given official status by any document until 1356, when difficulties encountered by German trading posts in Bruges led the towns to meet in Lübeck and decide on the measures to be taken.

It is not always easy to determine whether or not a given town belonged to the Hanseatic League. There were almost 200 members between the 14C and 16C and no comprehensive list was ever drawn up. However, contrary to many claims, it is known that Amsterdam was not a member.

In the middle of the 15C, the Low Countries included some 20 Hanseatic towns, in particular Deventer, Groningen, Nijmegen and **Kampen**. The latter, located at the mouth of the IJssel, was the busiest port in the region during the Middle Ages (in c 1400 it had a population of 12 000 compared to 5 000 in what is now the country's capital city). Admission criteria for would-be members of the Hanseatic League were draconian because the League feared unfair competition, especially from the Dutch. Transactions between the League and Kampen were so protracted that the town did not finally become a member until 1441. Amsterdam, on the other hand, was one of the two main centres of trade with the Hanseatic League, Dordrecht being the other; it just goes to prove that there is no insurmountable obstacle to trade.

A tulip field near Lisse: an alternative to counting sheep?

The suburbs

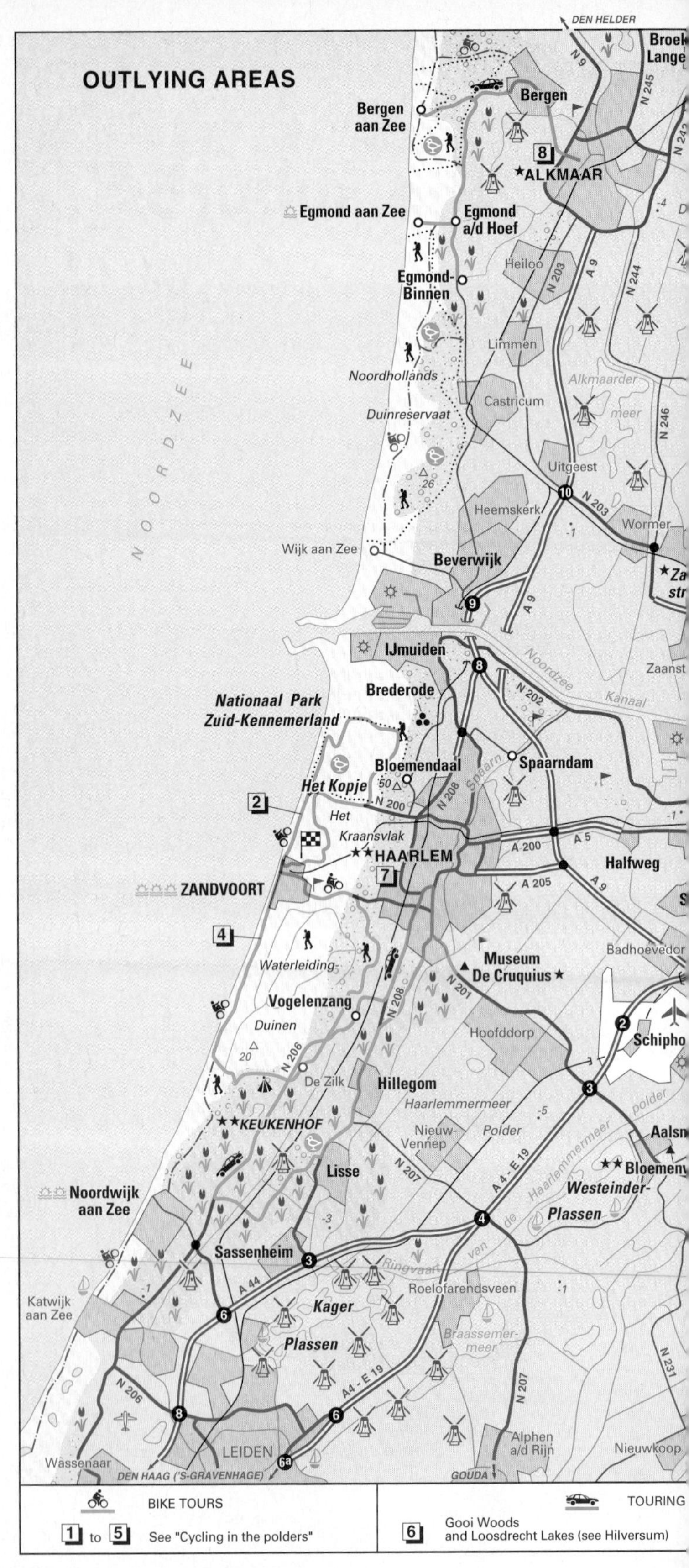

OUTLYING AREAS
DEN HELDER
Bergen aan Zee
Bergen
8
★ALKMAAR
Egmond aan Zee
Egmond a/d Hoef
Heiloo
Egmond-Binnen
Limmen
Noordhollands
Duinreservaat
Castricum
Alkmaarder meer
NOORDZEE
Uitgeest
Heemskerk
Wormer
Wijk aan Zee
Beverwijk
IJmuiden
Noordzee Kanaal
Zaanst
Brederode
Nationaal Park Zuid-Kennemerland
Bloemendaal
Spaarndam
Het Kopje
Het Kraansvlak
★★HAARLEM
7
2
ZANDVOORT
Halfweg
4
Badhoevedor
Waterleiding-
Museum De Cruquius★
Vogelenzang
Duinen
Hoofddorp
Schipho
De Zilk
Hillegom
Haarlemmermeer
Polder
★★KEUKENHOF
Nieuw-Vennep
Lisse
Aalsm
★★Bloemen
Westeinder-Plassen
Noordwijk aan Zee
Sassenheim
Ringvaart
Roelofarendsveen
Katwijk aan Zee
Kager Plassen
Braassemer-meer
LEIDEN
Wassenaar
Alphen a/d Rijn
Nieuwkoop
DEN HAAG ('S-GRAVENHAGE)
GOUDA
BIKE TOURS
1 to 5 See "Cycling in the polders"
TOURING
6 Gooi Woods and Loosdrecht Lakes (see Hilversum)

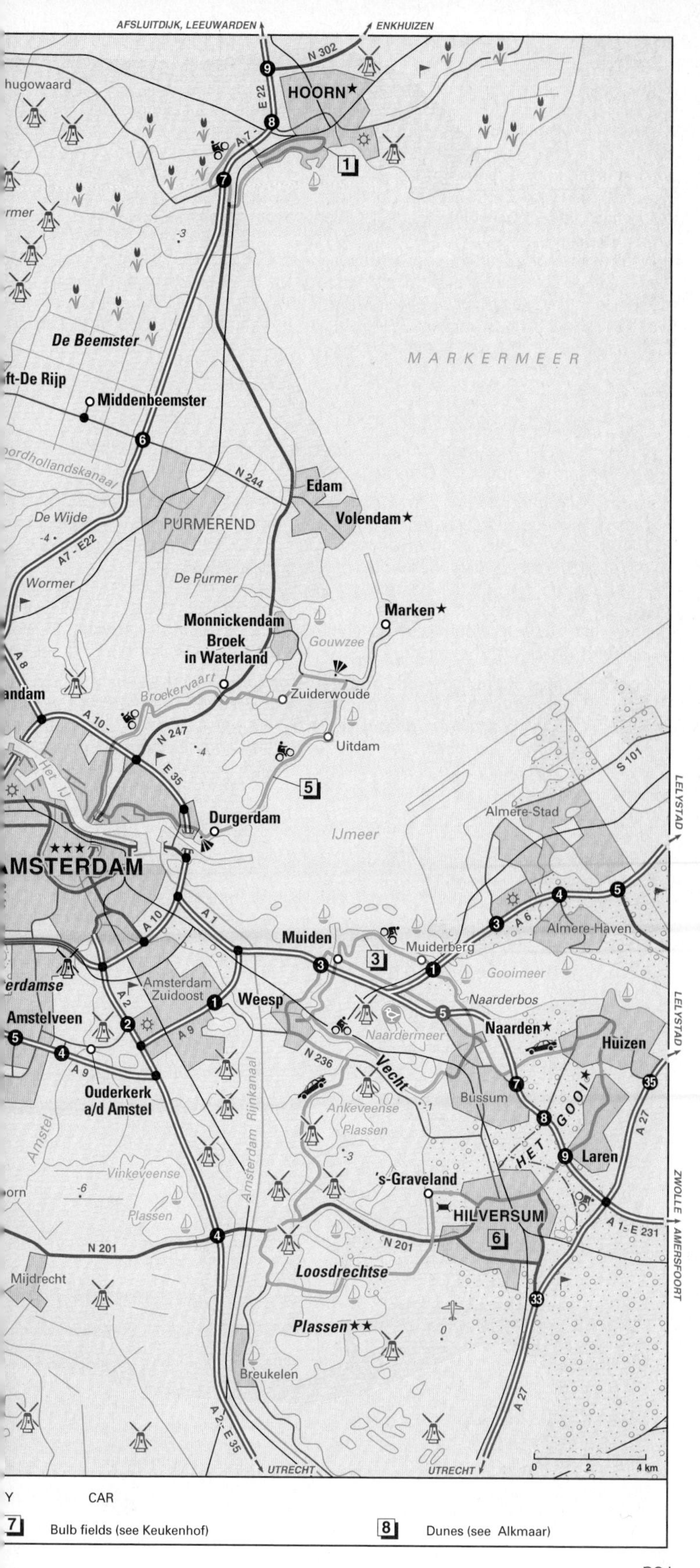

CAR

7 Bulb fields (see Keukenhof)

8 Dunes (see Alkmaar)

CYCLING IN THE POLDERS

In the vicinity of Amsterdam there are countless possibilities for cycle rides, since the area is criss-crossed by a multitude of cycle paths. Our suggestions for rides include the widest possible variety of landscapes: beaches and sand dunes along the shore, a bird sanctuary inland, polders dotted with lakes and fields full of grazing cows and sheep, a fortified town or former port of the Dutch India Company, canals with houseboats or rivers spanned by swing bridges, fields of tulips and dikes dotted with windmills. Noord-Holland has an unsuspected diversity of scenery.
For information on other rides, we recommend a visit to the VVV shops *(Vereniging voor Vreemdelingenverkeer, or Tourist Association)* or to any good bookshop where you can purchase the *Noord-Holland/Noord* or *Noord-Holland/Zuid Fietsgids*. These two cycling guides each contain 20 tours which, although described in Dutch, are clearly depicted on the corresponding maps.

1 TOUR FROM HOORN: 14km/9mi

1hr 30min to 2hr (not including visits of museums and stops).

From Amsterdam: by car or train from the central station. Cycle hire at the railway station in Hoorn (right on exiting the station).

Hoorn – *From the station turn into Veemarkt and left into Gedempte Turfhaven, then follow the route on the Hoorn map. Beyond Hoofdtoren, continue along Hoofd and turn right into Achter op het Zand overlooking the yachting marina. At the end, turn right along Westerdijk opposite Markermeer.*
This delightful port on the Markermeer, has an old district which is very pleasant to tour by bike *(see HOORN)*. Cycle at will through the streets and alleyways in the old town of Hoorn and leave the prescribed route if you want to. You will not regret it. At the road junction, Westerdijk continues left out of the town.

In the vicinity of Hoorn: reeds and fields of tulips – *Approximately 2km/1mi on, turn right onto the cycle path (Berkhout direction). Then follow the cycle path on the left just before the railway crossing. In Scharwoude, turn right and cross the railway line then follow the cycle track on the right to Hoorn and Berkhout. Further on, ignore the path returning to Hoorn and take the path signposted Berkhout (it runs under the motorway). Beyond the tunnel, turn right then right again into Oosteinde. Return to Hoorn and the station via Middelweg.*
The route runs along the Markermeer and passes Beeldenpark Hoorn, where there is an exhibition of modern sculptures. The cycle path runs through a shady park and along the banks of a canal before entering an area of reed beds. The route then turns inland, moving away from the railway lines and main roads to cross fields of tulips (in season) and meadows filled with grazing sheep.

Fields of tulips in Berkhout

R. Dechamps/MICHELIN

In the sand dunes of the Nationaal Park Zuid-Kennemerland

2 TOUR FROM ZANDVOORT: 23km/14mi

2hr 15min to 2hr 45min (not including stops).

From Amsterdam: by car or train from the central station. Cycle hire at the railway station in Zandvoort (right on exiting the station).

Zandvoort and the sea – *Follow Koper-Passerei opposite the station and turn right into J van Heemskerckstraat continuing into Barnaart Boulevard. Just beyond Bloemendael aan Zee, turn left and follow the sand dune on the coast.*
This brings you face to face with the North Sea, in the northern part of a seaside resort with a population of approximately 15 000 which attracts an additional 150 000 visitors on Sundays in the summer. Behind the long beach in Zandvoort are sand dunes, among which is a motor racing circuit which used to be used for the Dutch Formula One Grand Prix.

Nationaal Park Zuid-Kennemerland ⓥ – *At the car park of the Parnassia Café, turn right along the track signposted "Vogelmeer 2km". Pass the lake and turn right towards Ingang Bleek en Berg. Continue in this direction until you reach the following junction. Turn right and head for Ingang Koevlak which is signposted at 3km/2mi. On leaving the park, turn right along the cycle path that skirts Zeeweg (N 200). Just before Bloemendaal aan Zee, at the junction with the path you took earlier when heading for the park, cross the road and cycle down it for some 60m.*
The 3 800ha estate situated within the wide string of sand dunes flanking and hiding the sea is crisscrossed with footpaths and cycle tracks. The small lakes attract numerous birds protected by several organisations which work in the park and attempt to encourage the reproduction of these species. There are several steep gradients along the cycle tracks, which also run through a pine wood on the western edges of Bloemendaal on the outskirts of Haarlem.

Het Kraansvlak – *The cycle track begins with a chicane. At the end of the track pass the roundabout and turn left then right to return to the station at Zandvoort.*
In days gone by, potatoes were grown in the sand dunes flanking the motor racing circuit.

3 TOUR FROM WEESP: 28km/17mi

2hr 30min to 3hr (not including stops and visits).

From Amsterdam: by car or train from the central station. Cycle hire at the railway station in Weesp (left on exiting the station).

Weesp and the Vecht Valley – *After leaving the station, turn left into Herenweg then right along the Vecht. Cross the swing bridge on the left and turn left along Langmuiderweg in the Muiden direction.*
The centre of Weesp *(see HILVERSUM)*, crossed by the Vecht, is absolutely charming, a real picture postcard spot. The tour continues along the waterway lined by boatyards and houseboats with meticulously kept gardens, through a landscape filled with polders.

Cycling does not prevent a spot of fishing

Muiden and the shores of Ijmeer – *In Muiden, follow the signs to Muiderslot and continue to the castle. Head east from Muiden and turn left into Noordpolderweg just before Muiderslot. Then leave Noordpolderkade and continue along Noordpolderweg and Dijkweg. Beyond Muiderberg follow the Muiden Route signposts which will take you under the A 6 motorway to Naarden (NB the Flevo Route signs coincide with the Muiden Route signs for some distance but suddenly change direction before the A 6).*
Located at the mouth of the Vecht, Muiden is a delightful yachting marina with a red-brick fortress. The route continues through the polders, protected by one of the oldest of the Zuiderzee dikes. The IJmeer does not come into view until Muiderberg. Before reaching Naarden, the route crosses the Naarderbos (Naarden Woods) on the edge of which is an extensive yachting marina.

Naarden and Naardermeer – *Leave Naarden by the gate to the right of the Nederlands Vestingmuseum (Westwalstraat 6) and head for Naarden via Koningin Wilhelminalaan, continuing along this street after the traffic lights. Beyond the railway line, turn right into Verlengde Fortlaan (ignore the signpost indicating that this is a cul-de-sac). Cross the narrow bridge and turn left into Naarderweg. The cycle path then turns right and rejoins the Vecht which it flanks until it reaches Weesp.*
Set on the edge of the Gooi Woods, Naarden is an old fortified town with an admirable defence system surrounded by water. The old town is an ideal place for a stop. We are not describing the town in this route plan; use the corresponding chapter in this guide book to see all that it has to offer. After a short stop at Naarden, the route enters the Naardermeer polder which has a large lake in the centre (1m/3.25ft below sea level). In 1906, this polder was the first to be turned into a nature reserve. It is now a bird sanctuary filled with cormorants and purple herons. In summer, visitors may be lucky enough to see spoonbills, a very rare sight in Western Europe. Beyond the Naardermeer and the lock at the end of the lake, the route follows the Vecht and passes a superb rotating cap mill before returning to Weesp.

4 TOUR FROM ZANDVOORT: 28km/17mi

3hr 15min to 3hr 45min (not including stops).

See indications for tour no 2.

Zandvoort and the sea – *Follow Koper-Passerei opposite the station and turn left into Burg. Engelbertsstraat continuing into Thorbeckestraat (at the foot of the Uitzichttoren where a café at an altitude of 60m/195ft provides a panoramic view). Turn into Boulevard Paulus Loot. At the end of the boulevard there is a bend in the road; the cycle track runs off the road to the right (the street changes its name to Brederodestraat).*
The route runs through the town before skirting the seafront on which small villas overlook the beach and sea.

The sand dunes – *At the end of the nature reserve, follow the cycle track that runs along the road and, 1.5km/1mi further on, turn left onto another cycle track (signposted De Zilk).*

The view no longer extends out to sea, but over the sand dunes of the Waterleidingduinen which have been built up by the wind over the centuries. These accumulations of sand are only possible in places where the wind reaches speeds of 4m/13ft to 5m/16ft per second, and this is not always conducive to cycling. Here and there, access to the beach can provide an excuse for a swim. The next stop along the way, Langevelderslag, has three cafés and access to the beach.

The fields of flowers – *At the end of the cycle track, turn left under the N 206 bridge and follow the signs to De Zilk on the left (the cycle track runs between two roads). At the crossroads turn right to De Zilk (Deeklaan). Turn left before the church in Regenvlietweg. Cross the village and turn right at the stop sign to Vogelenzang. Beyond the fields of flowers, turn left at the end of the bend onto a narrow road (2.2m/7ft), Tweede Doodweg.*

The cycle track is pleasantly shaded as it skirts the Waterleidingduinen (dunes). From the gliding club, there is an attractive view of the tulip fields (in season) in the Lisse region.

Vogelenzang and the woods on the outskirts of Haarlem – *Turn right into Bekslaan. At the road junction, turn left onto the cycle track. Some 600m further on, cross the road (just beyond the Frans Rozen car park) onto the cycle track that runs into the woods (beyond the house with the red tiled roof). At the end of the woods, turn left and go straight on. Turn left at the white house. At the end of the estate, turn right and follow the track that runs alongside the road. When the road bends to the right, cross it and continue along the cycle track on Nachtegalenlaan. Turn left into Zwaluwenweg and follow the Zandvoort direction, turning right into Leeuwerikenlaan. At the road junction, turn left and return to Zandvoort station.*

At Vogelenzang, of which the bell-tower is visible, the countryside changes again. This route takes you along the edge of an elegant private estate full of trees and shrubs. In the woods, the cycle track crosses private property here and there, with no boundary fencing or walls. This is the edge of the particularly wealthy outskirts of Haarlem.

5 TOUR FROM AMSTERDAM: 35km/22mi

3hr 30min to 4hr (not including stops and visits).

From Amsterdam-Noord to Broek in Waterland – *After leaving the central station in Amsterdam, take the (free) ferry to the district known as Amsterdam-Noord. Continue along Noordhollands Kanaal to the ferry (2fl) across to the other bank of the canal. On the other bank, turn right and follow the signposts to Broek in Waterland. The cycle track runs along the Broevkaart, a small drainage canal.*

Cut off from the bustle of the city centre, the district of Amsterdam Noord has a mainly working-class population. The Northern Holland Canal is 80km/50mi long; it links the IJ to Den Helder. It was inaugurated in 1825 but its traffic dropped considerably after the refurbishment of the North Sea Canal in 1876.

The Broekvaart Canal, which is lined with houseboats, leads to Broek in Waterland, flanking the Broekermeer on the right as it does so. This polder lies 5m/17ft below sea level; it was drained in the early 17C.

R. Dechamps/MICHELIN

There may not be any hills but there is plenty of wind

Houseboats have spread into the country: this is Broek in Waterland

Polders and dikes on Gouwzee and Markermeer – *Cross N 247 and take the Zuiderwoude direction (along the left bank of a small drainage canal). In Zuiderwoude, follow the signs to Monnickendam. At the Waterlandse Zeedijk, turn right to Marken. If you wish, you can continue to Marken (+ 8km/5mi); otherwise turr right to Uitdam before the windmills. Beyond Uitdam continue along the Uitdammerdijk to Durgerdam then follow the signs indicated in Route 6 in CYCLING IN AMSTERDAM to return to Amsterdam.*
The town of Waterland also includes Zuiderwoude; in fact it consists of a succession of small towns or villages with timbered housing. The villages are surrounded by peaty land crossed by small canals that flow into the lakes. All this constitutes a vast nature reserve which is a haven for birds. On the northern limits of the polder, there is a superb view of the Gouwzee and the island of Marken. Uitdam, further south, is a charming little village consisting of only a few houses, most of them built of timber. It is also a popular place with bathers because of the nearby "holiday village". The return to Amsterdam includes a wonderful view down across the polder *(right)* and the Markermeer *(left)*. This is a splendid beauty spot and is worth the ride. In the distance is the Flevoland polder. This is where cycling becomes more difficult, because the wind usually blows from the south.

Bird Life in the Polders

The **oyster catcher** (45cm/18in) has a reputation of being a sociable bird; it never moves very far away from the sea. It can be seen in mudflats or in fields where it digs its long reddish-orange beak into the earth in search of food.
The **skylark** (20cm/8in) is the commonest of the larks. It is easily recognisable for its short erectile crest and, more particularly, for the melodious, sustained song it produces when in flight.
The **curlew** (60cm/24in) is the largest of the European limicolae. It has a characteristic, long curved beak. Its name is said to come from its call, "curl-you". It frequents marshland, moors and sand dunes.
The **peewit** or **lapwing** (30cm/12in) is a very common sight in the polders of Noord-Holland and is easily recognisable for its raised crest. It lives in pastures and wetlands where it nests on the ground.
With its yellow beak ending in a red spot, the **herring gull** (60cm/24in) is a common sight in northern Europe. It nests in colonies, mainly along coasts and estuaries.
The **reed warbler** (12cm/5in) is most easily recognised by its repeated alarm calls. As its name suggests, it lives in reed beds where it frequently uses the plants as perches.
The **snipe** (28cm/11in) has a sturdy body and a long, straight beak. If surprised by walkers, it cowers then suddenly rises into the air with a shrill cry, following a zig-zag flight path.
The **shelduck** (60cm/24in) is noisy during the mating season but silent for the remainder of the year. It lives on sandy coasts and in mudflats. Sometimes it nests in rabbit burrows in sand dunes.

Bird Life in the Polders

Oyster catcher

Skylark

Curlew

Peewit or Lapwing

Herring gull

Reed warbler

Snipe

Shelduck

M. Guillou/MICHELIN

AALSMEER

Plan p 200 – Michelin map no 211 N 9

Aalsmeer lies on the edge of the Haarlemmermeer, the area once covered by a lake and now drained but crisscrossed by canals and centring on a large lake known as Westeinder Plassen. It is a small town with a Gothic church built to a central layout (16C). However, the town is world famous for its flower auction which is held on the outskirts five days a week.
The **floral procession** from Aalsmeer to Amsterdam is renowned *(see Practical Information at the beginning of the guide)*.

★★ **Bloemenveiling Aalsmeer** – *Legmeerdijk 313.* The "Aalsmeer Auction Sale Cooperative" is very well signposted for visitors arriving by car *(the car park is at Begane Grond)*; it is a gigantic complex of sheds occupying 766 000m² and it is difficult to miss because it is located on the Amsterdam road. If you really have difficulty finding it, the Aalsmeer flower centre is indicated by a stylised red tulip.

Tour – It is advisable to visit the market early. Auction sales are open to visitors from 7.30am to 11am, but it is best to arrive before 9am. Monday is the liveliest day, Thursday the quietest. From the **long walkways** above the division and distribution shed visitors look down on four salerooms, a sea of flowers, most of which come from the greenhouses on the outskirts of the town. It is a constantly moving sea; the need to keep the products fresh requires speedy sales.

Shall I? Shan't I? Decision time at the auction sale

Sales "against the counter" – The VBA has five salerooms. The four that can be seen through soundproofed glass walls are reserved for cut flowers. The rooms are shaped like amphitheatres and equipped with electronic counters, each assigned daily to a single type of product. From control desks bristling with buttons, buyers decide whether or not to participate in the sale announced and select the counter corresponding to the required product. Purchasers are identified by means of a magnetic card and can therefore participate as and when they wish in the sales at decreasing prices displayed on the counter faces (indication of producer, product quality, currency, number of flowers per batch etc). By pressing a button when the required price is displayed, purchasers can buy their products.

Westeinder Plassen – This vast lake is one of the most popular water sports centres in the Amsterdam area during the summer season. From the route skirting the lake via Kudelstraat, there are some **fine views**.

The largest flower market on earth

Superlatives demand to be backed up by figures, which are often more edifying than any adjective. Every day 19 million cut flowers and 2 million pot plants are sold here. The star of the show is not the tulip! It is the rose (1.7 billion flowers), followed, far behind, by tulips (569 million), chrysanthemums (421 million), gerberas (272 million) and carnations (178 million). The Bloemenveiling Aalsmeer is the main national market, known by its abbreviation **VBA**. It achieves an export turnover of 3 billion guilders (1999 figure) with an average of 50 000 transactions every day.

ALKMAAR★

Plan p 201 – Michelin map no 210 N 7

Alkmaar is a historic town which owes its present reputation to its colourful weekly cheese market *(from mid-April to mid-September)*.
The moat surrounding the town walls constitutes part of the North Holland Canal; within the walls the old town has retained almost all its 17C layout and its many old houses. The former fortifications have been turned into gardens. Today Alkmaar is the main agricultural centre in the Noord-Holland peninsula.

A SHORT HISTORY

Alkmaar was founded in the 10C in the middle of marshland and lakes. Its name is thought to mean "All Lake" or "Alk Lake", a strange name referring to the species of auk living on the lake.

A heroic siege – In August 1573, during the Eighty Years War, the town was attacked by 16 000 Spaniards under the command of Frederick of Toledo, son of the Duke of Alba. Heavy autumn rains flooded the surrounding countryside, forcing the attackers to withdraw on 8 October, after a siege lasting seven weeks. Alkmaar was the first town to withstand attack by the Spanish troops, so "Victory began in Alkmaar" has become a traditional saying repeated for hundreds of years to anybody suffering long-standing difficulties.

Boat trips ⓥ – Boat trips are available on the canals of Alkmaar. There are also excursions to Amsterdam and the Zaan area known as Zaanstreek.

★★ KAASMARKT (CHEESE MARKET) ⓥ

This traditional market has been held since the 17C on Waagplein, overlooked by the public weigh-house, and still takes place every Friday in the summer. Loads of round Edam and Gouda cheeses arrive on the square in the morning and are carefully arranged in piles. From 10am onwards purchasers begin tasting and comparing the various cheeses, before negotiating prices and concluding their agreement with the vendor with a vigorous handshake.
The famous **cheese porters**, or *kaasdragers*, then begin their work. They are dressed in white as they were in days gone by, and they wear a straw hat. From the outset, they have been members of a guild comprising four companies distinguished by colour (green, blue, red and yellow). Each company comprises six porters and one weighman or "piler" *(tasman)*.
Once a batch of cheese has been sold, it is placed on a stretcher in the company's colour. Much to the delight of onlookers, the porters then run the load (which can weigh as much as 160kg/352lb) to the public weights and measures office where the "piler" is waiting for them. Finally, the cheeses are taken to the lorries nearby.

OTHER SIGHTS

Waag – *Waagplein 2*. In 1582 the former chapel dedicated to the Holy Spirit (14C) was turned into the public weigh-house. The chancel at the east end of the building has been replaced by a Renaissance building with ornate gable decorated, since the 19C, with a tablet of lavastone from the Auvergne depicting trade and industry. The tower built in the late 16C to the same design as the one on the Oude Kerk in Amsterdam contains a peal of bells and mechanical figures which act out a tournament every hour.

Pratt-Pries-DIAF

The famous cheese porters of Alkmaar

Hollands Kaasmuseum ⓥ – The public weigh-house contains the Dutch Cheese Museum (start your visit on the second floor), which covers the history of the production of cheese and butter. The material on the first floor illustrates current production techniques, both on farms and in dairies, as well as showing the importance of dairy products to the Netherlands' economy.

Nationaal Biermuseum De Boom ⓥ – *Houttil 1.* This museum, housed in a 170 brasserie, shows old methods of brewing beer.

Huis met de Kogel – The Cannonball House, situated above the canal, has a corbelled wooden frontage and, lodged in the gable, a Spanish cannonball fired in 1573.

From the neighbouring bridge, there is an attractive view of the public weights and measures office.

Mient – There are numerous old houses on this square and on the banks of the canal. The Vismarkt (fish market) is on the south side of the square.

Langestraat – This pedestrian precinct is the town's main shopping street.

ALKMAAR

Street	Grid	No.
Bierkade	BZ	
Boterstraat	BZ	3
Breedstraat	AZ	
Canadaplein	AY	4
Costerstraat	AZ	
Dijk	BY	6
Doelenstraat	AY	7
Eilandswal	BZ	
Emmastraat	AZ	
Fnidsen	BZ	
Frieseweg	BY	
Gasthuisstraat	AY	9
Gedempte Nieuwesloot	ABY	10
Geestersingel	AY	
Geesterweg	AY	
Helderseweg	AY	
Heul	AY	
Hofstraat	ABZ	12
Hoogstraat	AY	13
Houttil	BZ	15
Huigbrouwerstr.	BZ	16
Kanaalkade	BY	
Kennemersingel	AYZ	
Kennemerstraatweg	AZ	
Koedijkerstraat	BY	
Koningsweg	ABY	
Kooltuin	BZ	18
Koorstraat	AYZ	19
Korte Vondelstr.	BZ	
Kwakelkade	BY	
Laat	ABZ	
Langestraat	AYZ	
Luttik Oudorp	BZ	21
Lyceumstraat	AZ	
Mient	BZ	22
Nassaulaan	AZ	
Nieuwe Schermerweg	BZ	24
Nieuwlandersingel	AZ	
Noorderkade	BY	
Oude Gracht	ABZ	
Paternosterstr.	AY	25
Payglop	AZ	27
Pettemerstraat	BY	
Randersdijk	BY	
Ridderstraat	AZ	28
Ritsevoort	AZ	
Schaepmankade (Dr.)	BZ	
Scharlo	AY	
Schoutenstraat	AYZ	30
Snaarmanslaan	AY	
Stationsweg	AY	
Tesselsebrug	AY	
Varnebroek	AZ	
Vrouwenlaan	AY	
Waagplein	BYZ	31
Wageweg	BYZ	
Zevenhuizen	AY	33
Zilverstraat	AZ	34

Sight	Grid
Huis met de Kogel	BZ D
Grote of St.-Laurenskerk	AY
Kaasmarkt★★	BYZ
Stadhuis	AYZ H
Nationaal Biermuseum De Boom	BY M[1]
Stedelijk Museum	AY M[2]
Waag (Het Hollands Kaasmuseum)	BZ

Stadhuis ⓥ – The town hall has a delightful Gothic façade with a flight of steps. To one side is an elegant octagonal tower with white limestone banding. Adjacent to the town hall is a 17C façade. Inside the town hall there is an interesting collection of porcelain.

Grote of St.-Laurenskerk ⓥ – The Great Church or St Lawrence Church is a fine building with nave and side aisles, transept and ambulatory (late 15C and early 16C). It was commissioned by members of the Keldermans family, famous architects from Mechelen in Belgium.

The impressive interior has wooden vaulting from which hang magnificent 17C chandeliers. Note, in the chancel, a painting by Cornelis Buys who may be the Master of Alkmaar *(see RIJKSMUSEUM)*. It depicts *The Last Judgement*. The main **organ loft★** was made in 1645 by Jacob van Campen, architect of the royal palace in Amsterdam. It is decorated with shutters illustrating the *Triumph of King Saul*. The **small organ★** to the left of the ambulatory dates from 1511; it is one of the oldest instruments in the country. More than 1 700 gravestones cover the floor. **Floris V**, Count of Holland and Zeeland, is buried in this church *(for further information about Floris, see MUIDEN)*. Since 1996 this building has been the setting for a variety of events (organ concerts, exhibitions, fairs and conventions).

Stedelijk Museum ⓥ – This municipal museum contains some interesting collections relating to the town's history (gold and silverware, pewter, frontage stones, sculptures) and paintings from the 16C and 17C including a large number of paintings of the civic guards and works by Maarten van Heemskerk, Pieter Saenredam, Gerard van Honthorst, Willem van de Velde the Elder and Van Everdingen. Also on display is a collection of toys dating from the late 19C. The modern art collection, which includes works from the Bergen School, is displayed in temporary exhibitions.

IN THE VICINITY OF ALKMAAR

Broek op Langedijk – *8km/5mi north*. This is the site of the largest European wholesale vegetable market accessible by boat, the **Broeker Veiling** ⓥ. From 1847 to 1973 the market gardeners of the Kingdom of a Thousand Islands, the nickname of this region which is so rich in waterways, brought their vegetables to the market by boat. No time was wasted in loading and unloading. Originally the barges remained moored to the bank, but since 1903 they go right into the saleroom! Visitors can buy vegetables by activating the clock in the saleroom themselves, or they can go for a boat ride through the fields.

Graft-De Rijp – *17km/11mi south-east*. These two towns amalgamated in 1970. **Graft** still has its fine Town Hall (1613) with stepped gables. **De Rijp**, a major herring fishing and whaling harbour in the 16C and 17C, also has a town hall (1630) designed by a local man, **Jan Adriaenszoon Leeghwater** (1575-1650), the architect and famous hydraulics engineer *(see HAARLEM and below)*. The building is elegantly decorated with gables and scrolls; it houses the public weights and measures office. Note the houses built in regional style with a wooden gable and the church, **Hervormde Kerk** ⓥ, decorated with stained-glass windows made in the 17C.

Beemsterpolder – *22km/14mi south east*. Its impeccably rectilinear plots of land and the remarkable history of its development earned this polder a place in Unesco's World Heritage list in 1999. In Middenbeemster you can visit the **Museum Betje Wolff** ⓥ housed in the presbytery where the celebrated woman of letters lived between 1759 and 1777.

The Beemster: a masterpiece of 17C planning

The draining of Beemster lake was decided on at the beginning of the 17C due to the high water level and the shortage of good quality agricultural land. Thanks to the financial aid of Amsterdam's merchants and the ingenious talent of the hydraulics engineer **Jan Adriaenszoon Leeghwater**, this ambitious project was completed in 1612, creating 7 200 ha/17 791 acres of fertile land. Conforming to the Renaissance ideals of order and harmony adhered to in the 17C, the new land was divided into squares with perfect right angles. These in turn were divided into plots measuring 185m/607ft by 903m/2 962ft, ideal dimensions for the purposes of agriculture. Since then this regular landscape, made up of paths, canals, dykes and trees, has not undergone any change, making it truly exceptional. Between the fields and the pyramid-shaped farms, landowners from Amsterdam built opulent country houses which they used in the summer to escape the stench of the city. Some of these can still be seen today.

THE DUNES

35km/22mi trip – Approximately 2hr – Leave by Scharlo.

Bergen – Also known as Bergen-Binnen to distinguish it from the nearby seaside resort (*binnen* means "interior"), Bergen is a pleasant holiday venue. Its luxurious villas flank tree-lined streets. It has a popular university housed in the former manor of the lords of Bergen.

It was c 1915 that the Bergen School, or **Bergense School** (1910-40), was founded. Its members (Leo Gestel, the Matthieu brothers, and Piet Wiegman) were influenced by the French artists Cézanne and Le Fauconnier and contributed to the introduction of new trends in Netherlandish painting. Some of their works can be seen in the **Museum Kranenburgh** ⓥ *(Hoflaan 26)*. Today Bergen is still home to many artists whose work can be seen at the Kunstenaarscentrum Bergen (Bergen Arts Centre) which organises art sales in the summertime.

The junction with the Egmond road marks the start of the **Noordhollands Duinreservaat** ⓥ, a private bird sanctuary covering an area of 4 760ha running from the dunes to the sea.

Bergen aan Zee – This seaside resort, founded in 1906, is pleasantly situated on a coastline with extensive beaches backed by tall sand dunes dotted with villas. From the boulevard there is an extensive view of the dunes, broken up on the horizon by woodland.
The **Zee Aquarium Bergen aan Zee** ⓥ contains 43 aquaria containing a fine selection of fish and crustaceans from various seas and oceans worldwide. The collection of shellfish is very attractive. Note also the skeleton (14m/46ft long) of one of the sperm whales which was beached in November 1997 on the island of Ameland.

Egmond aan den Hoef – This small town lies in the heart of the bulb-growing region to the south of Alkmaar. To the east, on the old Alkmaar road *(Slotweg)*, beyond the church and just beside a chapel *(Slotkapel)*, stand the ruins of a castle, the **Slot van Egmond** (or Slot op den Hoef). In fact, only the red-brick foundations surrounded by water are still visible. The 17C French philiosopher **René Descartes** stayed in this castle whose foundation stone was laid in the early 13C.

The courageous Count of Egmont

Among the lords of Egmond Castle was **Lamoral, Count of Egmont** (spelt with a "t" in English). He was born near Ath (Belgium) in 1522. He married Sabine of Bavaria, the daughter of the Count of the Rhineland Palatinate. He covered himself in military glory and was named Commander of the Spanish Armies in the Low Countries by Philip II.
He demanded the abolition of the Inquisition and protested against the measures taken against the Calvinists since 1539. With the **Count of Hornes**, he requested a pardon for confederate noblemen. The policy of repression instigated by the Duke of Alba led the Council of Troubles to sentence the two counts to death and they were beheaded on Grand-Place in Brussels on 5 June 1568, neither of them having sought to flee.

Egmond aan Zee – In days gone by, the cottages and church in this resort found favour with the great landscape painter Jacob van Ruisdael. Now, Egmond aan Zee is a small seaside resort lost amid the sand dunes.
At the foot of the lighthouse is a statue of a lion symbolising the heroism of Lieutenant **Jan Carel Josephus van Speijk** (1802-31), who blew up his gunboat near Antwerp on 5 February 1831, sending it to the bottom with all hands rather than surrendering to the Belgians. Relics are kept in the Amsterdams Historisch Museum.

Egmond-Binnen – In 1935, the famous Egmond **Abbey** was rebuilt; it had been demolished by the Beggars in 1573. The **Museum Abdij van Egmond** ⓥ *(Abdijlaan 26)* contains the items uncovered during the building work (most of the exhibits date from the 16C). They include ceramics, coins and fabrics.

BROEK IN WATERLAND

Plan p 201 – Michelin map no 210 O 8

Broek in Waterland is part of the vast locality of Waterland, an area of lakes and pasture. Broek is a flower-decked village that has always been famous for its cleanliness. Indeed, in days gone by, visitors were required to take off their clogs before entering the village. It is said that **Napoleon** himself took his shoes off when he came for discussions with the mayor on 15 October 1811. Several 17C and 18C timbered houses add a pleasant touch to the village. Some of the 17C houses have two doors; the one on the façade was only used for weddings and funerals.

Napoleonhuisje – On the shores of the lake is a pavilion where the Emperor of the French was received. It dates from 1656 and is a small white wooden construction in the shape of a pagoda.

St.-Nicolaaskerk – The Reformed Church (14C) near the canal was burnt down by the Spaniards in 1573 and rebuilt between 1628 and 1639. The north aisle has an interesting stained-glass window (1640) divided into five sections depicting the stages in the destruction and rebuilding of the church. The organ was built in 1832 by Wander Beekes. Historically, only women sat on the chairs in the church; the pews were for the men. This custom served as a reminder of the sermons preached in the open air when the women and children were defended by the men, all of them armed.

C. Valentin/HOA QUI

Napoleonhuisje where the Emperor was received

EDAM

Plan p 201 – Michelin map no 210 P 7

Edam, a major centre of cheese production, is a quiet, charming little town. Towering above it is the **Speeltoren**, a tall bell-tower. It is all that remains of a church demolished in the 19C. Canals flow through the town and are still lined by a few superb 17C houses. This was once a bustling Zuiderzee harbour, famous for its shipyards.

Edam cheese – This cheese used to be produced only in Edam; now it is made throughout Noord-Holland. It is prepared from lightly skimmed milk and its smoothness is reminiscent of Gouda. Edam, though, has a drier taste and it also differs from Gouda in its shape: a sphere in yellow rind, covered with red wax if it is designed for the export market. Edam cheese has been exported since the 16C.

SIGHTS

Damplein – In the centre of the town crossed by the Voorhaven Canal is the main square. Overlooking it is the 18C **town hall** topped by a bell turret.

In the Eet-café *Prinsenbar* (Prinsenstraat 8) you can grab a sandwich while you play darts *(vogelpick)*.

Edams Museum – *Damplein 1-8.* The small museum in a delightful 16C house on the square provides an insight into the town's history.

Kaasmarkt – The **Kaaswaag** ⓥ or cheese weigh-house stands on the square. It was here that the cheese was weighed. Decorated with painted panels, it contains an **exhibition** relating to the production of Edam cheese. In summer *(Wednesdays in July and August)* the square is the setting for the Kaasmarkt, the traditional cheese market like the one in Alkmaar.

Grote of St.-Nicolaaskerk ⓥ – The Great or St Nicholas Church dates from the 15C. It is famous for its attractive, colourful stained-glass **windows** created in the early 17C in Gouda.

HAARLEM★★

Plan p 200 – Michelin map no 211 M 8

Haarlem, the historical capital of the County of Holland and the main town in the province of Noord-Holland, lies on the River Spaarne. It was the birthplace of Thierry Bouts and Adriaen van Ostade as well as the city of adoption of Frans Hals. Haarlem was once a major centre of the arts and now lies at the heart of a vast region that is famous for its bulbs *(see KEUKENHOF)*. In the springtime there is a floral procession which starts in Noordwijk *(see Practical Information at the beginning of the guide)*.

Although it lies close to the North sea, Haarlem is well protected from sea breezes by the string of dunes. It is a delightful little town some 20km/12mi from Amsterdam but is quite different in atmosphere to its near neighbour. It has all the tranquillity and elegance that are characteristic of some of the towns in inland Holland.

HISTORICAL NOTES

Founded in the 10C, which makes it older than Amsterdam, Haarlem was fortified in the 12C and then became the residence of the Counts of Holland.

In the 13C it was granted borough status. Its people took part in the fifth Crusade and the capture of the fortress in Damietta (1219), the main harbour on the great Phatnitic Branch of the Nile. The bells on the church dedicated to St Bavo are still known as "damiettes" in memory of this event.

In the 14C Haarlem underwent expansion. All that remains of its town wall is the Amsterdam Gate (late 15C) to the east of the Spaarne.

Heroic defence – During the uprising that opposed the Netherlands and Spain (1572-73), Haarlem was besieged for seven months by Don Frederico, the Duke of Alba's son. During the winter, William the Silent succeeded in supplying food to the town thanks to the Gueux, the Dutch guerillas who skated across Lake Haarlem but despite a heroic defence by the entire population the town was forced to capitulate in June 1573. In 1577 Haarlem expressed support for the States General which appointed William stathouder of the United Provinces in November 1576 under the terms of the Pacification of Ghent.

Haarlem's golden age was the 17C, when the town took advantage of the decline in Flemish towns to develop a linen industry and produce a fabric that was sold throughout Europe under the name of holland.

Haarlemmermeer – This huge lake covering an area of some 18 300ha resulted from the working of the peat bogs. Because of the storms that occurred there, the lake represented a threat for Amsterdam and Leyden. In 1641, the celebrated hydraulics engineer **Jan Adriaenszoon Leeghwater** (1575-1650) suggested that the lake could be drained using dozens of windmills; the land could then be turned into polders. He had already performed the same task on Beemster Lake which he had drained in 1612. The work was not undertaken until two centuries later. Steam pumps gradually replaced the windmills. Three enormous pumping stations were built, with a force equivalent to that of 160 mills (one of them is in Cruquius, *see Museum De Cruquius*). Having drained off 88 million m³ of water, the work was completed on 1 July 1852. The area corresponding to Haarlem Lake has become a town, and Schiphol Airport has also been built on the reclaimed land. On average, town and airport both lie 6m/19ft below sea level. The maritime clay beneath the ancient peat bogs is very fertile.

The artists' town – Haarlem was probably the birthplace of **Claus Sluter** (c 1345-1406). His name was recorded in the register of stonecarvers in Brussels as Claes de Slutere van Herlam. The sculptor entered the service of the dukes of Burgundy and created highly realistic statues for the Carthusian monastery of Champmol near Dijon. His work was quite unlike the international Gothic style of the day, and it was to exercise a strong influence on 15C art. One of those born in the town during that century was **Dirk Bouts** (c 1420-75), who settled in Leuven (Louvain) just before 1450 and produced paintings that were both ascetic and full of a luminous quality. Another was

Jan Mostaert (c 1475-c 1556), a painter of religious works who worked for Margaret of Austria. As to Gérard de Saint-Jean (c 1465-c 1495), he was born in Leyden but came to live in Haarlem; he showed enormous skill in the way he treated draped fabrics.

In the 16C, **Maarten van Heemskerck** (1498-1574), who painted in the Italian style, studied under Jan van Scorel during the artist's stay in Haarlem from 1527 to 1529. The Mannerist painter **Cornelis van Haarlem** (1562-1638) and **Willem Claeszoon Heda** (1594-1680), who was famous for his still-life works, were both born in the town. Among those who died there were engraver **Hendrick Goltzius** (1558-1617), **Pieter Claeszoon** (1597-1661), the creator of the monochrome still life, and **Pieter Saenredam** (1597-1665) who was so skilled at reproducing the serenity that fills the great empty interiors of Protestant churches. Another inhabitant of Haarlem (he may also have been born there) was the outstanding landscape artist, **Hercules Seghers** (c 1590-1638). **Lieven de Key** (c 1560-1627) was born in Flanders and was one of the leading architects of the Renaissance. *(For information on Frans Hals, see insert below.)*

In the 17C Haarlem was the birthplace of the portrait artist **Bartholomeus van der Helst** (1613-70), **Philips Wouwerman** (1619-68) who specialised in painting horses and was imitated by his brother Pieter, and **Nicolaes Berchem** (1620-83) who produced some 300 paintings, mainly landscapes. Another of the town's sons, **Adriaen van Ostade** (1610-84) excelled in genre paintings; all his works are steeped in rigorous realism. **Salomon van Ruysdael** (c 1600-70), who was born in Naarden but settled in Haarlem, was one of the earliest great Dutch landscape painters, with Jan van Goyen. Salomon's nephew and pupil, **Jacob van Ruysdael** (c 1629-82) or **Ruisdael** was born in Haarlem. His landscapes were more tormented, pointing the way to Romanticism.

Haarlem is now home to a dynasty of contemporary artists, the Andriessen family. Composed mainly of musicians, it also includes a sculptor, **Mari Andriessen** (1897-1979).

AROUND GROTE MARKT

★ **Grote Markt** – The market square is flanked by the church dedicated to St Bavo, the town hall and the former meat market. The bronze statue of **Lourens Janszoon Coster** (1405-84) by Louis Royer has stood on this spot since 1856. In the Netherlands, Coster is regarded as the inventor of printing (in 1423, 17 years before Johann Gutenberg). In fact it was the Chinese who first developed a system of separate mobile letters, in the 7C.

★★ **Grote of St.-Bavokerk** – *Entrance: Oude Groenmarkt 23.* The first document to mention a church dedicated to St Bavo in Haarlem dates from 1313. The early church, however, was destroyed by a terrible fire in 1328.

Reconstruction work did not begin until half a century later. The chancel was completed in 1390, the transept in 1455 and the nave in 1481. The "Great Church", so called because it was larger than its predecessor, was given a bell-tower designed by Antoine Keldermans in 1506. The tower was demolished eight years later because it was too heavy for the transept crossing to support. Rising to a height of 80m/260ft, the superb **lantern tower**★ dates from 1520; it was designed by Michiel Bartssoen in wood completely covered in lead. The construction of this harmoniously planned building took almost 150 years.

The entrance is among the stalls built against the south wall. These stalls were rented out by the clergy and the proceeds were used to maintain the church. The narrow corridor skirts the former sacristy and opens onto the ambulatory.

R. Dechamps/MICHELIN

The fine lantern tower on St Bavo's Church

The interior of this Gothic church appears in many a work by artists of the Haarlem School. The most immediately striking features are its fine **starry vault★** made of cedar wood and its floor paved entirely with gravestones. Proceed left and stand in front of the chancel to see the grave of artist **Pieter Saenredam** (slab no 6, in front of the 17C map of Haarlem hanging on the wall). The chancel can only be glimpsed through the splendid brass **screen★** (1517), a remarkable work by a craftsman from Mechelen, Jan Fierens (note also the fine oak railing in the chancel). It contains a copper lectern (1499) in the shape of a pelican by the same craftsman, some fine choir stalls (1512) bearing amusing sculptures, and the tomb of **Frans Hals** marked by a lantern that is constantly lit.
The nave and side chapels include a few noteworthy features of which the most interesting is undoubtedly the **great organ★** built by a craftsman from Amsterdam, Christian Müller, in 1738 and decorated with carvings by Jan van Logteren. The instrument, one of the finest in the world, consists of 5 068 pipes, three keyboards and 68 stops; it reaches a height of 30m/98ft. The full, rounded sound attracted several famous composers including Handel, the young Mozart and Saint-Saëns. International organ competitions are held here every two years. Before leaving the church, note the pulpit (1679) supported on the wings of an eagle symbolising St John; the pillars in the transept and chancel in which the 15C paintings are reminiscent of carpets; and the three models of Dutch warships (fifth span in the south aisle).

Vishal ⓥ – The fish market was built in 1769 against the north side of St Bavo's Church. This building also belongs to the Frans Halsmuseum. Temporary exhibitions.

★**Vleeshal** ⓥ – The meat market is an elegant Mannerist building, erected between 1602 and 1604 to plans by Lieven de Key. Note the heads of cattle and sheep decorating the front and the pinnacles on the stepped gable. The building has belonged to the Frans Halsmuseum since 1961. In the cellar are temporary exhibitions and the **Archeologisch Museum Haarlem** ⓥ.

Verweyhal ⓥ – This building, again the property of the Frans Halsmuseum, is named after the Impressionist painter Kees Verwey, who was born in Haarlem. There are numerous examples of his work in the museum collections. There is also a permanent collection of modern Netherlandish art.

★**Stadhuis** ⓥ – The 14C Gothic town hall is flanked by a turret. Numerous changes have been made to the building over the years. The pilastered projection on the right is topped by an elegant gable decorated with volutes; it includes a niche containing an allegory of Justice (early 17C). On the left, above the steps, is a delightful little Renaissance balcony.

The Banquet of the Officers of the Civic Guard of St George, Frans Hals

The Chamber of the Counts or Gravenzaal on the first floor has retained its original splendour. The decorative paintings are old copies of frescoes in the Carmelite convent; they represent the counts of Holland.

★★★ FRANS HALSMUSEUM ⏲ *Groot Heiligland 62*

The museum lies in the heart of Old Haarlem. Since 1913, it has been located in a former almshouse built in 1610, probably to designs by Lieven de Key. From 1810 to 1908, the buildings were used as an orphanage. They have undergone numerous transformations over the years.

The frontage is typical of this type of institution, with a succession of small houses topped by stepped dormer windows to each side of the entrance. The main façade looks onto the main courtyard and its garden. Around it are the rooms.

This attractive architectural ensemble of houses with stepped gables opposite the museum formed part of **St Elizabeth's Hospital** *(see below)*, whose governors were painted by Frans Hals.

The Civic Guards in Haarlem

In the 17C, the town had two companies of civic guards (St George's and St Hadrian's), whose members were drawn from the wealthiest citizens. They were responsible for defending the town and for maintaining law and order. Every three years, a new commanding officer was appointed. The members were then immortalised in a group portrait and, in some instances, a ceremonial banquet was given to mark the occasion.

The works of Frans Hals – The paintings of civic guards *(room 21)* and regents or governors constitute the most outstanding part of the collection. They are an excellent illustration of the developments in the artist's style.

The Banquet of the Officers of the Civic Guard of St George★★★ (1616) is an undeniable masterpiece which breathed new life into the painting of traditionally stiff group portraits. This is easy to see by comparing it with the earlier works of the same type painted by Dirck Barendszoon or Cornelis Corneliszoon van Haarlem. The position of the officers reflects their rank within the guard. Yet today's visitors see the bearer of the folded flag as the main character; this is due partly to his almost nonchalant stance and partly to the fact that the placing of the banner diagonally through the window gives a remarkable impression of depth. This work was so successful that Hals was commissioned to paint a further six portraits of companies. The composition, now regarded as a particularly fine example of Dutch painting, is striking for the richness of its colouring and the animation of the people represented in it. Hals had been a member of this company of guards since 1612; he painted this work at the age of 34. It shows such ease and skill that many art historians believe he must already have painted other large canvases before this one.

Frans Halsmuseum

The ***Meeting of the Officers and Non-Commissioned Officers of the Civic Guard of St Hadrian***★★ (1633), another painting of exceptional quality, reflects the role of hand movements in bringing the composition together. The lieutenant in the foreground, for example, is handing the captain a quill pen, an act which has fully captured the attention of the lieutenant holding the register. Actually, the latter is the artist Hendrick Pot who replaced the captain after his death. One may ask whether Hals did not wish to symbolise the handing over of power, an idea strengthened by the hand movement of the man behind the artist. If this is the case, the presence of the captain, who seems to be fixing his gaze on those who look at the work, would be a posthumous homage.

Room 21 has several other exhibits worthy of admiration: ***Officers and Non-Commissioned Officers of the Civic Guard of St George***★ (1639), containing what is presumed to be a self-portrait (upper left corner, character no 19); ***The Banquet of the Officers of the Civic Guard of St George***★ (1627), in which the meal is of secondary importance; ***The Banquet of the Officers of the Civic Guard of St Hadrian*** (1627).

Frans Hals

Although born in Antwerp c 1582, Frans Hals is nevertheless one of Haarlem's sons. His family settled in the town just before 1591. Like Vermeer, he was a weaver's son. He studied with the Mannerist painter Karel van Mander from 1600 to 1603. In 1610, he married Anneke Harmensdochter. That same year, he was registered with the Guild of St Luke as a master painter. The earliest known work by Hals is the *Portrait of Jacobus Zaffius*, painted in 1611.

Frans Halsmuseum

Self-Portrait in *Officers and Non-Commissioned Officers in the Civic Guard of St George* (1616)

In 1616, he was admitted to the Society of Rhetoricians. Contrary to appearances, this was a major event in the artist's life for the Chamber was the Dutch equivalent of the *sociétés précieuses* that flourished in 17C France. It meant great social recognition for the artist, shortly before his second marriage, to Lysbeth Reiniers, in the following year. Hals' entire career as an artist centred on Haarlem. Even his earliest works bear his characteristic mark; they were produced quickly, underlining the importance of the face. The artist shows great alertness. Although Hals painted a few genre scenes as a result of the influence of the Mannerist movement in the town, he was first and foremost a portrait artist. The 240 paintings attributed to him are all indicative of this fact, including the works described as genre paintings. His homogeneity is another characteristic of his work.

His 195 portraits overturned the traditions that had been associated with this type of work until that time. Hals found a totally new approach to portraiture. Before him, composition had been stiff and lacking in depth. He introduced a degree of disorderliness, more natural attitudes (e g a conversation) and a sense of space. His paintings are expressive and spontaneous. The touch is rapid; his brushwork is daring and, in many cases, irregular.

His technique is an essential quality of his paintings. It enabled him to create the impression of having captured the animation of his subjects and to produce almost a snapshot of their lives. Indeed, he had no hesitation in depicting them as they really were, showing off their corpulence and detailing their ugliness. Nor had he any hesitation in juxtaposing dazzling colours and representing the gaudy brilliance of scarves and flags. Because of all this, he was sometimes referred to as an "untidy painter".

His collective portraits of guilds and brotherhoods are an excellent illustration of his skilful use of naturalism, a feature which he introduced into the art of his country. Frans Hals, who died in Haarlem in 1666 aged 84, should be seen as the founder of the Dutch Realist School.Among his numerous pupils Judith Leyster (1609-60), the Flemish painter Adriaen Brouwer and Adriaen van Ostade (1610-85) are the most noteworthy.

The *Portrait of Jacobus Zaffius* (1611) *(26)* is probably a fragment of a larger painting. It is the earliest known work of the artist whose huge talent is evident in the intensity of the subject's expression.

In 1641 Frans Hals began to develop a tendency towards austerity and solemnity, a trend which was already noticeable in the works of *Nicolaes van der Meer* and his colleague, *Cornelia Vooght* (1631) *(26)*. Perhaps justifiably, there are those who claimed that this change resulted from the influence of Flemish works (the artist was born in Flanders); its most obvious manifestation is the marked liking for black. The *Governors of the St Elizabeth Hospital* (1641) *(26)*, which no longer bears any of the lightness and gaiety of the portraits of guards, is a very good example of those compositions in which the dark shades underline the facial expressions and the very studied attitude of the hands.

Hals was over 80 years of age when, in 1664, he created two masterpieces that highlighted his consummate skill: ***The Lady Governors of the Old Men's Home at Haarlem*★** and ***The Governors of the Old Men's Home at Haarlem*★★** *(28)*. The first of these paintings is slightly unnerving to the observer, perhaps because of its rigid Protestant austerity; the second one is a daring study of six people with status and authority. The third person on the right is not drunk, as has often been said; he was suffering from facial paralysis. The humanist attitudes of the day would normally have required that he be tactfully painted in profile or from a three-quarters view, but Hals was careful to echo reality, through absolute truthfulness.

The museum's other collections – Apart from the works by Hals, the museum has extensive collections of paintings, furniture, and objets d'art (including 17C and 18C silverware) and a manuscript decorated with a painting of a tulip by **Judith Leyster** (1609-60), a pupil of Hals and the wife of Jan Molenaer, another of the town's artists.

Older works include a *Lamentation* by Jan Mostaert *(8)*, an *Ecce Homo* by Maarten van Heemskerck and ***The Baptism of Christ in the Jordan*** ★ by Jan van Scorel *(9)*, a baffling and satirical work entitled *The Monk and the Beguine* by Cornelis Corneliszoon van Haarlem and *Mercury* by Hendrick Goltzius *(11)*, ***Estuary Landscape*** by Hendrick Vroom and *Landscape of Dunes in Haarlem* by Jacob van Ruysdael *(13)*, ***River with Fishing Boats in the Foreground*** by Salomon van Ruisdael *(14)*, *The Nieuwekerk in Haarlem* by Pieter Saenredam *(20)*, *Interior of St Bavo's Church* by Jacob Berckheyde *(22)*, *The Merry Drinker* by Judith Leyster and a very amusing *Allegory of Tulipmania or The Tulip Trade*, in which the figures are apes, by Jan Brueghel *(24)*, ***Portrait of an Unknown Woman*** ★ by M van Heemskerck *(25)*, ***Portrait of a Man*** by Johannes Verspronck *(26)*, and works by Carel van Mander, Jan van Goyen, Cornelis van Wieringen, Reijer Suycker, Adriaen van Ostade, Willem Claeszoon Heda, Jan de Bray, Jan Bruegel II, Dirck Hals (the artist's brother) and Reynier Hals (the artist's son).

Among the modern works, note those by Piet Mondrian (figurative period) and **Karel Appel** *(4 and 5)*.

ADDITIONAL SIGHTS

★ **Teylers Museum** ⓥ – *Spaarne 16*. The Netherlands' oldest public museum was opened in 1784, by virtue of a bequest from Pieter Teyler van der Hulst (1702-78), a cloth and silk merchant in Haarlem who wanted to use his fortune to promote the sciences and the arts. **Napoleon** visited the museum in 1811.

The superb rooms in this vast neo-Classical mansion, among them the **oval room** (1784) decorated with stucco work and wood panelling, have retained their original charm, thanks to a museum display that is pleasantly old-fashioned. They contain fossil and mineral collections, as well as instruments used in physics, including the largest electrostatic machine ever built (Cuthpertson, 1791).

The Water Colour Room was turned into a prints and engravings room in 1996. A magnificent collection of **drawings** ★★ is exhibited here on a rota basis. The collection includes some 2 500 drawings by the Dutch masters (Goltzius, Rembrandt, Schelfhout, etc), over 1 500 drawings by the Italian School (Michelangelo, Raphael, Pietro Testa alias Il Lucchesino, Annibale Carracci), some of which belonged to Queen Christina of Sweden, and works by Dürer, Watteau, Boucher etc.

Two other rooms *(9 and 10)* will be of interest to those who appreciate The Hague School. They contain: *Winter Landscape* (1837) by BC Koekkoek, *Storm at Sea* by JC Schotel, *Storm on the Zuiderzee at Medemblik* (1840) by PJ de Schotel, *The Lek near Elshout* by HJ Weissembruch and ***Dusk at Sea*** by HW Mesdag.

The display cases in the numismatics section contain Dutch medals (16C-20C), many of which date back to the days of the Republic of the United Provinces.

Since 1996 the new wing *(12)* has been used solely for temporary exhibitions.

Waag – *Corner of Damstraat and Spaarne*. Built in 1598, the former public weighhouse was designed in the Mannerist style and is attributed to Lieven de Key.

Waalse Kerk – *Begijnhof 28*. The French-speaking church in Haarlem was the chapel used by the Beguines until 1586. This is the oldest church in the town.

Amsterdamse Poort – Building began on the Amsterdam Gate in 1425, but was not completed until the end of the century. On the side facing the town, the gate is preceded by two turrets. The construction also served as a water gate controlling traffic up and down the Spaarne. Note the town motto carved into the masonry on the outside: *Vicit vim virtus*. When still complete, the town fortifications included 11 gates and the walls rose to a height of 7.5m/24ft.

Haarlem Station – In 1839, the first railway link in the Netherlands was opened between Amsterdam and Haarlem. The luxurious Art Nouveau style station building (1908) is still used today.

Voormalig Sint-Elisabeth Gasthuis (Former St Elizabeth's Hospital) – *Groot Heiligland 47, opposite the Frans Hals Museum*. The institutions listed below are housed in the old hospital.

Historisch Museum Zuid-Kennemerland ⓥ – This small museum covers the history of the town. It includes a model of the town as it was in 1822. Haarlem's history is evoked by Laurens Janszoon Coster in an audio visual presentation.

HAARLEM

Amsterdamstr. . . . . CZ
Anegang . . . . BCY
Baan . . . . BZ
Bakenessergracht. . . . . CY 6
Barrevoetestr.. . . . . BY 7
Barteljorisstr. . . . . BY 9
Botermarkt. . . . . BYZ 13
Brouwerskade . . . . BY
Brouwersvaart . . . . BY
Burgwal . . . . CZ
Damstr. . . . . CY 18
Donkere Spaarne . . . . CY 19
Duvenvoordestr.. . . . . BX
Dyserinckstr. (A. L.) . . . . . . CZ
Eedenstr. (van) . . . . BZ
Frans Halsplein CX
Frans Halsstr.. . . . . CX 25
Friese Varkenmarkt . . . . . CXY 27
Gasthuisvest . . . . BZ 28
Gedempte
Oostersingelgracht. . . . . CY
Gedempte Oude Gracht . . BYZ
Gedempte Raamgracht . . . . BZ
Gedempte Voldersgracht . . BY 30
Gierstr.. . . . . BZ 31
Gravestenenbrug . . . . CY
Groot Heiligland . . . . BZ 33
Grote Houtstr. . . . . BYZ
Hagestr.. . . . . CZ 34
Harmenjansweg . . . . CY
Herensingel . . . . CZ
Herenstr. CX
Hoogstr.. . . . . CZ 39
Hooimarkt . . . . CY
Houtplein . . . . BZ
Jacobstr. . . . . BY 40
Jansstr. . . . . CY
Jansweg CX
Kampersingel . . . . BCZ
Kampervest . . . . BCZ
Keizerstr. . . . . BY 45
Kennemerpl. CX
Kinderhuissingel. . . . . BXY
Kinderhuisvest . . . . BY
Kleine Houtstr. . . . . BZ
Kleine Houtweg . . . . BZ
Klokhuisplein . . . . CY 48
Kloppersingel CX
Koningstr. . . . . BY 49
Koudenhorn . . . . CY
Kruisstr. . . . . BY
Kruisweg . . . . BX
Lange Herenvest . . . . CZ
Leidsevaart . . . . BY
Lorentzplein . . . . BZ
Marumstr. (van) . . . . CZ
Nassaulaan . . . . BY
Nassaustr. . . . . BY 54
Nieuwe Gracht. . . . . BCY
Nieuwe Groenmarkt . . . . . . BY 55
Oranjekade. . . . . BZ
Ostadestr. . . . . BX 57
Oude Groenmarkt . . . . . . BCY 58
Oudeweg . . . . CXY
Papentorenvest . . . . CY
Parklaan . . . . BCX
Pieter Kiesstr. . . . . BXY
Prinsen Bolwerk. CX
Raaks . . . . BY
Raamsingel . . . . BZ
Raamvest. . . . . BZ
Ridderstr.. . . . . BCY
Rozenhagenstr. CX
Rozenstr.. . . . . BX
Santpoorterstr.. . . . . BX
Schalkwijkerstr. . . . . CZ
Schotersingel. . . . . BCX
Smedestr. . . . . BY 66
Spaarndamseweg . . . . CX 67
Spaarne . . . . CZ
Spaarnwouderstr. . . . . CZ 69
Staten Bolwerk. . . . . BX
Tuchthuisstr. . . . . BZ 72
Verspronckweg . . . . BX
Verwulft. . . . . BYZ 75
Wilhelminastr. . . . . BZ
Wouwermanstr. . . . . BX
Zijlsingel . . . . BY 79
Zijlstr.. . . . . BY
Zijlweg . . . . BY
Zomerkade. . . . . CZ
Zomervaart. . . . . CZ

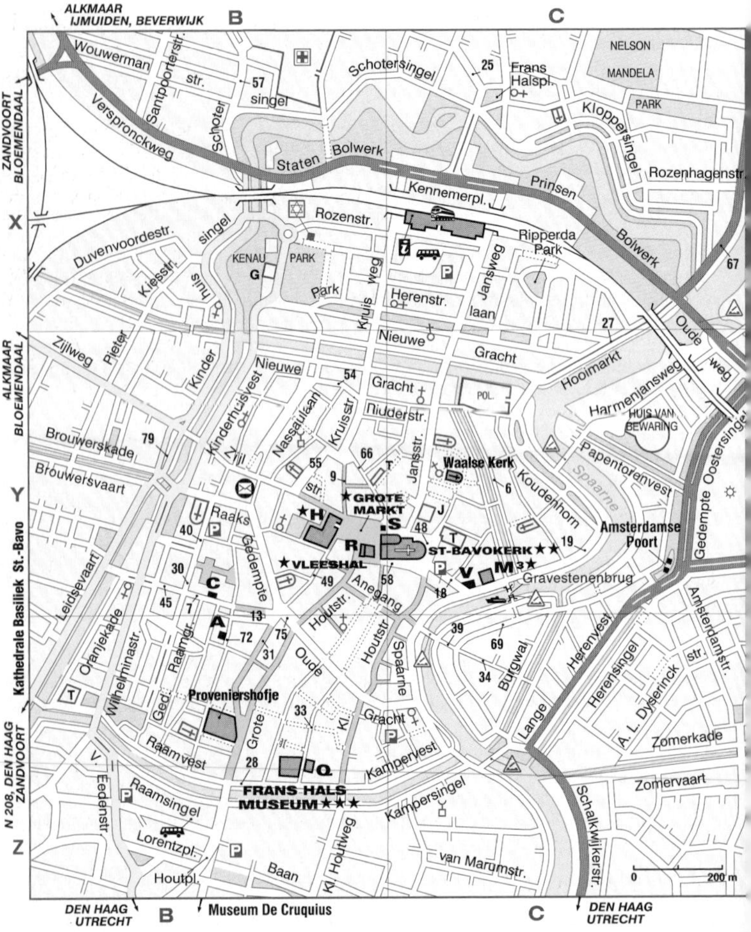

Amsterdamse Poort . . . . CY
ABC Architectuur centrum . . . . BZ Q
Brouwershofje. . . . . BZ A
Frans Halsmuseum★★★ . . BZ
Grote Markt★ . . . . BY
Historisch Museum Zuid-Kennemerland . . . . BZ Q
Hofje van Loo . . . . BY C
Proveniershofje . . . . BZ
Sint-Bavokerk★★ . . . . BCY
Spaarnestad Fotoarchief . . . BZ Q
Stadhuis★ . . . . BY H
Station Haarlem CX
Teylers Museum★. . . . . CY M[3]
Verweyhal. . . . . BY R
Vishal. . . . . BCY S
Vleeshal★ . . . . BY
Waag . . . . CY V
Waalse Kerk . . . . CY

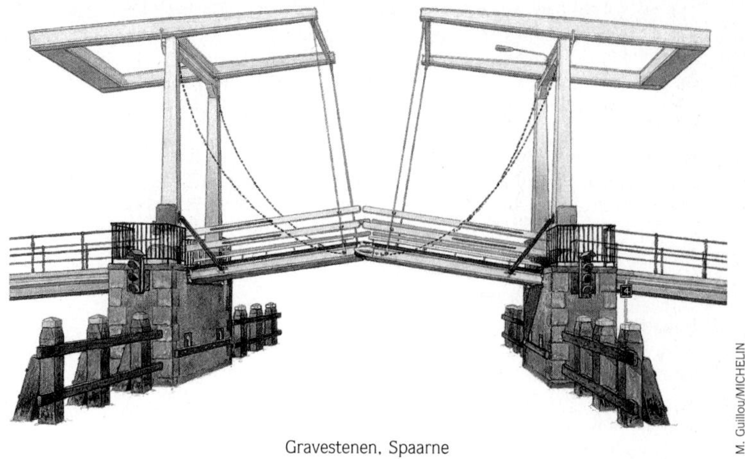

Gravestenen, Spaarne

M. Guillou/MICHELIN

ABC Architectuurcentrum ⓥ – This centre of architecture organises exhibitions devoted to old and new architecture.

Spaarnestad Fotoarchief ⓥ – *First floor.* This constitutes the largest photographic archive in the Netherlands, with more than 3 000 000 photographs. The collection starts with material dating from 1870 and covers the entire 20C. Temporary exhibitions offer diverse surveys of the collection.

Former Almshouses – Among the many charitable institutions in the rich town of Haarlem from the 15C onwards, there were the **Proveniershuis** (1592), with a wide porch opening onto Grote Houtstraat, the **Brouwershofje** (1472) in Tuchthuisstraat and the delightful **Hofje van Loo** (1489) named after its architect, Sijmon van Loo, in Barrevoetestraat.

Kathedrale Basiliek St.-Bavo ⓥ – *Leidsevaart 146.* Haarlem, a Catholic bishopric, has two churches dedicated to St Bavo. This one was built between 1895 and 1906 to designs by Jos Cuypers, the son of PJH Cuypers who designed the Rijksmuseum and the central station in Amsterdam; the two towers on the west front date from 1930. The sacristy contains the treasure consisting of an extensive collection of church plate, especially gold and silverware dating from the 15C to the 20C. Note the early 16C liturgical ornaments which come from one of the town's old Beguine convents.
Organ concerts are held here every Sat from 1 Apr to 1 Oct at 3pm.

EXCURSIONS

Stoomgemaal Halfweg (Halfweg steam pump) ⓥ – *8km/5mi east via A 5, in the direction of Amsterdam (Zwanenburg exit).* This is the oldest active steam pump in the world. It was constructed in 1852 and originally had a pumping capacity of 25 000 litres/5 500gal per second. One of the two boilers has been removed allowing one to see the pump's mechanism.

Spaarndam – *8km/5mi north-east via Spaarndamseweg which turns into Vondelweg. After a bend in the road turn right onto Vergierdeweg.* This fairly picturesque village is famous for its smoked eels served with a good beer. The houses huddle along each side of a dike including a number of locks; it links the River Spaarne and River IJ.
On one of the locks stands the statue of Hans Brinker. Legend has it that the young boy plugged a hole in the protective dike with his finger for an entire night, thereby saving the town from flooding. The origin of the story is actually a children's book written in 1873 by the American authoress, Mary Mapes Dodge. It was entitled ***Hans Brinker of the Silver Skates***.
Beyond the small memorial is a yachting marina. A footpath leads to the basin in Oost-en Westkolk where there are some attractively restored houses.

Ijmuiden – *13km/9mi north-west via Verspronckweg.* Situated at the mouth of the North Sea Canal, IJmuiden is the Netherlands' largest fishing harbour and the seventh largest in Western Europe. The fish auctions are particularly lively here. However, the town is best known for its three **locks**★ or *sluizen* which enable even the largest ships (up to 80 000t) to sail upriver to Amsterdam. The north lock or *Noordersluis*, is the most recently built; work began on the lock in 1919 and it was officially opened on 29 April 1930. It is 400m/433yd long, 40m/130ft wide and 15m/49ft deep.

The landscape is marked by industry for, like Tarente in Italy, IJmuiden has been a major centre of maritime iron and steelmaking since 1924. The Koninklijke Nederlandsche Hoogovens en Staalfabrieken (KNHS) was set up by central government, the city of Amsterdam and a number of private companies; it produces steel and aluminium. The town's seaside resort suffers somewhat as a result of the unwelcome presence of chimney stacks and billowing smoke.

Beverwijk – *13km/9mi north-west via Verspronckweg.* Located on the north bank of the canal, Beverwijk constitutes, with Heemskerk, the residential area of the tiny Ijmond region, an area of only $90km^2$ which plays a leading role in the Dutch economy and which is one of the most heavily industrialised regions in the country. The **Beverwijkse Bazaar** *(open weekends only)* is a large covered market with 3 000 stalls. Blast furnaces concealed by trees and shrubs separate Beverwijk from the seaside resort of **Wijk aan Zee**.

Bloemendaal – Behind the string of sand dunes is an elegant residential area with villas scattered across wooded hillsides. The open-air theatre or *Openluchttheater (Hoge Duin en Daalseweg 2)* stages shows in the summer. Not far away is the highest sand dune in the country, **Het Kopje** (50m/162ft), literally "the small head". Further north are the ruins of **Brederode**, a castle destroyed by the Spaniards in 1573.

Nationaal Park Zuid-Kennemerland – *There is a reception area near the south-eastern entrance at Overveen. Also see CYCLING IN THE POLDERS, tour no 2.* This national park has a surface area of 3 800ha and is formed by vast stretches of dunes bordering the North Sea. It has a network of footpaths and cycling paths. Many migratory birds stop off here on their way south.

☆☆☆ **Zandvoort** – *11km/7mi west via Leidsevaart. See CYCLING IN THE POLDERS, tours no 2 and 4.* This is one of the most popular and most elegant seaside resorts in the Netherlands. Since 1976, Zandvoort has had a **casino** only a few yards from the seafront.

To the north of the town is its 4.252km/2.5mi motor racing circuit which is famous among sports enthusiasts as the site of the Formula 1 Dutch Grand Prix until 1985. That year, the race was won by the Austrian driver Niki Lauda, in a McLaren-Porsche. The track still hosts Formula 3 races.

★ **Museum De Cruquius** ⏲ – *Cruquiusdijk 27. 7km/4.5mi to the south-east via Dreef. The museum stands to the north-east of a large bridge, on the Vijfhuizer road. Local map, see KEUKENHOF.* Standing on the banks of the former Haarlem Lake *(see Haarlemmermeer)*, the museum is laid out in one of the three pumping stations used to drain the lake between 1849 and 1852. The station is named after **Nicolas Cruquius** (1678-1754), the Latinised name of Nicolaas de Kruik, a surveyor and the designer of a project (1750) aimed at draining the lake which had expanded dangerously after the collapse of dikes and intensive extraction of peat from the local bogs. The other two stations are called Leeghwater and Lynden.

The museum contains interesting documents concerning technical developments in the fight against water and the creation of the polders. This aspect is particularly well illustrated by an animated map-cum-model showing the waterways network in the Netherlands and the areas that would be under water if there were no dikes and dams. Among the machines on display are two of special interest: a Watt-type Cockerill pump which is the oldest of its kind in the Netherlands (1826) with an output of $45m^3$ per minute *(ask at reception if you wish to operate it)*, and the actual **pumping station**★ equipped with eight pendulum arms and eight pumps with piston. Its output was $250m^3$ per minute. This is the largest steam-operated machine ever built (in Cornwall); it was inaugurated in 1849. The American Society of Mechanical Engineers acknowledged its worth by designating it as an International Historic Landmark in 1991. It ceased operation on 10 June 1933.

HILVERSUM

Plan p 201 – Michelin map no 211 Q 9

Set in the heart of moorland and the picturesque Gooi Woods, Hilversum, once known as the capital's *achtertuin* (back garden or hunting ground), can now be considered as Amsterdam's main residential suburb. The town was directly inspired by the garden cities designed by Englishman Ebenezer Howard. It forms a very widespread community, with villas dotted among the trees. It is also the main centre of Dutch television and radio broadcasting. Since 1951 Hilversum and the immediate vicinity (in the Bussum direction) have accommodated the equipment and studios used by the national channels and stations.

WM Dudok (1884-1974), the most important exponent of cubist architecture in the Netherlands, was associated with the city of Hilversum. He built the town hall, the municipal sports park, several residential districts and about twenty schools.

SIGHTS

★ **Raadhuis** – *Hoge Naarderweg.* Built between 1927 and 1931, the town hall was designed by **Willem Marinus Dudok** (1884-1974) and was his most important work. He produced a formalist yet romantic building that was a rarity in the late 1920s, a period more typical for the aggressively modern style.

It consists of terraced cubic structures whose varying volumes form a harmony of horizontal and vertical lines. This gives the building a different aspect depending on the viewpoint from which it is observed. The clock tower soars over the building to a great height.

The bare walls are built of brick (a regional tradition rather than a manifesto of regionalism). Supporters of international architecture would have made greater use of concrete here, since concrete is a more rational and, therefore, more functional material. The vertical joins between the bricks are flush with the level of the brick while the horizontal joints are more deeply embedded, giving a streaked look. Inside rationalism and functionalism are also predominant. Furniture, clocks, lighting and even the wooden mallet were designed by Dudok. The basement houses the **Dudok Centrum**, a collection of documents on the life and work of the architect.

Goois Museum ⏱ – *Kerkbrink 6.* Accommodated in the former town hall, this museum has archeological and geological collections and a record of the folklore of the vast Gooi Woods. There are a few display cases containing local porcelain *(see Weesp, below)*.

★ THE GOOI WOODS AND LOOSDRECHT LAKES

A 72km/45mi trip through the northern section of the Gooi – allow approximately one day. Leave Hilversum by Hilversumeweg and follow the Laren signs (N 525).

The Gooi woods and the surrounding area are steeped in reminders of the Golden Age when the merchants constituting the elite of Amsterdam owned properties in the country, either "relaxation homes" *(lusthuizen)* or "leisure homes" *(speelhuizen)*. The most highly prized areas were on the banks of the Amstel and Vecht, between Muiden and Utrecht, and around 's-Graveland. In some ways, the area was a bourgeois arcadia of holiday homes in which wealthy merchants and traders came to spend the summer months.

Laren – This small residential town lies in very pleasant surroundings. It is a symbol of the region's wealth. At the end of the 19C, the **Laren School** *(Larense School)* attracted several painters under the leadership of Neuhuys and Anton Mauve, a cousin of Vincent van Gogh. Several of the artists were also members of the Hague School.

Around the villa (1911) belonging to the American artist **William Henry Singer** (1868-1943), an arts centre was set up in 1956 by the widow of the artist who inherited the industrial empire that bears his name.

Singer Museum ⏱ – *Oude Drift 1 via Naarderstraat.* The Singer Museum contains some interesting collections displayed on a rota basis. They are regularly replaced by excellent temporary exhibitions. In addition to Singer's own works, which reveal Impressionist tendencies, the museum exhibits paintings by the Amsterdam and Hague schools (Maris, Bosboom, Isaac Israëls) and others by the local school (Hart Nibbrig). The garden contains a few sculptures.

Huizen – Since the closure of the Zuiderzee, this town has become an industrial centre; it also has a large yachting marina. Between Huizen and Naarden, the Gooi has remained somewhat wild; it is not yet overrun by the spread of luxury estates such as those being built between Hilversum and Laren or Hilversum and Bussum.

★ **Naarden** – *See NAARDEN*

Muiden – *See MUIDEN*

Vecht Valley – This river has regained its erstwhile tranquillity since the building of the Rhine-Amsterdam Canal. It wends its way hither and thither through the quiet country landscape.

Weesp – This small walled town, which was already prosperous in the 14C, is famous for its beer and spirits, and for its porcelain.

The first porcelain factory established in the country was opened in Weesp in 1758. **Gemeentemuseum Weesp** ⏱ – *Nieuwstraat 41.* Housed in the town hall, this museum has a fine **collection** (1758-70). Although Delft pottery is world famous, only Weesp, Loosdrecht *(see below)*, Ouder-Amstel and Nieuwer-Amstel produce porcelain in the Netherlands.

Leave Weesp via N 236 and turn right after the bridge over the Vecht (N 523). After Nederhorst den Berg, cross the bridge over the Vecht and turn right into Vreelandseweg to Vreeland.

★★ **Loosdrechtse Plassen** – The tour crosses the northern part of the Loosdrecht Lakes (3 600ha) stretching towards Utrecht (which is outside the area covered by this guide). The description below will probably encourage some readers to consult the Green Guide to the Netherlands in which there is a full description of the area of former peatbogs.

Loenen – This delightful little town with flower-decked houses has (in the north) a tall mill with a balustrade known as De Hoop *(Hope)*.

Oud-Loosdrecht – This is the region's main tourist centre. Oud Loosdrecht has a large yachting marina.

Kasteel-Museum Sypesteyn ⌚ – *Nieuw-Loosdrechtsedijk 150.* Located just outside Nieuw-Loosdrecht, the castle was rebuilt between 1912 and 1927 (after an old watercolour) by the last descendant of the Van Sypesteyn family, Henri who wanted to revive the former glory of his family. The castle has been turned into a museum. It contains collections of furniture, clocks, silverware, family portraits by Nicolaes Maes and Cornelis Troost, and antique objets d'art (in particular **Loosdrecht porcelain**).
The grounds include a rose garden, orchards and a maze decorated with arbours.

's-Graveland – Numerous manor houses embellish the outskirts of this small town nestling in the Gooi Woods. The most elegant of all is the **Trompenburg** (Tromp Castle, *not open to visitors*), built for Admiral Cornelis Tromp, son of the illustrious Admiral Maarten Tromp (1597-1653), who defied the Spanish Armada at the famous Battle of the Downs in 1637. The manor is almost completely surrounded by water. It consists of a rectangular building and a domed pavilion whose graceful outline is reflected in the waters of a lake.

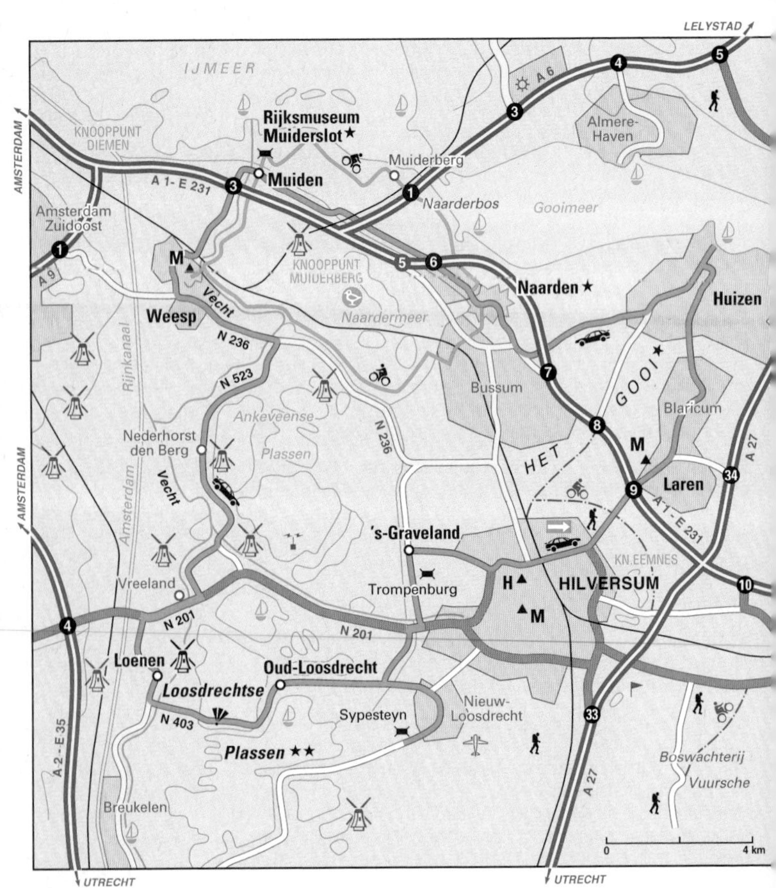

See "Cycling in the polders", Tour no. 3

HOORN★

Plan p 201 – Michelin map no 210 P 7

'his is one of the most traditional harbours on the old Zuiderzee. It lies on the shores f the IJsselmeer. Hoorn, co-founder of the Dutch East India Company, is a delightful ttle town with a very busy shopping centre. The marina is very lively.

tourist train **(Museumstoomtram** ⓥ**)** runs between Hoorn and Medemblik; it is a sort of ravelling museum and the railway journey can be combined with a boat trip from Aedemblik to Enkhuizen *(see the tourist office for details)*.

HISTORICAL NOTES

Founded c 1300 around a natural harbour, Hoorn soon became the main town in West Friesland. In fact for some time it was the capital of the region, under the name of *Hoarne*. It owed its prosperity to fishing and overseas trade, mainly with Scandinavia. It was in Hoorn in 1416 that the first large herring net was made. This led to a flourishing fishing net industry. To the north, wide canals laid out as gardens mark the site of the moat round the town walls built in the early 16C.

In October 1573 a famous naval battle took place offshore from the town, the "Battle of the Zuiderzee" which resulted in the defeat of the Spanish Admiral **Bossu** by the fleets from Hoorn, Enkhuizen, Edam and Monnikendam, towns which were supporters of the dissenting Gueux faction.

In the 17C Hoorn enjoyed a period of splendour when it was the administrative and trading centre of the area of Holland north of Amsterdam. This was also one of the six harbours, or chambers *(kamer)*, of the Dutch East India Company founded in 1602 *(see Introduction, The Golden Age)*.

The town has had a number of famous sons: **Willem Schouten** (1580-1625) *(see insert below)* and **Jan Pieterszoon Coen** (1587-1629), Governor General of the Dutch East Indies from 1617 to 1623 and from 1627 to 1629, who founded Batavia (now known as Djakarta) and is also regarded as the founder of the colonial empire of the Dutch East Indies (Indonesia).

From Hoorn to Cape Horn

It was a native of Hoorn who, with his compatriot Jacques Le Maire (1585-1616), was the first man to sail round the southernmost tip of the Americas, south of the Magellan Strait. **Willem Schouten** named the last island of Tierra del Fuego after the town in which he was born, and it became the storm-racked Cape Horn whose meridian marks the boundary between the Atlantic and Pacific Oceans.

★THE OLD TOWN *Allow 3hr*

The original town centre provides an opportunity for a historic tour past old houses. Some of the frontages are decorated with superb stone carvings relating, in most cases, to seafaring and navigation.

Achterstraat – The **Doelengebouw** at no 2 was once the guildhall for two guilds of archers (St George's and St Sebastian's). Above the entrance (1615) is a bas-relief illustrating the martyrdom of St Sebastian, patron saint of archers.

Onder de Bompjes – At the eastern end of the canal at no 22 are two warehouses (1606) with stepped gables. They were once used by the Dutch East India Company (*Verenigde Oostindische Compagnie* or VOC) as is obvious from the fine carving of two ships on the **façade**. In order to prevent thefts and burglaries, these spice warehouses were built away from the more easily accessible seafront.

Korte Achterstraat – At no 4 in this narrow street is the entrance to a former orphanage, the **Weeshuis** (1620). A commemorative plaque recalls that Admiral Bossu spent 3 years' imprisonment in this building.

Nieuwstraat – The former **town hall** (1613) (voormalig Stadhuis) is situated in a shopping street. Its beautiful, ornate façade rises to a double stepped gable.

At the top of the frontage on **no 17** is a carving of Poseidon, god of the sea, and Amphitrite, his wife, accompanied by two dolphins. The inclusion of these marine mammals is not due solely to the sculptor's whim. When they are shown with a trident (which, in this case, is one of the attributes of Poseidon), they symbolise free trade and the navy.

Kerkplein – At no 39, opposite a church that has been turned into a clothes store, stands the butter market **(De Boterhal)**, once the St John Hospice *(Sint Jansgasthuis)*. It is a fine building dating from 1563; its stepped gable is decorated with sculptures.

Kerkstraat – There is an attractive façade dating from 1660 on the house at no 1.

R. Dechamps/MICHELIN

A frontage stone relating to the Dutch East India Company, Onder de Boompjes 22

★**Rode Steen** – Towering ove this delightful square are th wonderful façade of th West Friesland Museum an the public weights and meas ures office. The square' strange name (literally "re stone") has a somewhat ter rifying origin. It comes from the blood spilt here during public executions.
In the centre is a statue o Jan Pieterszoon Coen. Th house front at no 2 include a stone carving of a smith hence the name of th dwelling: *In dyser Man* (T the man of iron).

Westfries Museum ⏱ – *Rod Steen 1.* Erected in 1632 the building that houses th West Friesland Museum is majestic Baroque construc tion with an outstanding ta **façade★**. It is impressive fo its large windows, coloure coats of arms of the Hous of Orange *(top)* and of Wes Friesland *(bottom)*, and it entablatures topped b lions holding the coats o arms of seven towns in th region. This feature wa designed by an unknow architect. The seven towns are Alkmaar, Edam, Enkhuizen, Hoorn, Medembli Monnickendam and Purmerend. The building was once the seat of the College c States consisting of delegates from the seven towns. This was the body which hel executive power in West Friesland and the "Northern District" *(Noorderkwartier)* Once beyond the wonderful wrought-iron gate dating from 1729, visitors acces the museum collections described by author Aldous Huxley in 1925 as a "mess c bric-a-brac". The bric-a-brac may have disappeared but the variety of exhibits ha remained unchanged.
On the ground floor, note the ceiling in the Louis XVI drawing room; it consists c fake stucco work made of wood, which is fairly uncommon. The main receptio room, the *Grote Voorzaal*, is decorated with a superb fireplace and four large paint ings of the national guard by Jan Rotius (1624-66); the beams are supported b brackets carved with the coats of arms of various towns in the region.
The Admiralty Room on the 1st floor contains models and weaponry, as well as portrait of Admiral Bossu. The most interesting exhibit on this floor, however, i the painting in the following room, ***View of Hoorn***★ (1622) by Hendrik Corneliszoo Vroom (1566-1640), a work which shows the extent to which the harbour ha retained its original appearance for those who arrive here by boat. The roor relating to the Dutch East India Company has a strong scent of cloves introducin visitors to the fascinating world of the ships that used to sail to the Orient. Th room also contains some interesting paintings such as *The Directors of th Chamber of Hoorn* (1682) by Johan de Baen, and two portraits by Jacob Wabe hung one opposite the other; they depict Jan Pieterszoon Coen and his wife, Ev Ment.
The attic includes two cells dating back to the days of the French occupation a the end of the 18C when the building was used as a local courthouse.
The cellar includes archaeological artefacts from the town and surrounding areas

Waag – It is generally thought that the public weigh-house was designed by Her drick de Keyser, the architect of the Zuiderkerk and the Westerkerk (i Amsterdam). It is a fine building dating from 1609, built of blue stone (limestone and now a restaurant. In a niche is a statue of a unicorn holding a shield deco ated with a cornucopia (the unicorn is the town's emblem).

Grote Oost – In this street, the houses nearest the square all have a pronounce slope. Some of them (such as the one at no 20) are topped by impressive carve balustrades in the Rococo style. Another (no 7) is decorated with a delightful frieze

Foreestenhuis – At no 43 there is the Foreest house, named after Nanning va Foreest, one of the town's most illustrious governors. The elegant Louis XVI façad (1724) is adorned with telamones (male figures as pillars) supporting a balcony

Oosterkerk – *Grote Oost 60.* Founded in 1453, the "East Church", dedicated to St Anthony, has a Renaissance west front (1616) in the style of Hendrick de Keyser. On the top is a charming little wooden belfry. This was once the sailors' church; now it is used mainly for cultural events.

Slapershaven – The Bossu houses *(Bossuhuizen, Grote Oost 132 and Slapershaven 1 and 2)* date from the early 17C. The façades of those in Slapershaven are decorated with a carved frieze illustrating the naval battle of 1573 at which Admiral Bossu was defeated.

The **façade** on the left is typical of the old shops along the quaysides. Above the ground floor are tall, narrow bays separated by carved wooden pilasters.

> It would be a pity to leave Hoorn without tasting the excellent smoked eels served in the D Wormsbecher en Zoon establishment, in Wijdebrugsteeg. Eat them at the counter or, in fine weather, on the small terrace.

Binnenluiendijk – At no 3, visitors can see the office of the chamber of the Dutch East India Company which purchased two houses in 1629. The house at no 2 has a frontage built in 1784; no 3 dates from 1624.

Oude Doelenkade – Stand on the little bridge for a wonderful **view** of the basin and quaysides lined with old warehouses. The **inner harbour★** *(Binnenhaven)* is particularly picturesque. A traditional boat with a double centreboard is often tied up alongside. As soon as the fine weather returns, the owners of the craft put to sea so that they can tidy up the hull of their boat before taking part in the regular regattas on the IJsselmeer.

HOORN

Achter de Vest .... Y
Achterstraat .... Y 2
Appelhaven .... Z
Bierkade .... Z 4
Binnenluiendijk .... Z 5
Breed .... Y
Breestraat .... Z 6
Draafsingel .... Y
Eikstraat .... Y
Gedempte Turfhaven .... Y 9
Gerritsland .... Z
Gouw .... Y
Grote Noord .... YZ
Grote Oost .... Z
Hoge Vest .... Y 10
Italiaanse Zeedijk .... Z
J.D. Pollstr. .... Y
Joh. Messchaertstr. ...... Y 12
Keern .... Y 15
Kerkplein .... Z 17
Kerkstraat .... Z 18
Kleine Noord .... Y
Kleine Oost .... Z
Koepoortsplein .... Y 20
Korenmarkt .... Z 23
Korte Achterstr. .... Y 24
Lange Kerkstraat .... Z 26
Muntstraat .... Y 29
Nieuwendam .... Z 30
Nieuwsteeg .... Y 32
Nieuwstraat .... YZ 33
Noorderstraat .... Y 35
Noorderveemarkt .... Y 36
Onder de Boompjes .... Y 38
Oude Doelenkade .... Z 39
Pakhuisstr. .... Y
Scharloo .... Y 41
Slapershaven .... Z 42
Spoorsingel .... Y 44
Stationsplein .... Y 45
Veemarkt .... Y
Veermanskade .... Z 47
Venenlaan .... Y
Vollerswaal .... Y
West .... Z
Westerdijk .... Z 48
Wijdebrugsteen .... Z 50
Zon .... Z 51

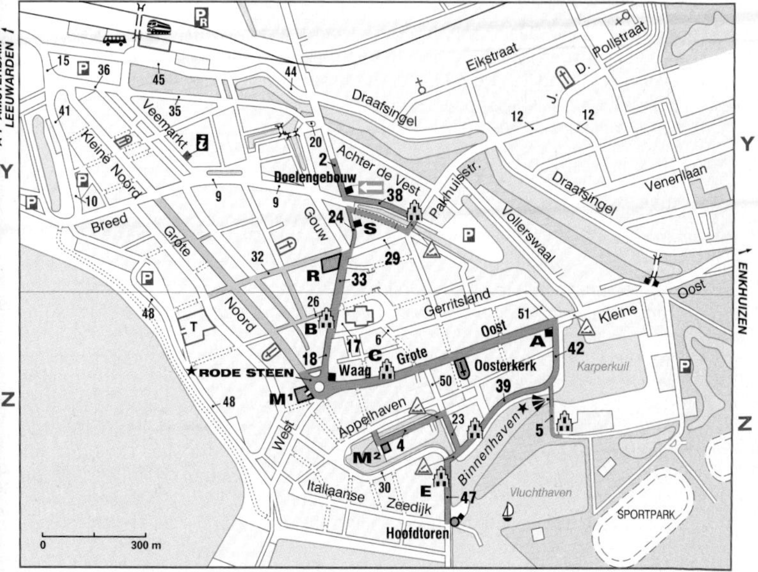

Bossuhuizen .... Z A
Boterhal .... Z B
Doelengebouw .... Y
Foreestenhuis .... Z C
Hoofdtoren .... Z
In de Bonte Koe .... Z E
Museum van de Twintigste Eeuw .... Z M²
Westfries Museum ...... Z M¹
Oosterkerk .... Z
Rode Steen★ .... Z
Voormalig stadhuis .... Y R
Waag .... Z
Weeshuis .... Y S

The harbour in Hoorn, or the perpetual tranquillity of the shores of the IJsselmeer

At nos 21 (1618) and 17-19 (1616), note the stone frontages illustrated with scenes connected with sea voyages to the Indies.

★**Veermanskade** – Along this quayside is a fine row of restored houses. Most of them were once the homes of traders. Some have attractive wood carvings on the façade, a feature characteristic of Hoorn. Others have delightful stone façades and five have stepped gables. No 15, the house known as "*In de bonte koe*", was the birthplace of seafarer **Willem Bontekoe** (1587-1657). This explains the presence of the piebald *(bonte)* cow *(koe)* on the frontage.

Hoofdtoren – Built in 1532 to stand guard over the main entrance *(hoofd)* to the harbour, this tower was given a wooden bellcote in 1651. On the rear of the building is a sculpture representing the town's emblem, a unicorn.
Since 1968, a bronze sculpture by Jan van Druten and known as "Bontekoe's cabin boys" has stood near the tower, looking out to sea. The three lads are the heroes of the children's book written by Johan Fabricius, *De Scheepsjongens van Bontekoe (see above)*.

Bierkade – "Beer Quay" gets its name from the goods that were once offloaded here by ships from Hamburg and Bremen. It has some interesting façades, especially at nos 10 and 13. No 4 houses the **Museum van de Twintigste Eeuw** ⓥ (Twentieth Century Museum) which is interesting for its architecture. The museum is housed in two old cheese stores built in 1903.

Willem Ysbrantszoon Bontekoe, one of Hoorn's heroes

In 1646, a book was successfully published and was even translated into several languages. It was the *Journael ofte gedenckwaerdige beschrijvinghe van de Oost-Indische Reyse van Willem Ysbrantszoon Bontekoe*, a consummate example of a maritime epic.
Bontekoe, who sailed with the Dutch East India Company, described his adventures between 1618 and 1625. The first part (the trip between Hoorn and Batavia) is particularly famous. The 206 passengers were subjected to the worst possible difficulties: the mast snapped just before the ship left, then scurvy was diagnosed and finally the ship exploded off Batavia. Bontekoe narrates the tale of his escape and describes how he succeeded in reaching Batavia with 54 other survivors. The second part of the diary deals with his years sailing the seas round Asia and the struggles between the Portuguese and the Chinese. In the third part, Bontekoe describes his stay in Madagascar. Bontekoe remained a source of inspiration even in the 20C. Even though his role was not as important as he implied in his *Journael*, he remains one of the heroes of Fabricius' book. *De Scheepsjongens van Bontekoe*, which was published in 1924 and was also highly successful.

KEUKENHOF and the BULB FIELDS★★★

Plans pp 200 and 234 – Michelin map no 211 fold 4

THE TULIP

"The tulip, white, did for complexion seek;
And learned to interline its cheek.
Its onion root they then so high did hold,
That one was for a meadow sold."

The Mower against Gardens
Andrew Marvell (1621-78)

The story of a huge success – The plant is said to have first been brought back from Turkey by Ogier Ghislain de Busbecq (1522-92), Ambassador of Austria. In 1554, he saw not far from Andrinople a field of tulips in bloom belonging to Soliman the Magnificent, and he is said to have had bulbs sent to the court of Vienna. What is certain is that **Charles de l'Ecluse** (1526-1609), better known as Carolus Clusius, a scientist responsible for the Imperial garden of medicinal plants in the Austrian capital, was the first man to write a botanic description of the tulip after receiving the first bulbs. When he became a professor at the University of Leiden in 1593, he brought his small collection of bulbs with him and began growing tulips on the damp, sandy soil along the shores of the North Sea between Leiden and Haarlem.

Success was rapid and far-reaching, despite the very high price demanded by the eminent botanist. Other flowers such as hyacinths and gladioli were introduced, but it was the tulip that attracted the highest prices. Between 1630 and 1636, speculation reached senseless proportions. A rare tulip bulb that produced a multi-coloured flower was sold for 6 000fl. People even began exchanging a tulip bulb for a carriage and two horses, for acres of land, or for a house. Tulipmania reached such a height that "tulip lawyers" began monitoring speculation on the Stock Exchange based on the flower. The States of Holland put an end to this commercial folly in 1636 and the industry was regulated. Meanwhile tulips had become known throughout Europe and, although they were briefly replaced in the popularity ratings in the late 17C by hyacinths, they remained very sought-after plants.

Frans Halsmuseum

Allegory of Tulipomania, Jan Bruegel

Tulip, who art thou? – Its name comes from the Persian word *tulipan* which itself comes from the Turkish *tülbend* meaning *a turban*. It was Ogier Ghislain Busbecq who gave the flower its name in his *Itinera constantinopolitanum et amasianum* published in 1581. Later, the name appeared in a Flemish-Latin-French dictionary published during the Golden Age (17C). A tulip is a member of the **liliaceae** family; it is a bulb with an annual growth cycle. After flowering, in the spring, the bulb produces another bulb (which will flower the following year) and a number of bulblets. It then dies. There are now some 125 varieties of tulip in 15 major families – single early tulips, double early tulips, Mendel tulips, Triumph tulips, Darwin tulips, hybrids of Darwin tulips, lily-flowering tulips, late or "cottage" tulips, late double tulips, Rembrandt tulips, parrot tulips, *Kauffmannania* tulips, hybrids of *fosteriana* tulips, hybrids of *greigii* tulips, and wild or self-setting tulips.

Naming cultivars

When a new cultivar appears on the market, it must be accompanied by the name of its creator, the year in which it was obtained, a detailed description of the flower and its colour, and the number of chromosomes.

The decorative value of the flower and the increased commercial interest show in tulips over the centuries have led horticulturalists to undertake extensive hybrid isation work in order to obtain tulips that are more and more impressive. Fo example, multicoloured cultivars are produced by the introduction of viruses. Som 2 300 cultivars have been recorded by the Dutch Royal Bulb Growing Association

From ornament to symbol – The tulip was the emblem of the Ottoman Empire i the 14C – and has been the emblem of the Islamic Republic of Iran since 1993. It wa used as a stylised decorative feature, especially in Anatolia which produced the famou Iznik ceramics (tiles adorned with tulips decorate the mosques of Istanbul). It also dec orates the wool carpets from the Ladik region. Moreover, the lily-flowering tulip, whic was much appreciated by the sultans, became an inherent part of Turkish art.
In Europe, tulips began to appear on a large number of everyday objects in th 17C, especially pottery and tapestries; they also decorated table linen and pewter ware. Yet it was in art that the flower was most often depicted, mainly in th superb bouquets painted by the Flemish and Dutch schools of the 17C and 18C.

BULB-GROWING AND FIELDS OF TULIPS

The commonest varieties of bulbs in the Netherlands are tulips, narcissi, hyacinths irises and crocuses although many other flowers are also grown, including gladi oli, lilies, grape hyacinths, dahlias, anemones and freesias.
At the present time, the bulbs cover a total of 14 400ha over the country as whole. The main areas of production are to the south of Haarlem and the nort of a line between Alkmaar and Hoorn. The bulbs are exported to countries in bot the northern and southern hemispheres; the exports result in a turnover of som one billion guilders per year.

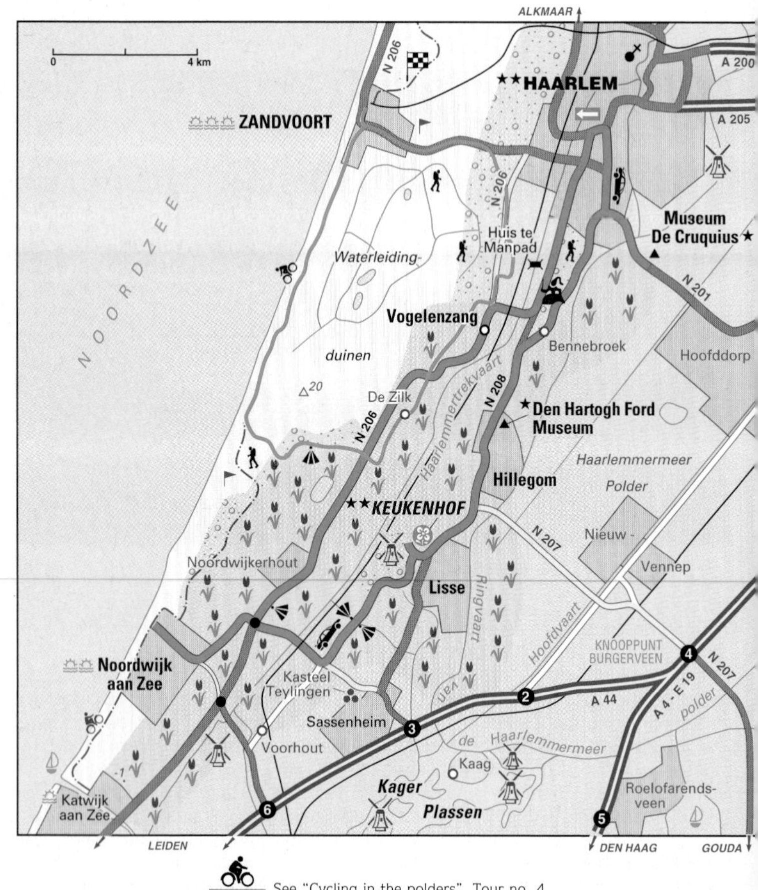

See "Cycling in the polders", Tour no. 4

When to visit the bulb fields – Towards mid-March the bulb fields take on their first colours when the yellow or purple **crocus** come into bloom, followed by the white and yellow **narcissi** at the end of March. By mid-April, the **hyacinths** are beginning to flower, with the first **tulips**. A few days later, the finest of all the tulips burst into bloom and it is, therefore, at the end of April that the flat expanse of fields is at its most beautiful. It is divided into multicoloured strips separated by narrow irrigation canals, resembling a vast mosaic of often brilliant colours. It is at this time that the grand flower procession is held, on the road from Haarlem to Noordwijk aan Zee. Later, the fields disappear beneath a carpet of **irises** then **gladioli**, in August. Another procession is held in September, between Aalsmeer and Amsterdam.
Shortly after the flowering season, the plants are mechanically dead-headed in order to strengthen the bulb and prevent the formation of seeds. The large bulbs are harvested at the end of June and sold to private gardeners or businesses wishing to grow the flowers. The bulblets are replanted in the autumn.

★★ THE KEUKENHOF

Set in a vast area of flower-decked fields, the Keukenhof is, in some ways, a temple to bulbs. They cover an area of 32ha in a delightfully wooded setting. An admission fee is charged for the Keukenhof, however, and it should not be confused with the vast, geometrical fields of tulips to be seen between Haarlem and Leiden.

The History of the Gardens – From 1401 to 1436, the Keukenhof was the hunting ground of the turbulent **Jacqueline of Bavaria** who inherited the counties of Hainaut, Holland and Zeland on the death of her father, William IV of Bavaria. She not only hunted here; she also grew herbs and spices for use in the dishes served in her castle where she had her court (the Kasteel Teylingen whose red-brick ruins can be seen near Sassenheim; it was here that Jacqueline died in 1436). This explains the strange name of the park, which literally means **"kitchen garden"**.
In 1830 the German landscape gardener Zocher *(see VONDELPARK)* was commissioned to create a landscaped park here in the "English" style, so named because it originated in England. Its aim was to imitate nature. This is why the gardens are slightly undulating, with narrow canals and a man-made lake that is the haunt of swans. There are several different varieties of trees, and a magnificent beech-lined avenue. In 1949, the town of Lisse set up an open-air flower show which has now made the Keukenhof the largest spring garden in Europe.
This is the setting for the Keukenhof national floral exhibition **(Nationale Bloemententoonstelling Keukenhof** ⏱**)** which has taken place in springtime since 1949. Initially created to give horticulturists the chance to show their clients the full spectrum of their production, this exhibition has proved to be an ever-growing success, attracting nearly 900 000 visitors a year in this magnificent park.

Tour – The "kitchen garden" is a magnificent showcase for Holland's horticulturalists. More than **6 million bulbs** forming magnificent splashes of colour against a green background of lawns and foliage can be seen here – and admired, for the quality of the floral layouts is absolutely perfect. Although the Spring Garden *(Lentetuin)* is open to visitors for only two months of the year, it takes 10 months for the 90 or more registered suppliers to prepare the display. At the end of May, the park's 30 gardeners pull up the bulbs, redesign the beds to suit future varieties, select and plant the new bulbs before the first frosts, prune the trees and maintain the many rhododendrons and azaleas. They also sow new lawns. The care taken with the preparation is obvious to visitors entering the park with its ocean of flowers at the end of March; the results of their labours are quite simply spectacular.
Various flower displays (the "Parades") in the pavilions round off the visit. This is an opportunity to admire an amazing variety of flowers including roses, chrysanthemums, narcissi, hydrangea and lilacs. The Queen Beatrix Pavilion houses a **permanent orchid exhibition**. The park also includes flowering bushes, **themed gardens** (nature garden, music garden), fountains and ornamental lakes. The park is also adorned with about 50 **sculptures**.
Remember to leave time to climb to the platform of the windmill constructed in 1957, from which there is a superb **view**★ of the neighbouring fields of flowers.
Since 1999 the extension of the park also stages an annual exhibition in the summer. This summer garden **(Zomerhof)**, a 7ha expanse of summer flowers, is mainly composed of a water garden, a dune landscape and an artificial hillock. Every year in October there is also a **bulb market**.

★★ EXCURSION THROUGH THE BULB FIELDS

Haarlem to Haarlem: allow a full day for this trip. The roads flanking the bulb fields have, unfortunately, very few lay-bys from which to admire the scenery. Because of this, it is preferable to take the train from Amsterdam or, best of all, to have a flight over the fields.

★★ **Haarlem** – *See HAARLEM.*

Leave Haarlem via Van Eedenstraat.

A few fine houses line the road before the first bulb fields come into view. Note the castle on the right: **Huis te Manpad**.

Take the first road on the right then turn left beyond the railway crossing.

M. Guillou/MICHELIN

Vogelenzang – The village set in a woodland near the coastal dunes has some luxury homes.

To the south of De Zilk, the pale sand dunes come into view, forming a pleasant contrast to the vivid colours of the carpets of flowers.

Beyond Noordzijkerhout, the road climbs a hill before the slip road. This provides some wonderful **views★** of the bulb fields.

Noordwijk aan Zee – *See plan in The Red Guide Benelux.* Preceded by some vast camp sites, this chic seaside resort consists mainly of a seafront covered with concrete apartment blocks overlooking tall sand dunes and a long beach. Noordwijk lies on the route of the flower processions (amongst others on the last Saturday in April). Behind the Noordwijk dunes stands the technical centre (ESTEC) of the European space agency Esa. This is where satellites are tested, and the technical management of European space projects is organised from here. Further afield, the **Noordwijk Space Expo** ⊙ *(Keplerlaan 3)* traces the history of international (particularly European) space navigation in an exhibition which includes models of rockets, real satellites, space suits and a slide show. Children can follow an exploration route and will be given an astronaut's diploma signed by Wubbo Ockels, the first Dutch astronaut.

Follow the signs to Lisse/Sassenheim and turn left into Loosterweg just after the Voorhout sign to the right.

★★ Keukenhof – *See above.*

The Black Tulip

Alas, this is mere legend, for the simple reason that the colour does not exist naturally in the plant world. Although the heart of certain tulips can look black, for example in certain cultivars of the famous Darwin tulip that is the ancestor of many modern flowers, it is more by way of contrast with the red and yellow of the petals.
However, a few tulips get very close to this colour, including the "Black Parrot" or the "Queen of the Night", which is a very dark purple. Dutch breeders have announced a tulip of an almost black, very dark violet shade although this is not yet available.

Lisse – One of the principal sights in this region of bulb fields. An old house in the centre of the town is home to the **Museum de Zwarte Tulp** ⏲ (Black Tulip Museum). Although its permanent collection is essentially anecdotal (but the tools and delightful jars containing tulips preserved in formol are worth particular attention), there are some interesting little exhibitions devoted to bulb growing.
Lisse is the departure point for boats going to **Kagerplassen** (Kager Lakes) and the insular, picturesque little village of **Kaagdorp**.
The neighbouring village of **Sassenheim** also lies at the heart of the bulb field region. Jacqueline of Bavaria spent the last years of her life in a castle **(Kasteel Teylingen)** situated nearby which is now in ruins.

Hillegom – This is the home of the **Den Hartogh Ford Museum** ⏲★, *(Haarlemmerstraat 36)*, a museum containing some 185 vehicles bearing the famous trade mark of Detroit produced between 1903 and 1948. Fans cannot fail to be impressed by the pristine condition of all the cars on show including a Ford N (1906), a Ford S (1908), several model T Fords (more than 15 million of them rolled off the assembly lines between 1908 and 1927), a Lincoln 160 (1929), a Ford 181 Phaeton (1930), a Ford 40 Roadster (1932), a Ford 720 coupé (1936) and a whole series of commercial vehicles grouped in the last room.

Continue to Haarlem and follow the signs to Cruquius.

★ **Museum De Cruquius** – *See HAARLEM, Museum De Cruquius.*

MARKEN★

Plan p 201 – Michelin map no 210 P 8

Marken was separated from the mainland in the 13C by the formation of the Zuiderzee. Originally, it was occupied by Frisian monk-farmers. Until 1957 it was an island situated 2.5km/1.5mi from the shore. It is now linked to the coast and lies on the shores of the Gouwzee, a sort of inland sea.
From the outset Marken, which has a Protestant population, has formed a closed community. It still has its old charm, firstly because of its wooden houses and secondly because its people wear traditional costume in the high season.
Before the creation of the IJsselmeer as a result of the building of the Afsluitdijk in 1932, the population earned its income from fishing. Now, the peninsula lives mainly from tourism, even though it has not made as many concessions to this industry as Volendam.

P. Duval/HOA QUI

★ **The village** – The picturesque village has two districts: Havenbuurt near the harbour and Kerkbuurt (sometimes referred to as "the capital") around the church. From the vaulted roof in the church hang two scale models of boats: a *haringbuis*, which was used for herring fishing, and a sailing smack.

In order to afford protec-tion against high tides, the houses are built on smal man-made hillocks *(wer-ven)* and on piles which were visible before the clos-ure of the Zuiderzee; the purpose of the piles is to leave the way open for the waves. The small houses are, for the most part made of timber and painted dark green, with slightly projecting side gables. Some of the houses are covered in pitch and roofed with tiles.

TRY A LOCAL SPECIALITY

The *erwtensoep* is a typical dish, pea soup which is served in the restaurant called *De Tanderij*, Havenbuurt 1. There is an excellent view of the IJsselmeer from the restaurant.

The **interiors** are painted and waxed. They gleam with cleanliness and are richly dec-orated with crockery and ornaments. The beds are built in recesses where there is also a small drawer that was used as a cradle.

★ **The costumes** – The women wear a striped petticoat, wide skirt and black apron. The striped bodice worn in the summer is covered with a waistcoat and a printed bib. The headdress is simple: a striped lace and cotton cap. The men are dressed in a short waistcoat, baggy knee breeches and black socks. The children are more rarely seen in costume. Both boys and girls wear a skirt and bonnet; only the shapes and colours are different.

The costume worn on feast days, especially at Whitsun, is more refined and elegant.

Marker Museum ⏱ – *Kerkbuurt 44.* Installed in four fishermen's cottages where once herring and eels were smoked, the museum has a small permanent exhib-ition telling the history of Marken.

Eel nets belonging to the fishermen of the Gouwzee

MONNICKENDAM

Plan p 201 – Michelin map no 210 P 8

Like Broek in Waterland, this is part of the vast Waterland community. It has a marina on the Gouwzee, but still there are some delightful fishermen's cottages and some fine 17C and 18C mansions *(see Kerkstraat and the town hall in Noordeinde)*.

The town gets its name from a Premonstratensian monastery (*monnick* means "monk"), which has now disappeared, and from the *middendam*, a dike built by the brothers.

Museum De Speeltoren ⓥ – *Noordeinde 4*. This small local history museum stands at the foot of the fine brick **tower** (1591) which has a beautiful animated carillon. It was once part of the old town hall.

Waag – *Middendam*. The public weigh-house (c 1600) is decorated with pilasters and a heavy carved gable.

If you do not mind queuing, take advantage of your visit to eat a plate of smoked eels at *Stuttenburgh* (Haringburgwal 2-5). The decor is sure to amaze you.

Grote of St-Nicolaaskerk – The Great or St Nicholas Church is a "hall church", a Gothic construction with nave and side aisles 70m/228ft long. Its vaulting is shaped like an upturned boat. Note the carved oak **screen** in the chancel; it dates from 1653 despite its style which is typical of the mid-16C.

MUIDEN

Plan p 201 – Michelin map no 210 P 9

Muiden is a small harbour that is very popular with yachtsmen. It is an age-old community set on the banks of the IJmeer at the mouth of the Vecht, the river that was once a major route for maritime traffic. Since 1952, it has lain parallel to the Rhine-Amsterdam Canal.

This is a historic town, with an old castle surrounded by a moat. The castle still seems to be standing guard over the harbour mouth.

★HET MUIDERSLOT (MUIDEN CASTLE) ⓥ

Founded in 1205 by the Bishop of Utrecht then rebuilt by Count Floris V of Holland in 1280, the castle in Muiden resembles an old brick fortress with sturdy corner towers surrounded by a moat.

Once upon a time, there was an ambitious nobleman... – In about 1290, William II's successor, **Floris V**, Count of Holland and Zeeland, took advantage of the opening of the Zuiderzee which had formed in the late 12C to seize control of Western Friesland. He immediately set up a system of authority based on the wealthy middle classes rather than on the nobility whose right to mete out justice was, like other traditional rights, gradually diminished. Although this policy was modern, it soon created tension within the Count's entourage, especially among his vassals who were distressed by so much power. Floris conquered the Amstel region and granted Amsterdam its first privilege in 1275. The Count of Holland's power was then at its peak; in 1296, his vassals put him permanently to sleep, well away from watching eyes, somewhere in the castle in Muiden.

... and a poet who wrote love sonnets – From 1621 onwards, the castle housed an intellectual and literary circle called the Muiderkring. Led by the castle's owner, the circle brought together musicians and writers such as Maria Tesselschade and Anna Roemersdr Visscher, daughters of the writer Roemer Visscher. The owner, the son of Amsterdam's burgomaster and himself Bailiff of Muiden, was none other than **Pieter Corneliszoon Hooft** (1581-1647), a diplomat, historiographer, and dramatist whose works marked the first decades of the Golden Age. Although the Dutch literature of the day, created by the governing elite and filled with the spirit of the French Pléiade, was steeped in alexandrines and elegies, it was unusual in making the Dutch language acceptable. Celebrities such as the great poet and tragic actor Joost van den Vondel and Constantijn Huygens, secretary to the Prince of Orange as well as a poet and musician, frequented the castle standing proudly at the mouth of the Vecht.

Tour – The fortress, saved from destruction by King William I and abandoned after the passage of French troops in the late 18C, has been turned into a museum.

An interesting opportunity to imagine yourself in the world of the local noblemen

Guided tours (available in several languages) reveal the history of the building and enable visitors to see, in particular, a Flemish tapestry woven in Audenaarde and depicting the meeting of Alexander the Great and the daughters of Darius III, Emperor of Persia.
In front of the castle is a garden of herbs and medicinal plants.

NAARDEN★

Plan p 201 – Michelin map no 211 P 9

The former capital of the Gooi area *(see HILVERSUM)* once stood on the banks of the Zuiderzee. The town was originally situated about 3km/1.9mi northeast of its current location and was reduced to ashes after the conflict between the Hameçons and the Cabillauds in 1350. Having also been flooded repeatedly, the town was rebuilt further inland. In 1572 Naarden was captured by the Duke of Alba. The Spanish troops massacred the population and razed the town to the ground. In 1673 the town was occupied by Louis XIV's army who had been garrisoned in Utrecht.
Today Naarden is a pleasant little town still enclosed by its magnificent **fortifications**★ shaped like a 12-pointed star (six bastions and six islands), with a double ring of ramparts and ditches. They date from the 17C and were designed by an architect from Amsterdam, **Adriaan Dortsman**.
Naarden boasts a few celebrities in its past. The artist **Salomon van Ruysdael** (c 1600-70) was born here. Jan Amos Komensky (1592-1670), a Czech Humanist who was better known under the Latin name of **Comenius**, found his final home here after a life dogged by political and religious hatred. **Frank Martin** (1890-1974), a Swiss musician who was a contemporary of Honegger, settled here after the Second World War.

SIGHTSEEING

★**Stadhuis** ⓥ – *Markstraat 22.* This fine Renaissance town hall has a double stepped gable; it dates from 1601. Behind the beautiful façade decorated with bonding and medallions lies an interior furnished in the antique style and adorned with 17C paintings. It also contains a model of the 17C fortifications.

Grote Kerk ⓥ – *Kerkpad.* The Great Church is dedicated to St Vitus; its east end faces the town hall. Inside the barrel vault is decorated with some wonderful 16C **paintings**★ representing scenes from the Old and New Testaments. From the top of the tower (45m/146ft) above the Gothic church built between 1380 and 1440, there is a superb **view**★ which will delight those with an interest in military architecture.

Comenius Museum ⓥ – *Kloosterstraat 33.* The objects, documents and works exhibited here concern the life and work of Comenius, the most influential figure in Czech culture after Jan Hus.

A universal man – Comenius was a philosopher, theologian, teacher, poet and pastor. Born in Moravia, he was ordained into the priesthood then banished in 1621 (he was a Protestant). He left Bohemia six years later and travelled across Europe until 1656, when he arrived in Holland at the request of patrons of the arts (the Van Geer family). His major work is the *Didactica magna* (*The Great Didactic Treatise* 1632) which made him the father of the western concept of teaching.

Comenius Mausoleum – *Enter via Kloosterstraat 33.* This former Walloon chapel contains the tomb of this highly-educated man who died in Amsterdam. He provided inspiration for Leibnitz.

Het Spaanse Huis – *Turfpoortstraat 27.* The frontage stone on the Spanish House (1615) depicts the massacre of the townspeople by the Spaniards in 1572.

★ **Het Nederlands Vestingmuseum** ⓥ – *Westwalstraat 6.* The Fortress Museum is housed in the five casemates of one of the six bastions in the Turfpoort, or Peat Gate. It owes its name to the fact that peat, used as fuel, was stored here. The fortifications in Naarden were directly inspired by the ideas mooted by engineer **Menno van Coehoorn** (1641-1704). He won fame by publishing a modern project for fortifications for the town of Coevorden (Drenthe), but he has remained famous for the invincibility of his masterpiece, Bergen op Zoom (Noord-Brabant), albeit an invincibility that was badly dented by the French in 1747 during the War of the Austrian Succession. In addition to a historical look at fortified towns and fortresses in the Netherlands, the museum contains various weapons, uniforms, engravings and an audio-visual programme illustrating the eventful history of the town. The most exciting parts of the visit, though, are the **listening passage** (61m/200ft long) from which the defendants could listen to the enemy at night, and the demonstration firing of a cannon *(ask for information at the entrance)*.

SHOPPING IN AN ARSENAL...

...can be done in Naarden. Lovers of art, design and fine dining won't want to miss a visit to Het Arsenaal (Kooltjesbuurt 1), a group of 17C buildings which used to serve as an arms and munitions warehouse. In 1993 this complex was transformed into a Design Centre by the cabinetmaker Jan des Bouvrie. Luxury shops, a tastefully decorated restaurant and a modern art gallery border the pretty internal garden. Markstraat and Cattenhagestraat also have many pleasant boutiques.

SCHIPHOL

Plan p 200 – Michelin map no 211 N9

The literal meaning of *schiphol* is "shelter for ships". The former Haarlem Lake formed a cove that provided safe mooring for shipping until it was drained in the 17C. **Schiphol Airport**, which is 18km/11mi southwest of the capital, was built on land 4.5m/12ft below sea level, and is now one of the largest and most modern airports on the continent of Europe with four runways. A fifth runway is due to be opened shortly, enabling the airport to cater for 432 000 movements per year, ie an average of 82 landings per hour and an average passenger throughput of 40 million.

Nationaal Luchtvaartmuseum Aviodome ⓥ – *Westelijke Randweg 201.* This museum, located a mere 10min walk from the great central Schiphol Plaza terminal, consists of an aluminium geodesic dome resembling a strange parachute that has floated down not far from the runways (it is beyond the WTC and the Sheraton). Beneath the dome with its star-shaped honeycomb structure are the collections belonging to the National Museum of Aviation. Among the machines juxtaposed to show technical developments, visitors are first confronted with some superb **replicas**★: a glider (1893) used by pioneer Otto Lilienthal; the Wright Flyer, a glider turned into a biplane which enabled the two famous brothers to launch the history of aviation on 17 December 1903; and the Blériot XI with which the famous aviator flew from Calais to Dover on 29 July 1909. Another section honours **Anthony Herman Gerard Fokker** (1890-1939), a great Dutch aviator and aircraft designer (he worked mainly in Germany). His designs included the Fokker Spin (1911) and the triplane Dr1 (1917) used by the much feared Red Baron, Manfred von Richthofen. The company still produces planes such as the Fokker F28 and F100, subsonic aircraft used for civilian transport.

VOLENDAM★

Plan p 201 – Michelin map no 210 P8

Volendam lies to the south-east of Edam at the entrance to an inlet known as the Gouwzee. It still has a small eel-fishing fleet, but in days gone by it was a very famous harbour on the Zuiderzee. The town has become a major tourist centre since the construction, in 1932, of the dike closing off the IJsselmeer, the Afsluitdijk, built between the coast of Friesland and the former island of Wieringen.
In the summer months, the local population (most of them Roman Catholics, unlike the people of nearby Marken) wear a traditional costume that has now become one of the characteristic images of the Netherlands in foreign countries.

The village – The long street that runs along the top of the tall dike has nothing but a row of souvenir shops offering a whole range of junk. However, down below behind the dike there are some picturesque, narrow streets winding here and there between small brick houses with wooden gables.

★ **The traditional costume** – The men wear black breeches with silver buttons, short jackets over striped shirts, and round caps. The women's costume includes a black skirt with striped apron or a striped skirt with a black apron, a blouse with a floral bib, a short-sleeved black jacket and heavy coral necklace with gold clasp concealed in the winter months by a blue and white scarf. When they are not wearing their pointed black bonnet, they put on the tall lace cap with "wings" kept for festive occasions, the headdress for which the Netherlands are famous. Both men and women wear clogs or shoes with buckles. If possible, watch the people leaving the church after Mass or Vespers on Sundays or feast days. They then cross the little wooden bridge in front of the Catholic church.

Volendams Museum ⓥ – *Zeestraat 37.* Installed in two small houses (one a shop and the other a classroom), the museum displays mainly traditional costumes, jewellery, fishing tackle and cigar rings.

ZAANSTREEK★

Plan p 200 – Michelin map n° 210 N 8

The region crossed by the River Zaan includes several towns and villages which, since 1974, have been regrouped into the community of **Zaanstad** (population 135 126). The population of this district, situated on the north-western boundaries of Amsterdam, increased by 30% between 1960 and 1970, while the population of the capital city itself went into a decline. Now Zaanstad should be seen as a residential suburb of Amsterdam, a suburb full of greenery and man-made lakes.
Originally, the people of the Zaan area earned their living from fishing. In 1592, Cornelis Corneliszoon built the first timber mill here. Thereafter, industrial mills began to develop and there were almost 600 in the region c 1760, making the Zaan region one of the principal industrial centres of the world.
Working with timber was greatly facilitated by the use of timber mills, and this in turn enabled the development of shipbuilding. Their yards were so famous that the Czar **Peter the Great** came here incognito in 1697 to train with one of the local boat- builders.
There are still a great number of **mills** today. They used to be used mainly for the production of mustard, paper, oil, paint and tobacco.
The **wooden houses** are also typical of the region. The instability of the ground makes the use of stone for building impossible. Nowadays most of the surviving old houses are to be seen in Zaanse Schans.

★ DE ZAANSE SCHANS (The Zaan Redoubt)

A fortification built in the late 16C as a defence against the Spanish troops has given its name to this site, which was gradually developed over the 1960s and 1970s. As for the "Zaan Redoubt" itself, it disappeared many years ago.
The Zaanse Schans is still inhabited, a village with utilitarian buildings and houses dating from the 17C and 18C. They were brought here from various localities nearby, in particular Zaandam, then rebuilt and renovated on site, forming an area which is still lived in and where the windmills still operate.
The village is built in a row along the **Kalverringdijk** which is flanked by a ditch crossed by small humpbacked bridges. A few houses stand on the banks of the secondary canals lined with paths such as Zeilenmakerspad. Most of the houses are built of wood and painted green or covered in pitch. The doors, windows and gables are outlined in white, a feature typical of the Zaan area. At the top of the gable is a small wooden decoration, the *makelaar*.
Several houses, shops or windmills in the folk museum are open to the public. There are demonstrations of typical Dutch trades and local products are on sale. Although the site is picturesque, its commercialised aspect makes it somewhat artificial. There are also **boat trips** ⓥ on the Zaan *(for information ask at the reception area)*.

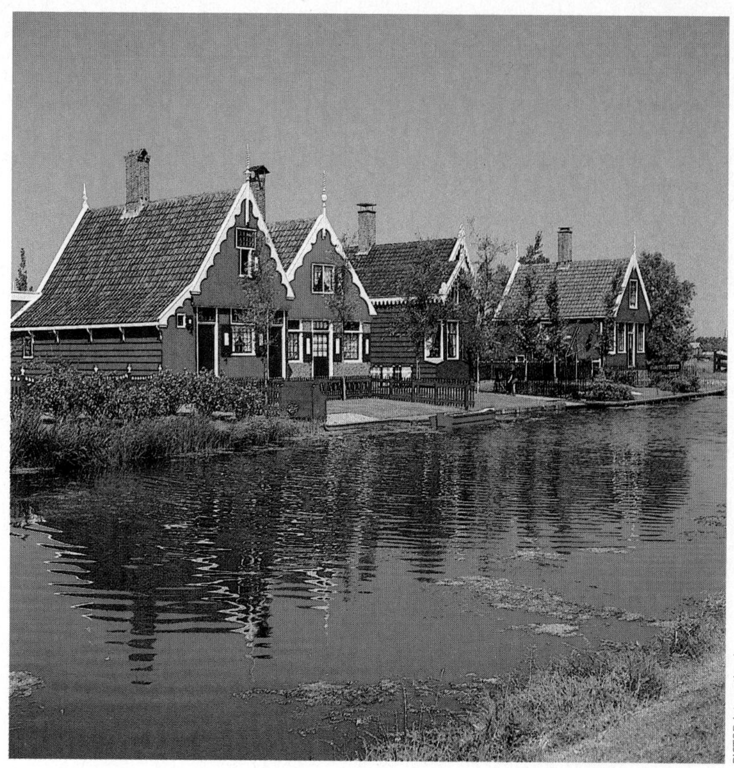

PICTOR International

These houses, which are typical of Zaanstreek, bear a resemblance to dolls' houses

Zaans Museum ⓥ – The museum is devoted to the history of the Zaan area. A life-size model of the region is the starting point of an "audio tour" that includes seven areas where all sorts of objects are on display: clogs, reading boards, ploughs etc. Each of these areas illustrates a particular theme (the wood industry, the importance of the fire brigade etc). Audiovisual presentations, computers and interactive terminals provide visitors with additional information. There is a good view of the factories, canals and mills of the surrounding area from the *Z-watch* situated on the top floor.

Ambachtencentrum ⓥ – A glass-blowing centre and a Delft ceramic workshop are housed in this old De Lelie warehouse.

Klompenmakerij ⓥ – This warehouse from Westzaan is called "De Vrede", or "Peace". It dates from 1721. Clogs are made here in the traditional manner, using green poplar wood.

Scheepswerf – Small wooden boats are repaired or built in this late-18C shed.

Tinkoepel – This is a rotunda-shaped pavilion at the end of a garden where tea used to be served. It houses a **pewter foundry** ⓥ (tingieterij).

Museum van het Nederlandse Uurwerk ⓥ – The clock museum is situated in a house from Assendelft dating from the second half of the 17C. It has a collection of all the kinds of clocks produced in the country. Note the chiming clock with 31 bells (c 1700) *(24)*, a fine clock from the Zaan area (c 1770) *(33)*, a clock designed by the Amsterdam clockmaker Paulus Bramer (c 1770) *(63)* and a replica of an Egyptian hour glass (c 1550 BC) *(upstairs)*.

Museumwinkel Albert Heijn (Grocery Museum) ⓥ – Located in a house that is a reconstruction of **Albert Heijn**'s first grocery shop which was opened in Oostzaan in 1887, this charming old shop displays some rather old-fashioned products such as candied sugar, medicinal mint, or pitchforks made of steam-treated wood.

De Hoop Op d'Swarte Walvis – The former Westzaan orphanage (18C) was rebuilt in 1966. It now houses a famous restaurant: "The Hoped-For Black Whale".

Het Noorderhuis ⓥ – "North House" (1670) is an authentic Zaandijk merchant's house. It has an attractive neck gable. It contains a small museum exhibiting costumes and antique dolls.

Mosterdmolen De Huisman (Mustard mill) – This octagonal smock mill (1786) is used to make the famous traditional Zaan mustard.

Bakkerijmuseum In de Gecroonde Duyvekater (Bakery museum) ⏲ – This 17C house bears the name of a type of local brioche known as "duyvekater". Note the marble flooring.

Weidemolen De Hadel – This small "hollow post mill" or **wipmolen** is situated at the end of the Zeilenmakerspad path.

Het jagershuis (Hunter's house) – This merchant's house (1623) is the oldest building in the Zaanse Schans. It houses an antiques shop.

Kaasboerderij Catharina Hoeve ⏲ – This cheese-making plant is housed in a replica (1988) of a typical eastern Zaan farm. Visitors (including Chinese visitors who are given a guided tour in their own language!) are shown the various stages in the traditional production of Edam and Gouda cheeses.

Houtzaagmolen De Gekroonde Poelenburg – This timber mill (1869) is of the Paltrok type. It is mounted on a large workshop which rotates with the mill when the sails are directed into the wind. It gets its name from its wide, mobile base resembling the Pfalzrock, the skirt worn by women from the Rhineland Palatinate who once sought refuge in the Low Countries.

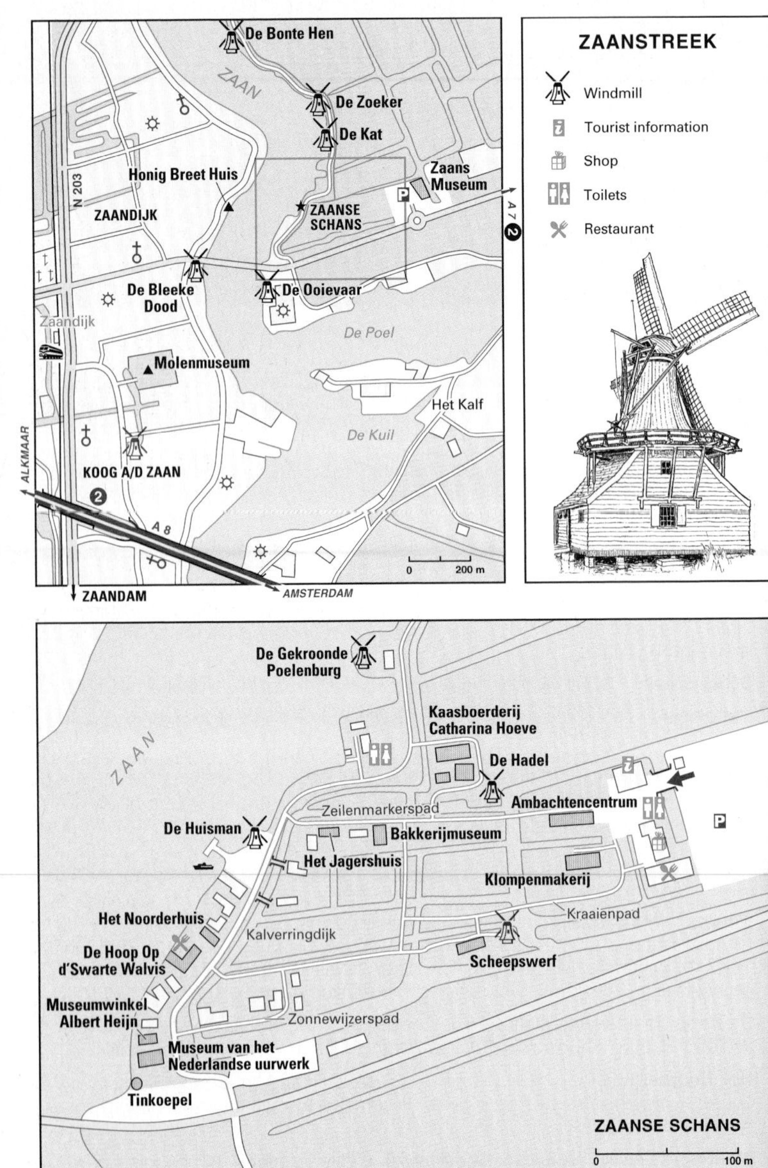

Verfmolen De Kat ⓥ – This windmill has been nicknamed "The Cat". It was originally built in 1646, then rebuilt in 1782 and brought here in 1960. Actually, it consists of two mills: the lower section is original and was part of an oil mill whereas the upper section came from a dye mill. In the past, the area had 55 dye mills, for in the 17C the Netherlands imported large quantities of tropical woods from which colouring agents were extracted.
On windy days, it is worth climbing to the external platform in order to appreciate the speed and noise of the sails from close by. In Force 9 winds, they can rotate at speeds of up to 130kph/81mph.

A sometimes uncouth guest

When **Czar Peter the Great** returned to the Low Countries in 1717, he lived at 527 Herengracht, in Amsterdam, in a house that he rented for his ambassador. The house was later purchased by the King of Holland, Louis Bonaparte.

The Czar was welcomed in French by the city's dignitaries but immediately showed he still had excellent memories of his stay in 1698. He soon began to swear in Dutch and drink beer straight from the jug during the celebratory banquet given in his honour.

Oliemolen De Zoeker ⓥ – This windmill, known as "The Searcher", grinds various types of grain to produce salad oil. It was built in 1607 and was brought here from the Zaandijk area.

Oliemolen De Bonte Hen – This is another oil mill, built in 1693.

Oliemolen De Ooievaar – To the south of the village museum, is an oil mill nicknamed "The Stork".

OTHER SIGHTS

Zaandijk – This small town lies on the opposite bank of the Zaan. It has a clearly visible flour mill called *De Bleeke Dood* (White Death) which was built in 1656. There is also a noticeable smell of chocolate (depending on the wind direction) coming from the *De Zaan* cocoa factory.

Honig Breet Huis ⓥ – *Lagedijk 80.* This 18C brick mansion has little to distinguish it, in terms of style, from more modest houses built in the same period. The main difference lies in the interior decoration. Merchants' houses often have wood carvings, murals and tiled fireplaces. A tour of this museum gives an insight into the home of a wealthy merchant's family. Note the furniture and the superb porcelain collection. The summer room overlooking the Zaan was added in the 19C.

Koog aan de Zaan – Situated immediately to the south of Zaandijk, this village has an interesting museum devoted to windmills.

Molenmuseum ⓥ – *Museumlaan 18.* The Windmill Museum was opened in 1928 in two elegant 17C and 18C houses. The **models★** room is of particular interest since it gives visitors an opportunity to see the various types of mill in the Noord-Holland region. The finest of these scale models is the model of a paper mill, *De Eendracht* (Concord), made in 1900 by seven people, a task that took six months to complete. A large map indicates the geographical locations of the 1 000 mills still to be seen in the Netherlands; the country had some 9 000 in c 1850 *(See Introduction, Windmills)*.

Zaandam – This industrial town on the Zaan has been served, since 1876, by the North Sea Canal (Noordzeekanaal). In itself the town is of no special interest, but it does have one amazing place to visit: a small house in which **Peter the Great**, Czar of Russia (1672-1725), lived in 1697 when he came here, incognito, to train with a boat-builder. This explains the presence on the Dam (the central square in Zaandam) of a statue of the Czar.

One Pierre Michaëlof – This son of Czar Alexis Mikhaïlovitch, who profoundly influenced the history of his country, leaves the impression of a rather eccentric person. He was a giant of a man, more than 2m/6ft tall, endowed with extraordinary physical strength, and he was very much an entrepreneur. At the age of 25, he came to Zaandam determined to learn the art of shipbuilding. Accompanied by a few compatriots, he found himself a job under the name of Pierre Michaëlof and had no hesitation in sharing the modest lifestyle of the other workers. They soon nicknamed him Pieterbaas, ie Master Peter. He returned to Zaandam in 1717, in an official capacity this time, as a king who had gloriously conquered Sweden. He was accompanied by his wife, Czarina Catharina.

Czaar Peterhuisje ⓥ – *Krimp 23. Follow the street opposite the Apollo Theatre then turn into the street on the left (Czaar-Peterstraat) and turn left again.* This was the house where Peter the Great lived incognito for some time in 1697 when he was apprenticed to a shipbuilder. Originally built in wood, in 1895 the house was incorporated into a brick construction, a gift from Czar Nicholas.

Admission times and charges

Because of increases in the cost of living and the constant changes in the opening times of most of the places to visit, the information given below is intended only as a guideline. When we have been unable to obtain updated information, we have reprinted the details included in the previous edition of this guide. In this case, the information is printed in italics.

The information applies to tourists travelling on their own and not entitled to any reductions. For parties, it is usually possible to obtain special rates and different opening times by prior arrangement.

Churches are not open to visitors during services. They are usually closed between noon and 2pm. Admission times and/or charges are indicated if the interior is of particular interest.

Guided tours are organised on a regular basis during the high season. Contact the tourist office or VVV. Prices are indicated in guilders (fl) and euro (€). In the descriptive section of the guide, places to visit that are subject to specific admission times and charges are marked with the symbol ⓥ.

Although admission prices are given in guilders (fl), visitors should be aware that in Jan 2002 the guilder will be replaced by the euro, with 1€ equal to approximately 2.2fl. *See conversion table below.*

Fl	€	€	Fl
2.00	0.91	1	2.20
6.00	2.72	3	6.61
10.00	4.54	5	11.02
15.00	6.81	7	15.43
20.00	9.08	10	22.04
25.00	11.34	11	24.24
30.00	13.61	15	33.06
50.00	22.69	20	44.07

Amsterdam

ℹ De Ruyterkade 5 – 1013 AA – ☎ (0900) 400 40 40 – fax (020) 625 28 69 – www.visitamsterdam.nl

CYCLING IN AMSTERDAM

Heineken Brouwerij – Temporarily closed for restoration. Due to re-open May 2001. For more information call ☎ (020) 523 96 66.

AMSTELVEEN

ℹ Th. Cookstraat 1 – 1181 ZS – ☎ (020) 441 55 45 – fax (020) 647 19 66

Cobra Museum voor Moderne Kunst – ♿ Open daily (except Mon), 11am-5pm. Closed New Year's Day, 30 Apr and Christmas Day. 7.50fl, 3.40€. ☎ (020) 547 50 50. www.cobra-museum.nl

AMSTERDAMSE BOS

Bezoekerscentrum het Bosmuseum – Open daily, 10am-5pm. No charge. ☎ (020) 676 21 52.

Elektrische Museumtramlijn Amsterdam – Open Easter to end Oct, daily. 6.60fl, 3€. ☎ (020) 673 75 38, go.to/trammuseum.

ANNE FRANK HUIS

Anne Frank Huis – Open daily, 9am-7pm (9pm early Apr to end Aug). Closed Yom Kippur. 10fl, 4.54€. ☎ (020) 556 71 00, www.annefrank.nl

Multatuli Museum – Open Tues, 10am-5pm; Sat-Sun, noon-5pm. Closed bank holidays. No charge. ☎ (020) 638 19 38.

BEGIJNHOF

Amsterdams Historisch Museum – Open daily, 10am (11am Sat-Sun)-5pm. Closed New Year's Day, 30 Apr and Christmas Day. 12fl, 5.45€. ☎ (020) 523 18 22. www.ahm.nl

BIJLMERMEER

Ajax Museum – Open daily, 10am-6pm. Closed New Year's Day, 30 Apr, Christmas Day, Boxing Day and during matches and other events. 12.50fl, 5.67€. ☎ (020) 311 14 44, www.ajax.nl

BLOEMENMARKT

Universiteitsmuseum De Agnietenkapel – Open Mon-Fri, 9am-5pm. Closed 25 to 31 Dec and bank holidays. 2.50fl, 1.13€. ☎ (020) 525 33 39, www.uba.uva.nl

Allard Pierson Museum – ♿ Open Tues-Fri, 10am-5pm, Sat-Sun and bank holidays, 1pm-5pm. Closed Mon, New Year's Day, Easter, 30 Apr, Whitsun and Christmas Day. 9.50fl, 4.31€. ☎ (020) 525 25 56, www.uba.uva.nl/apm.

DAM

Koninklijk Paleis – Open at regulated times and during exhibitions. It is advisable to find out in advance. 9fl, 4.08€. ☎ (020) 620 40 60, www.kon-paleisamsterdam.nl

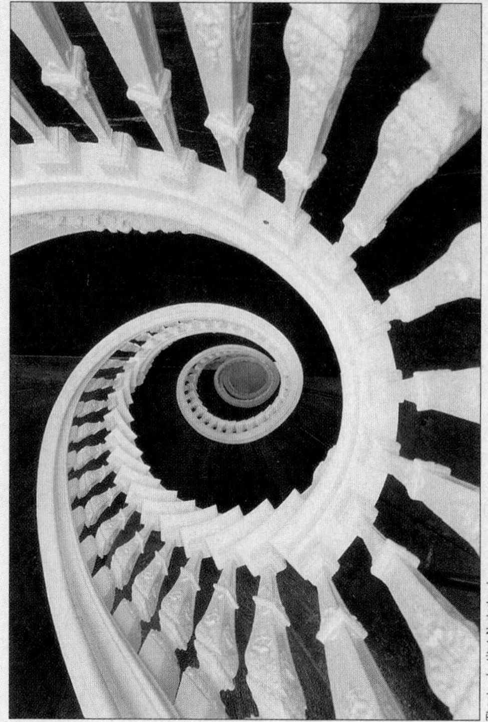
Theater Instituut Nederland

Staircase in the Theatermuseum, Herengracht 168

Nieuwe Kerk – Open daily, 11am-5pm. ☎ (020) 638 69 09, www.nieuwekerk.nl

Madame Tussaud Scenerama – Open daily, 10am-5.30pm; July and Aug, 9.30am-7.30pm. Closed New Year's Day, 30 Apr and New Year's Eve. 19.95fl, 9.06€. ☎ (020) 522 10 10.

HERENGRACHT

No 168: Theatermuseum – Open Tues-Fri, 11am-5pm; Sat-Sun, 1-5pm. Closed Mon and bank holidays. 8.50fl, 3.86€. ☎ (020) 551 33 00, www.tin.nl

Bijbels Museum – Open Mon-Sat, 10am-5pm; Sun and bank holidays, 1-5pm. Closed New Year's Day and 30 Apr. 8fl, 3.63€. ☎ (020) 624 24 36, www.bijbelsmuseum.nl

De Appel – ♿ Open daily (except Mon), noon-5pm. Closed New Year's Day, Easter, Whitsun, 30 Apr, Christmas Day and Boxing Day. 2.50fl, 1.13€. ☎ (020) 625 56 51, www.deappel.nl

Kattenkabinet – Open Mon-Fri, 10am-2pm; Sat-Sun 1-5pm. Opening times may differ in winter months. Closed New Year's Day, Christmas Day and Boxing Day. 10fl, 4.54€. ☎ (020) 626 53 78, www.kattenkabinet.nl

No 605: Museum Willet-Holthuysen – Open Mon-Fri, 10am-5pm; Sat-Sun and bank holidays, 11am-5pm. Closed New Year's Day, 30 Apr and Christmas Day. 8fl, 3.63€. ☎ (020) 523 18 22, www.ahm.nl/willet.

JAVA-EILAND

Open Haven Museum – Open Wed-Fri, also Sun, 1-5pm. Closed Mon, Tues, Sat and bank holidays. 4fl, 1.82€. ☎ (020) 418 55 22.

JORDAAN

Looier Kunst- en Antiekcentrum – ♿ Open daily (except Fri), 11am-5pm. Closed Fri, New Year's Day, 30 Apr, Christmas Day, Boxing Day and New Year's Eve. ☎ (020) 624 90 38, www.looier.nl

Theo Thijssen Museum – Open Thur-Sun, noon-5pm. Closed bank holidays. 2.50 fl, 1.13€. ☎ (020) 420 71 19.

KEIZERSGRACHT

Museum Van Loon – Open Fri-Mon, 11am-5pm. Closed Tues-Thurs. 7.50fl, 3.40€. ☎ (020) 624 52 55, www.musvloon.box.nl

LEIDSEPLEIN

Max Euwe-Centrum – Open Tues-Fri and first Sat in the month, 10.30am-4pm. Closed Sun and bank holidays. No charge. ☎ (020) 625 70 17, www.maxeuwe.nl

MUSEUMPLEIN

Coster Diamonds – Open daily, 9am-5pm. ☎ (020) 305 55 55, www.costerdiamonds.com.

NEDERLANDS SCHEEPVAART MUSEUM

Nederlands Scheepvaartmuseum – Open Tues-Sun, 10am-5pm from mid-June-end Sept and during school holidays Mon 10am-5pm. Closed New Year's Day, 30 Apr and Christmas Day. 14.50fl 6.58€. ☎ (020) 523 22 22, www.scheepvaartmuseum.nl

NIEUWE ZIJDE

Beurs van Berlage Museum – Open daily (except Mon), 10am-5pm. 7fl, 3.18€. ☎ (020) 530 41 41, www.beursvanberlage.nl

OOSTERDOK

Nemo – ♿ Open Tues-Sun and during school holidays, 10am-5pm. Closed Mon, New Year's Day and 30 April. 20fl, 9.08€. ☎ (0900) 919 11 00, www.e-nemo.nl

OUDE ZIJDE

Museum Amstelkring Ons' Lieve Heer op Solder – Open Mon-Sat, 10am-5pm; Sun and bank holidays, 1-5pm. Closed 30 Apr. 10fl, 4.54€. ☎ (020) 624 66 04.

Oude Kerk – Open daily Apr to end-Dec, 11am (1pm Sun)-5pm. 7.50fl, 3.40€. ☎ (020) 625 82 84, www.oudekerk.nl

Hasj Marihuana Museum – ♿ Open daily, 11am-10pm. 8fl, 3.63€. ☎ (020) 623 59 61.

Koffie- en Theemuseum – Open Tues and Sat, 2-4pm. Closed Mon, Wed, Thu, Sun and bank holidays. No charge. ☎ (020) 624 06 83.

Tropenmuseum

Bis masts, Tropenmuseum

OUDERKERK AAN DE AMSTEL

Oudheidkamer – ♿ Open Tues-Fri, 10am-noon; first Sunday of the month, 1-3pm. Closed bank holidays. No charge. ☎ (020) 496 43 65.

De PIJP

Gemeentearchief Amsterdam – Open weekdays (also Sat from Sep to June), 10am-5pm. Closed Sun and bank holidays, also Sat in July and Aug. ☎ (020) 572 02 02, www.gemeentearchief.amsterdam.nl

PLANTAGE

Hortus Botanicus – Open weekdays Apr-Oct, 9am (11am-5pm Sat-Sun and bank holidays)-5pm (5pm early Apr to end Oct). From Nov to end Mar open weekdays 9am-4pm (11am-4pm Sat-Sun and bank holidays) Closed New Year's Day and Christmas Day. 7.50fl, 3.40€. ☎ (020) 625 84 11.

Hollandsche Schouwburg – ♿ Open daily, 11am-4pm. Closed Yom Kippur. No charge. ☎ (020) 626 99 45.

Nationaal Vakbondsmuseum – ♿ Open Tues-Fri, 11am (1pm Sun)-5pm. Closed Mon, Sat and bank holidays. 5fl 2.27€. ☎ (020) 624 11 66, www.deburcht-vakbondsmuseum.nl

Artis – ♿ Open daily 9am-5pm (6pm in the summer). 28.50fl, 12.94€. ☎ (020) 523 34 00, www.artis.nl

Stedelijk Museum

Summer Luxury (c 1900) by J van Looy, a painting in the Rijksmuseum

Verzetsmuseum – ♿ open Tues-Fri, 10am-5pm, Sat-Sun noon-5pm. 8fl, 3.63€. ☎ (020) 620 25 35, www.verzetsmuseum.org

Tropenmuseum – ♿ Open daily, 10am-5pm. Closed New Year's Day, 30 Apr, 5 May and Christmas Day. 12.50fl, 5.67€. ☎ (020) 568 82 15, www.kit.nl/tropenmuseum.

PRINSENGRACHT

No 281: Westerkerk – Open Apr-end Sept, Mon-Fri, 11am-3pm. Closed Sat, Sun and Oct-end Mar. ☎ (020) 624 77 66, www.westkerk.nl

Woonbotenmuseum – Open Tues-Sun, 10am-5pm. Closed New Year's Day, 30 Apr and Christmas Day. 3.75fl, 1.70€. ☎ (020) 427 07 50.

RAI

Peter Stuyvesant Stichting – Open Mon-Fri, 9am-noon and 1-4pm. Closed bank holidays. No charge. ☎ (020) 540 62 52.

REMBRANDTHUIS

Museum Het Rembrandthuis – Open Mon-Sat, 10am-5pm; Sun and bank holidays, 1-5pm. Closed New Year's Day. 12fl, 5.67€. ☎ (020) 520 04 00, www.rembrandthuis.nl

Holland Experience – Open daily 10am-6pm. 17.50 fl, 7.94€. ☎ (020) 422 22 33, www.holland-experience.nl

Zuiderkerk – ♿ Open Mon, 11am-4pm, Tues-Fri 9am-4pm (8pm Thur). Closed weekends and bank holidays. No charge. ☎ (020) 522 79 87, www.dro.amsterdam.nl

RIJKSMUSEUM

Rijksmuseum – ♿ Open daily, 10am-5pm. Closed New Year's Day. 15fl, 6.81€. ☎ (020) 674 70 47, www.rijksmuseum.nl

SLOTEN

Molen van Sloten – ♿ Open daily, 10am-4pm. Closed New Year's Day, 30 April, Christmas Day and Boxing Day. 6fl, 2.72€. ☎ (020) 669 04 12, www.molenvansloten.nl

STEDELIJK MUSEUM

Stedelijk Museum – ♿ Open daily, 11am-5pm. Closed New Year's Day. 10fl, 4.54€. ☎ (020) 573 27 37, www.stedelijk.nl

VAN GOGH MUSEUM

Van Gogh Museum – ♿ Open daily, 10am-6pm. 15.50fl, 7.04€. ☎ (020) 570 52 52, www.vangoghmuseum.nl

VONDELPARK

Filmmuseum – Shows daily at 7pm, 7.15pm, 7.30pm, 9.30pm, 9.45pm and 10pm; Sun from 3pm. 12.50fl., ☎ (020) 589 14 00, www.nfm.nl

WATERLOOPLEIN

Joods Historisch Museum – ♿ Open daily, 11am-5pm. Closed Yom Kippur. 10fl, 4.54€. ☎ (020) 626 99 45, www.jhm.nl

Portugees-Israëlitische Synagoge – Open Sun-Fri, 10am-4pm. Closed Sat and Jewish feast days. 5fl, 2.27€. ☎ (020) 624 53 51.

The Suburbs

CYCLING IN THE POLDERS

Nationaal Park Zuid-Kennemerland – Open Tues-Sun, 10am-5pm. Closed Mon, Easter, Whitsun and Christmas day. No charge ☎ (023) 541 11 23.

AALSMEER

Drie Kolommenplein 1 – 1431 LA – ☎ (0297) 32 53 74 – fax (0297) 38 76 76

Bloemenveiling Aalsmeer – ♿ Open weekdays, 7.30-11am. Closed Sat-Sun and bank holidays. 7.5fl, 3.40€. ☎ (0297) 39 21 85. www.vba.nl

ALKMAAR

Waagplein 2-3 – 1811 JP – ☎ (072) 511 42 84 – fax (072) 511 75 13

Boat trips – ♿ Trips early Apr-end Oct. Contact Rondvaart Alkmaar B.V. ☎ (072) 511 77 50. www.rondvaartalkmaar.nl

Kaasmarkt – Market open mid-Apr to mid-Sept, Fri, 10am-noon. ☎ (072) 511 42 84.

Hollands Kaasmuseum – ♿ Open early Apr to end Oct, 10am (9am Fri)-4pm. Closed Sun, bank holidays and early Nov to end Mar. 5fl, 2.27€. ☎ (072) 511 42 84. www.kaasmuseum.nl

Nationaal Biermuseum De Boom – ♿ Open daily (except Mon) 10am (1.30pm Sat-Sun) to 4pm. From early Nov to end Mar, open daily (except Mon), 1pm-4pm. Closed Mon and bank holidays. 4fl, 1.8€. ☎ (072) 511 38 01.

Stadhuis – Guided tours only, by prior appointment. ☎ (072) 511 42 84 (VVV).

Grote of St.-Laurenskerk – Open early June to mid-Sept, daily (except Sun and Mon) noon-5pm. ☎ (072) 514 07 07.

Stedelijk Museum – Open daily (except Mon), 10am-5pm (1pm Sat-Sun and bank holidays). Closed Mon, New Year's Day, 30 Apr and Christmas Day. 3fl, 1.36€. ☎ (072) 511 07 37.

Broeker Veiling – ♿ Open Apr to end of Oct, Mon-Fri, 10am-5pm, Sat-Sun, 11am-5pm. Closed Nov to end of Mar and 30 Apr. 9.50 fl, 4.31€. ☎ (0226) 31 38 07, www.broekerveiling.nl

Hervormde Kerk – Open early June to end Sept, daily (except Mon), 1.30-4.30pm. Closed remainder of year. ☎ (0299) 67 15 95.

Museum Betje Wolff – Open early May to end of Sept, Fri 11am-5pm, Sat-Sun 2-5pm. From early Oct to end of Apr, Sun 2-5pm. 4fl, 1.82€. ☎ (0229) 68 19 68.

Museum Kranenburgh – Open daily except Mon, 1-5pm. Closed Mon, New Year's Day and Christmas Day. 7.50fl, 3.40€. ☎ (072) 589 89 27.

Noordhollands Duinreservaat – Open daily dawn-dusk. 2fl, 0.91€. ☎ (0251) 66 22 66.

Zee Aquarium – ♿ Open early Apr to end of Sept, daily, 10am-6pm; Nov to Mar, 11am-5pm. 11.50fl, 5.22€. ☎ (072) 581 29 28, www.zeeaquarium.nl

Museum Abdij van Egmond – Guided tours only and by prior arrangement, daily, 11am-12.30pm and 2-5pm. ☎ (072) 506 14 15.

EDAM

Damplein 8 – 1135 BK – ☎ (0299) 31 51 25 – fax (0299) 37 42 36 – www.vvv-edam.nl

Edams Museum – Open Apr to end of Oct, Tues-Sat, 10am-4.30pm, Sun and bank holidays, 1.30pm-4.30pm. Closed Mon and from Nov to end Mar. 4fl, 1.82€. ☎ (0299) 31 51 25 (VVV).

Kaasweg – ♿ Open daily Apr to end of Oct, 10am-5pm. Closed Nov to end of Mar. ☎ (0299) 31 51 25 (VVV).

Grote of St.-Nicolaaskerk – Open daily Apr to end of October, 2pm-4.30pm. Closed Nov to end of Mar. ☎ (0299) 31 51 25 (VVV).

HAARLEM

ℹ Stationsplein 1 – 2011 LR – ☎ (0900) 616 16 00 fax (023) 534 05 37 – www.vvvzk.nl

Grote of St.-Bavokerk – Open daily except Sun, 10am-4pm. 2.75fl, 1.25€. ☎ (023) 532 43 99.

Vishal – ♿ Same conditions as Frans Halsmuseum. No charge. ☎ (023) 532 68 56.

Vleeshal – ♿ Same conditions as Frans Halsmuseum. 7.50fl, 3.40€. ☎ (023) 511 57 75, www.franshalsmuseum.

Archeologisch Museum Haarlem – Open Wed-Sun, 1pm-5pm. Closed Mon, Tues, New Year's Day, Christmas Day and Boxing Day. No charge. ☎ (023) 531 31 35.

Verweyhal – Same conditions as Frans Halsmuseum. 7.50fl, 3.40€. ☎ (023) 511 57 75, www.franshalsmuseum.

Stadhuis – Guided tours.on request. For more information call ☎ (023) 511 31 58.

Frans Halsmuseum – ♿ Open Mon-Sat, 11am-5pm; Sun and bank holidays, noon-5pm. Closed New Year's Day and Christmas Day. 8fl, 3.63€. ☎ (023) 511 57 75, www.franshalsmuseum.nl

Teylers Museum – Open Tues-Sat, 10am-5pm; Sun and bank holidays, noon-5pm. Closed Mon, New Year's Day and Christmas Day. 10fl, 4.54€. ☎ (023) 531 90 10. www.teylersmuseum.nl

Historisch Museum Zuid-Kennemerland – Open Tues-Sat, noon (1pm Sun)-5pm. Closed Mon and New Year's Day, 25, 26 and 31 Dec. No charge. ☎ (023) 542 24 27.

ABC Architectuurcentrum – Open Tues-Sat, noon-5pm, Sun 1-5pm. Closed Mon and bank holidays. No charge. ☎ (023) 534 05 84.

Spaarnestad Fotoarchief – Open Tues-Sat, noon-5pm, Sun 1-5pm. Closed Mon. No charge. ☎ (023) 518 51 52, www.spaarnefoto.nl

Kathedrale Basiliek St.-Bavo – Open early Apr to end Sept and during school holidays, Mon-Sat, 10am-4pm, Sun, 1pm-4pm. Closed for the remainder of the year. 2.50fl, 1.13€. ☎ (023) 553 33 77.

Stoomgemaal Halfweg – Open early Apr to end Sept, Wed and Thur, 1pm-4pm, Sat 10am-4pm. Closed early Oct to end Mar. 4fl, 1.82€. ☎ (020) 497 43 96.

Museum De Cruquius – ♿ Open early Mar to end Oct, Mon-Fri, 10am-5pm; Sat-Sun and bank holidays, 11am-5pm. Closed early Nov to end of Feb. 6fl, 2.72€. ☎ (023) 528 57 04.

HILVERSUM

ℹ Noordse Bosje 1 – 1211 BD – ☎ (035) 624 17 51

Goois Museum – ♿ Open daily (except Mon), 1-5pm. Closed New Year's Day, 30 Apr, Christmas Day and New Year's Eve. 3fl, 1.36€. ☎ (035) 629 28 26.

Singer Museum – Open Tues-Sat, 11am-5pm; Sun and bank holidays, noon-5pm. Closed Mon, New Year's Day, 30 Apr and Christmas Day. ☎ (035) 531 56 56.

Gemeentemuseum Weesp – ♿ Open mid-June to mid-Sept, Thur, 9.30am-12.30pm, Fri 9.30am-12.30pm, Sat, 1.30-4.30pm. From mid-Sept to mid-June, Tues and Thur 9.30am-12.30pm, Sat 1.30pm-4.30pm. No charge. ☎ (0294) 49 12 45.

Kasteel-Museum Sypesteyn – Guided tour only (1hr): Sat-Sun and bank holidays in Apr and Oct, noon-5pm; early May to end Sept, daily (except Mon), 10am (noon Sat-Sun and bank holidays)-5pm. Closed early Nov to end Mar. 10fl, 4.54€. ☎ (035) 582 32 08. www.sypesteyn.nl.

HOORN

ℹ Veemarkt 4 – 1621 JC – ☎ (0900) 403 10 55 – fax (0229) 21 50 23

Museumstoomtram – Departures Apr to end of October and during Christmas holidays Tues-Sun, 11am-3pm. July-Aug departures also Mon. Return: 23.50fl, 10.67€. ☎ (0229) 21 92 31. www.stoomtram.demon.nl

Westfries Museum – Open Mon-Fri, 11am-5pm; Sat-Sun and bank holidays, 2-5pm. Closed New Year's Day, 3rd Mon in Aug and Christmas Day. 5fl, 2.27€. ☎ (0229) 28 00 28. www.wfm.nl

Museum van de Twintigste Eeuw – ♿ Open daily (except Mon), 10am-5pm. Closed New Year's Day, 30 Apr, Christmas Day and Boxing Day. 6fl, 2.72€. ☎ (0229) 21 40 01. www.hoorngids.nl/museumhoorn.

KEUKENHOF and the BULB FIELDS

Nationale Bloemententoonstelling Keukenhof – ♿ Open end Mar to end May, daily, 8am-7.30pm. Closed remainder of year. 20fl, 9.08€. ☎ (0252) 46 55 55. www.keukenhof.nl

Noordwijk Space Expo – Open Tues-Sun 10am-5pm. Also open Mon during school holidays. Closed Mon, New Year's day and Christmas day. 15fl, 6.81€. ☎ (071) 364 64 46. www.12move.nl/space.

Museum de Zwarte Tulp – ♿ Open daily (except Mon), 1-5pm. Closed Mon, New Year's Day, Christmas Day, Boxing Day and New Year's Eve. 4fl, 1.82€. ☎ (0252) 41 79 00.

Den Harthogh Ford Museum – ♿ Open Wed-Sun, 10am-5pm. Closed Mon, Tues New Year's Day, Christmas Day, Boxing Day and New Year's Eve. 15fl, 6.80€ ☎ (0252) 51 81 18, www.fordmuseum.nl

MARKEN

Marker Museum – ♿ Open Easter to end Oct, daily, 10am-5pm (noon-4pm Sun) Closed early Nov to Easter. 4fl, 1.82€. ☎ (0299) 60 19 04.

MONNICKENDAM

Nieuwpoortslaan 15 – 1140 AA – ☎ (0299) 65 19 98 fax (0299) 65 52 68

Museum De Speeltoren – Open early June to mid-Sept, Tues-Sat, 11am-5pm (2-5pm Sun); mid-Apr to end of May, Sat, 11am-5pm, Sun, 2-5pm . 2.50fl, 1.13€. ☎ (0299) 65 22 03. www.ayllas.demon.nl

MUIDEN

Kazernestraat 10 – 1398 AN – ☎ (0294) 26 13 89

Het Muiderslot – Guided tour only (50min): early Apr to end Oct, daily, 10am (1pm Sat-Sun and bank holidays)-5pm; remainder of year, Sat-Sun only, 1-4pm. Closed early Nov to end Mar, Mon-Fri, also New Year's Day and Christmas Day. 10fl, 4.54€ ☎ (0294) 26 13 25. www.muiderslot.nl

NAARDEN

Adr. Dortsmanplein 1b – 1411 RC – ☎ (035) 694 28 36 – fax (035) 694 34 24

Stadhuis – Open early Apr to end Sept, Mon-Sat, 1.30pm-4.30pm. Closed Sun and bank holidays. ☎ (035) 695 78 11.

Grote Kerk – Same opening times as Comenius Museum below.

Comenius Museum – Open early Apr to end Oct, Tues-Sat, 10am-5pm, Sun and bank holidays, noon-5pm; remainder of year, daily except Mon, 1-4pm. Closed Christmas Day, New Year's Eve and New Year's Day. 4.50fl, 2.04€. ☎ (035) 694 30 45.

Het Nederlands Vestingmuseum – Open early Mar to mid-June and early Sept to end Oct, Tues-Fri, 10.30am-5pm, Sat-Sun, noon-5pm; mid-June to end Aug, daily, 10.30am (noon Sat-Sun)-5pm; remainder of year, Sun, noon-5pm. During school holidays, Tues-Fri 10.30am-5pm, Sat-Sun and bank holidays noon-5pm. Closed Christmas Day, New Year's Eve and New Year's Day. 10fl, 4.54€. ☎ (035) 694 54 59. www.vestingmuseum.nl

SCHIPHOL

Schiphol Plaza – ☎ (0900) 400 40 40 – fax (020) 625 28 6

Nationaal Luchtvaartmuseum Aviodome – Open early Apr to end Sept, daily, 10am-5pm; remainder of year, daily (except Mon), 10am (noon Sat-Sun)-5pm. Closed Mon from early Oct to end Mar, also Christmas Day, New Year's Eve and New Year's Day. 12.50fl, 6.81€. ☎ (020) 406 80 00. www.aviodome.nl

VOLENDAM

Zeestraat 37 – 1131 ZD – ☎ (0299) 36 37 47 – fax (0299) 36 84 84

Volendams Museum – Open Easter to All Saints Day holiday, daily, 10am-5pm. 3.50fl, 1.59€. ☎ (0299) 36 92 58. www.volendam.com/museum.

ZAANSTREEK

Gedempte Gracht 76 – 1506 CJ – ☎ (075) 616 22 21
fax (075) 670 53 81 – www.zaanseschans.nl

Boat trips – ♿ Departures daily, early Apr to end Oct, 11am-4pm (hourly departures); July and Aug, daily, 10am-5pm. ☎ (075) 614 67 62.

Zaans Museum – Open Tues-Sat, 10am-5pm, Sun 12-5pm. Closed Mon, New Year's Day and Christmas Day. 10fl, 4.54€. ☎ (075) 616 82 18.

Ambachtencentrum – Open daily 8.30am-6pm. ☎ (075) 635 46 22.

Klompenmakerij – ♿ Open daily, 8am-6pm. ☎ (075) 617 71 21.

Pewter Foundry – Open early Mar to end Oct 10am-5pm. The remainder of the year open 10am-4pm. Closed Christmas Day. ☎ (075) 617 62 04.

Museum van het Nederlandse Uurwerk – Open early Mar to end of Oct daily, 10am-5pm. The remainder of the year open Sat-Sun 12pm-4.30pm. 5fl, 2.27€. ☎ (075) 617 97 69.

Museumwinkel Albert Heijn – Open early Mar to end Oct, daily, 10am-1pm and 2-5pm; remainder of year, Sat-Sun and bank holidays 11am-1pm and 2-4pm. No charge. ☎ (075) 659 28 08.

Het Noorderhuis – Open early Mar to end Nov, daily (except Mon), 10am-5pm; remainder of year, July-Aug and Sat-Sun, 10am-5pm. 2fl 0.91€. ☎ (075) 617 32 37.

Bakkerijmuseum In de Gecroonde Duyvekater – Open daily except Mon 10am-5pm. 1.50fl, 0.68€. ☎ (075) 617 35 22.

EUREKA SLIDE

William of Orange's colours are still popular

Kaasboerderij Catharina Hoeve – Open daily, 9am-6pm. ☎ (075) 621 58 20. www.henriwillig.com

Verfmolen De Kat – Open early Apr to end Oct, daily, 9am-5pm, Sat-Sun and the remainder of the year 9am-5pm. 4fl, 1.82€. ☎ (075) 621 04 77.

Oliemolen De Zoeker – Open early Mar to end Sept, daily, 9.30am-4.30pm; remainder of year by prior arrangement. 4fl, 1.82€. ☎ (075) 628 79 42.

Honig Breet Huis – Open Tues-Sun, 1-5pm. Closed Mon, New Year's Day, Easter, Whitsun and Christmas Day. 2.50fl, 1.13€. ☎ (075) 621 76 26.

Molenmuseum – Open early June to end Sept, Mon, 1-5pm, Tues-Fri, 11am-5pm; Sat, 2-5pm; Sun and bank holidays, 1-5pm; early Oct to end May, Tues-Fri, 10am-noon and 1-5pm; Sat, 2-5pm; Sun and bank holidays, 1-5pm. 4.50fl, 2.04€. ☎ (075) 628 89 68.

Czaar Peterhuisje – Open early Apr to end Oct, Tues-Sun, 1pm-5pm and 2-5pm; remainder of year, Sat-Sun, 1.30-5pm. Closed Mon and bank holidays. 2.50fl, 1.13€. ☎ (075) 616 03 90.

Index

Haarlem Noord-Holland .... Towns, sights and tourist regions followed by the name of the province

Rembrandt .... People, historical events, artistic styles and local terms covered in the text

Mauritshuis .... An important sight listed and extensively described under a town or city

Individual sights (mountains, lakes, dams, abbeys, castles etc) appear under their own name.

E

F

G

H

I

J

K

S

T

U

V

W

Z

Notes